The President, the Public, and the Parties

D1411152

The President, the Public, and the Parties

SECOND EDITION

CONGRESSIONAL QUARTERLY INC.
WASHINGTON, D.C.

Book design and production by Kachergis Book Design,
Pittsboro, North Carolina

Printed and bound in the United States of America

The paper used in this publication meets the minimum requirements of the American National Standard for Information Science—Permanence of Paper for Printed Library Materials, ANSI Z 39.48-1984.

Cover illustration credits *(clockwise from top right):* Library of Congress; Library of Congress; no credit; Library of Congress; Franklin D. Roosevelt Library; David Hume Kennerly, White House

Illustration credits and acknowledgments: iii Library of Congress 3 Pete Souza, White House 4 Library of Congress 5 Library of Congress 7 Library of Congress 9 Library of Congress 10 Franklin D. Roosevelt Library 11 John F. Kennedy Library 13 Scott J. Ferrell 16 Reuters 18 Lyndon B. Johnson Library 22 National Archives 34 Library of Congress 35 Library of Congress 38 Library of Congress 45 (both) Library of Congress 49 Library of Congress 55 no credit 58 Franklin D. Roosevelt Library 63 National Republican Congressional Committee 67 Ray Lustig, *Washington Post* 75 (top) The Bettmann Archive, (bottom) Franklin D. Roosevelt Library 77 Library of Congress 81 no credit 88 Library of Congress 91 Library of Congress 93 Illinois State Historical Library 97 Library of Congress 103 Franklin D. Roosevelt Library 104 *Washington Post* 106 White House 107 Jimmy Carter Library 115 David Valdez, White House 116 AP/Wide World Photos 118 David Hume Kennerly, White House 119 no credit 128 R. Michael Jenkins 134 National Archives 136 Reuters 139 Library of Congress 141 R. Michael Jenkins 147 Library of Congress 149 George Bush Presidential Materials Project 156 Library of Congress 160 Pete Souza, White House 163 Franklin D. Roosevelt Library 165 Ronald Reagan Library 169 R. Michael Jenkins 173 Library of Congress

LIBRARY OF CONGRESS CATALOGING-IN-PUBLICATION DATA
The president, the public, and the parties.—2nd ed.
        p.   cm.
    Rev. ed. of: The presidents and the public. 1990.
    Includes bibliographical references and index.
    ISBN 1-56802-313-8 (alk. paper)
    1. Presidents—United States—Public opinion. 2. Public opinion—United States. 3. Press and politics—United States. 4. Pressure groups—United States. 5. Political parties—United States. I. Presidents and the public.
JK516.P665 1997
351.73'0223—DC21   96-30004

Table of Contents

Preface

THE PRESIDENT IS the nation's most prominent public figure, and much of the power of the presidency is drawn from the support or acquiescence of influential groups outside the federal government. *The President, the Public, and the Parties* examines the presidential relationships with these important groups—namely, the American public, political parties, the mass media, and interest groups.

The first chapter, Presidential Appearances, looks at the history of presidential appearances and speech making up to the present day. The ability of presidents to persuade through the use of rhetoric—to "go public"—to attain support for their presidential agendas is one of the most important tools of the presidency. The types of speeches required in the varying roles of the presidency are also discussed in the chapter.

Chapter 2, The President and Political Parties, looks at presidential party leadership. Although presidents seldom act solely as chiefs of their political parties, their exercise of party leadership is intertwined with most of their executive decisions and actions. It is through the political parties that presidents maintain connections in the political order, both inside and outside the government. This party leadership extends to how presidents support or oppose legislation in Congress and how they make appointments to the executive branch and to the judiciary.

Presidents from George Washington to Bill Clinton have been greatly dependent on the news media to publicize the goals of their administrations and to get their messages to the public.

Chapter 3, The President and the News Media, looks at the crucial relationship between presidents and the press, which can be advantageous or hostile at times. Beginning with a historical overview of the press coverage of the White House, this chapter explores the modern-day arrangements the press maintains with the president and the White House communications personnel.

The public gives its consent to be governed when it elects a president—but presidential elections occur only every four years. To maintain public support, presidents must be attentive to public opinion. Chapter 4, Public Support and Opinion, looks at how public opinion is continually communicated—by demonstrations, letter writing, electronic mail, poll taking—to the president. The chapter shows how presidents make use of public opinion polls, particularly important in the modern era, to advance their programs and how their public support is affected by different circumstances and cycles in governing.

Americans have often formed private associations or groups to attain their political or policy goals. Chapter 5, The President and Interest Groups, looks at the historical relationship between interest groups and the presidency and executive branch. Balancing the demands of these special groups has become one of the most difficult parts of being president.

Many of the discussions in *The President, the Public, and the Parties* are supported by tables of historical data. Each chapter concludes with a note section and a selected bibliography for further reading. A comprehensive index is also provided.

Contributors

HAROLD F. BASS JR. is the Moody Professor of Pre-Law Studies and chair of the department of political science at Ouachita Baptist University. He has written numerous articles in professional journals and chapters for collections on the presidency and political parties.

CHARLES C. EUCHNER is an assistant professor of political science at Holy Cross College. He has written several books, including *Extraordinary Politics: How Protest and Dissent Are Changing American Democracies* (1996).

MARTHA JOYNT KUMAR is professor of political science at Towson State University and senior fellow at the Center for Political Leadership and Participation at the University of Maryland. She has written extensively on the president and the media and is co-author of *Portraying the President: The White House and the News Media* (1981) and author of *Wired for Sound and Pictures: The President and White House Communications Policies* (forthcoming). She also serves as co-editor of the journal *Congress and the Presidency* and as president of the American Political Science Association's Presidency Research Group.

CHAPTER 1

Presidential Appearances

BY CHARLES C. EUCHNER

RESIDENTS ALWAYS WORK at a distance from the American public. Public opinion polls, interest groups, the media, and relations with Congress and the bureaucracy give presidents indirect access to their constituents. While speaking directly to the population helps presidents to create at least the illusion of a direct relationship, it does not help them to develop the relationships needed to assemble coalitions and to govern. To build coalitions, presidents must appeal to many separate groups, or separate publics, as much as to the public at large. Presidents' frequent public appeals have made presidential governance an extension of electoral campaigns.

The President as Public Figure

The president occupies the most prominent position in American politics largely because, with the exception of the vice president, the United States has no other nationally elected leader. A related reason for the president's prominence is the availability of what Theodore Roosevelt called the "bully pulpit." The president's unique ability to promote a national vision and to influence actors in both the public and private spheres has been crucial in disproving the predictions of some observers of early America that the presidency would play a minor role in national government.

In the twentieth century, the president's prominence in American politics has increased not only with the growing involvement of the White House in domestic policy and the rise of the United States to international leadership, but also with the expansion of the president's role as the starring preacher in the "bully pulpit" of American politics.[1] Using words and images as well as the actions of the administration, the president plays a major role in setting the terms of debate for the entire political system.

Public speaking is one of the most important ties between the president and the public. For many citizens, the clearest memory of the president is of the president delivering a speech.[2] Between 1945 and 1994, public speeches by presidents increased by about 500 percent. (See Table 1-1.) A 1972 report estimated that "a half million words annually flow out of the White House in a torrent of paper and ink."[3] Not only presidents' words but also their appearances are important in communicating with the public. Academic studies conclude that nonverbal signs, such as physical appearances, have four to ten times the effect of verbal signs on "impression formation."[4]

Political scientist Richard E. Neustadt has argued that the president can exert influence by command only rarely. A more important tool of power is the "power to persuade."[5] Neustadt concentrated on the president's power to persuade other members of the Washington establishment, but the breakdown of many stable institutions has moved presidents to use their persuasive abilities more and more on the public. Even when presidents do not speak out, the threat of "going public" is an important tool.[6]

Communications expert Roderick P. Hart has argued that ubiquitous presidential speech has transformed not only the presidency and the rest of the national government but also the way people perceive politics. The president dominates the public sphere. Working within a "matrix of countervailing forces," the president must maneuver with speech. "Virtually every activity in the modern White House is designed to shape or reshape something that the president has said or will say."[7]

Even when urging change, the president's themes are basically conservative. Political scientist Philip Abbott has written: "President after president, whether advocating reform or retrenchment, attempt[s] to justify policy by calling America back to its origins, restating its basic values, applying them to current problems by seeking to establish an underlying unity amidst current conflict through a call to rededication and sacrifice."[8]

TABLE 1-1 Level of Public Activities of Presidents, 1945–1994

President[a]	Total activities	Yearly average	Monthly average
Truman, I	248	62	5.2
Truman, II	520	130	10.8
Eisenhower, I	330	83	6.9
Eisenhower, II	338	85	7.0
Kennedy	658	219	18.8
Johnson[b]	1,463	293	24.0
Nixon, I	634	159	13.2
Nixon, II	204	113	10.2
Ford	756	344	26.0
Carter	1,047	262	22.0
Reagan, I	1,194	299	24.9
Reagan, II	852	213	18.0
Bush	1,244	311	26.0
Clinton[c]	713	357	29.7

SOURCE: Lyn Ragsdale, *Vital Statistics on the Presidency* (Washington, D.C.: Congressional Quarterly, 1996), 179.

NOTES: Public activities are defined as including all domestic public appearances by a president, including major speeches, news conferences, minor speeches, Washington appearances, and U.S. appearances but not political appearances. a. For two-term presidents: I (first term); II (second term). b. Includes full term from November 1963 to January 1969. c. 1993–1994 only.

The development of a voluble presidency stems from changes in the U.S. political system as well as from advances in communications and transportation technologies. The president no longer can depend on the traditional bases of support such as Congress, party organizations, the print media, or the bureaucracy. Without those mediators of public policy, presidents increasingly must rely on their own ability to move people with words.

The connection between presidential speech and the absence of institutional bases was underscored by Richard Nixon's handling of the Watergate scandal in the early 1970s. As the president lost support in Congress, in public opinion polls, and among interest groups, he depended increasingly on his rhetorical powers. Nixon's last year in office was dominated by behind-the-scenes strategy sessions on how to respond to charges of law-breaking and by the carefully crafted release of information and public statements.[9]

The disparate parts of the American federal system—from states and localities to the wide variety of economic and social groups—regularly turn to the president for rhetorical as well as administrative and legislative leadership. As political scientist E. E. Schattschneider has noted, battles that originate in a restricted setting often move to higher and higher levels as the combatants seek to attract powerful allies.[10] The president exerts rhetorical force on almost every possible political and economic issue that Americans face, even when the White House plays no direct role in the issue.

Communicating complex policies to the American public is one of the most important—and difficult—tasks of the president. Issues such as interest rates, budget deficits, health care, and trade policy can be numbingly difficult taken alone. When discussed as part of a comprehensive, long-term program, they become even more difficult. Jimmy Carter suffered when he could not explain his complex energy proposals. Carter also addressed so many issues—energy, deregulation, taxes, the Middle East, détente with the Soviet Union, reorganization of the bureaucracy, the environment, urban development—that he could not stay focused in his efforts to sell his policies to the public. Ronald Reagan, in contrast, provided a simple and coherent world view.

President Bill Clinton faced some of the same problems as Carter. Democratic constituencies pressed the new president to address concerns that had been suppressed during the previous twelve years of Republican rule. But Clinton's ambitious agenda often got lost in the minutiae of political battles and policy calculations. At an early meeting of the Clinton cabinet at Camp David, the Maryland presidential retreat, Clinton's communications advisers and his wife, Hillary Rodham Clinton, tried to get the president's communication with the public back on track. Mrs. Clinton told the group that Clinton's success as governor of Arkansas had hinged on his ability to describe his policy initiatives as a "story" with a beginning, middle, and end, so that the people could follow complex policy initiatives. Clinton had to do the same as president, Mrs. Clinton declared. The story would depict the long journey that the people would travel together—by way of the president's policy initiatives—and it would include tangible signs of progress at regular intervals. Without a coherent story line, the president would confuse and scare the people who supported him.[11] Clinton used the strategy successfully in his campaigns for the deficit-reduction bill and the North American Free Trade Agreement. The approach was unsuccessful, however, in the administration's push to reform the nation's health care system.

Presidents apply rhetoric to politics in a variety of ways. They meet regularly with reporters and other media representatives, give speeches on television and radio, address large crowds, hold informal meetings with leaders of interest groups, travel abroad to meet foreign leaders, meet and speak by telephone with members of Congress and other elected officials, and attend events that feature celebrities. Every president also commands large research and public relations operations in the White House and federal agencies. Finally, presidential appointees promote the administration's policies.

What presidents say is often less important than how they say it. In other words, the potency of presidential remarks lies not in their content but in the ceremonial way they are delivered. Deference to the president is the norm. As Hart has noted: "Precious few of these ten thousand texts [presidential addresses from Eisenhower to Reagan] were remembered by listeners even a day after their delivery. But what was recalled was the speech event itself—the crowds and the color and the dramaturgy and the physical presence of the chief executive."[12]

Political scientist Murray Edelman has argued that the stage on which a president appears can provide a rhetorical advantage because the stage removes the audience from its daily routine. "Massiveness, ornateness, and formality are the most common notes struck in the design of these scenes, and they are presented upon a scale which focuses constant attention on the difference between everyday life and the special occasion," Edelman writes. Such backgrounds make for heightened sensitivity and easier conviction in onlookers, for the framed actions are taken on their own terms. They are not qualified by inconsistent facts in the environment.[13]

Presidents bask in the regal splendor of the presidency whenever they make a public appearance. The podium usually features the presidential seal, and flags often hang somewhere within the audience's frame of vision. Standing alongside the president will likely be a line of dignitaries who look on with respect and even reverence. The distance between the president and the audience increases the sense of the president's "untouchable" status.

When presidents give their annual State of the Union address, they face a rare assemblage of both houses of Congress, the Supreme Court, and the cabinet; the vice president and Speaker of the House are seated behind the president, and a huge flag hangs in the background. The address provides a backdrop for national unity—however brief. Political scientist H. Mark Roelofs notes: "The general impression is of massed

The setting for a president's speech can be even more important than the words uttered. President Ronald Reagan's speech at the Statue of Liberty celebration on July 3, 1986, is a prime example. Nancy Reagan stands at the president's side.

cooperation, of forces of every sort coming centripetally together in the president's very person from every corner of the government, the nation, and even the world."[14] When presidents visit military officials, the backdrop might include an assemblage of highly disciplined officers and troops, an impressive-looking navy ship, or a military band. When they visit a foreign country, presidents are treated to welcomes from dignitaries and bands as well as formal dinners and presentations. When they welcome the winners of the World Series or Super Bowl, they are surrounded by the team's banners and other trappings of the sport.

Even in the most unceremonial situations, the president can use a particular setting to evoke strong national sentiment. After President Kennedy was assassinated in 1963, Lyndon Johnson took the oath of office on an airplane to emphasize the suddenness of the tragedy and the swift assumption of power. Soon after the truck-bombing of marine barracks in Lebanon in 1983, President Reagan stood in the drizzling rain with his wife and somberly read a statement of tribute to the murdered men and a warning to the forces responsible for the attack.

Although the major television networks occasionally refuse to broadcast an address, presidents almost always have the prestige to gain a wide electronic audience for their speeches and informal discussions. Radio stations always agree to broadcast short speeches and special events, such as Jimmy Carter's call-in show. The importance of televised speeches has increased since the 1960s as the number of press conferences has declined. The more formal talks give the president greater control over the agenda and tempo of the appearance than does the give-and-take of press conferences. *(See Chapter 3, The President and the News Media.)*

Early Eras of Presidential Appearances and Rhetoric

Even though the president always has been the preeminent single figure in American politics, only since the rise of an activist national government and vast systems of communications and transportation has the president been at the center of constant, partisan, policy-oriented rhetoric. In the early days of the Republic, presidents usually confined their public appeals to written messages and addressed only matters of broad national interest. Presidential messages, at least until Woodrow Wilson's administration (1913–1921), took on the quality of a national civics lesson in constitutional government rather than open appeals for political support.

The nation's history of presidential rhetoric can be divided roughly into three periods: the age of the Founders, the age of economic expansion and reform, and the age of presidential leadership. Abraham Lincoln's speech at Gettysburg in 1863 was a turning point in presidential rhetoric.

THE AGE OF THE FOUNDERS

The president's role in the nation's rhetoric was set by George Washington (1789–1797) and the rest of the "Virginia Dynasty," which ruled the young nation from 1789 to 1825. Everything Washington did was a conscious precedent for later presidents. Washington's immediate successors—John Adams, Thomas Jefferson, James Madison, and James Monroe—all had direct ties to the nation's founding. They all experienced the same fears about the dangers of democratic or "mob" rule and recognized the importance of the national leadership avoiding rhetorical excess. Thus the same impulse that led the Founders to set limits on democratic rule also led the first presidents to set limits on presidential rhetoric to avoid demagogy.

George Washington delivers his inaugural address, April 30, 1789, in New York's old City Hall.

The sense of rhetorical limits that guided presidential rhetoric for its first century began with Washington's first inaugural address. After hearing recommendations from his advisers, Washington discarded plans to include a seventy-three-page set of policy recommendations in his inaugural speech. Instead, he used the occasion to deliver a more general lecture on virtue and the need for guidance from the Constitution and from God. Washington was the only president to deliver his inaugural address to a select crowd of members of Congress and other dignitaries rather than to the people at large. As was true throughout his presidency, Washington tried to offer leadership by example, not by argumentation. Fearing that the regal ceremony of his inauguration might give later presidents dangerous dreams of monarchy, Washington issued a simple two-paragraph address at his second inaugural.[15]

With the exception of John Adams (1797–1801), later presidents until Abraham Lincoln (1861–1865) used the inaugural address to explain and extol the principles of republican government, complete with warnings about the potential excesses of democracy. Discussion of specific policy matters was infrequent and was always linked directly to the president's conception of American constitutional values. Of the early presidents, James K. Polk (1845–1849) was the most explicit on policy questions; in his inaugural address he pushed for lower tariffs and annexation of Texas and Oregon and opposed creation of a third national bank.

Early presidents also issued a variety of proclamations, mostly written. Those proclamations rarely argued any points; they usually stated government policies, from the institution of Thanksgiving Day to the emancipation of slaves in the South during the Civil War. As political scientist Jeffrey K. Tulis has noted, the proclamations derived their force not from argumentation but from appeals to the Constitution, the nation's sacred document.[16]

The most outstanding example of argumentation in a proclamation was Andrew Jackson's statement denying states the right to "nullify," or declare invalid, laws passed by the national government. Jackson's proclamation was more like a Supreme Court decision, explaining the rationale for an irrevocable decision, than like an attempt to persuade people to join a coalition.

Perhaps the most ceremonious speech presidents deliver regularly is the State of the Union address. Until Woodrow Wilson, however, presidents from Thomas Jefferson on had met the constitutional requirement to address the nation's affairs with a written report. Congressional leaders followed up the written report with a response to each of the president's points. The State of the Union address, then, was just the beginning of a formal dialogue about government policies based on constitutional and republican principles.

The nation's early years saw some presidential appeals to the people, but the rhetoric was restrained and the audience limited. Below the level of presidential politics, however, debate could be bitter and divisive. As historian Michael E. McGerr has noted, political debate took place as a public spectacle: "Through participation in torchlight parades, mass rallies, and campaign clubs and marching companies, men gave expression to the partisan outlook of the [fiercely partisan] newspaper press."[17] Political discussions in speeches, pamphlets, and newspapers could be personal and invective. Debates in Congress often took violent turns. City politics was organized by the gangs and political machines that operated in the streets. Mass demonstrations over slavery, labor, and U.S. involvement in wars were a regular part of the American landscape in the nineteenth century. People who worked for presidential campaigns often resorted to caustic language and threats. Through it all, however, the president stood above the fray, speaking little publicly about some of the most important issues of the day.

Up through the administration of Herbert Hoover, presidents spent several hours a week at the White House shaking hands with citizens. Right, the general public is admitted for a New Year's Day reception.

The Founders resisted unbridled democracy, and their rhetoric sought to dampen whatever political passions might exist at the time. The Constitution includes many mechanisms for blocking democratic processes, such as a federal system, an independent executive, a bicameral legislature, indirect election of presidents and (until 1913) senators, and an independent and tenured judiciary. The ideal political leader was not the man of the people, but rather the statesman who could guide the nation. Alexander Hamilton expressed this ideal in *Federalist* No. 71:

The republican principle demands that the deliberative sense of the community should guide the conduct of those to whom they entrust the management of their affairs; but it does not require an unqualified complaisance to every sudden breeze of passion, or to every transient impulse which the people may receive from the arts of men, who flatter their prejudices to betray their interests. . . . [W]hen occasions present themselves in which the interests of the people are at variance with their inclinations, it is the duty of the persons whom they have appointed to be the guardians of those interests to withstand the temporary delusion in order to give them time and opportunity for more sedate reflection.[18]

The president was expected to account for his actions in public, but not necessarily popular, messages. Written messages explaining vetoes and the "state of the union" would be available to Congress and anyone else educated and interested enough to seek them out, but presidents would not aggressively seek public support.

From the administration of George Washington through that of Herbert C. Hoover (1929–1933), the president spent several hours a week at the White House shaking hands with any citizen interested in glimpsing him. The "open house," usually held on Sundays after church services, did not communicate anything of substance, but it conveyed the message that the president would not be monarchical and removed from the people. After the sounding of trumpets and bands and the announcement that the president was on his way to meet the peo-

ple, single-file queues would move rapidly through the public room of the Executive Mansion. Presidents often tried to calculate just how many hands they would shake in an afternoon, as well as the handshake-per-minute rate. The conversation consisted of little more than greetings and best wishes, although some citizens occasionally tried to convey an opinion about a pressing policy question.[19]

The change in presidential rhetoric was marked by the way biographers treated presidents before and after 1930. Later biographers expressed puzzlement that the earlier presidents did not turn to rhetoric as a tool of leadership. But earlier biographers underscored the value of the "custom" of limiting public remarks since such remarks would "sacrifice [the president's] dignity to beg in person for their support."[20]

Tulis found evidence of some one thousand presidential speeches before the twentieth century. Of the twenty-four presidents who served during that period, only four attempted to defend or attack a specific piece of legislation, and only three—Martin Van Buren, Andrew Johnson, and Grover Cleveland—made partisan speeches. Only Lincoln addressed the war in which the nation was engaged at the time; Madison and Polk did not. Only nine presidents indicated the general policy directions of the nation in popular speeches. Eighty percent of the speeches were brief.[21]

Throughout the period, presidential rhetoric was circumscribed by the mores that Washington had established. The mores may have changed somewhat—policy issues crept into presidential speeches, even if they were tethered to constitutional principles—but they remained strongly in force. Just how strong the mores remained was underscored by the miserable failure of President Andrew Johnson (1865–1869) in his attempt to rally the public through a national speech-making tour in the early years of Reconstruction.

Washington, the nation's greatest public figure and a symbol of the new nation's unity, made several public tours in which he put himself on display, but the purposes of these excursions were limited. Washington traveled in order to gather information, ease tensions, and simply show himself to the people. He treated the tours "as auxiliary to the president's narrow executive function of carrying out the law and preserving tranquility, rather than his legislative responsibility to initiate new policies."[22] Washington set an important precedent by insisting on making written replies to the remarks of others after his speeches.[23] His farewell address was more scholarly than rhetorical—a document open for careful analysis.

The second president, John Adams, occasionally met with small groups but did not make public tours. Some historians suggest that Adams lost his chance to improve his public standing on issues, particularly foreign affairs, because of his public reticence. Thomas Jefferson (1801–1809), considered the most democratic theorist of early America, limited his public statements to a few meetings with American Indians and his formal, written messages to Congress. Despite a difficult war with Great Britain, James Madison (1809–1817) continued the practice of presidential communication by proclamation rather than speech.

James Monroe (1817–1825) reinstituted Washington's practice of the national tour, but otherwise stayed within the limits of unity appeals and limited speech. Despite his background as a teacher of rhetoric at Harvard College, John Quincy Adams (1825–1829) refused to do more than put himself "on display" in public gatherings. His public remarks were simple statements of greetings and congratulations. Adams almost never even referred to the public issues of the day before popular audiences.

After the bitter controversy surrounding the 1824 election of John Quincy Adams over Andrew Jackson (1829–1837), the nation experienced major pushes to expand the idea of democratic rule. Suffrage barriers related to property fell during this period as the nation moved westward and politicians from different regions competed for control over the nation's development. Political parties, which put forth radically different views of development and protection, gained legitimacy for the first time and created a regular public clash of ideas. The sectional tensions finally led to the bloody Civil War, which consumed the nation from 1861 to 1865.

Jackson rarely gave speeches. He enjoyed popular discourse, but once elected president he limited the number of his appearances and contained his argumentation within the limits set by his predecessors. Jackson's most public campaigns—those against the Bank of the United States and the doctrine of nullification—were quite limited. His public appeals were mediated—that is, he spoke to the public through the formal channels of official documents and proclamations. Jackson's annual messages and the nullification proclamation to Congress were all written appeals.

Jackson's successors also were reluctant to speak. Martin Van Buren (1837–1841) faced a boycott of council members in three New York towns after he delivered a slightly partisan remark, then abandoned any more such rhetoric. John Tyler (1841–1845) delivered no public addresses. James Polk (1845–1849) took one public tour but considered other public appearances a nuisance and therefore avoided them. Zachary Taylor (1849–1850) took one tour but avoided being seen; the journey was more a fact-finding tour than a public relations effort.

Millard Fillmore (1850–1853) became the first president after Washington to discuss policy in public when he defended the Compromise of 1850 in a series of short speeches. But these speeches took place after policy had been determined; they were not intended to sway action during the policy-making process. Franklin Pierce (1853–1857) expanded presidential rhetoric, discussing the role of tariffs and federalism. As a lame-duck president just before the Civil War, James Buchanan (1857–1861) discussed the nominating process of the Democratic Party and the role of property and popular rule in the states.

LINCOLN, RHETORIC, AND THE NEW NATIONAL IDEAL

Abraham Lincoln (1861–1865) carefully adhered to the limits of presidential rhetoric. But Lincoln's ruminations about the nation's fragility and destiny during the Civil War challenged Americans to adopt new values to give meaning to the Civil War.

Lincoln appeared before a number of groups but averred that he could not speak about policy except in an appropriate setting. Tulis has outlined five reasons for Lincoln's infrequent public rhetoric: modesty before his inauguration about his own "wisdom," a desire to let problems sort themselves out, the need for flexibility, the dramatic effect that his statements might have, and a desire to lend greater authority to the few public pronouncements he eventually would make.[24]

Still, Lincoln's addresses were an important part of his leadership. As Philip Abbott has noted, Lincoln's speeches focused on specific political problems, such as the lynching of an abolitionist journalist and the economic aspects of slavery. Lincoln carefully articulated principles to guide public opinion on these matters.[25]

Many scholars consider the Gettysburg Address to be the pivotal moment of Lincoln's presidency. The address provided a coherent way for Americans to understand the bitter Civil War that still threatened the Union. More important for the long term, the address helped to change the way Americans understood their government and changed the way in which all politicians talked with the people.

Lincoln appeared at Gettysburg, Pennsylvania, on November 19, 1863, months after the bloody battle that claimed more than forty thousand lives and provoked deep uncertainty on both sides about the strategy and objectives of the war. The occasion was the dedication of the battlefield's cemetery. Realizing the symbolic potency of cemeteries and the uneasy state of the nation one year before his reelection campaign, Lincoln prepared intensely for his appearance. *(See box, Gettysburg Address, p. 7.)*

Although he was not the main speaker at the dedication of the Union cemetery at Gettysburg, Pennsylvania, on November 19, 1863, Abraham Lincoln's short speech there has become one of the most cherished of the nation.

THE GETTYSBURG ADDRESS

On November 19, 1863, Abraham Lincoln rode a train from Washington to Gettysburg, Pennsylvania, to attend the next day's dedication of a cemetery in which six thousand casualties of the Battle of Gettysburg were buried. The battle, fought in early July, had helped to turn the tide of the Civil War in the Union's favor. Lincoln was not the main speaker at the dedication—that honor fell to former senator and renowned orator Edward Everett, who delivered a lengthy and moving address. Instead, Lincoln spoke briefly after Everett was finished.

The brilliance of the Gettysburg Address is that in the space of 272 words it solemnly and honestly acknowledges the awful pain of "these honored dead" while placing the war in which they had fought into the context of the struggle to attain "government of the people, by the people, for the people" that had begun "four score and seven years ago" in 1776. That struggle, Lincoln urged, must continue into "a new birth of freedom" so that the soldiers would "not have died in vain."

Four score and seven years ago our fathers brought forth on this continent, a new nation, conceived in Liberty, and dedicated to the proposition that all men are created equal.

Now we are engaged in a great civil war, testing whether that nation or any nation so conceived and so dedicated, can long endure. We are met on a great battle-field of that war. We have come to dedicate a portion of that field, as a final resting place for those who here gave their lives that that nation might live. It is altogether fitting and proper that we should do this.

But, in a larger sense, we can not dedicate—we can not consecrate—we can not hallow—this ground. The brave men, living and dead, who struggled here, have consecrated it, far above our poor power to add or detract. The world will little note, nor long remember what we say here, but it can never forget what they did here. It is for us the living, rather, to be dedicated here to the unfinished work which they who fought here have thus far so nobly advanced. It is rather for us to be here dedicated to the great task remaining before us—that from these honored dead we take increased devotion to that cause for which they gave the last full measure of devotion—that we here highly resolve that these dead shall not have died in vain—that this nation, under God, shall have a new birth of freedom—and that government of the people, by the people, for the people, shall not perish from the earth.

Garry Wills and other scholars argue that Lincoln's mere 272 words dramatically changed the basic creed of American politics.[26] In the address, Lincoln raised the Declaration of Independence above the Constitution as the nation's guiding light, stressed the notion of equality of citizens, and began the process of rebuilding the nation so bitterly consumed by the Civil War.

Lincoln's brief remarks gave the war a transcendent meaning that was not obvious amid the war's confusion and misery. He declared that the United States was a nation constantly in the process of becoming, not a nation already completed with the establishment of a constitutional system of government. Lincoln called on citizens to undertake "the great task remaining before us," which was to remake the nation.

Edward Everett, an Ivy League scholar, former senator, and diplomat, was the major speaker at Gettysburg. He spoke for more than two hours before Lincoln delivered his remarks and attracted the most press notice. Lincoln worked within the narrow constraints of presidential rhetoric, delivering only general remarks that made no direct reference to such divisive issues as slavery, parties, and elections. But Lincoln's Gettysburg Address was so infused with national symbolism that it eventually became one of the nation's greatest creedal statements. In fact, the abstractness of Lincoln's language elevated the speech above addresses that deal with the particulars of controversies.

The major theme of the speech was the equality of men in the experimental and uncertain American republic. Lincoln had always hedged on the question of the position of blacks in America, expressing opposition to slavery but acceptance of the idea of white superiority over blacks. Lincoln's statement that the Declaration "dedicated [the United States] to the proposition that all men are created equal" established a new foundation for the nation's ongoing struggle to order its affairs.

Lincoln's reference to "government of the people, by the people, for the people" forever fused the notions of liberty, equality, and democracy in American political thought. The importance of that rhetorical move can be appreciated only when the early American aversion to democracy—derisively called "mobocracy" or "Jacobinism" in the years after the Constitution was adopted—is recalled.

The style of Lincoln's speech also changed American discourse. Wills argues that Lincoln's fondness for the new medium of long-distance communications, the telegraph machine, shaped his speech patterns. "The language is itself made strenuous, its musculature easily traced, so even the grammar becomes a form of rhetoric. . . . Lincoln forged a new lean language to humanize and redeem the first modern war."[27]

But to call Lincoln's words simple would be wrong. The speech uses Latinate terms to elevate the basic simplicity of the message. Lincoln stated that "four score and seven years ago" the nation was "conceived in Liberty" and "dedicated to the proposition," and that the soldiers "consecrated" the battlefield. If he had wanted to make an ordinary speech, Lincoln would have used more ordinary words. But his goal was to lift the nation to a new public philosophy. Wills comments: "He was a Transcendentalist without the fuzziness."[28]

THE AGE OF ECONOMIC GROWTH AND REFORM

As the nation recovered from the Civil War, economic growth resumed on a scale never before imagined. Transportation and communications networks stretched across the country, and businesses grew in size and geographic importance. The national government played an important role in the expansion but did not address the negative consequences of rapid industrialization and urbanization. It responded to the economy's swings of boom and bust, but its role was limited by the constrained rhetoric and vision of public action. As politicians recognized the need for more concerted national action, both the rhetoric and the vision expanded.

When Abraham Lincoln was assassinated, Andrew Johnson became president. As a former Southern Democrat, Johnson had no real base of power in Washington. When he found himself under attack from all sides, he fought back with words. But his rhetorical thrusts further undermined his position.[29]

The dilemmas that Andrew Johnson faced after succeeding President Lincoln resembled the situation of modern presidents. Bereft of a strong party organization, dealing with an independent-minded Congress, facing deep sectional divisions, and lacking control over patronage, Johnson desperately needed a way to build his political strength. Like presidents in the twentieth century, Johnson sought that strength by appealing over the heads of political elites to the power of public opinion. But because the system was not accustomed to such appeals, Johnson's attempt to go public failed. He was the only president in history to be impeached, and one of the counts against him actually concerned the style of his "intemperate" rhetoric. Johnson

committed the most important rhetorical "crimes" while trying to rally public support for his policies toward the defeated states of the Confederacy. Tulis has described Johnson's rhetorical style:

Like contemporary electoral campaigns, Johnson had one rough outline, carried in his head, on which he rendered variations for particular audiences. In the typical speech, Johnson would begin by disclaiming any intention to speak, proceed to invoke the spirits of Washington and Jackson, claim his own devotion to the principles of Union, deny that he was a traitor as others alleged, attack some part of the audience (depending on the kind of heckles he received), defend his use of the veto, attack Congress as a body and single out particular congressmen (occasionally denouncing them as traitors for not supporting his policies), compare himself to Christ and offer himself as a martyr, and finally conclude by declaring his closeness to the people and appealing for their support.[30]

Johnson's tour, which received bad notices in the Republican-dominated press, was avoided even by Johnson's cabinet and aides. When on February 24, 1868, the House of Representatives resolved to impeach Johnson, the tenth and last article concerned Johnson's bad rhetoric. The Senate acquitted Johnson (by one vote), but no major political figure disagreed with the notion that his public appeals were improper. The lessons from Johnson's bitter experience were clear: politics is a dirty game, and presidents who become involved in the nasty rhetoric put themselves in danger of getting tarred in the process.

Ulysses S. Grant (1869–1877) and Rutherford B. Hayes (1877–1881), the two presidents immediately after Johnson, limited their public speech making to official greetings and plaudits to veterans and other groups. Both presidents refused to campaign for the White House and issued written statements to indicate policy preferences. Hayes delivered more than one hundred speeches, but they were limited to greetings to groups. This real but unsubstantive expansion of presidential speech might be attributed to the need to shore up national confidence because of the controversy surrounding Hayes's election by the House. (A House electoral commission had resolved disputed electoral returns from three southern states in Hayes's favor in an agreement to remove federal troops from the South and end Reconstruction.) Hayes also took several tours of the country and delivered speeches that addressed policy within the larger philosophical framework of republicanism.

James A. Garfield (1881) campaigned for the White House but did not speak on policy as president. His successor, Chester A. Arthur (1881–1885), also limited his talks to symbolic statements at public ceremonies. Grover Cleveland (1885–1889, 1893–1897) discussed taxes, civil service, and labor during his presidential campaigns but made few public remarks as president. He also wrote extensively on many issues. Benjamin Harrison (1889–1893) broke with tradition when he discussed policy issues such as the railroads and the postal service during his public tours; still, he was reluctant to go too far. He told a Kingston, New York, crowd, for example: "You ask for a speech. It is not very easy to know what one can talk about on such an occasion as this. Those topics that are most familiar to me, be-

Seeking to build his political strength, President Andrew Johnson made a speaking tour of the country in 1866.

cause I am in daily contact with them, namely, public affairs, are in some measure prohibited to me."[31]

William McKinley (1897–1901) vowed to talk on a wide range of issues, but his speeches were formal and philosophical in character like those of the nineteenth-century presidents. McKinley did not make any speeches on the Spanish-American War, the sinking of the battleship *Maine*, the Philippines, or southern race laws.

Theodore Roosevelt (1901–1909), the feisty former New York governor who assumed the presidency upon McKinley's assassination, was the first president since Andrew Johnson to go over the head of Congress to the people, but Roosevelt did not overturn the longtime balance of power between the two branches of government. As political scientist Elmer E. Cornwell Jr. has noted, Roosevelt's tours in behalf of specific policies began and ended before Congress took up the matter.[32]

Roosevelt's handpicked successor, William Howard Taft (1909–1913), increased presidential leadership of public opinion. Taft regularly issued lists of legislative initiatives he favored. He was more adept as an administrator than as a rhetorician, however. Although his antitrust and environmental policies were in line with Roosevelt's, his hortatory deficiencies were one of the reasons Roosevelt opposed him in the 1912 election.

Woodrow Wilson (1913–1921) was a crucial figure in the transformation of the national government from a congressional to a presidential system. He argued for a more unified system of government with the president as the leader, overcoming the fragmented, plodding committees in Congress. Moving public policy from the darkness of the committee meeting to the bright light of public debate was central to Wilson's system. He argued that the public could judge the president's character; if the public could find a leader to trust, the president could be entrusted with a wide grant of power. Wilson wrote: "Men can scarcely be orators without the force of character, that readiness of re-

source, that clearness of vision, that earnestness of purpose and that instinct and capacity for leadership which are the eight horses that draw the triumphal chariot of every leader and ruler of free men. We could not object to being ruled by such men."[33]

Wilson's ambitious domestic programs and involvement in World War I and the Versailles peace conference put the presidency in the middle of the nation's rhetorical battles. As historian David Green has argued, Wilson's public comments on the European war left room open for eventual U.S. involvement in the conflict. He promised to keep the United States out of war but contrasted American "liberty" with German "authoritarianism."[34]

Once the United States entered the war and the Allied powers won, Wilson took an active public role. His depiction of the war as the "war to end all wars" helped to overcome many of the deep internal divisions within the United States based on the nationalities of U.S. immigrant citizens. Wilson's 1919 trip to Versailles and his later parade through the streets of Paris were rare occurrences. The climax of this public role was his tour of the United States to build support for U.S. membership in the League of Nations. Wilson's moralistic campaign ended, however, when he collapsed from a stroke and the Senate rejected the treaty.

The presidents who succeeded Wilson—Warren G. Harding (1921–1923), Calvin Coolidge (1923–1929), and Herbert C. Hoover (1929–1933)—were less active rhetorically. Harding, nominated for president because of a backroom bargain at the Republican convention in 1920, limited his public appearances and statements and instituted a written-questions-only policy for the media. He died of a heart attack two years into his term. Coolidge—"Silent Cal"—was best known for his taciturn manner. In his press conferences, Coolidge continued Harding's policy of written press questions. Hoover was the first president to use radio extensively, but the audience was too small and

President Franklin D. Roosevelt gives one of his "fireside chats" national broadcasts from the White House, November 14, 1937.

Hoover's speaking style too formal for a strong president-public relationship to develop around his speeches. *(See Chapter 3, The President and the News Media.)*

THE AGE OF PRESIDENTIAL LEADERSHIP

During the Great Depression, which began in 1929, the nation turned to Franklin D. Roosevelt (1933–1945) for presidential leadership. Roosevelt was tireless in his efforts to expand the government's involvement in domestic and international politics.

Both Roosevelt's programs and his rhetoric emphasized the need for strong central direction that only a president could provide. For the first time, the government in Washington moved from its traditional role as patronage state to welfare state.[35] As the government became involved in all aspects of everyday life, the need for strong executive direction increased. In the meantime, sophisticated systems of communication tightened the bond between the president and the public. From Franklin Roosevelt to Bill Clinton some fifty years later, the president became more a rhetorical leader on a wide range of issues than an executive who dealt with a limited set of fundamentally national concerns.

By the time FDR took office, millions of American homes were tied together by the airwaves of radio broadcasting. Politics moved from the crowds to the smaller units of a radio-listening audience. Political speeches, once bombastic, became more conversational and intimate. As communications expert Kathleen Hall Jamieson has noted, this shift was reflected in the metaphors used to describe human relations. Warlike words such as *armed, forceful, take, hold, yield, marshal, battle, weapons,* and *onslaught* had often been used to describe political debates.

With the dawn of the media age came such warm, electrical words as *wavelength, relayed, channeled, transformed, turned on, fused,* and *defused.*[36]

Roosevelt was the perfect president to begin the new style of debate. Over the radio he delivered a series of "fireside chats" to the nation that identified him with everyday concerns. Roosevelt's secretary of labor, Frances Perkins, described the talks:

When he talked on the radio, he saw them gathered in the little parlor, listening with their neighbors. He was conscious of their faces and hands, their clothes and homes. His voice and his facial expression as he spoke were those of an intimate friend. . . . I have seen men and women gathered around the radio, even those who didn't like him or who were opposed to him politically, listening with a pleasant, happy feeling of association and friendship. The exchange between them and him through the medium of the radio was very real. I have seen tears coming to their eyes as he told them of some tragic episode, of the sufferings of the persecuted people in Europe, of the poverty during unemployment, of the sufferings of the homeless, of the sufferings of the people whose sons had died during the war, and they were tears of sincerity and recognition and sympathy.[37]

Since the end of World War II, presidents have spoken in public more than ten thousand times—an average of one speech every working day.[38]

Harry S. Truman (1945–1953) used rhetoric as a tool in his relations with Congress, but it always was directed toward specific policy aims. Truman relied on rhetoric to promote his policies on European redevelopment, relations with the Soviet Union, aid to Greece and Turkey, and civil rights. Truman's 1948 election campaign was a marathon of public speaking, a whistle-stop excoriation of Congress and a call for public support. Perhaps the Truman administration's most important legacy was its rhetoric about the Soviet Union. Truman acknowledged overstating the Soviet threat to arouse the public during the

Greece-Turkey crisis of 1947—after a congressional leader had advised him to "scare the hell out of the country."[39] Harsh anti-Soviet rhetoric starting with the Truman administration may have contributed to the bitterness of U.S.-Soviet relations and the costly nuclear arms race.

Because of improved air transportation, modern presidents have traveled regularly both within the United States and around the world. Presidents through Dwight D. Eisenhower (1953–1961) felt obliged to justify their trips abroad, but international travel has become a regular, expected, and even desired part of the office.

In addition to advanced systems of transportation and communication, the president's expanded role in national politics has stemmed from, among other things, the decline of political party strength, the development of popular nominating systems, the rise of political consultants, the fragmentation of Congress, and the "nationalization" of politics and policy.

Modern Presidential Appearances and Rhetoric

Presidential rhetoric in the postwar years shifted fundamentally with the ascension of John F. Kennedy to the White House. Harry Truman and Dwight Eisenhower used public speech almost solely in pursuit of a specific policy initiative, but later presidents spoke out regularly on a wide range of matters. Indeed, speech became a daily fact of life for modern presidents, who appeared willing and even compelled to talk about every possible aspect of political and social issues—even those about which they were ignorant. Presidents also began to speak before a greater variety of groups.[40]

Today, presidential speech is more personal than ever. Presidents even feel compelled to discuss their own emotions.

Whereas earlier presidents spoke formally about issues of great national importance, modern presidents talk in a conversational, intimate way.[41] The shift to the informal style was gradual. Eisenhower spoke formally, but, generally, presidents after Roosevelt at least tried to connect with the public in a casual way.

The number of self-references a president makes increases throughout the term of office. Typical are the following statements by Jimmy Carter: "I've always been proud of the fact that when I came to Virginia to begin my campaign a couple years ago and didn't have very many friends, I went to Henry Howell's home, and he and Betty were nice enough to. . . ." "I would like very much to tell my grandchildren that I slept in the same bed that was used by the governor of Virginia."[42]

Modern political discourse has become deeply personal in other ways as well. Jimmy Carter talked openly about his experiences as a sinning Christian Baptist; Ronald Reagan described his alcoholic father and "Huck Finn" childhood; and George Bush discussed the childhood death of his daughter Robin and offered that he had become "born again." Bill Clinton was often the most intimate of all, speaking emotionally about his fatherless childhood and his own lapses of marital fidelity.

THE KENNEDY STYLE

John Kennedy (1961–1963) may be considered the founder of modern presidential speech making. Indeed, he rose to the presidency in part because of his favorable television appearance during the 1960 election debates with Richard Nixon. Once he occupied the White House, Kennedy used his humor and his ease on camera and in group settings to disarm opponents.

Kennedy was the first president to make regular appearances year-round. Previous presidents and politicians had appeared publicly during elections and campaigns to tout specific policies, but Kennedy stayed in public view even during the slow

President John F. Kennedy developed a personal relationship with the public by pioneering the frequent use of televised press conferences.

summer months. Television—which by the early 1960s was in 90 percent of all American households—presented a powerful new opportunity for speaking directly to Americans.

President Kennedy used the presidential news conference to appear on television more frequently than previous presidents. The conferences usually took place during the day because White House aides worried about overexposure and the effect that mistakes would have on the president's public standing. Despite this reluctance, Kennedy was aware that the occupant of the Oval Office intrigued the public, and he moved to exploit that interest. Kennedy's wit played a central part in meetings with the press.

Beyond the development of a personal relationship with the public, speeches were at the center of the most important policy developments of the Kennedy years. The Bay of Pigs invasion, the Cuban Missile Crisis, the presidential visit to the Berlin Wall, the decision to accelerate the space program, relations with the Soviet Union, and the civil rights movement—all were marked by important addresses. Unlike the addresses of later presidents, the Kennedy speeches remain important today for their content as much as for the atmosphere in which they were delivered.

Kennedy's inaugural address was one of the most memorable in history because it was a new expression of national purpose and energy. Kennedy won the presidency in 1960 with the narrowest margin of victory ever, and he needed a rallying cry to establish his leadership. Congress was skeptical and moved slowly throughout Kennedy's presidency, making the president's stirring calls to action all the more important.

The speech after the failed Bay of Pigs invasion of Cuba in April 1961 is a classic statement of presidential responsibility for failed policy. The invasion by Cuban exiles, who were trained and equipped by the Central Intelligence Agency during the Eisenhower administration, was designed to topple Cuban leader Fidel Castro. Kennedy's response to the fiasco was one of his first tests as a world leader. Kennedy quickly reported the incident to the nation and took full responsibility for its failure. The report itself was viewed as an important test of the young president's ability to persevere and learn from mistakes.

In a nationally televised speech, Kennedy told the nation: "There is an old saying that victory has a hundred fathers and defeat is an orphan. . . . I am the responsible officer of government and that is quite obvious."[43] After the speech, Kennedy's poll support increased by 10 percentage points. Other presidents—most notably Ronald Reagan—have copied the technique of accepting responsibility for a failed undertaking, thereby defusing difficult political situations.

In 1962 President Kennedy used his television address on the Cuban Missile Crisis as a negotiating tool with the Soviet Union. Kennedy's selective use of information about the stalemate over Soviet placement of nuclear missiles in Cuba gave him flexibility in his private negotiations with Soviet leader Nikita Khrushchev. Later presidents all used dramatic television speeches as levers in their international bargaining. Nixon's speeches on the Vietnam War and Reagan's speeches on arms control are important examples.

The tension over the status of Berlin—a city in the middle of East Germany that was occupied by the four World War II Allied nations—produced two important kinds of public speech. As part of their own strategy of public diplomacy, Soviet leaders had threatened the status of the city's "free" sectors. Kennedy responded with a threatening television speech. The speech was not an ultimatum, but it evoked the possibility of nuclear war and even discussed the advisability of Americans building bomb shelters. One critic called it "one of the most alarming speeches by an American president in the whole, nerve-wracking course of the cold war."[44] The speech provided an impetus for Congress to mobilize and was a stark warning to the Soviets.

In June 1963, Kennedy visited Berlin. The famous "Ich bin ein Berliner" speech at the Berlin Wall was a classic statement to foreign publics and a warning to U.S. adversaries. The speech spoke through symbols in a very personal way about major issues of world politics. President Kennedy stood at the wall the Soviets had constructed to halt the free movement of citizens in the city and declared himself and the rest of the Western world citizens of the troubled city.

President Kennedy's speech at American University in Washington, D.C., the same month helped to establish a framework for the later policy of U.S.-Soviet détente. Few presidential speeches have helped to chart major changes in policy as much as that address.

JOHNSON AND NIXON

Lyndon Johnson (1963–1969) was a less graceful speaker than Kennedy, but he spoke even more frequently. Johnson's appearance before a joint session of Congress after Kennedy's assassination was crucial in restoring confidence and stability in the government. After winning election as president on his own in 1964, Johnson used a State of the Union address to outline his ambitious "Great Society" domestic programs.

Johnson also increased the number of domestic ceremonies, which already had quadrupled from the Eisenhower to the Kennedy administrations. He made a ceremony of the activities of every conceivable group that could be identified with the nation. Like later presidents, Johnson took refuge in ceremony, especially when polls showed low levels of public support.

Richard Nixon (1969–1974) ran his public relations campaign on two tracks: national television, where he gave regular addresses and press conferences, and local community and White House meetings, where he appeared before groups likely to support him. On the three issues that occupied Nixon the most—foreign policy (especially the Vietnam War), the economy, and Watergate—Nixon's strategy was closely tied to the way he presented himself to the public. From the time of his successful 1968 campaign, Nixon used public relations to bypass the Washington "establishment." Nixon's presidency was plebiscitary in that he sought public approval after acting on important issues.

Nixon was adept at using foreign travels to build public support. His 1972 trips to the Soviet Union and the People's Republic of China attracted unprecedented television and print coverage and established him as an epoch-making world leader.

Toward the end of his presidency, Nixon's public support fell precipitously—he had the approval of just 23 percent of the public before his resignation—and he tried to revive his fortunes with carefully orchestrated trips to small, friendly communities. Domestic trips to such places as Nashville's Grand Ole Opry gave the president a chance to get away from the insistent questioning of the national press corps. This strategy was lampooned in the newspaper comic strip "Doonesbury," which showed a fictional town called Critters, Alabama, awaiting a presidential motorcade.

Despite his reputation as a cold and even devious politician, Nixon often showed an emotional side to the public and to his staff. The emotional displays were at least partly responsible for many citizens' intense loyalty to the president. In his farewell talk to White House staff after his resignation, Nixon recalled his mother's guidance—he called her a "saint"—and his own setbacks as a politician. With tears in his eyes, he spoke of how Theodore Roosevelt fought to rebuild his life after the death of his first wife, implying that he would do the same after losing the presidency. Nixon's staff—and the television audience—was profoundly moved by the speech.

FORD AND CARTER

When Gerald R. Ford (1974–1977) inherited the presidency after Nixon resigned, his main job was to restore faith in the badly bruised presidency. In his first address to the nation, Ford declared that "our long national nightmare is over." Ford's relaxed style won him broad public support, but his popularity fell dramatically when he pardoned former president Nixon. Ford was unable to recover because of a lack of support in Congress and an inability to stir the nation with his words.

Ford was the nation's most voluble president, even if his many remarks did not win him much public support. Ford made public statements on 1,236 occasions in his less than two and a half years in office.[45] None of his speeches (except his first) was considered memorable, but that was not very important for Ford's immediate purpose of wrapping himself in the prestige of the presidency. The most memorable Ford statements were "gaffes," such as his declaration that Eastern Europeans did not consider themselves to be dominated by the Soviet Union. Ford's aborted public campaign to "Whip Inflation Now" also met with derision.

Jimmy Carter's rise to the presidency stemmed in part from his intimate statements during the 1976 campaign. Carter's presidency was filled with symbolic events and addresses to the nation; for example, he wore a cardigan sweater in his televised address asking the nation to make energy sacrifices. The crucial moment of the Carter term occurred when, after a ten-day consultation in July 1979 with more than one hundred government officials, economic advisers, business executives, and religious

Jimmy Carter's presidency was filled with symbolic addresses to the nation. Here he wears a cardigan sweater in his televised address asking the nation to make energy sacrifices.

leaders at Camp David, the president spoke on television about a "crisis of confidence" in the nation.

Carter, a tireless public performer, sometimes was very effective. Especially in small groups, Carter's grasp of facts and quiet manner were rhetorically impressive, but his halting speech and southern drawl did not serve him well on television and before larger groups. Moreover, the public did not always receive well his often gloomy assessments of world affairs, such as his descriptions of American moral decay, environmental dangers, human rights abuses, the Vietnam War's legacy, and nuclear war.

REAGAN, THE "GREAT COMMUNICATOR"

Ronald Reagan (1981–1989) presented a rosier picture of the future than Carter. Reagan's training as a movie actor, host of a television show, and speaker on the "mashed potato circuit" for General Electric served him well as a speaker both on television and before crowds. Reagan's optimism gained credibility from his upbeat reactions to such catastrophic events as the attempt on his life. After the 1981 shooting, Reagan told his wife, "Honey, I forgot to duck"—a line from an old Hollywood boxing movie.

President Reagan's reputation as the "Great Communicator" underscored the growing separation between the president and the message. All of Reagan's addresses were drafted by professional speechwriters, and even some of his apparently extemporaneous remarks, such as greetings to specific people and jokes, were scripted. Reagan held the fewest press conferences of any modern president because White House aides doubted his grasp of many policy issues and his ability to make statements that were not written out beforehand.

A number of embarrassing extemporaneous remarks seemed to suggest that Reagan was ill-informed about many of the subjects he addressed, such as the role of Americans in the Spanish Civil War, the effects of budget and tax cuts, weapons systems, the makeup of the nuclear "freeze" movement, Native Americans, monetary policy, and Central American and Soviet politics. Still, Reagan succeeded in promoting his policies because of his apparently deep and consistent convictions and his comfort with public speaking. With the possible exception of Kennedy, Reagan was the first president to have a well-developed affinity for the electronic media. That affinity carried over to live events because audiences in the media age are comfortable with public performances that resemble television appearances.

Reagan restored the pomp and ceremony stripped from the presidency in the reaction to Nixon's "imperial" administration. A hallmark of his appearances was the grand celebration of American icons, from the Statue of Liberty to ordinary citizens whom Reagan hailed as "heroes" during State of the Union addresses. Reagan basked unabashedly in hearing "Hail to the Chief" before his speeches, and his rhetoric about liberty and opportunity in America and the need to confront the Soviet Union in world politics was inspirational to many Americans weary of the apparent decline the United States had suffered in the 1970s.

Reagan's rhetoric failed conspicuously, however, when he tried to rally public support behind aid to the contra rebels, who were waging guerrilla warfare against the Nicaraguan Sandinista regime, between 1984 and 1986. Reagan delivered a total of thirty-two speeches during this period, all aimed at convincing the public that the Sandinistas posed a threat to their Central American neighbors. But the public did not budge in its opposition to military and financial aid to the rebels. Reagan's evocation of the "threat" posed by "communists," and his equation of the rebels with such groups as the Abraham Lincoln Brigade in the Spanish Civil War, did not resonate with the public. Reagan dropped his appeals after the so-called Iran-contra revelations.[46]

As Kathleen Hall Jamieson has argued, Reagan's speech making fit the intimate manner of public discourse during the age of mass media.[47] His descriptions of firsthand experiences and concrete events were lucid, but his remarks about more abstract policy matters often were disjointed. Earlier presidents had used first-person accounts, but Reagan's personal remarks were particularly effective because they used humor and modesty to portray him as a likable, stable figure. After brief periods in the hospital, Johnson and Nixon used personal anecdotes to attempt to connect with the public. But Johnson's words were cold, Nixon's

competitive. Reagan's presidency, by contrast, was a string of self-deflating cracks and yarns about his experiences in Hollywood and politics.[48]

BUSH

George Bush (1989–1993) had one of the hardest acts to follow in modern American history when he succeeded Ronald Reagan as president. Bush lacked Reagan's consistent ideology and affable storytelling technique. Partly as the result of a patrician upbringing, when he was taught not to talk about himself, Bush's attempts to relate to ordinary Americans were clumsy.

To make the best of his ordinary speaking ability, Bush's advisers cast him as a modest person who wanted to heal the divisiveness of American politics evident during the Reagan years. In accepting the Republican nomination, Bush promised a "kinder and gentler" nation in which opposing factions would be willing to work out compromises. Bush's inaugural address stressed a desire to work cooperatively with Congress. "The American people await action," he said. "They didn't send us here to bicker." The new president talked about the limits of governmental initiatives and resources: "We have more will than wallet." This modest demeanor continued after the ceremony. Bush and his wife greeted thousands of ordinary citizens in a receiving line at the White House.

Yet Bush was never able to develop a comfortable rapport with the American public. Conservatives in Bush's own party viewed the new president suspiciously, as did Democrats who charged that he conducted a dirty campaign in 1988. The problems confronting the nation—unprecedented budget and trade deficits, the breakdown of the savings and loan industry, economic stagnation, and uncertainty abroad from the Soviet Union to Nicaragua—did not lend themselves to sweeping programs. Articulation of the administration's purposes became difficult.

Bush vacillated between the rhetoric of confrontation and the rhetoric of conciliation. Overtures to groups that had been excluded in the Reagan years—African Americans, women, the disabled, urban dwellers—were countered by strident rhetoric on symbolic issues. Bush supported a constitutional amendment banning flag-burning as a mode of expression. His rhetoric on the measure was harsh.

Bush's most effective rhetoric—and ultimately his most damaging—was directed against the dictator of Iraq, Saddam Hussein. When campaigning in 1990 and 1991 for military action to expel Iraq from neighboring Kuwait, Bush compared Hussein to Hitler and warned that Iraq would obtain a nuclear weapon if Hussein was not defeated. Even though the U.S.-led coalition defeated Iraq decisively, Hussein remained in power. Bush's own rhetoric about Iraq was used against him in the 1992 election.

CLINTON

Bill Clinton provided a stark contrast to Bush, yet his rhetoric was not much more effective. Clinton appeared frequently in public to promote his activist agenda. But he jumped from issue to issue; many of his initiatives did not get the follow-up necessary to keep them in the public spotlight; and his rhetoric often strayed off the major themes of the administration.

Clinton's best performances came when he could use public appearances to display his vast knowledge of government. In his 1993 health care address to Congress, the TelePrompTer flashed the text of his earlier State of the Union message, but Clinton forged on with a detailed and spirited pitch for his health care reform plan. He also performed well in formal press conferences.

Clinton gave particularly effective speeches on what he called the moral crisis of the nation. In an address at a Memphis church, Clinton challenged African Americans to recover the spirit and aims of the civil rights movement and put an end to inner-city violence and family breakdown. He later gave a well-regarded speech on the breakdown of the American family and community. These addresses were intended to give the administration—and the nation—a focus for Clinton's far-flung agenda. But experts questioned whether rhetoric could make Clinton's agenda coherent in an age fragmented by interest group politics, an explosion of mass media outlets, growing cynicism, and decline in social mores.

Kinds of Presidential Speeches

The president has different ways and reasons to communicate with the public. How widely the president's remarks will be circulated is the main consideration for the tone and content of a speech. The audience's role in the president's past and future political battles is another consideration. Still another is the president's current political standing with the public and with various interest groups.

The deadlock in U.S. domestic politics may explain the shift in the content of televised speeches from foreign to domestic affairs. Presidents Carter and Reagan were more likely to devote air time to domestic affairs than were their predecessors. Both sought to overcome interest group alignments on such issues as energy, taxes, and budgetary matters through appeals to the public at large.[49]

The effect of presidential speech making is complex. In one respect, the greater emphasis on rhetoric centers the whole political system on the presidency; the other parts of the system—such as parties, interest groups, and regions—become subordinate to the White House. But as political scientist Samuel Kernell has argued, presidential speeches are neither a plebiscitary nor a leveling force in U.S. politics. Presidents "go public," in Kernell's words, to assemble temporary coalitions of many different groups on specific policies.[50] Indeed, the explosion in minor addresses supports Kernell's contention that the system remains complex despite the president's primacy. (See Table 1-2.)

Presidential speeches can be broken down by audience, mode of communication, purpose of the address, and political

TABLE 1-2 Minor Presidential Speeches by Year, 1945–1994

Truman, I		Nixon, II	
1945	4	1973	12
1946	0	1974	10
1947	1	Total	22
1948	0	Yearly average	12
Total	5	Monthly average	1.1
Yearly average	1		
Monthly average	0.1	Ford	
		1974	5
Truman, II		1975	36
1949	8	1976	36
1950	13	Total	77
1951	9	Yearly average	35
1952	9	Monthly average	2.7
Total	39		
Yearly average	10	Carter	
Monthly average	0.8	1977	21
		1978	15
Eisenhower, I		1979	22
1953	5	1980	24
1954	2	Total	82
1955	2	Yearly average	21
1956	2	Monthly average	1.7
Total	11		
Yearly average	3	Reagan, I	
Monthly average	0.2	1981	11
		1982	27
Eisenhower, II		1983	19
1957	5	1984	21
1958	7	Total	78
1959	2	Yearly average	20
1960	4	Monthly average	1.6
Total	18		
Yearly average	5	Reagan, II	
Monthly average	0.4	1985	6
		1986	2
Kennedy		1987	7
1961	6	1988	1
1962	7	Total	16
1963	17	Yearly average	4
Total	30	Monthly average	0.3
Yearly average	10		
Monthly average	0.9	Bush	
		1989	9
Johnson[a]		1990	2
1963–1964	11	1991	7
1965	9	1992	2
1966	11	Total	20
1967	4	Yearly average	5
1968	14	Monthly average	0.4
Total	49		
Yearly average	10	Clinton[b]	
Monthly average	0.8	1993	26
		1994	23
Nixon, I		Total	49
1969	5	Yearly average	24.5
1970	6	Monthly average	2.0
1971	10		
1972	4		
Total	25		
Yearly average	6		
Monthly average	0.5		

SOURCE: Lyn Ragsdale, *Vital Statistics on the Presidency* (Washington, D.C.: Congressional Quarterly, 1996), 171–172.

NOTES: For two-term presidents: I (first term); II (second term).   a. Includes full term from November 1963 to January 1969.   b. 1993–1994 only.

situation at the time of the speech. There are six basic categories of presidential addresses: ceremonial speeches, official state speeches, general persuasive speeches, hortatory or moralistic speeches, crisis speeches, and addresses to specific groups. Some speeches fit more than one category.

CEREMONIAL SPEECHES

As the symbolic embodiment of the nation, the president represents the United States in international affairs and in events held abroad and designed to underscore the country's unity and progress. The president also sets the tone for a number of domestic events, such as presentation of awards and space shuttle launchings, and issues, such as the fight against drug abuse.

As Roderick Hart has noted, the increase in presidential speech making since World War II is largely attributable to ceremonial events. The average number of monthly ceremonial speeches increased from 2.4 under Truman and 3.4 under Eisenhower to 15.2 under Ford and 10.7 under Carter.[51] The monthly average of ceremonial speeches by Reagan—7.85—was not as high as those of his predecessors, but it was still significant. Reagan also made ceremonies out of businesslike events, such as the State of the Union address and interest group speeches.

The chief of state role strengthens the president's efforts to build widespread support for policies and ideas that are part of his political program. Hart has noted: "To stand in this spotlight is to risk comparatively little, for in such situations listeners' defenses are down, the press is prohibited by cultural mandate from being excessively cynical, and the institution of the presidency—its traditions and its emotional trappings—insulate the chief executive from partisan attack."[52]

Hart has identified four kinds of presidential ceremonies.[53] *Initiating ceremonies* mark major transitions—signing legislation or treaties and swearing in government officials. *Honorific ceremonies* bestow some formal recognition of achievement. Testimonial dinners, awards of medals, and university commencements all fit into this category. *Celebrative ceremonies* pay tribute to important national events or values. They include eulogies, dinners for foreign dignitaries, patriotic remembrances, and building dedications. The Statue of Liberty celebration in New York in 1986 was a prime example. *Greeting and departure ceremonies* mark the important travels of presidents and foreign dignitaries.

Inaugural addresses (initiating ceremonies) are the premier ceremonial speeches of the presidency. A president sets the tone for the administration at the inauguration. Traditionally delivered at the steps of the Capitol right after the swearing-in, the inaugural address provides the most important hint of the kind of moral leadership the chief executive wants to provide. The president uses the inaugural address to unite a nation that has just undergone a partisan election campaign. In the address, the president asks the opposition for help and asserts that the nation's factions have common purposes despite disagreements about how to achieve goals.

The State of the Union address, delivered before a joint session of Congress, the Supreme Court, and the cabinet, has become a major forum for presidents to announce new initiatives or goals for their administrations. Here President Bill Clinton delivers his 1996 State of the Union address.

The content of most inaugural addresses is usually forgotten soon after the event. Some addresses have been so eloquent or poignant, however, that they have become part of the nation's "civic religion." Thomas Jefferson's first inaugural argued that the nation shared a common purpose despite the bitter battles of the Federalists and the Anti-Federalists. Andrew Jackson asserted the power of the common man in his inaugural. Abraham Lincoln's second inaugural was an eloquent appeal for national healing in the midst of the horrors of the Civil War:

With malice toward none, with charity for all, with firmness in the right as God gives us to see the right, let us strive on to finish the work we are in, to bind up the nation's wounds, to care for him who shall have borne the battle and for his widow and his orphan, to do all which may achieve and cherish a just and lasting peace among ourselves and with all nations.

Other famous inaugural addresses include Franklin Roosevelt's 1933 admonition that "the only thing we have to fear is fear itself" and John Kennedy's 1961 call for national sacrifice. Kennedy urged: "Ask not what your country can do for you; ask what you can do for your country." Kennedy also pledged to "friend and foe alike" that the United States would be an active force in international affairs.

Eulogies at state funerals (celebrative ceremonies) are considered above partisanship. The speaker attempts to associate with the person being eulogized and to rise above the nation's political divisions. Bill Clinton's eulogy of former president Richard Nixon in 1994 aimed to heal the lingering bitterness of the Vietnam War and the Watergate scandal. "May the day of judging President Nixon on anything less than his entire life and career come to a close," Clinton said.

Presidents' farewell addresses (departure ceremonies) can help to set the tone for the next administration and, more likely, help to shape the nation's memory and assessment of the outgoing executive. The farewell can be an emotional time for the president, the public, and the president's closest political allies. (*See "Speeches of Departing Presidents," p. 25.*)

When moving from active leader to historical figure, presidents are not subject to the same political pressures as an incumbent and cannot muster the same clout. The farewell address can exert great force over time but is not likely to have much of an effect on politics immediately. The purpose is to leave the nation with a lasting statement of principles from an elder statesman to which it can refer. George Washington's farewell set substantive policy and etiquette for future presidents. Other important farewell addresses were delivered by Jackson, Cleveland, Eisenhower, Nixon, and Carter.

OFFICIAL STATE SPEECHES

The Constitution requires the president to make a statement "from time to time" on the "state of the Union," and since Woodrow Wilson every president has personally addressed a joint session of Congress once a year to propose policies and to assess the nation's problems and achievements. (Thomas Jefferson discontinued the practice of personal, oral delivery of State of the Union reports, which George Washington had begun, choosing instead to present them in writing.)

The State of the Union address has become a major event in presidential leadership and congressional relations. Delivered before a joint session of Congress, the Supreme Court, and the cabinet, these addresses survey the range of budgetary and other policies that the administration plans to pursue. Even if the administration has not completed the design of its programs, presidents announce their major initiatives in the address.

Lyndon Johnson's Great Society and Vietnam initiatives; Richard Nixon's Vietnam, "New Federalism," and economic programs; Jimmy Carter's energy, civil service, welfare and tax reform, and foreign affairs initiatives; Ronald Reagan's tax, budget, regulatory, and military programs; George Bush's budget and foreign policies; and Bill Clinton's health care reform initiative—all were outlined in State of the Union addresses.

Because many programs are announced without thorough planning, there is a danger that the State of the Union address could create false expectations and eventual disappointment. Many of Johnson's Great Society programs, for example, were in their nascent stages when announced. The combination of warlike rhetoric and fragmented program designs contributed to the disappointment with many of the programs—among them, the Community Action program, which had been designed to "empower" the urban poor.

Other state speeches include addresses to foreign bodies such as the British Parliament and the United Nations General Assembly.

GENERAL PERSUASIVE SPEECHES

Most presidential addresses seek to develop a favorable environment for a wide variety of policies, but less than half of presidential speeches try to persuade the public to adopt specific policies and directions.

Woodrow Wilson's national campaign after World War I for Senate acceptance of the Versailles treaty and the League of Nations was perhaps the most dramatic example of persuasive oratory in U.S. history. Unwilling to bargain with the Republican leaders on the treaty, Wilson traveled eight thousand miles in a month, starting on September 3, 1919. He delivered thirty-seven speeches and attended even more public events at which he urged the treaty's passage. Wilson's tour ended when he collapsed of a stroke. The Senate defeated the treaty.

Reagan successfully urged passage of his tax and budget packages in 1981. On February 5, Reagan told a national television audience that the nation faced the "worst economic mess since the Great Depression." Less than two weeks later, Reagan told a television audience about his plans to deal with the problem. After an assassination attempt boosted his popularity, Reagan, in late April 1981, addressed an enthusiastic joint session of Congress. In July he returned to national television and asked viewers to pressure Congress to support administration policies. Reagan's appeal generated fifteen million more letters than Congress normally receives in a session.[54]

Other recent examples of major persuasive speeches include Kennedy's addresses on civil rights and economics; Johnson's addresses on Vietnam, social problems, and domestic disorder; Nixon's speeches on Vietnam, the economy, and Watergate; Ford's addresses on the economy and his pardon of Nixon; Carter's energy and economic speeches; Bush's speeches on the Gulf War; and Clinton's speeches on health care.

HORTATORY OR MORALISTIC SPEECHES

The president sometimes attempts to persuade Americans to set aside personal, selfish aims and to seek goals more in the interest of the general public. Like a high school football coach, the president also attempts to infuse the public with confidence and zeal for tasks that may seem difficult.

Presidential speech making in the nation's first century usually was confined to educational or moralistic messages. On their tours of the expanding nation, presidents discussed constitutional and republican principles, federalism, economic policies, and the place of American values in world politics.

Twentieth-century president Jimmy Carter spoke frequently on the energy crisis—so frequently that he began to worry that Americans were "inured" to the major problems that the issue presented. In 1979, after a ten-day retreat to Camp David, Carter delivered a speech about what he called the nation's "crisis of confidence" in an attempt to confront the public's blasé attitude.

The speech, with its choppy text, failed to offer a plan of action that matched the spiritual crisis Carter described. Thus, although delivered in an atmosphere of crisis, the address was quickly dismissed. Republican opponents in 1980 revived the speech as evidence of Carter's leadership failures.

Clinton's strongest speech was delivered in November 1993 at the Memphis pulpit where Martin Luther King Jr. gave his last speech before he was assassinated in 1968. Clinton challenged the congregation to live up to King's ideals of nonviolence at the community level and to end the gang and drug violence in the inner city. If Martin Luther King were to reappear, Clinton said, he would decry the violence in America's cities and the breakdown of the African American family.

He would say, "I did not live and die to see the American family destroyed. I did not live and die to see 13-year-old boys get automatic weapons and gun down 9-year-olds just for the kick of it. I did not live and die to see young people destroy their own lives with drugs and then build fortunes destroying the lives of others. This is not what I came here to do. I fought for freedom."

This address exemplified President Clinton's increasing tendency to use moral and religious themes in his rhetoric. Through moralistic speeches Clinton attempted to counter the growing cynicism and defeatism that he felt threatened his activist policy agenda.

CRISIS SPEECHES

The public turns to the president for leadership during crises and other difficult times, partly out of practical considerations—the president is the political figure most familiar to most Americans—and partly out of a psychological need for the reassurance that strong leadership can provide.

A presidential speech in times of crisis can mobilize the nation almost instantly. Franklin Roosevelt's call for war on the Axis powers in World War II after the December 7, 1941, bombing of Pearl Harbor, for example, changed the public's mood dramatically. Before the dramatic address to a joint session of Congress, the public and Congress were reluctant to enter the foreign war; after the speech, public opinion favored all-out involvement.

John Kennedy's addresses on the failed invasion of the Bay of Pigs, confrontations with the Soviet Union over the status of Berlin, and the Cuban Missile Crisis were among the most dramatic speeches in modern history. Each suggested the possibility of apocalyptic confrontations. The youthful Kennedy was able to use the speeches to build confidence in his own leadership, even on occasions when his administration had failed, as at the Bay of Pigs.

Lyndon Johnson's first presidential address was another major crisis speech. Both the traumatized Congress and the public watched the address not only for clues of Johnson's policy intentions but also for signs of the stability of the government five days after President Kennedy's assassination on November 22, 1963. Johnson and his aides worked on the speech almost without interruption throughout those five days and produced an address that reassured the nation of the government's stability and Johnson's own vigor. Johnson was able to outline his own legislative program while paying homage to the martyred Kennedy. "Let us continue," Johnson said, in a reference to Kennedy's "Let us begin."[55]

Richard Nixon delivered a number of addresses on the Vietnam War and the Watergate affair, but with mixed success. Nixon slowly developed a national consensus on the war and blunted opposition to his bombings of Laos and Cambodia.[56] He was unable to convince the nation of the credibility of his statements on the Watergate affair, however. In fact, his many television speeches on the campaign scandal gave rise to more questions and criticisms than they answered.

Carter's "crisis of confidence" speech may fit in this category as well as the hortatory category. Other crisis speeches Carter delivered included those on the Soviet invasion of Afghanistan, on the discovery of Soviet troops in Cuba, and on the American hostages in Iran.

Speeches marking national crises give the president the opportunity to rise above partisan disputes and represent the nation as a whole. President Gerald Ford's statement that "our long national nightmare is over," after Richard Nixon resigned the presidency in disgrace in August 1974, was credited with

Just five days after Kennedy's assassination, President Lyndon Johnson delivers a painstakingly worded speech to Congress. The address reassured the nation during a time of crisis.

healing the nation. Ronald Reagan's speech after the explosion of the *Challenger* space shuttle in 1985 promoted a sense of national community and loss.

The wide latitude that the public gives presidents during a crisis invites possible abuse of the crisis speech. President Johnson reported in 1964 that North Vietnam had attacked U.S. ships without provocation in the Gulf of Tonkin and quickly won congressional approval of a resolution that granted him almost unlimited war powers. But the evidence supporting the North Vietnamese attack was questionable at best, as Johnson privately acknowledged. The crisis atmosphere created by Johnson's speech may have been the most important element in the growing U.S. involvement in the war.

A crisis may give the president an opportunity for rhetorical leadership, but it does not guarantee success. President Carter's address after the Soviet invasion of Afghanistan eventually fueled the arguments of critics on both the left and the right that Carter was too naive and inexperienced to continue as president. Carter stated that the invasion fundamentally changed his perception of the nature of the Soviet Union.

Failure to give an address during a major crisis can undermine the president's support. Herbert Hoover's unpopularity after the Great Crash of 1929 was attributable not so much to his policies as to his inability to convey a sense of national purpose and sympathy for the victims of the economic depression.

ADDRESSES TO SPECIFIC GROUPS

As the government has become more complex and more interest groups have developed permanent ties to the government, presidents have spent more time addressing specific groups. The purpose of such addresses is often nothing more than flattery. Whether delivered to faithful supporters or to skeptical adversaries, such addresses are designed to create a feeling of goodwill toward the presidency. These addresses often include a specific appeal that is designed for media coverage.

The advantage of appearing before specific constituency groups is that remarks can be tailored to the group, and the president's words will be transmitted to the larger group membership for weeks after the speech. By merely accepting an invitation to address a particular group, a president tells the group that it is important.

Appearances before constituencies also allow the president to see how they might behave during the "bargaining" process over budgetary, tax, and other current legislative matters. The president can then fine-tune the White House approach on those issues. The National Association for the Advancement of Colored People (NAACP) provided presidents from Franklin Roosevelt on with strong signals about the civil rights initiatives it would find meaningful.

Perhaps more important, the president also can use interest group appearances to line up support for policy initiatives. Presidents frequently appear before business and labor groups to seek backing for their economic programs. Carter tried to build support for his energy program and Panama Canal treaties with appearances before interest groups, but he was opposed by a well-financed cadre of conservatives.[57]

Business organizations are perhaps the most constantly courted in the constellation of interest groups. Presidents of both parties need support from business to pursue their economic and social policies. Some presidents—such as Franklin Roosevelt, Harry Truman, and John Kennedy—publicly attacked business but eventually had to build support among businesspeople.

Other groups to be courted depend on the president's base of support. Almost half of all speeches by postwar presidents were "targeted" appeals to specific constituencies. Most such appeals take place in or around Washington, D.C., where national organizations are housed. Groups ranging from the AFL-CIO to the Christian Coalition attract the sporadic attention of the president.

Government workers are one of the most important interest groups the president addresses. Especially when morale is low in departments, the president's words can provide a big lift. Speaking before government groups also enables the president to lay out policy positions in the sanctified arena of officialdom. Because the president's words are usually reported widely, the government audience provides an opportunity to talk about a wide range of issues. Jimmy Carter spoke to government workers on the morality of couples living together outside marriage.

As the leader of the national party, the president also delivers a number of partisan addresses. These appeals usually take place during important election campaigns. President Reagan, for example, was tireless in campaigning for Republican congressional and gubernatorial candidates in the 1980s. An unpopular president is not asked to participate in other campaigns. Democratic candidates studiously avoided Carter in the 1980 campaign and Clinton in the 1994 midterm campaign.

Appearances before groups also can distract them so that the administration can pursue other priorities. During his tax and budget initiatives of 1981 and 1982, Reagan used rhetoric to allay the concerns of religious organizations, who wanted immediate action on abortion, school prayer, and other social issues. Reagan promoted state education reforms in a series of speeches in 1983 and 1984, defusing pressure for national initiatives and spending increases.

Presidents often appear before skeptical groups to co-opt whatever opposition they might present and to portray themselves as leader of all the people. Good examples are Carter's appearances before the Veterans of Foreign Wars and Reagan's speeches to the NAACP. Presidents sometimes deliberately even antagonize certain interest groups to solidify the alliances that have developed in opposition to those groups.[58]

The Imperative to Speak

Because the presidency is central to American politics, presidents are expected to offer authoritative opinions even on subjects about which they are ignorant or uncertain. As presidents move past the first year or so of their terms, the imperative to speak grows because they must shore up political standing after an inevitable decline.

Speech is an important strategic weapon for the president. Every new administration usually enjoys a honeymoon period of six months to a year in which Congress and the public are inclined to yield to presidential leadership on many important questions. Lyndon Johnson's Great Society legislation of 1965 and Ronald Reagan's budget- and tax-cutting initiatives of 1981 are notable examples.

After the initial period of goodwill, however, presidents begin to lose their appeal. The president is better known and develops disputes with more groups as the term progresses.

The president also must accept responsibility for many of the nation's problems that were previously blamed on Congress or on a former president. Political scientist John E. Mueller has asserted that the longer the president is in office, the more a "coalition of minorities" develops grievances that cut the president's base of support.[59]

Presidents tend to increase their speech making considerably from the first to the second year in office. For example, Carter delivered 282 speeches in his first year and 323 in his second year; Reagan delivered 211 in his first year and 344 in his second. As the reelection campaign nears, presidents give even more speeches. Ford increased the number of his speeches from 392 to 682 in the year of his reelection bid. The figures for Carter were 272 and 436; for Reagan, 384 and 421.[60]

Because presidents no longer can count on party machinery or congressional leadership for support, they turn to the public. Several presidents have appealed to the public "over the heads of Congress" when Congress has shown reluctance to go along with legislative initiatives. Carter's public statements on western water projects, the Panama Canal treaty, the nation's energy problems, relations with the Soviet Union, and economic problems were all intended to overcome resistance to unpopular programs on Capitol Hill. The psychological demands of the presidency probably contribute to the tendency to speak often, as political scientist Bruce Buchanan has suggested. Stress, deference from underlings, and the search for clear signs of success combine to push the president toward dramatic rhetoric. Frustrated presidents search for scapegoats to pummel in public in order to improve their own relative standing and their leverage over the political process.

The imperative to speak is self-generating. "Presidents have developed a rhetorical reflex, a tendency to resort to public suasion as an initial response to a political situation," Hart has written. Carter displayed the built-in push toward presidential speech. "Always he spoke, and the speaking justified its own continuance: if the coverage were favorable, it stood to reason that more speaking would generate even more flattering responses from the media; if the press disparaged him, more speaking would set matters right."[61]

If presidents need to go public to promote their political agendas, that does not mean they speak all the time about important policy issues. Much of the president's time is occupied with noncontroversial, almost trivial appearances, such as presentation of awards and proclamations of special days. Even if these talks appear trivial, they strengthen the president's public standing and symbolic hold on the nation and its different "publics."[62]

One of the reasons the president turns to rhetoric is the institutionalization of speech writing and public relations efforts in the White House. The president has a growing corps of aides who analyze the political situation and develop public campaigns for improving it.

The emergence of a public presidency presents dangers as well as opportunities for the chief executive. If the president is blamed by the media or the voters for problems, making regular appearances can aggravate rather than improve the president's position. The regular presence can serve as a constant reminder of the administration's failings.

Jimmy Carter suffered politically in 1980 because voters associated him with the Iranian hostage crisis, "stagflation," tense relations with the Soviet Union, and divided leadership in Washington. When Carter appeared on television or before groups, he struck many as tired and ineffectual. But the problem of "overexposure" did not begin with Carter. Both John Kennedy and Lyndon Johnson were criticized for speaking too much. During Clinton's first year in office, his proclivity to discuss any subject was seen as a liability by his advisers, who convinced the president to cut back on his daily exposure to the media.

Presidents are trapped by their public utterances in many ways. Because the media record every public word, presidents must carefully weigh the effect of their statements and take care not to get caught in a tangle of contradictory remarks.

Critics of the "Rhetorical Presidency"

Critics of the new rhetorical style argue that it has led to confusion on the part of both the president and the public about the difference between political action and political speech. The president's dominance in politics also "crowds out" other legitimate actors and issues.[63]

When a presidential address or "photo opportunity" is treated as a meaningful political event, attention is diverted from the complicated process of policy making and implementation that is the substance of politics. Not only the public but also the president can be deceived about the state of government activity. Media coverage of speeches reinforces the notion that speech is tantamount to substantive action.

As political scientist Bruce Miroff has argued, the president's dominance of U.S. politics starves the political actors and issues not in the president's orbit. That is, the president's "monopolization of public space," as Miroff put it, simplifies issues and distances politics from the average citizen; politics becomes a spectator sport. The citizen's "vicarious" relationship to important policy issues also reduces important policy decisions to a game. The suspense over Jimmy Carter's decision on whether to produce the B-1 bomber, for example, concerned the game-like political maneuvering and not the merits of the superbomber.[64]

Theodore J. Lowi points out that the movement toward a rhetorical presidency has led to an "oversell" of specific policies that breeds disappointment. "Such are the president's channels of mass communication that he must simplify and dramatize his appeals, whether the communication deals with foreign policy, domestic policy, or something else again. Almost every initiative is given a public relations name. Every initiative has to be 'new and improved.'"[65] Steps taken to simplify and dramatize policies remove them from their natural state of uncertainty and complexity—and produce frustration and cynicism when major improvements do not result.

Presidents have taken to more frequent speech in part to improve the chances of their legislative and other initiatives, but the link between speech and success has proved tenuous at best. Legislative success is no greater in the modern age of presidential talk than it was in the earlier periods of limited speech. Presidents Eisenhower, Kennedy, Johnson, and Nixon won close to three-quarters of their major tests in Congress while giving an average of 150 policy speeches a year between 1957 and 1972. Presidents Nixon, Ford, and Carter won less than 60 percent of the key issues between 1972 and 1979 while speaking more than 200 times a year.[66]

More frequent presidential communications—not only speech but also written material—do not appear to have increased the understanding between the leaders and the led. Americans continue to exhibit ignorance of most public policy issues despite the ubiquitous media "teaching" of the president. Even more revealing, Americans tell pollsters that they feel increasingly ignored. Voters sense that politicians talk to them but do not listen.[67]

Presidential speech making also reduces the president's control over the job. Because presidents speak so often, they cannot possibly write or even contribute significantly to the drafting of speeches. The White House speech-writing corps drafts all the president's words. If presidents do not have to work on the complex ideas they present to the public, they are less likely to have a thorough and nuanced understanding of issues.

One authority has argued that the "scripted presidency" might have contributed to Reagan's decision to trade arms to Iran in exchange for the release of American hostages in Lebanon. "President Reagan's reliance on speechwriters and before them [movie] scriptwriters played a role in his disposition to accept information about the Iran/Contra dealings uncritically and to trust his aides to act in his best interest."[68]

Proponents of constant presidential talk say it brings the political process into the open. Because presidents are such compelling figures, what they say attracts wide attention and makes politics a more open affair. But presidents must be cautious because their remarks are so thoroughly covered, and that caution can drain public politics of any meaningful content. The effect, ironically, is that open, public politics can drive important policy discussions underground.

The tendency to "go public" is one result of the decline of party strength in Congress. Since World War II, the president and Congress have been from different parties during all or part of the administrations of Eisenhower, Nixon, Ford, Reagan, Bush, and Clinton. Even when the president's party controls Congress, support for specific policies must be developed issue by issue. Public support has therefore become a crucial tool for prodding Congress.

The President and the Foreign Policy Debate

Every president since Theodore Roosevelt has traveled to foreign countries, but only since the Eisenhower administration have such trips become a regular part of the president's routine. (See Table 1-3.) Many of the trips have been related to diplomatic events, such as treaty negotiations, but most trips have been more for public relations.

The trips usually give the president a temporary lift in public opinion polls.[69] Longer trips—such as President Nixon's trip to China and President Reagan's trip to the Soviet Union—may have a more permanent effect on the president's standing. More important than the brief surge in popularity, however, is the presentation of the image of the president as a political leader in charge of world affairs.

Presidential travel once was considered a risky proposition with the voters. When President Eisenhower embarked on his first foreign trip, he felt obliged to explain the necessity for the trip in almost apologetic terms:

Now, manifestly, there are many difficulties in the way of a president going abroad for a period, particularly while Congress is in session. He has many constitutional duties; he must be here to perform them. I am

TABLE 1-3 Foreign Appearances by President, 1954–1994

President[a]	Days of travel	Number of appearances	Yearly average	
			Days	Appearances
Truman, I	10	7	3	2
Truman, II	0	0	0	0
Eisenhower, I	3	7	1	2
Eisenhower, II	50	115	13	29
Kennedy	28	77	9	26
Johnson[b]	29	55	6	11
Nixon, I	35	108	9	27
Nixon, II	17	25	9	14
Ford	30	63	14	29
Carter	52	69	13	17
Reagan, I	36	82	9	21
Reagan, II	48	51	12	13
Bush	86	113	24	29
Clinton[c]	38	62	19	31

SOURCE: Lyn Ragsdale, *Vital Statistics on the Presidency* (Washington, D.C.: Congressional Quarterly, 1996), 170.

NOTES: Foreign appearances are defined as the total number of appearances made by a president during travel outside the United States. An appearance includes formal remarks, toasts to other heads of state, airport greetings, remarks to reporters, and remarks to American citizens who reside in the host country.
a. For two-term presidents: I (first term); II (second term).   b. Includes full term from November 1963 to January 1969.   c. 1993–1994 only.

Presidents have often appealed to foreign publics and their leaders to increase their political capital. In December 1918, Woodrow Wilson made a successful European tour to promote his postwar foreign policy agenda.

able to go on the trip only because of the generous cooperation of the political leaders in Congress of both political parties who have arranged their work so that my absence for a period will not interfere with the business of the government. On my part, I promised them that by a week from Sunday, on July 24th, I shall be back here ready to carry on my accustomed duties.[70]

The surges in public approval that followed Eisenhower's trip led him—and later presidents—to make travel a regular part of the job.[71]

THE IMPORTANCE OF FOREIGN POLICY RHETORIC

Control of foreign policy always has been an important political "card" for the president. Especially since the United States became a world economic and military power at the turn of the century, presidents have been able to increase their prestige with military and diplomatic action. The public often defers to authorities because of its scant knowledge of foreign affairs, so presidents receive a boost in public support even when the action concerns an obscure nation or issue.

Presidents have been able to depend on foreign affairs even more than on economic or social events to enhance their political stock, because they are able to supersede temporarily the divisions engendered by the domestic struggle over "who gets what, when, and how." On foreign policy issues, the president acts for the nation as a whole, creating a situation in which "we" are acting, but domestic actions always create internal divisions. The president can argue that foreign policy involves outside threats to the security of all of the people and therefore requires a unified response.

Simply appearing at great international events can lend the president a bit of glory. In 1993 President Bill Clinton hosted the signing ceremonies in which the Palestine Liberation Organization and Israel ended their formal state of war. Clinton also hosted a ceremony marking the end of hostilities between Israel and Jordan in 1994. The peace talks leading to the White House ceremony occurred long before Clinton became president, but he basked in the rapprochement.

The boost that the president gets from foreign policy is usually short-lived. Nevertheless, the president can use a series of foreign events and rhetoric about foreign policy to develop a general disposition among the public to defer to presidential leadership.

Foreign policy action can be a double-edged sword. If presidents do not appear to assert control over crises after the initial period of emergency, the public might develop suspicions about presidential expertise and control. Presidents also can lose on foreign policy if their actions create or aggravate internal divisions—usually by asking for difficult sacrifices of important domestic constituencies.

Bill Clinton, who struggled to gain credibility in foreign affairs, confronted his credibility gap head-on with speeches before hostile groups. For example, Clinton, who avoided military service in the Vietnam War, became in 1993 the first president to speak at the Vietnam War Memorial in Washington. "Let us continue to disagree, if we must, about the war, but let us not let it divide us as a people any longer," the president told a Memorial Day audience. Some veterans opposed Clinton's appearance, but others expressed respect for his "courage" in speaking to a hostile crowd.[72]

The administration exerts extensive control over the foreign policy agenda through its control over information held in the federal bureaucracy. The president benefits from the huge operations of the public relations offices of the Pentagon, State Department, and Central Intelligence Agency. Through the power of classification, the president can also control how much information journalists, scholars, and political activists have at their disposal.

Scholars have raised concerns about the effects of the executive's control over information. A constant tension exists between the democratic value of openness and the strategic value of secrecy. Even as the president speaks more and more in public, the president and government also hold more matters in secrecy. This development may be attributed to the need for different strategies to overcome and control a growing bureaucracy. Political scientist Francis E. Rourke has written:

To be sure, the bureaucracy did not invent secrecy in American government. The Founding Fathers found it expedient to conduct the deliberations of the Constitutional Convention at Philadelphia in 1787 in private [and] presidents have, through the development of "executive privilege," contributed a great deal to the secrecy surrounding executive activities. . . . But it remains true that the growth of bureaucracy in American government has brought about an enormous expansion in the secretiveness with which policy is made.[73]

The erection of a "national security state," critics have argued, gives the president almost unchallenged power over foreign affairs and even many areas of domestic policy. Presidents always can assert that "national security" requires withholding information.

Presidents clearly enjoy an important advantage in deciding what information they want released and how they want to do it. President Nixon justified both the "secret" bombing of Cambodia in 1970 and his handling of the Watergate affair on the grounds of national security requirements. The Reagan administration's refusal to allow reporters to witness the invasion of Grenada was based on similar claims. But perhaps more important is the routine information that presidents can keep secret.

REACHING FOREIGN PUBLICS

American presidents have "gone public" not only to speak over the heads of their own government, but also to speak directly to foreign publics. Presidents sometimes speak directly to other nations' populations in order to strengthen their negotiating positions with those nations' leaders. More often, presidents simply try to foster goodwill abroad with their public appeals.

The cold war and its aftermath provided the backdrop for dramatic moments in rhetoric to foreign audiences. John Kennedy's 1963 "Ich bin ein Berliner" speech, Ronald Reagan's challenge to Soviet leader Mikhail Gorbachev twenty years later to "tear down this wall," and Bill Clinton's 1994 challenge to the Russian leadership to fight resurgent nationalism provided a clear narrative—complete with beginning, middle, and end—of the American struggle with the Soviet empire.

Some of the boldest appeals to foreign audiences took place during President Reagan's 1988 visit to Moscow. During his trip, Reagan spoke to Soviet citizens on television; later, with Gorbachev at his side, he met crowds at Red Square—an event televised to millions of homes in both the United States and the Soviet Union. Reagan was most outspoken at the University of Moscow. Standing before a huge Soviet flag and a portrait of V. I. Lenin, Reagan challenged the nation to restructure its political and economic institutions and praised the U.S. system.

During his tenure, Reagan also spoke several times about the protests against the placement of American nuclear missiles on European soil. The U.S. missiles were strongly opposed by peace activists in Great Britain and West Germany, and Reagan alternately sought to win over opponents of the missiles and to undercut their legitimacy.

A speech at Normandy, France, commemorating the fortieth anniversary of the 1944 U.S. invasion was a dramatic statement of solidarity among Western nations and values. President Reagan spoke movingly of the soldiers who died in the invasion and their families and of the need for nations to avoid another world war. Bill Clinton's 1994 speech at Normandy was greeted skeptically because of Clinton's avoidance of the military draft as a young man. But Clinton's speech convinced some critics that he was up to the job of commander in chief.

Reagan's foreign appeals sometimes backfired. His trip to Bitburg, West Germany, in 1985 was intended to symbolize the development of ties between the former World War II foes, the United States and Germany. The visit was controversial from the time of its scheduling, however. The discovery that former officers of an elite Nazi brigade were buried in the Bitburg cemetery insulted Jews and others who had fought the Nazis. Reagan defended the trip by saying that German soldiers "were victims, just as surely as the victims in the concentration camps."[74] Despite calls for him to cancel the trip, Reagan went.

George Bush's 1992 trip to Tokyo was supposed to project an image of strength as Bush demanded trade concessions from Japan. But when an exhausted Bush vomited and passed out at a state dinner, he made a poor impression on his Japanese hosts.

Presidential statements to foreign publics sometimes take the form of threats. Presidents speak frequently about other nations' weapons buildups, terrorist actions, human rights problems, military actions, and trade policies. Although such statements often are intended for domestic consumption, they also offer flexible ways to communicate with other governments outside the normal channels of diplomacy.

Speeches to foreign bodies such as the United Nations and the Organization of American States—meetings well covered by media across the world—offer additional opportunities to address foreign publics. Because many nations practice censorship, presidents often try to embed their true messages in larger statements that will be reported. Reagan, who sharply criticized the United Nations, also took advantage of the platform of the international body. In his farewell speech in 1988 he attempted to promote internal Soviet political reforms and arms control agreements. Reagan and his UN ambassadors used the body to criticize the Soviet Union, Nicaragua, and third world countries. George Bush used the United Nations to make a case first for sanctions and then for war against Iraq after Iraq's invasion of Kuwait in 1990.

The president leads the world with words in other ways as well. At summit meetings and economic conferences with foreign leaders, the president speaks for the nation on a wide variety of issues. The "news" from most conferences is that the leaders will try to cooperate in pursuit of common goals. But if a president can visibly "take charge," it helps to provide the authority the president needs in world affairs.

Presidents do not speak to other nations only through their own appearances and statements. The U.S. government includes a number of agencies designed to appeal to the "hearts and minds" of foreign peoples. The president's appointments to these agencies can put a distinctive mark on the way the rest of the world sees the United States.

The U.S. Information Agency promotes U.S. foreign policy through media, libraries, speakers, and programs. With 199 posts in 143 countries, the nation's chief propaganda agency operates a radio service called Voice of America (VOA). The VOA broadcasts 900 hours of news and other programs in forty-seven languages each week. The State Department and Central Intelligence Agency also disseminate information to foreign nations.

An administration's policy on government information—what documents and information should be classified (that is, made secret) or made public—can have a profound effect on the nation's foreign policy. As the commander in chief and head of a huge national security apparatus, the president has access to information about foreign affairs that people outside the government lack.

The president enjoys a huge advantage in the sheer size of the public relations operations of the government. The public information office of the Pentagon, for example, spends more money each year than any of the major news services. Especially considering that the wire services devote only a small part of their operations to foreign affairs, the Pentagon's public relations work gives the government an awesome advantage in communicating its point of view.

The Terms of Presidential Discourse

Besides dominating the political stage and tilting the balance of opinion on many specific public issues, the president's rhetoric is important in shaping the way political issues are discussed. The president's prominence is crucial in establishing the terms of debate for other participants in the political system.

Many linguistic experts have argued that shaping the political vocabulary is the most important element in gaining public support for a wide range of policies. The president is perhaps the most important political figure in defining and creating a context for such widely used terms as *conservative, progress, lib-*

eralism, economic growth, national security, and *free trade.* The meanings of such terms change over time, sometimes helping and sometimes hurting presidents' abilities to promote their agendas.

Even the most fundamental ideas in American political discourse are constantly changing. The rise and fall of such terms as *people* and *interests* closely parallel the historical development of the nation and the evolution of the presidency. The regular public use of the word *interests,* for example, in the nation's early years was tied to the decline of notions of public virtue and the development of more competitive ideals of politics and society. Theodore Roosevelt and Woodrow Wilson, leaders of the national Progressive movement, used the rhetoric of interests both to decry what Roosevelt called "the ferocious, scrambling rush of an unregulated and purely individualistic industrialism" and to propose government remedies. The upshot was the "pluralistic" idea that a clash of interests managed by popular government would redound to the national interest.[75]

Political scientist Murray Edelman has argued that political terms always have multiple meanings that contradict each other. But because people have self-contradictory interests and beliefs, they need catch-all words that cover up the contradictions. These words help to overcome "cognitive dissonance"—the unsettling feeling produced by the realization that one's thoughts are contradictory. These words also provide enough "signposts," or guides for living, enabling people to get along in life without having to reassess their situations and alternatives constantly.

An example of a self-contradictory word is *conservative,* which in U.S. politics is used to denote both stability (family, neighborhoods, local control) and turbulence (economic growth, mobility, exploration, and research). President William McKinley described his "Open Door" policy, which reduced trade and cultural barriers among nations, as conservative. Although the policy augured unprecedented changes in world trade activities, it also was said to be the surest policy for maintaining traditional American values. President Reagan wove together the contradictory meanings of conservatism. His rhetoric and policies for "unleashing" the dynamic forces of capitalism contradicted his denunciations of the decay of traditional "values" and practices regarding religion, family life, sexual mores, and authority.

The complex and changing definitions of political words give presidents wide latitude in shaping the way people talk about political issues at all levels of society. Presidents not only have a "bully pulpit" from which to promote their choices in important policies, as Theodore Roosevelt asserted, but also the ability to shape the way the population thinks about those choices in the first place.

David Green has chronicled the way twentieth-century presidents have used labels to give themselves a privileged position in policy debates. According to Green, presidents have attempted to use such words as *progressive, liberal, isolationist,* and *conservative* to give their own actions greater legitimacy and to undercut the legitimacy of their opponents.

Franklin Roosevelt's presidency is a thorough case study of adapting, avoiding, and switching labels. Roosevelt avoided using the label *progressive* because it had connotations of confiscation for many members of the older generation. Roosevelt labeled his policies "liberal" and fended off attacks on his policies as "fascist," "socialist," and "communist." The liberal label connoted openness, generosity, and popular support. Roosevelt branded his opponents "conservative" and "reactionary." When it became apparent that the New Deal policies were not ending the Great Depression, Roosevelt stepped up his attacks on opponents, particularly business interests and the wealthy, whom he called "economic royalists."

Roosevelt also went beyond the debate over domestic and economic policy with a move into international affairs. As the United States inched toward involvement in World War II, Roosevelt branded opponents of the war "isolationists," "appeaser fifth columnists," and "propagandists of fear," and linked those terms to his broader argument about reactionaries. Critics who questioned the war or specific tactics found themselves undercut.[76]

What goes around usually comes around in rhetoric. By the 1980s, the word *liberal* was poison. President Reagan's constant labeling of Democrats as "tax and spend liberals" helped to make *liberal* the scarlet letter of politics in the 1980s and early 1990s. Politicians were so scared to identify themselves as liberal, because of the word's negative connotations, that pundits took to calling it the "L-word" as if it were profanity.

Twentieth-century presidents have tended to use catch-all phrases to describe their policy programs. Among the phrases are Square Deal (Theodore Roosevelt), New Freedom (Wilson), New Deal (Franklin Roosevelt), Fair Deal (Truman), New Frontier (Kennedy), Great Society (Johnson), New Foundation (Carter), New Federalism (Nixon and Reagan), and New Covenant (Clinton). Such phrases can give the president's program a sense of coherence and completeness, but they also can create false expectations about what the president's policies can accomplish. Johnson's Great Society, for example, was a collection of relatively small and uncoordinated programs, many of which had no viable support system in the state and local governments where they were to be administered. The policies were prepared hurriedly, and funding was restricted before many of the programs were fully implemented. The potent rhetorical force of the Great Society label, David Zarefsky argues, left the domestic programs vulnerable to attack: "The very choices of symbolism and argument which had aided the adoption of the program were instrumental in undermining its implementation and in weakening public support for its basic philosophy."[77]

The use of vague slogans and "sentiments" to promote policies, rather than precisely defined programs, fundamentally undermines the entire U.S. political system, according to Theodore Lowi.[78] When the policies do not work as promised and interest groups gain control over programs, the president is left with the impossible job of gaining control of the federal leviathan. Only clearly defined and circumscribed programs—in the place of sweeping promises—can restore the government's legitimacy and authority.

Speeches of Departing Presidents

Among the most prominent speeches of any presidency are the addresses delivered at the end of the administration. The farewell addresses of many presidents are remembered long after other speeches have been lost in the bog of presidential rhetoric. Such speeches also gain prominence because they are so infrequent and because they depict politicians jousting to determine their places in history.

George Washington delivered the first and most famous farewell address. Washington's most lasting advice to the country was to avoid becoming entangled in European alliances, which he predicted would sap the strength and resources of the young nation. Much of the speech was written by Alexander Hamilton, but Washington himself took an active hand in its drafting. Experts agree that it reflects his values and character.

The most influential modern farewell address was Dwight Eisenhower's valedictory of 1961. He warned the nation against the "military-industrial complex," which, he argued, was beginning to dominate the American system and could endanger democratic processes and liberties. Eisenhower said:

We must never let the weight of this combination endanger our liberties or democratic processes. We should take nothing for granted. Only an alert and knowledgeable citizenry can compel the proper meshing of the huge industrial and military machinery of defense with our peaceful methods and goals, so that security and liberty may prosper together.[79]

Farewell addresses give presidents the opportunity to speak more freely than they did as incumbents. Eisenhower's farewell provided a poignant coda to a career in the military and politics. Most presidents, however, simply try to cast their administration in a good light and set challenges for their successors.

NOTES

1. Along with the explosion in presidential speech making has come an explosion of research about the development. See Theodore Otto Windt Jr., "Presidential Rhetoric: Definition of a Field of Study," *Presidential Studies Quarterly* 16 (winter 1986): 102–116.

2. Roderick P. Hart, *The Sound of Leadership* (Chicago: University of Chicago Press, 1988), 1.

3. Quoted in Kathleen Hall Jamieson, *Eloquence in an Electronic Age* (New York: Oxford University Press, 1988), 212–213.

4. Lloyd Grove, "Dukakis: If He Only Had a Heart," *Washington Post*, October 9, 1988, D1.

5. Richard E. Neustadt, *Presidential Power* (New York: Wiley, 1976).

6. Samuel Kernell, *Going Public: New Strategies of Presidential Leadership*, 2d ed. (Washington, D.C.: CQ Press, 1993), 31.

7. Hart, *Sound of Leadership*, 2.

8. Philip Abbott, "Do Presidents Talk Too Much? The Rhetorical Presidency and Its Alternative," *Presidential Studies Quarterly* 18 (spring 1988): 335.

9. Hart, *Sound of Leadership*, 5.

10. E. E. Schattschneider, *The Semisovereign People* (Hinsdale, Ill.: Dryden, 1975).

11. Bob Woodward, *The Agenda: Inside the Clinton White House* (New York: Simon and Schuster, 1994), 109–110.

12. Hart, *Sound of Leadership*, xix.

13. Murray Edelman, *The Symbolic Uses of Politics* (Urbana: University of Illinois Press, 1985), 96.

14. H. Mark Roelofs, *The Poverty of American Politics: A Theoretical Interpretation* (Philadelphia: Temple University Press, 1992), 116.

15. Jeffrey K. Tulis, *The Rhetorical Presidency* (Princeton, N.J.: Princeton University Press, 1987), 47–49.

16. Ibid., 51–55.

17. Michael E. McGerr, *The Decline of Popular Politics* (New York: Oxford University Press, 1986), 22–23.

18. Alexander Hamilton, *Federalist* No. 71, in *The Federalist Papers*, quoted in Tulis, *Rhetorical Presidency*, 39.

19. Calvin Coolidge once commented on this practice: "At twelve thirty, the doors were opened and a long line passed by who wished merely to shake hands with the president. On one occasion, I shook hands with nineteen hundred in thirty-four minutes." (Quoted in Gary King and Lyn Ragsdale, *The Elusive Executive: Discovering Statistical Patterns in the Presidency* [Washington, D.C.: CQ Press, 1988], 249.)

20. Tulis, *Rhetorical Presidency*, 63.

21. Ibid., 67, 64–65.

22. Ibid., 69.

23. Ibid., 67–68.

24. Ibid., 79–83.

25. Abbott, "Do Presidents Talk Too Much?" 333–334.

26. See Garry Wills, *Lincoln at Gettysburg: The Words That Remade America* (New York: Simon and Schuster, 1992). Wills's argument that Lincoln's address fundamentally changed the national creed was anticipated by Willmoore Kendall, *The Conservative Affirmation* (New York: Henry Regnery, 1963), 252; and by M. E. Bradford, *Remembering Who We Are: Observations of a Southern Conservative* (Athens: University of Georgia Press, 1985), 145.

27. Wills, *Lincoln at Gettysburg*, 172, 174.

28. Ibid., 174.

29. Tulis, *Rhetorical Presidency*, 87–93.

30. Ibid., 88.

31. Quoted in Tulis, 86.

32. Elmer E. Cornwell Jr., *Presidential Leadership of Public Opinion* (Bloomington: Indiana University Press, 1965), 24–25.

33. Quoted in Tulis, *Rhetorical Presidency*, 131.

34. David Green, *Shaping Political Consciousness* (Ithaca, N.Y.: Cornell University Press, 1987), 81.

35. Theodore J. Lowi, *The Personal President* (Ithaca, N.Y.: Cornell University Press, 1985), 22–66.

36. Jamieson, *Eloquence in an Electronic Age*, 45–53.

37. Quoted in Daniel J. Boorstin, *The Americans: The Democratic Experience* (New York: Random House, 1973), 475.

38. Hart, *Sound of Leadership*, xix.

39. Kernell, *Going Public*, 22.

40. Hart, *Sound of Leadership*, 11.

41. Ibid., 12–14; see also Jamieson, *Eloquence in an Electronic Age*, 165–201.

42. Quoted in Hart, *Sound of Leadership*, 36.

43. Quoted in Theodore C. Sorensen, *Kennedy* (New York: Harper and Row, 1965), 346.

44. Herbert S. Parmet, *JFK: The Presidency of John F. Kennedy* (New York: Dial Press, 1983), 197.

45. Hart, *Sound of Leadership*, 8. In calculating the total number of Ford's speeches, Hart counted all public occasions at which the president made remarks, including press conferences, dinners, and welcoming ceremonies.

46. Judith D. Horton, "Ronald Reagan's Failure to Secure Contra Aid: A Post-Vietnam Shift in Foreign Policy Rhetoric," *Presidential Studies Quarterly* 24 (summer 1994): 531–541.

47. Jamieson, *Eloquence in an Electronic Age*, 182–200.

48. Kathleen Hall Jamieson contrasts the more awkward style of Johnson and Nixon with the casual, modest style of Reagan (ibid., 186–187). The media critic Mark Crispin Miller makes the same point: "Reagan is unfailingly attractive, not at all like a predator, nor, in fact, like anything other than what he seems—'a nice guy,' pure and simple. . . . We, too, should appreciate the spectacle, after all the bad performances we've suffered through for years: LBJ, abusing his dogs and exposing his belly; Richard Nixon, hunched and glistening like a cornered toad; Jimmy Carter, with his maudlin twang and interminable kin. While each of these men, appallingly, kept lunging at us from behind the mask of power, Reagan's face and mask are as one." (Mark Crispin Miller, *Boxed In* [Evanston, Ill.: Northwestern University Press, 1988], 82.)

49. Kernell, *Going Public*, 93.

50. Ibid., 98.

51. Hart, *Sound of Leadership*, 51.

52. Ibid., 50.

53. Ibid., 219–220.

54. Kernell, *Going Public*, 131.

55. Patricia D. Witherspoon, "'Let Us Continue': The Rhetorical Initiation of Lyndon Johnson's Presidency," *Presidential Studies Quarterly* 17 (summer 1987): 531–540.

56. Kernell, *Going Public*, 89.

57. Craig Allen Smith, "Leadership, Orientation, and Rhetorical Vision: Jimmy Carter, The 'New Right,' and the Panama Canal," *Presidential Studies Quarterly* 16 (spring 1986): 317–328.

58. King and Ragsdale, *Elusive Executive*, 255.

59. John E. Mueller, *War, Presidents, and Public Opinion* (New York: Wiley, 1973); Lowi, *Personal President*, 11.

60. Hart, *Sound of Leadership*, 8.

61. Ibid., 33.

62. Ibid., 19.

63. A good overview of the criticism of the trend is James W. Ceaser et al., "The Rise of the Rhetorical Presidency," *Presidential Studies Quarterly* 11 (spring 1981): 158–171. For a response, see Abbott, "Do Presidents Talk Too Much?"

64. Bruce Miroff, "Monopolizing the Public Space: The President as a Problem for Democratic Politics," in *Rethinking the Presidency*, ed. Thomas E. Cronin (Boston: Little, Brown, 1982), 226. Also see Richard Sennett, *The Fall of Public Man* (New York: Vintage, 1974), 150–194, for an analysis of the way politics dominated by personalities affects discussion of complex issues.

65. Lowi, *Personal President*, 170.

66. Hart, *Sound of Leadership*, 32.

67. Ibid., 30.

68. Jamieson, *Eloquence in an Electronic Age*, 220–222.

69. Robert E. Darcy and Alvin Richman, "Presidential Travel and Public Opinion," *Presidential Studies Quarterly* 18 (winter 1988): 85–90.

70. Quoted in Hart, *Sound of Leadership*, 58.

71. Kernell, *Going Public*, 105.

72. Ana Puga, "Amid Boos, Clinton Asks War Healing," *Boston Globe*, June 1, 1993.

73. Francis E. Rourke, *Bureaucracy, Politics, and Public Policy* (Boston: Little, Brown, 1984), 155.

74. Quoted in David I. Kertzer, *Ritual, Politics, and Power* (New Haven, Conn.: Yale University Press, 1988), 94.

75. Daniel T. Rodgers, *Contested Truths* (New York: Basic Books, 1987), 182.

76. Green, *Shaping Political Consciousness*, 119–163.

77. Quoted in Tulis, *Rhetorical Presidency*, 172.

78. Theodore J. Lowi, *The End of Liberalism* (New York: Norton, 1979).

79. Dwight D. Eisenhower, "Farewell Address to the American People," in *Great Issues in American History: From Reconstruction to the Present Day, 1864–1969*, ed. Richard Hofstadter (New York: Vintage, 1969), 451.

SELECTED BIBLIOGRAPHY

Green, David. *Shaping Political Consciousness.* Ithaca, N.Y.: Cornell University Press, 1987.

Hart, Roderick P. *The Sound of Leadership.* Chicago: University of Chicago Press, 1988.

Jamieson, Kathleen Hall. *Eloquence in an Electronic Age.* New York: Oxford University Press, 1988.

Kernell, Samuel. *Going Public: New Strategies of Presidential Leadership.* 2d ed. Washington, D.C.: CQ Press, 1993.

The Library of Congress Presents: Historic Presidential Speeches (1908–1993), Rhino, compact disk.

Ragsdale, Lyn. *Vital Statistics on the Presidency.* Washington, D.C.: Congressional Quarterly, 1996.

Tulis, Jeffrey. *The Rhetorical Presidency.* Princeton, N.J.: Princeton University Press, 1987.

Windt, Theodore Otto, Jr. "Presidential Rhetoric: Definition of a Field of Study." *Presidential Studies Quarterly* 16 (winter 1986): 102–116.

CHAPTER 2

The President and Political Parties

BY HAROLD F. BASS JR.

THE PRESIDENT-PARTY RELATIONSHIP gives rise to a significant presidential leadership role, party chief. It also generates noteworthy opportunities and problems for both presidency and party.

National political parties did not exist when the presidency was created in 1787. The emergence of political parties in the decade of the 1790s, however, brought about both an enduring link with the presidency and presidential responsibilities for party leadership. Two centuries later, in the wake of numerous institutional transformations in both the presidency and the political parties, the linkage and the leadership persist.

Political parties connect citizens with rulers. They also link various public officeholders within the constitutionally designed separated-powers, checks-and-balances federal system that disperses the officers into different branches and levels of government and further positions them as rivals.

In turn, presidential leadership involves role playing. In Harry S. Truman's apt analogy, the president wears many hats: chief executive, chief of state, commander in chief, chief diplomat, chief economic manager, legislative leader, and chief of party. Presidential role playing is simultaneous, however, rather than sequential. A president wears several hats at a time.

This recognition is especially meaningful in considering the presidential role of party chief. Rarely will a president act solely as party leader. It is also rare that other roles will be performed without regard for party leadership.

Paradox pervades the presidential role of party leader. Party chieftainship both stands apart from and connects diverse presidential roles. It is simultaneously on the periphery yet at the center of presidential leadership. It clearly divides, and yet more subtly and significantly it complements and integrates. It is less a power than an opportunity; yet under certain conditions it becomes an obstacle.

The Constitution does not authorize party leadership. It developed outside the framework formed by the constitutionally enumerated presidential powers. Moreover, the assignment of presidential leadership responsibilities over a specific part of the public conflicts with the general expectation that as head of state the president presides over the entire nation.

Yet, because parties play significant linkage roles in politics, party leadership is central to the varied array of presidential responsibilities. Through the party, the president establishes and maintains connections with other elements in the political order, both inside and outside the government. These connections produce cohesion rather than division.

The exercise of presidential party leadership is often shrouded because of perceived presidential role conflicts and public antagonism toward the concept of partisanship. Given the structure and character of the United States political order, however, Woodrow Wilson's observation remains pertinent: the president's responsibility as chief of party is virtually inescapable.[1]

Party chieftainship calls for particular leadership skills. Political scientist James MacGregor Burns identifies two basic types of leadership: *transactional* and *transforming*. Transactional leadership operates within the framework of exchange. It features bargaining and negotiation. The more complex and potent transforming leadership has an elevating, even moralistic quality. Burns places party leadership in the transactional category.[2] And yet, certain exercises of party leadership are surely transformational—for example those that effect a realignment of electoral forces, or those that institute and implement a new policy agenda.

The concept of a major political party in the United States embraces three analytically separate structural elements of membership: the party organization, the party in office (sometimes referred to as "the party in the government"), and the party in the electorate. The party organization consists of the variably linked network of activists who hold membership and leadership positions in party headquarters throughout the country. The party in office comprises the public officials who hold their positions under the banner of the party along with those who aspire to do so. This group includes both elected officials and those appointed under partisan auspices. According to political scientist Frank Sorauf, the president is chief among the officeholders who have "captured the symbols of the party and speak for it in public authority."[3] The party in the electorate refers to those voters who with varying degrees of intensity support the party's candidates and causes.

Origins and Development of Presidential Party Leadership

The presidential role of party leader emerged outside the constitutional framework of expectations and powers established in 1787. As noted earlier, national political parties were

ORIGINS OF PARTY LABELS AND SYMBOLS

Our understanding of political party development in the United States is complicated by considerable confusion surrounding the names of the parties. Contemporary Democrats trace their partisan ancestry back to Thomas Jefferson. In Jefferson's day, however, the party went by two different names, either *Republican* or *Democratic-Republican*. By 1830 the dominant wing of a divided Democratic-Republican Party, led by President Andrew Jackson, abandoned the *Republican* portion of their label, leaving *Democratic* standing alone ever since.

A quarter-century later, in 1854, antislavery sympathizers forming a new party appropriated the name *Republican*. Today's Republicans are their descendants.

The term *democrat* comes from the Greek word *democratia,* a combination of *demos,* meaning "common people," and the suffix *-kratia,* denoting "strength, power." Thus *democratia* means "power of the people," or "the people rule."

The term *republican* derives from the Latin phrase *res publica.* It literally means "public thing," or "public affair," and it connotes a government in which citizens participate. Both party names thus suggest the Democrats' and Republicans' common belief in popular government, conducted by representatives of the people and accountable to them.

Gilded Age political cartoonist Thomas Nast endowed the two major political parties with enduring symbols: the Democratic donkey and the Republican elephant. The association of the Democrats with the donkey actually dates back to the 1830s when Andrew Jackson was characterized by his opponents as a jackass. In the 1870s Nast resurrected this image in a series of compelling political cartoons appearing in *Harper's Weekly.* The donkey aptly symbolized the rowdy, outrageous, tough, durable Democrats. Nast portrayed the Republican Party as an elephant. His initial employment of this symbol lampooned the foolishness of the Republican vote. Nast and other cartoonists later likened the elephant's size and strength advantages over other animals to the GOP's domination of the post–Civil War political landscape. The symbol came to suggest such elephant-like attributes as cleverness, majesty, ponderousness, and unwieldiness.

In an age when literacy rates were much lower than today, and when information about specific party candidates and their policies was in short supply for the mass public, these party symbols came to serve as valuable cues to prospective voters, providing them with an easy way to distinguish candidates of one party from those of another. For modern electorates, these traditional symbols have diminished significance, but they endure as part of the popular culture.

not then a part of the political order. Moreover, to the extent that the Founders' generation contemplated the prospect of political parties, it was generally antagonistic toward them. George Washington, the first president, stood second to no one in upholding this position.

Looking from a distance at the Whig and Tory parliamentary factions in Great Britain, the Framers perceived them as divisive and detrimental to national unity. In contrast, the appropriate model of executive leadership appeared in the concept of a patriot king provided a half-century earlier by the British author and statesman Lord Bolingbroke. Such an ideal figure stood above party and faction and ruled benevolently in the public interest.

Nevertheless, almost immediately after the onset of the new government, political parties appeared on the national scene. At least in part, their origins can be found in an increasingly acute division within the newly formed cabinet of executive department heads convened by President Washington. This division pitted the secretary of the Treasury, Alexander Hamilton, against the secretary of state, Thomas Jefferson.

Their conflict had roots in ambition, interest, and ideology. Each saw himself as heir to President Washington. Moreover, each realized that the new constitutional order provided a skeletal framework for development that would inevitably need to be fleshed out; and their respective visions of what the new nation should become were at odds.

Hamilton glorified the urban areas and their resident merchants and financiers; Jefferson idealized the rural setting and saw the real America embodied in the hard-working farmer. Hamilton perceived the need for strong, dynamic national government; Jefferson professed not to be the friend of energetic central government.

During the early years of the Washington administration, conflict between these two principals rocked the cabinet. Among the issues of controversy were those of assumption of the state debts, establishment of a bank of the United States, and the protective tariff. Subsequently, foreign policy differences arose that intensified the cleavage.

In the federal framework created by the Constitution, with its decentralized separation of powers, these disputes could not be contained within the national executive branch. Inevitably, they extended beyond its bounds into Congress and the states.

Consequently, organization of the respective Hamiltonian and Jeffersonian interests took place. The Hamiltonians took the name *Federalists,* which previously had been used by those who favored ratification of the Constitution. Jefferson's followers were variously titled *Republicans* or *Democratic-Republicans.* *(See box, Origins of Party Labels and Symbols, left.)* In contrast to Hamilton, Jefferson was not especially visible in the early stages of this process. Rather, his long-standing ally James Madison, a member of the House of Representatives, propelled their common cause and opposed Hamilton's measures in Congress.

EARLY PRESIDENTS' ATTITUDES TOWARD PARTIES

President Washington viewed these developments with alarm and despair, in keeping with his virulent antipathy toward party. He implored Hamilton and Jefferson to mute their differences, steadfastly holding himself above the emerging partisan battles dividing the government and indeed the entire political community. The president could not remain oblivious, however, to the disputes over policy. Indeed, his office forced him to take a stand. Regularly, he opted for the Hamiltonian alternative, even as he denied the legitimacy of partisan conflict. Washington's legacy to presidential party leadership was to reject emphatically its propriety while tentatively embracing its inevitability.

Washington's successor as president, John Adams, found himself in an exceedingly awkward position in the ongoing party conflict, which was not of his making. In contrast to Washington, Adams viewed parties as natural and inevitable in a free society. However, his theory of government was built on a similar foundation of disinterested executive leadership. He viewed the executive as the balance wheel in a political order featuring a bicameral legislature that represented distinct class interests.

During the Washington administration, Vice President Adams generally had supported Hamilton's public policies while maintaining his distance from the latter's organizational maneuvers. Personally, he was far closer to Jefferson than to Hamilton. Adams's vice presidency made him the logical successor when Washington chose to retire; and the Federalists readily embraced his candidacy in 1796, claiming him as their own. Nevertheless, he had not played any significant organizational role within the party—this was indisputably Hamilton's domain. Meanwhile, Jefferson was thrust forward as a candidate by Madison and other Democratic-Republican partisans. Adams won a narrow electoral vote victory in the first presidential election conducted along partisan lines.

During his presidential term, Adams's exercise of party leadership foundered on his own theoretical objections to the president's assumption of the role and on Hamilton's ongoing claims. The tension between Adams and Hamilton and their respective followers grew until, by the end of Adams's term, the Federalist Party clearly had split into two wings. Thus President Adams can be said to have been the leader of, at most, a party faction.

The third president, Thomas Jefferson, is truly the father of presidential party leadership.[4] By the time Jefferson ascended to the presidency, partisan institutions had begun to take shape. Within the executive, appointments to federal positions were being made with party affiliation in mind. Inside the legislature, assemblies or caucuses of like-minded partisans were meeting, not only to plot legislative strategy but also to nominate party candidates for president. Finally, at the state and local level, electoral organizations had formed to secure the selection of candidates to public offices.

The Democratic-Republicans looked unequivocally to Jefferson for leadership. While sharing many of his predecessors' prejudices against presidential party leadership, he nevertheless exercised it in a pioneering and exemplary fashion that established high expectations of his successors.

Early on in Washington's presidency, Jefferson acknowledged partisan division as natural but nevertheless deplored its presence. In the ensuing years, he came to defend and justify party activity on grounds of expediency and even honor. Confronted with the realities of Hamilton's initiatives, and disagreeing profoundly with so many of them, he increasingly saw party organization as an exigent and appropriate response. He did not retreat from his antiparty position so much as he superimposed on it a temporary acceptance of party.

For Jefferson, republicanism, or representative government, was preferable to monarchism, which he associated with arbitrary, hereditary government. Republicanism derived governmental authority from popular sovereignty and held public officials accountable to popular control. As such, it had distinctly democratic implications, although Jefferson was not an advocate of direct democracy. The Jeffersonian party promoting this cause was labeled "Republican" or "Democratic-Republican."

Significantly, Jefferson did not clearly endorse the notion of institutionalized party competition. He was never really willing to accord legitimacy to those who opposed him and the republican cause he associated with his party. Furthermore, he demonstrated no abiding commitment to the institution of the Democratic-Republican Party. Instead, he viewed the party as dispensable once it had accomplished the restorative tasks for which it had been formed.

EXECUTIVE-LEGISLATIVE RELATIONS

Jefferson's party leadership had its chief influence on executive-legislative relations. For Jefferson, presidential party leadership enabled him to overcome an ideological restraint well established in republican thought—namely, an antipathy toward executive power, combined with a corresponding preference for legislative autonomy. Although Jefferson never embraced this position with the enthusiasm and extremism of some of his fellow partisans, still he honored it.

For Jefferson, the problem was how to exercise positive presidential leadership in the face of republican ideological objections. Here, the presence of party provided a convenient façade facilitating leadership on his part without compromising a fundamental position of his republican followers. He could justify actions taken under the protection of party that, according to republican ideology, might be considered inappropriate under purely executive auspices. In this sense, from many of his followers' perspectives, President Jefferson the party leader had more legitimacy than President Jefferson the chief executive. In adding party leadership to the president's powers, he substantially increased the president's strength in the political arena.

The tactics and techniques Jefferson developed in using party leadership in legislative relations remain part of the standard presidential repertoire after almost two centuries. He participated in recruiting candidates. He enlisted members of the legislature as his agents and worked through them in pursuit of his objectives. He deployed the executive department secretaries who constituted his cabinet as emissaries on Capitol Hill.

Not content to rely exclusively on surrogates, Jefferson sought to establish personal relations with rank-and-file legislators. He corresponded extensively with members of Congress. He also regularly scheduled dinner parties in which the guest lists were limited to small groups of senators and representatives who shared his partisan affiliation.

Further, the president sought to generate cooperation and goodwill with Democratic-Republican legislators through patronage. Although departmental secretaries and state and local officials also were involved in this process, he consistently solicited recommendations and evaluations from individual legislators for prospective appointees.

Jefferson discontinued the formal practice inaugurated by his two predecessors of delivering an annual address to Congress in person. Instead, he simplified his relations with Congress and preferred to work informally, behind the scenes, and through his agents. From this vantage point, however, he was quite willing to make suggestions about details of proposed legislation. Indeed, he often provided trusted legislators with drafts of actual bills for them to introduce according to prescribed procedures, accompanying these communications with admonitions of secrecy and disavowals of meddling.

During his presidency, the opposition Federalist press alleged that Jefferson met with and oversaw the deliberations of the Democratic-Republican Party caucus. *Caucus* was the term used to refer to the meetings of the partisan legislators. One well-documented practice was the quadrennial meeting to nominate party candidates for the presidential ticket. In addition, numerous reports mention informal assemblies of sizable numbers of legislators to plot legislative strategy and tactics. However, the historical record cannot clearly establish the nature and extent of the president's relationship with this early partisan institution.

In exercising party leadership through these various processes, President Jefferson based his partisan appeals for support on four main foundations. The first was principle. His correspondence is replete with references to the promotion of common republican principles. The mirror image of this appeal was one that invoked the specter of the Federalist opposition. Often nothing produces unity so well as a common adversary, and Jefferson frequently sought to keep his followers together by denouncing the other party. Third, Jefferson traded on the immense personal regard in which he was held by his fellow Democratic-Republicans. Finally, as president, he tried to make legislators see that his preferences were in their own self-interests.

EFFECT OF PARTIES ON THE PRESIDENCY

By the end of Jefferson's presidency, some twenty years into the constitutional era, the unforeseen emergence of political parties had transformed the character of the presidency and the larger U.S. political system. The parties' assertion and assumption of nominating responsibilities for the presidential ticket necessitated a formal change in the balloting arrangements of the electoral college. Originally, the Constitution required presidential electors to cast a single ballot with the names of two presidential candidates listed on it. After the counting of the assembled ballots, the candidate with the most votes, provided that number was a majority, was elected president. The candidate with the next largest number of votes became vice president.

Under this procedure, the election of 1800 produced a tie. The Democratic-Republican Party objective before the election was to secure the selection of presidential electors committed to the slate of Jefferson for president and Aaron Burr for vice president. It did so to ensure that as president Jefferson might not be bedeviled by the presence of a Federalist adversary in the secondary slot, as he himself had acted in quiet opposition to President Adams.

The party effort was too successful. Every elector who voted for Jefferson also voted for Burr, and vice versa; and more electors voted for Jefferson and Burr than for any other contenders. The electoral college tie sent the presidential election to the House of Representatives, where the lame-duck Federalist majority eventually consented to the choice of Jefferson.

Before the next presidential election in 1804, Congress proposed and the state legislatures ratified the Twelfth Amendment. The change separated the ballots for president and vice president, allowing presidential electors effectively to vote for party tickets. This amendment fundamentally altered the status of the electors. They quickly lost the independent agent status envisioned by the Framers. Instead, they became instruments of party will.

Moreover, the parties' monopoly over presidential selection had the result of adding a new, extraconstitutional presidential eligibility requirement above and beyond those enumerated in the Constitution: a party nomination. The expectations and requirements for presidential candidates, heretofore considerable public service and esteem, came to include not only party affiliation but also party nomination.

In turn, the presence of a party's candidate for president at the head of the party ticket for elective public offices conferred on that individual the status of party leader. Once elected, that figure could presume to be something more than the head of the executive branch. Indeed, there was now a basis for claiming government chieftainship, with the idea and organization of party unifying separated national institutions under the leadership of the president.[5]

The emergence of political parties had a profound and transforming effect on the executive office. The constitutional principle of separation of powers envisioned a clearly divided governmental structure with three distinct branches: executive, legislative, and judicial. Checks and balances, while blurring these divisions, nevertheless were intended to inhibit cooperation by encouraging rivalries among the branches. The appearance of national political parties altered this setting. They provided a foundation and an opportunity for coordination, cooperation, and unity in government.

EVOLVING PRESIDENT-PARTY RELATIONSHIPS

Although aspects of presidential party leadership as developed by Thomas Jefferson endure to this day, the president-party relationship has not been static since the first decade of the nineteenth century. Rather, the relationship has gone through a number of changes. Few of these changes have been sudden and dramatic. Instead, they have been mostly gradual and evolutionary, occurring over several presidencies with their essences emerging in clear form only in retrospect.

After Jefferson's retirement in 1809, the congressional party caucus that had responded in a generally positive fashion to his leadership proved to be less accommodating to his immediate successors. Indeed, the caucus came to perceive its role in nominating and, absent noteworthy interparty competition, in effect, electing presidents as subordinating the president to congressional authority.

By 1828, however, the caucus was in disarray; and the new president, Andrew Jackson, presided over important transformations in the president-party relationship. Two developments in particular were taking form at this time: the growth of national party organization and the emergence of a mass party—ordinary citizens who identified with a political party and provided electoral support for a party's candidates.

Initially, in the 1790s, American political parties were governmental factions. By 1800, however, they were developing organizational means to appeal to the electorate to support the parties' candidates for public offices. Party organization was taking shape, primarily in the form of loosely linked campaign committees, complemented by the partisan press.

In reaching out to the citizenry, positioning themselves as intermediary institutions linking citizens and government, political parties recognized that the constitutional order rested in part on a foundation of popular sovereignty. By the standards of the day, the states' suffrage requirements were liberal and becoming more so, making it easier for the rank and file to vote. Religious tests had been abandoned in the revolutionary era, and property requirements were largely eliminated in the decade of the 1820s. Further, the voters' involvement in presidential selection was enhanced by post-1800 changes in the operation of the electoral college, most notably the trend toward popular selection of party-nominated presidential electors.

The establishment of the citizen-government link dramatically increased the president's political power. By virtue of the selection process, nationwide in scope and increasingly popular in operation, the president could claim a national, popular constituency above and beyond that of any governmental rival. The "people connection" allowed the president to tap into the wellsprings of popular sovereignty that nourished the exercise of political authority in an increasingly democratic society. As "tribune of the people," the president could claim a prerogative not specifically enumerated in the constitutional allocation of governmental power.

These developments significantly enhanced the president's party leadership role. The presidency became linked with a national party organization that in turn connected state and local party organizations throughout the country. This came about with the advent of the national party convention as the nominator of the president. Further, the presidency became directly tied to the citizenry of the republic. With Jackson, a general and a popular hero, paving the way, the presidency became the focus of popular attention and representation. Meanwhile, under the astute direction of Jackson's vice president and successor in the White House, Martin Van Buren, presidential patronage assisted the creation and strengthening of the party organizational machinery.

The next important shift in the character of president-party relations occurred in the immediate aftermath of the Civil War. The congressional Republicans reacted against President Abraham Lincoln's assertive wartime leadership by restraining his successors. Also, party leaders at the state and local levels—fortified by patronage resources and strong party identifications and loyalties in the electorate—increased in stature and significance in national politics in the latter part of the nineteenth century. They came to dominate the presidential nomination process, and the presidential nominee was usually beholden to the party organization sponsors.

After the turn of the twentieth century, the balance of power began to shift in favor of the president. Strong, assertive occupants of the White House such as Theodore Roosevelt and Woodrow Wilson invigorated the presidency by dint of personality. An increasing world role for the United States enhanced the visibility and power of the presidential office. Further, advancing communications technology focused more popular attention on the president. In keeping with these developments, the president's party leadership position gradually became more commanding.

Franklin D. Roosevelt ushered in the modern era in president-party relations with his long presidential tenure, 1933–1945. In responding to the Great Depression and World War II, Roosevelt presided over a dramatic increase in the size and scope of the federal executive. This had important implications for party relations, because Roosevelt came to rely on executive branch personnel to perform many of the political and social service roles that had traditionally been the province of the political party.

In the first appearance of the Democratic donkey, this unfavorable 1837 political cartoon shows President Martin Van Buren walking behind his predecessor, Andrew Jackson, who rides the donkey.

Since then, further advancements in communications technology, especially television, have served to connect the president even more directly with the public. This weakened the party's traditional position as intermediary between the two. In addition, and partly in response, party identification in the electorate began to decline. Party reforms reduced the power of the party organization in the nomination of the president.

Thus, the president-party relationship has gone through a number of twists and turns over the years. Jefferson's legacy persists, but it has been augmented by numerous additional trends. The current status of the relationship has been shaped by and remains rooted in these various and conflicting patterns. Further changes, no doubt, will be forthcoming.

THE PRESIDENCY AND TWO-PARTY COMPETITION

The emergence of parties transformed American political contention. At first, such conflict mainly divided states. But these rivalries quickly came to be supplanted by competition between parties. Moreover, contests pitted two major parties against each other. This paradoxically promoted consensus by reducing the potential for fragmentation from among thirteen states to between two parties.

The enduringly dualistic character of party competition in the United States (and in Britain) is in contrast to the multiparty competition prevalent in many European countries, and the absence of party competition in the few remaining communist countries and in many of the nation-states of the developing world. In seeking to explain the two-party phenomenon, scholars have pointed to diverse factors such as tradition, culture, and electoral arrangements. Early on, the political conflicts in America divided the participants into opposing pairs: patriots versus loyalists, Federalists versus Anti-Federalists, Federalists versus Democratic-Republicans. The resulting tradition of two-party competition hindered the emergence of alternatives.

The American political culture contributes to the sustenance of the two-party system because it is supportive of accommodation and compromise. The culture encourages diverse interests to ally under a party banner despite significant differences. Absent this spirit of concession, the various groups would likely form their own, separate political organizations, and a multiparty system would prevail.

Finally, electoral arrangements are critical to understanding the persistence of the two-party system. American elections are for the most part organized on the principle of single-member district, winner take all. Electoral units designate a single individual—the one who receives the most votes—to occupy a public office. The winner-take-all provision frustrates minor parties that may be capable of assembling sizable numerical minorities but cannot realistically aspire to triumphing in an absolute sense over the two entrenched major parties.

The presidency can be viewed as a special case of, and credited with a critical contribution to, the electoral arrangements explanation. The constitutional standard of an electoral college majority (not just a plurality) to elect the president discourages competition from parties that cannot hope to attain the high level of support necessary for victory. As such, it supports the maintenance of the two-party system.

In the early years of the Republic, party competition matched the Federalists led by Alexander Hamilton against the Democratic-Republican followers of Thomas Jefferson. In the wake of the Federalists' demise—caused by Jefferson's triumphs

The Republican elephant made its first appearance in a Thomas Nast illustration for *Harper's Weekly* on November 7, 1874.

in 1800 and 1804 and reinforced by the victories of his lieutenant, James Madison, in 1808 and 1812—a brief period of one-party rule ensued. Jeffersonian heir James Monroe presided over this so-called Era of Good Feelings.

By the mid-1820s, however, intraparty conflict had resulted in the emergence of two rival Democratic-Republican factions. These factions reflected personal ambitions and rivalries in the party leadership, pitting Andrew Jackson and his advocates against an alliance of John Quincy Adams, Henry Clay, and their combined supporters. The Jackson faction represented the emerging claims of the growing southwestern region in party and national politics, as well as those of the lower classes, including immigrants; Adams spoke for the more traditional regional and socioeconomic elements within the party coalition.

The factions quickly evolved into competing political parties. Jackson and his followers styled themselves *Democrats,* the party of the people. Their adversaries borrowed the label *Whigs* from the British. There, Whigs had long supported the cause of legislative supremacy against expansive executive claims, a concern of Jackson's opponents. The partisan battle between the Democrats and the Whigs raged for more than two decades.

About the time the Whigs died out in the 1850s, a new party, the *Republicans,* appeared on the scene to challenge the Democrats. Their competition has endured ever since.

Two-party competition has typically taken the form of sustained periods of dominance by one party, measured in terms of control of the presidency. From 1800 to 1860 the Democratic Party, in its Jeffersonian and Jacksonian incarnations, ordinarily prevailed in presidential elections.

Amid the upheaval of the Civil War, this pattern gave way to one of Republican ascendancy. The rise of the Republican Party can be attributed initially to the demise of the Whigs and the self-destruction of the Democrats, both precipitated in large part by the slavery controversy. The ultimately successful prosecution of the Civil War under Republican auspices allowed the party to seize the banner of patriotism, while the Democratic opposition was stained in the North and West by its southern roots. Increasingly in the postwar years, the Republican Party developed lasting ties with business interests that provided it with solid financial support. The Republican era endured until 1932, when it was undermined by the Great Depression. That year marked the beginning of a new era of Democratic domination that clearly lasted two decades.

The presidential elections from 1952 until 1988 departed from the previous patterns in that no party was able to sustain its hold on the White House for more than eight years. If two-party competition is measured in terms of alternation in the occupancy of the White House, these years constituted an unprecedented era of competitiveness. In 1988 Republican nominee George Bush's quest to succeed retiring incumbent Ronald Reagan met with electoral approval, providing the Republicans three consecutive four-year terms in control of the White House.

However, suggestions of the presence of a new era of Republican dominance in presidential politics were challenged by the 1992 and 1996 electoral victories of Democratic candidate Bill Clinton. Although the Republican Party took control of both chambers of Congress during the 1994 midterm congressional elections (the first time the GOP has controlled both since the Eisenhower administration) and maintained control after the 1996 elections, a clear, enduring realignment of electoral forces in the GOP's favor has not emerged. Moreover, the strong showing of third-party candidate H. Ross Perot (19 percent of the popular vote in 1992 and 8.5 percent in 1996) called into question the extent to which the two major parties could continue to monopolize access to the presidency.

PARTIES AS COALITIONS

Political parties appeal to interest groups, or collections of individuals who share common concerns. Indeed, parties can be seen as broad coalitions of diverse interests: geographic, social, economic, ethnic, and issue. Particularly in presidential elections, parties seek to achieve victory by attracting sufficient electoral support from voters who are members of these varied groups.

Presidential party leadership is part and parcel of the linkages between president and public, and between parties and groups. For example, during the decade of the 1930s, under the New Deal policies of Franklin Roosevelt, the Democratic Party assembled under its umbrella a formidable electoral coalition that generally included the South, racial minorities, blue-collar laborers, farmers, Catholics, Jews, and middle-class elements brought low by the ravages of the Great Depression. This party coalition successfully supported Roosevelt's presidential candidacies an unprecedented four separate times. It remained sufficiently intact in 1948 to bring victory to his successor, Harry S. Truman. Vestiges of the declining Roosevelt coalition could still be observed in the electoral support for the victorious Democratic presidential nominees since Truman: John Kennedy, Lyndon Johnson, Jimmy Carter, and Bill Clinton.

Republican responses to this era of Democratic domination entailed successful presidential campaigns by Dwight D. Eisenhower, Richard Nixon, Ronald Reagan, and George Bush that appealed to traditionally Democratic voters. The Eisenhower and Reagan appeals in particular were personalistic. Both of these individuals enjoyed popularity that transcended partisanship. In addition, all but Bush benefited from public dissatisfaction with the performance of the Democratic incumbents who preceded them. In each instance, the dissatisfaction was fueled by foreign policy problems besetting Democratic administrations: Korea in 1952, Vietnam in 1968, and Iran in 1980.

As presidents, the four Republicans followed up with efforts to reshape electoral alignments into a new winning coalition of interests under the party banner. Over the years, they achieved significant defections to the GOP in the white South, the middle class, and among blue-collar workers that enabled Reagan's vice president, George Bush, to win the 1988 presidential election campaigning as a successor. The gains proved ephemeral in 1992 and 1996, in large part because Clinton was able to halt, at least temporarily, these inroads.

President Clinton's challenge after 1996 was to expand the electoral coalition that carried him to victories with 43 percent of vote in 1992 and 49 percent in 1996. As party leader, his 1996 reelection was pursuant to a larger goal: to engineer the emergence of an enduring Democratic coalition that can prevail over time not only against Republican onslaughts but also against

forces producing fragmentation in the party system and undermining its persistent two-party character.

The President and the Party Organization

In the United States, the organizational machinery of a major political party parallels government organization. At every level of government in our federal system—national, state, and local—there is a corresponding unit of party organization. Generally, the lower levels of the organization choose members of the higher levels.

Throughout the nineteenth century, and well into the twentieth, preponderant party power rested with the state and local organizations. They dominated the national parties, which acted essentially as holding companies. In recent years this balance has shifted, centralizing power at the national level. For the Democrats, centralization has been achieved through a codification of national party responsibilities in the party's formal rules and procedures. For the Republicans, a similar result has occurred with less resort to rules changes.

The institutions of party organization are the convention, the committee, the chair, and the headquarters staff. The first three typically exist at all levels, but local parties seldom have headquarters or staffs.

PARTY ORGANIZATION

National party organization activity traditionally centered on the presidency. The national unit had relatively little control over the operations of the state and local entities. More recently, the Democratic and Republican national committees have become increasingly superfluous to presidential politics and removed from them. However, they have assumed increasing supervision over the lower levels. In the wake of these historic shifts, national party organization today appears stronger and more vital in many respects than ever before, though less relevant to the presidency.

Within a quarter-century of Jefferson's retirement from the presidency in 1809, a new arena of presidential party leadership opened up with the establishment of national party organizations.[6] These institutions arose after the collapse of the congressional party caucus as a nominating device. Beginning in the 1790s congressional party caucuses had assumed responsibility for nominating the parties' presidential tickets. The gradual demise of the Federalist Party following the electoral success of Jefferson and the Democratic-Republicans in 1800 left the latter party's caucus as the designator of the president, with the electoral college eventually ratifying its choice.

The caucus effected reasonably smooth party leadership transitions from Jefferson to James Madison in 1808–1809, and from Madison to James Monroe in 1816–1817. The culmination of the Virginia dynasty following Monroe's retirement from the White House in 1824 left the party caucus without an obvious

FIGURE 18–1   American Political Parties 1789–1992

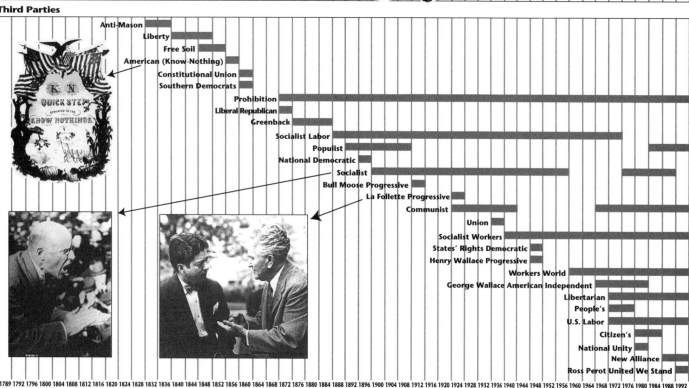

consensus choice. Internal division ensued. The decline of inter-party competition had served eventually to heighten intraparty competition for the presidential nomination that was tantamount to election.

Further, the very concept of the caucus came under attack from various outside sources. States and congressional districts not in the hands of the dominant Democratic-Republican Party had no voice in the caucus proceedings. These areas found themselves excluded from meaningful participation in presidential selection.

In 1824 the supporters of Andrew Jackson's presidential candidacy assaulted the caucus procedure as elitist. Embracing values of popular participation and reflecting the interests of outsiders in the political order, Jackson's cause drew little support from the members of the Washington-based caucus.

Alternatively, others perceived the caucus to be a de facto denial of the constitutional principle of separation of powers, since it allowed a congressional majority to choose the president. Under the weight of these onslaughts, the caucus as a nominating device virtually disintegrated in the mid-1820s, although for a brief time state legislative party caucuses engaged in nominating activities.

The controversy over the caucus was part of a larger issue, the growing division within the dominant Democratic-Republican Party. Jackson's 1824 candidacy, followed by his successful run for the presidency in 1828, clearly split the party into two irreconcilable wings. Before the 1832 presidential election, with the caucus discredited and inoperative, a new format for presidential nominations came into being.

The Jackson faction, now styling itself the Democrats, along

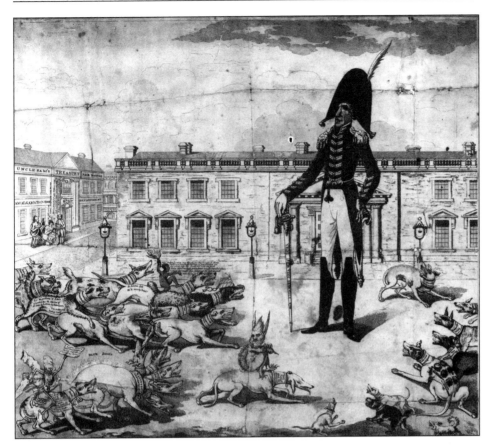

This 1824 political cartoon criticizes the treatment of Andrew Jackson by the hostile press and the practice of nominating candidates by caucus (especially Republican nominee William Crawford). The snarling dogs are labeled with the names of critical newspapers.

with the anti-Jackson elements, calling themselves National Republicans, and a third group, the Anti-Masons, separately convened to name their presidential tickets. These conventions, the first in U.S. history, brought together delegations from state parties, opening up participation in the nominating process to representatives of the rank-and-file party members. The concept took hold, and since then the quadrennial conventions have been a standard feature of the presidential nominating process.

Convention

The appearance of the nominating convention during the Jacksonian era also marked the beginning of party organization at the national level. Replacing the discredited congressional caucus as a nominating device, the quadrennial convention brought together state delegations to name the party's presidential ticket.[7]

The convention delegates also agreed upon a statement of party principles and issue stances, or platform, on which the party's nominees could run in the upcoming election. The gathering served as a massive party rally where rival factions could be conciliated and unified, and enthusiasm generated, in preparation for the general election campaign. The convention provided a national institutional identity, serving as the party's voice and authority.

In the nineteenth century, state representation at the national convention followed the electoral college formula, which itself was an extension of the Constitutional Convention's Great Compromise on congressional apportionment. Under the compromise, the House of Representatives was apportioned according to population, and the Senate according to state equality, two senators for each state. Similarly, delegate seats at the early nominating conventions were allocated according to the states' representation in Congress: a mixture of population plus state equality.

In the twentieth century, both major parties adopted formulas that also weight representation in part according to the states' previous electoral support for the party. In other words, a positive record of support for the party's nominees produces bonus representation at the convention.

For example, for the Republicans in the 1990s, a state delegation included base, district, and perhaps bonus delegates. Each state began with six at-large delegates as its base. It then received three delegates for each of its congressional districts. Bonus delegates were added for states that supported the GOP nominee in the previous presidential election, along with additional delegates for each state that had elected Republican governors, senators, and party majorities in its congressional delegation and/or its state legislative chambers since the previous presidential election. States could also receive additional bonus delegates for having increased the party representation in a state legislative chamber by at least 25 percent. Nonstate units (District of Columbia, Puerto Rico, Virgin Islands, and Guam) received varying bases of at-large delegates.[8] In 1992 California had the largest delegation, with 201 delegates, while American Samoa, Guam, and the Virgin Islands had the smallest, four apiece. For 1996 California was again to have the largest delegation, 163, with the three U.S. territories still having four delegates each.

The Democrats in recent years have moved beyond the bonus system to embrace two alternative representational principles. First, they have systematically sought through affirmative action to give representation to a variety of population groups. These include women, racial minorities, and age cohorts. Second, they have seated ex officio "superdelegates," party office-holders chosen apart from the normal delegate-selection processes.

Over the years, the conventions have grown dramatically. Early conventions drew fewer than three hundred delegates. In contrast, contemporary Democratic conventions bring together more than four thousand, and today's Republicans assemble about two thousand. Twenty cities have been the convention sites through 1992, many more than once. A twenty-first city joined the list with the Republicans' selection of San Diego for their 1996 convention. The Democrats chose Chicago, site of twenty-four previous conventions, most of them by the GOP. (See Table 2-1.)

In the nineteenth century, state party organizations tightly controlled the selection of convention delegates. Early in the twentieth century the progressive movement pushed for popular selection of delegates through a party primary. Although a few state parties adopted this mechanism, most kept the party organization in charge.

After 1968, however, some epochal reforms within the Democratic Party lodged far more effective party authority at the national level than previously had been the case and dramatically increased the number of state parties electing delegates through primaries. These reforms helped to transform the character of convention decision making. Party voters essentially choose the nominee in primaries and caucuses, leaving the convention little to do except ratify the voters' choice.

As a result, every major party convention since 1952 has produced a first-ballot victory. In 1996 Democrat incumbent Bill Clinton and Republican challenger Bob Dole wrapped up convention majorities through delegate-selection contests in the states well in advance of the convention. For them and their parties, the convention's presidential nominating role was a mere formality.

Increasingly, the modern convention has become a media event, heightening its traditional party rally function. The target of attention has shifted, however, from the party activists in the hall to the vast television audience viewing the prime-time proceedings. The convention gives the nominee a forum to kick off the general election campaign by demonstrating presidential leadership qualities to both party and public. This can be achieved through actions such as the choice of a running mate, acceptance of the nomination with a forceful speech, and skill-

TABLE 2–1 National Party Nominees, Convention Sites, and Dates, 1944–1996

Year	President	Democrats	Republicans
1944	Roosevelt (D)	Chicago July 19–21 Roosevelt[a]	Chicago June 26–28 Dewey
1948	Truman (D)	Philadelphia July 12–14 Truman[a]	Philadelphia June 21–25 Dewey
1952	Truman (D)	Chicago July 21–26 Stevenson	Chicago July 7–11 Eisenhower[a]
1956	Eisenhower (R)	Chicago August 13–17 Stevenson	San Francisco August 20–23 Eisenhower[a]
1960	Eisenhower (R)	Los Angeles July 11–15 Kennedy[a]	Chicago July 25–28 Nixon
1964	Johnson (D)	Atlantic City August 24–27 Johnson[a]	San Francisco July 13–16 Goldwater
1968	Johnson (D)	Chicago August 26–29 Humphrey	Miami Beach August 5–8 Nixon[a]
1972	Nixon (R)	Miami Beach July 10–13 McGovern	Miami Beach August 21–23 Nixon[a]
1976	Ford (R)	New York July 12–15 Carter[a]	Kansas City August 16–19 Ford
1980	Carter (D)	New York August 11–14 Carter	Detroit July 14–17 Reagan[a]
1984	Reagan (R)	San Francisco July 16–19 Mondale	Dallas August 20–23 Reagan[a]
1988	Reagan (R)	Atlanta July 18–21 Dukakis	New Orleans August 15–18 Bush[a]
1992	Bush (R)	New York July 13–16 Clinton[a]	Houston August 17–20 Bush
1996	Clinton (D)	Chicago August 26–29 Clinton[a]	San Diego August 12–15 Dole

NOTE: a. Won election.

ful management by the nominee and the campaign staff of the events of the convention week.[9]

The national convention endures as the formal, legally empowered nominator of the presidential ticket and as the apex of authority within the party. It remains a quadrennial event, though the Democrats experimented with midterm conventions in 1974, 1978, and 1982. The party has since abandoned these experimental meetings, which were designed to stimulate discussion and development of party positions on issues. Instead, they became divisive and harmful to party unity. The party dropped them, restoring the traditional four-year gap between conventions.

Committee

An institution convening for a few days every four years can hardly exercise effective power and authority within a political party. Early on, in the 1840s, the Democratic national convention established a national committee to oversee the conduct of the presidential campaign and to guide the party's fortunes between conventions. Subsequently, when the Republican Party formed a few years later, it adopted a similar organizational arrangement.[10]

These national committees consisted of representatives of the state and local parties. At the outset, the principle of state equality prevailed: one member from each state party. In the 1920s both parties expanded committee membership to two representatives from each state—one man and one woman. This revision clearly responded to the Nineteenth Amendment that denied states the power to discriminate according to sex in establishing voter qualifications.

In 1952 the Republican Party departed from the historical commitment to state equality as a representational principle. That year, its national convention voted to give ex officio national committee membership to party chairs from states that (1) supported the Republican nominee for president, (2) selected a majority of GOP House members and senators, or (3) selected a Republican governor. This reform gave added weight to those states that consistently voted Republican. Subsequently, the GOP returned to the principle of state equality by designating all state party chairs as committee members. Additionally, the District of Columbia, Guam, Puerto Rico, and the Virgin Islands were treated like states for representational purposes.

In the 1970s the Democrats abandoned state equality by adopting weighted representation and greatly expanding the committee's membership. Table 2-2 compares the much larger Democratic National Committee with its GOP counterpart.

Although the convention formally designates the national committee, in practice it ratifies state-level decisions regarding membership. State parties use a variety of means for choosing their representatives, usually according to their own rules or state laws. In most states, the state convention selects them. Alternatively, the state committee, the national convention delegation, or the party voters through a primary may be authorized to do so. Members serve a four-year term beginning with adjournment of the national convention and ending with adjournment of the next convention.

Party rules require the Democratic National Committee to meet at least once a year, whereas the Republican National Committee is supposed to meet at least twice a year. Typically, the party chair calls meetings, but each party provides for alternative avenues whereby meetings can be called, such as by the executive committee or a stipulated percentage of the national committee membership (at least sixteen members or 10 percent for the RNC; 25 percent for the DNC).

TABLE 2–2 Composition of the National Party Committees, 1996

	Number of Members
DEMOCRATIC NATIONAL COMMITTEE	
Chair and highest-ranking officer of opposite sex from each state and from District of Columbia and Puerto Rico	104
Members apportioned to states on same basis as delegates to national convention (at least two per state)	200
Chair of Democratic Governors Conference and two additional governors	3
Democratic leader and one other member from each chamber of Congress	4
Officers of the National Committee	9
Chair of Democratic Mayors Conference and two additional mayors	3
President of Young Democrats and two additional members	3
Chair of Democratic County Officials Conference and two additional officials	3
Chair of National Democratic Municipal Officials Conference and two additional officials	3
President of National Federation of Democratic Women and two additional members	3
President and vice president of College Democrats	2
Chair and vice chair of National Association of Democratic State Treasurers	2
Chair and vice chair of National Association of Democratic Lieutenant Governors	2
Chair and vice chair of Democratic Association of Secretaries of State	2
Additional members (up to 65)	65
Guam, the Virgin Islands, and American Samoa have four members each. The four share the single vote allotted to each entity.	12
Democrats Abroad has eight members who share the two votes allotted to Democrats Abroad	8
TOTAL	428
REPUBLICAN NATIONAL COMMITTEE	
National committeeman, national committeewoman, and the chair from each state and from American Samoa, District of Columbia, Guam, Puerto Rico, and Virgin Islands	165

SOURCES: *The Charter and Bylaws of the Democratic Party of the United States*, and *The Rules of the Republican Party*.

The committee's major collective function is the election of officers, chief of which is the party chair. Otherwise, the committee has little to do. Most of its assigned functions are undertaken by the chair and headquarters staff, with the committee customarily authorizing and ratifying these decisions.

One noteworthy assignment is to fill vacancies that occur before the election in the nominations for president and vice president. If a convention's nomination is vacated for any reason, it falls to the national committee to meet and fill it. In 1972, when Democratic vice-presidential nominee Thomas Eagleton withdrew, the Democratic National Committee, on the recommendation of presidential nominee George McGovern, formally nominated R. Sargent Shriver for the second spot on the ticket. A somewhat similar situation had developed for the Democrats in 1860, when their vice presidential nominee declined the nomination and the national committee replaced him.

Chair and Other Officers

The national chairman or chairwoman presides over the committee and administers the party headquarters. The position of national chair has high visibility and significance within the party organization, which looks to that individual for leadership. *(See Table 2-3, p. 42.)*

To the general public, the occupant of the national chair stands as a symbol and spokesperson for the party. To the president, the chair is a top-level presidential appointee who links White House and party and through whom the president traditionally has exercised considerable party leadership.[11]

The national committee formally elects its top officer. Traditionally, it did so at a meeting immediately after the national convention. This established the presumption that the chair's term of office was four years. In practice, few national party chairs have served that long. Within-term vacancies have been the normal occurrence, especially in the chair of the party that lost the presidential election.

In the decade of the 1980s, both Republicans and Democrats departed from tradition and opted to elect their chairs after the presidential election instead of after the nominating convention, somewhat separating chair selection from the contest for the party's presidential nomination. The Republicans further established a two-year term for their chair, providing for an election after the midterm elections.

There is an important distinction between the status and activities of the national chair whose party nominee occupies the White House and the one whose party does not. The in-party's chairs serve under the party leadership of the president.

Besides designating a chair, the national committee selects a number of other officers. The Democrats elect five vice chairs (three of whom are of the opposite sex of the chair), a treasurer, a secretary, a finance chair, and other appropriate officers as the committee deems necessary. The full committee is also empowered to choose an executive committee, determining its size, composition, and term of office.

The Republicans choose a cochair of the opposite sex, along with eight vice chairs—a man and a woman from each of four different regional state associations: West, Midwest, Northeast, and South. They also select a secretary, treasurer, and such other officers as they desire. Other collective leadership structures include the chair's executive council and the executive committee, with party rules stipulating procedures for selection and responsibilities.

Headquarters

In the nineteenth century, party operations were conducted largely within the context of the convention and the presidential campaign.[12] The chief responsibilities of the committee and its chair were to prepare and conduct the quadrennial nominating convention and direct the ensuing presidential campaign. Once the nominations were completed, headquarters would be established, usually in New York City, and the campaign led by the party chair. After the election, the organization would largely disband. The committee would meet perhaps once a year; at other times the national party would exist in the person of the chair. The pace would pick up again when plans had to be made for the forthcoming convention.

In the 1920s both national parties established year-round headquarters operations with paid staff. The Republicans took the lead here and have continued to emphasize organizational development more than their Democratic counterparts. Initially, both parties rented office space in Washington, D.C. During the Nixon administration, the Republicans moved into their own building adjacent to the House office buildings on Capitol Hill. In the 1980s the Democrats did the same, opening their permanent offices just a few blocks away.

Both parties have expanded their staffs and scope of operations, which swell temporarily before presidential elections. In the intervening years, the staff size remains relatively high. Political scientists Cornelius Cotter and John Bibby have assembled figures indicating that since 1950 the Republicans have never had fewer than eighty paid employees, and the Democrats, never fewer than forty. These figures are for the national party headquarters only. The congressional parties have campaign organizations, and occasionally the party headquarters will subsidize a White House employee. Further, off-year staffing for both parties has averaged in excess of seventy.[13]

With this increased staff capacity, the national party has been shifting its emphases away from its traditional presidency-related responsibilities toward party-building activities. But tasks related to the planning and conduct of the convention persist. The committee issues the convention call, which stipulates procedures for delegate apportionment and selection, along with temporary convention rules. It designates the membership and leadership of preconvention committees and designates convention presiders and speakers. It establishes the site, date, and order of business, though with in-party committees the White House normally has a significant say in these determinations.

The national headquarters retains some presidential campaign responsibilities. The Democratic Party charter formally authorizes it to conduct that campaign.[14] The nominee's own campaign organization, however, typically assumes the brunt of the campaign effort, relegating the party organization to the periphery. Nevertheless, operations of a contemporary presidential campaign are sufficiently broad that there is plenty of activity to occupy the time and energy of an expanded national committee staff throughout the fall campaign.

It is outside the arena of presidential politics, however, that party headquarters now are making increasingly significant contributions, primarily in campaign assistance and other services to the state and local parties. The national parties are now

TABLE 2-3 National Party Chairs

<table>
<tr><td colspan="3">DEMOCRATIC PARTY</td><td colspan="3">REPUBLICAN PARTY</td></tr>
<tr><td>*Name*</td><td>*State*</td><td>*Years of service*</td><td>*Name*</td><td>*State*</td><td>*Years of service*</td></tr>
<tr><td>B. F. Hallett</td><td>Massachusetts</td><td>1848–1852</td><td>Edwin D. Morgan</td><td>New York</td><td>1856–1864</td></tr>
<tr><td>Robert McLane</td><td>Maryland</td><td>1852–1856</td><td>Henry J. Raymond</td><td>New York</td><td>1864–1866</td></tr>
<tr><td>David A. Smalley</td><td>Virginia</td><td>1856–1860</td><td>Marcus L. Ward</td><td>New Jersey</td><td>1866–1868</td></tr>
<tr><td>August Belmont</td><td>New York</td><td>1860–1872</td><td>William Claflin</td><td>Massachusetts</td><td>1868–1872</td></tr>
<tr><td>Augustus Schell</td><td>New York</td><td>1872–1876</td><td>Edwin D. Morgan</td><td>New York</td><td>1872–1876</td></tr>
<tr><td>Abram S. Hewitt</td><td>New York</td><td>1876–1877</td><td>Zachariah Chandler</td><td>Michigan</td><td>1876–1879</td></tr>
<tr><td>William H. Barnum</td><td>Connecticut</td><td>1877–1889</td><td>J. Donald Cameron</td><td>Pennsylvania</td><td>1879–1880</td></tr>
<tr><td>Calvin S. Brice</td><td>Ohio</td><td>1889–1892</td><td>Marshall Jewell</td><td>Connecticut</td><td>1880–1883</td></tr>
<tr><td>William F. Harrity</td><td>Pennsylvania</td><td>1892–1896</td><td>D. M. Sabin</td><td>Minnesota</td><td>1883–1884</td></tr>
<tr><td>James K. Jones</td><td>Arkansas</td><td>1896–1904</td><td>B. F. Jones</td><td>Pennsylvania</td><td>1884–1888</td></tr>
<tr><td>Thomas Taggart</td><td>Indiana</td><td>1904–1908</td><td>Matthew S. Quay</td><td>Pennsylvania</td><td>1888–1891</td></tr>
<tr><td>Norman E. Mack</td><td>New York</td><td>1908–1912</td><td>James S. Clarkson</td><td>Iowa</td><td>1891–1892</td></tr>
<tr><td>William F. McCombs</td><td>New York</td><td>1912–1916</td><td>Thomas H. Carter</td><td>Montana</td><td>1892–1896</td></tr>
<tr><td>Vance C. McCormick</td><td>Pennsylvania</td><td>1916–1919</td><td>Mark A. Hanna</td><td>Ohio</td><td>1896–1904</td></tr>
<tr><td>Homer S. Cummings</td><td>Connecticut</td><td>1919–1920</td><td>Henry C. Payne</td><td>Wisconsin</td><td>1904</td></tr>
<tr><td>George White</td><td>Ohio</td><td>1920–1921</td><td>George B. Cortelyou</td><td>New York</td><td>1904–1907</td></tr>
<tr><td>Cordell Hull</td><td>Tennessee</td><td>1921–1924</td><td>Harry S. New</td><td>Indiana</td><td>1907–1908</td></tr>
<tr><td>Clem Shaver</td><td>West Virginia</td><td>1924–1928</td><td>Frank H. Hitchcock</td><td>Massachusetts</td><td>1908–1909</td></tr>
<tr><td>John J. Raskob</td><td>Maryland</td><td>1928–1932</td><td>John F. Hill</td><td>Maine</td><td>1909–1912</td></tr>
<tr><td>James A. Farley</td><td>New York</td><td>1932–1940</td><td>Victor Rosewater</td><td>Nebraska</td><td>1912</td></tr>
<tr><td>Edward J. Flynn</td><td>New York</td><td>1940–1943</td><td>Charles D. Hilles</td><td>New York</td><td>1912–1916</td></tr>
<tr><td>Frank C. Walker</td><td>Pennsylvania</td><td>1943–1944</td><td>William R. Wilcox</td><td>New York</td><td>1916–1918</td></tr>
<tr><td>Robert E. Hannegan</td><td>Missouri</td><td>1944–1947</td><td>Will Hays</td><td>Indiana</td><td>1918–1921</td></tr>
<tr><td>J. Howard McGrath</td><td>Rhode Island</td><td>1947–1949</td><td>John T. Adams</td><td>Iowa</td><td>1921–1924</td></tr>
<tr><td>William M. Boyle Jr.</td><td>Missouri</td><td>1949–1951</td><td>William M. Butler</td><td>Massachusetts</td><td>1924–1928</td></tr>
<tr><td>Frank E. McKinney</td><td>Indiana</td><td>1951–1952</td><td>Hubert Work</td><td>Colorado</td><td>1928–1929</td></tr>
<tr><td>Stephen A. Mitchell</td><td>Illinois</td><td>1952–1954</td><td>Claudius H. Huston</td><td>Tennessee</td><td>1929–1930</td></tr>
<tr><td>Paul M. Butler</td><td>Indiana</td><td>1955–1960</td><td>Simeon D. Fess</td><td>Ohio</td><td>1930–1932</td></tr>
<tr><td>Henry M. Jackson</td><td>Washington</td><td>1960–1961</td><td>Everett Sanders</td><td>Indiana</td><td>1932–1934</td></tr>
<tr><td>John M. Bailey</td><td>Connecticut</td><td>1961–1968</td><td>Henry P. Fletcher</td><td>Pennsylvania</td><td>1934–1936</td></tr>
<tr><td>Lawrence F. O'Brien</td><td>Massachusetts</td><td>1968–1969</td><td>John Hamilton</td><td>Kansas</td><td>1936–1940</td></tr>
<tr><td>Fred Harris</td><td>Oklahoma</td><td>1969–1970</td><td>Joseph W. Martin Jr.</td><td>Massachusetts</td><td>1940–1942</td></tr>
<tr><td>Lawrence F. O'Brien</td><td>Massachusetts</td><td>1970–1972</td><td>Harrison E. Spangler</td><td>Iowa</td><td>1942–1944</td></tr>
<tr><td>Jean Westwood</td><td>Utah</td><td>1972</td><td>Herbert Brownell Jr.</td><td>New York</td><td>1944–1946</td></tr>
<tr><td>Robert Strauss</td><td>Texas</td><td>1972–1977</td><td>Carroll Reese</td><td>Tennessee</td><td>1946–1948</td></tr>
<tr><td>Kenneth Curtis</td><td>Maine</td><td>1977–1978</td><td>Hugh D. Scott Jr.</td><td>Pennsylvania</td><td>1948–1949</td></tr>
<tr><td>John White</td><td>Texas</td><td>1978–1981</td><td>Guy George Gabrielson</td><td>New Jersey</td><td>1949–1952</td></tr>
<tr><td>Charles Manatt</td><td>California</td><td>1981–1985</td><td>Arthur E. Summerfield</td><td>Michigan</td><td>1952–1953</td></tr>
<tr><td>Paul Kirk</td><td>Massachusetts</td><td>1985–1989</td><td>C. Wesley Roberts</td><td>Kansas</td><td>1953</td></tr>
<tr><td>Ronald H. Brown</td><td>Washington, D.C.</td><td>1989–1993</td><td>Leonard W. Hall</td><td>New York</td><td>1953–1957</td></tr>
<tr><td>David Wilhelm</td><td>Illinois</td><td>1993–1994</td><td>H. Meade Alcorn Jr.</td><td>Connecticut</td><td>1957–1959</td></tr>
<tr><td>Christopher Dodd
(general chair)</td><td>Connecticut</td><td>1994–1997</td><td>Thruston B. Morton</td><td>Kentucky</td><td>1959–1961</td></tr>
<tr><td>Donald Fowler</td><td>South Carolina</td><td>1994–1997</td><td>William E. Miller</td><td>New York</td><td>1961–1964</td></tr>
<tr><td>Roy Romer
(general chair)</td><td>Colorado</td><td>1997–</td><td>Dean Burch</td><td>Arizona</td><td>1964–1965</td></tr>
<tr><td>Steven Grossman</td><td>Massachusetts</td><td>1997–</td><td>Ray C. Bliss</td><td>Ohio</td><td>1965–1969</td></tr>
<tr><td></td><td></td><td></td><td>Rogers C. B. Morton</td><td>Maryland</td><td>1969–1971</td></tr>
<tr><td></td><td></td><td></td><td>Robert Dole</td><td>Kansas</td><td>1971–1973</td></tr>
<tr><td></td><td></td><td></td><td>George Bush</td><td>Texas</td><td>1973–1974</td></tr>
<tr><td></td><td></td><td></td><td>Mary Louise Smith</td><td>Iowa</td><td>1974–1977</td></tr>
<tr><td></td><td></td><td></td><td>William Brock</td><td>Tennessee</td><td>1977–1981</td></tr>
<tr><td></td><td></td><td></td><td>Richard Richards</td><td>Utah</td><td>1981–1983</td></tr>
<tr><td></td><td></td><td></td><td>Paul Laxalt
(general chair)</td><td>Nevada</td><td>1983–1986</td></tr>
<tr><td></td><td></td><td></td><td>Frank Fahrenkopf</td><td>Nevada</td><td>1983–1989</td></tr>
<tr><td></td><td></td><td></td><td>Lee Atwater
(general chair)</td><td>South Carolina</td><td>1989–1991
1991</td></tr>
<tr><td></td><td></td><td></td><td>Clayton Yeutter</td><td>Nebraska</td><td>1991–1992</td></tr>
<tr><td></td><td></td><td></td><td>Richard Bond</td><td>New York</td><td>1992–1993</td></tr>
<tr><td></td><td></td><td></td><td>Haley Barbour</td><td>Mississippi</td><td>1993–1997</td></tr>
<tr><td></td><td></td><td></td><td>Jim Nicholson</td><td>Colorado</td><td>1997–</td></tr>
</table>

SOURCE: Hugh A. Bone, *Party Committees and National Politics* (Seattle: University of Washington Press, 1958), 241–243; updated by author.

actively engaged in candidate recruitment. They offer training sessions and make available a wide variety of information and expertise for the benefit of the parties' nominees. These include research, polling, data processing, direct mail, consultants, and money in vast amounts.[15]

Here again, the Republicans were the pioneers, initially under the leadership of Ray Bliss, party chair from 1965 to 1969. The same approach was emphasized by William Brock, chair from 1977 to 1981. The Democrats have followed suit since the late 1970s.

ROLES AND INTERACTIONS WITH THE WHITE HOUSE

The traditional patterns of interaction between presidents and national party organizations emerged out of mutual needs. A presidential aspirant needed the party nomination to legitimize the candidacy. Further, a nominee needed the resources of the party organization to conduct the general election campaign. After a successful effort to elect its nominee, the party organization could then justifiably claim the fruits of federal patronage distributed through the executive to its loyal laborers.

During the past half-century, three important developments have altered the traditional nature of that relationship. The structure of the presidential campaign organization has changed, relegating the party organization to peripheral status; civil service has been extended, reducing the number of political patronage jobs; and the White House Office has been established and expanded, lessening the president's reliance on outside help.

Vast patronage resources once awaited the victorious party assuming control of the executive branch, but the extensive coverage of civil service has reduced drastically the number of political appointments. The remaining appointments are at such high and specialized levels that the party organization is less often able to provide qualified candidates.

Finally, the establishment and expansion of the White House Office has provided the president with an in-house assembly of loyalists willing and able to do the sorts of political chores previously delegated to the national party organization. Their close presence to the Oval Office and the president's reliance on them, render the party organization less meaningful in presidential politics.

The president and the national party organization interact chiefly in selecting and deploying the party chair. Other avenues include managing party headquarters, establishing financial and organizational plans, arranging and running the convention, and managing the nominating and election campaigns.

Selection of the Party Chair

At the beginning of the twentieth century, custom and practice clearly dictated that the national committee defer to the party's presidential nominee in electing its postconvention chair. The usual procedure was for a delegation from the committee to call on the nominee to solicit a recommendation. The committee would then convene to ratify that choice. This practice initially developed to tie the nominee's campaign with the national party effort. It had the effect of placing the party organization leadership under the nominee's authority.

After the election, the president-elect could continue to claim that prerogative. Under the revised calendar currently in effect, the party that won the presidency in November defers to its victorious nominee in selecting its chair in January. Thereafter, for the party in power, the position of chair remains in effect a presidential appointment. The incumbent serves at the pleasure of the president, with the national committee compliantly endorsing the president's choice.

The full significance of the recent bipartisan reforms realigning and limiting the term of the party chair for presidential party leadership is not yet clear. Deferring the formal takeover of the party organization by the presidential nominee until after a victory in the presidential election enables the party organization to avoid the assertion of control over it by an unsuccessful nominee. For the victor's party, however, it is doubtful that these reforms will fundamentally reorient established patterns and practices.

In the 1970s both major parties established the position of chair as full time and salaried. This action appears to have been in response to an accelerating tendency to place legislators in that office, making it a part-time job. The change both contributes to and results from the increasing institutionalization of the national organization, whose members consider themselves ill-served by part-time leaders with primary loyalties to other elements within the party. Moreover, with the increasing amount of responsibility and activity located at the national level, the party headquarters requires full-time leadership. Since the imposition of these rules, however, both a Republican president (Reagan) and a Democratic president (Clinton) have managed to circumvent them and install an incumbent U.S. senator (Paul Laxalt by Reagan and Christopher Dodd by Clinton) in a newly created position of general chair.

Backgrounds. Traditionally, the eligibility requirements for the position of national party chair have been very loose, affording the president considerable discretion. Presidents have typically recruited party chairs out of three overlapping categories: state party leaders, officeholders, and the preconvention campaign organizations of the presidential nominee. George Bush, a former House member who headed the GOP in the last two years of the Nixon administration, has been the only national chair to date who has gone on to become president. Another former GOP chair, former Senate majority leader Bob Dole, was unsuccessful as the Republican presidential nominee in 1996. (See box, *The Party Chair as Candidate for National Office, p. 44.*)

Presidential nominees and incumbents have frequently looked to the ranks of the state party organizations in choosing party chairs. Among former state party leaders chosen while their party controlled the White House after World War II were Republicans H. Meade Alcorn Jr., Mary Louise Smith, Richard Richards, and Frank Fahrenkopf; Democrats Robert E. Han-

Traditionally, the national party chair performed in the arena of organizational politics and eschewed personal participation in electoral politics at the presidential level. Democratic national chair James A. Farley's candidacy for the 1940 presidential nomination constituted a major and singular departure from established practice. Since 1960, however, the incumbent national party chair frequently has figured in speculation surrounding the composition of the party's presidential ticket. This connection has taken three forms: (1) the chair's availability for the vice-presidential nomination; (2) consideration of the party chair position as a consolation prize for a loser in the vice-presidential sweepstakes; and (3) the presence of former party chairs in the field of contenders for the party's presidential nomination.

These modern patterns first emerged in 1960 when Sen. Thruston B. Morton of Kentucky, the Republican national chair, was a finalist on nominee Richard Nixon's list of vice-presidential prospects. Passed over in favor of Henry Cabot Lodge, Morton retained the chairmanship.

On the Democratic side in 1960, nominee John F. Kennedy placed Sen. Henry M. Jackson of Washington on his short list of potential running mates. After he chose Lyndon B. Johnson, Kennedy tapped Jackson to be the DNC chair for the duration of the campaign. When Johnson's nomination met with vocal opposition at the convention, the Kennedy camp sent word to Johnson that he could have the party chair job if he declined the offer of the vice-presidential nomination.

In 1964 Republican nominee Barry M. Goldwater named as his running mate the incumbent national party chair, Rep. William E. Miller of New York. To date, Miller remains the only incumbent chair ever named to a major party ticket.

The year 1968 marked the return of Richard Nixon to the Republicans' presidential ticket. Nixon seriously considered Rep. Rogers C. B. Morton of Maryland, younger brother of Thruston, as his vice-presidential partner, before settling on Spiro T. Agnew. When a vacancy occurred in the party chair following the general election, Nixon recommended Rogers Morton for the post.

In the Democratic contest that year, Sen. Fred Harris of Oklahoma lost out to Edmund S. Muskie as Hubert H. Humphrey's choice of running mate. Harris then unsuccessfully sought the party chair post, which on Humphrey's suggestion went to Lawrence F. O'Brien. Harris's persistence paid off when he was named chair in January 1969 amid speculation that he was positioning himself for a future presidential bid.

In 1972 O'Brien figured prominently in convention-week speculation for the vice-presidential spot on the ticket with George McGovern that went to Sen. Thomas Eagleton of Missouri. When Eagleton resigned the nomination shortly afterward, O'Brien again

was mentioned as a possible choice, but the vice-presidential slot eventually went to R. Sargent Shriver.

When President Nixon resigned in 1974, Gerald R. Ford became president, creating a vacancy in the vice presidency. Ford seriously considered nominating George Bush, then the Republican national chair, but instead he chose Nelson Rockefeller. Ford dumped Rockefeller from the 1976 ticket, replacing him with a former national chair, Sen. Robert J. Dole of Kansas. One of the individuals Ford passed over, John B. Connally, was offered the party chair as a consolation prize, but Connally rejected the offer. The Democratic presidential field that year included former party chair Harris.

The 1980 Republican nominating contest featured the candidacies of two former party chairs, Bush and Dole. After both lost out to Ronald Reagan and Bush became Reagan's running mate, the ticket's victory made Bush the first former party chair to be elected vice president.

In 1988, with Reagan's second term due to expire, former party chairs Bush and Dole resumed their presidential rivalry. Early in the campaign season rumors had former senator Paul Laxalt of Nevada, who held the position of general chair of the Republican Party from 1982 through 1986, as a possible contender for the GOP nomination; but Laxalt never entered the fray. Bush prevailed, and his November victory made him also the first former party chair to be elected president.

In 1992 the Democratic presidential nomination went to Arkansas governor Bill Clinton, who had been prominently mentioned as a possibility to chair the Democratic National Committee a decade earlier and who did chair the Democratic Leadership Council in 1990–1991. Incumbent party chair Ronald H. Brown figured in speculation regarding the vice-presidential nomination that went to Sen. Al Gore of Tennessee.

The emergence of the persistent connection between the party chair and the national ticket was rooted in the practice from the late 1950s through the mid-1970s of naming House and Senate incumbents as national party chairs. The visibility of the office made it attractive to electoral figures who sought the role of party spokesman.

The decision by both parties in the 1970s to make the chair a full-time position seemingly diminished this electoral connection. On two occasions, however, presidents have circumvented this practice by naming incumbent senators as general chairs serving at the same time as the national chairs, thus potentially reinstating the linkage. Moreover, in the modern media age, even the nonelected officials who serve as party chair have heightened public visibility, which promises to make the connection between the party chair and the national ticket an enduring one. Indeed, in 1996 former national chair Dole captured the Republican presidential nomination before losing the general election to President Clinton.

Jean Westwood, left, was the first woman to head the Democratic National Committee; Ronald Brown, right, was the first African American to hold the post.

negan, J. Howard McGrath, Frank E. McKinney, John M. Bailey, and Donald Fowler. Such state party leaders have often already been members of the national committee they are being tapped to head.

A congressional connection can be found for a number of national chairs. Post–World War II chairs of the in-party who had congressional experience before or during their party leadership service included Republicans Leonard W. Hall, Thruston B. Morton, Rogers C. B. Morton, Robert Dole, George Bush, and general chair Paul Laxalt, and Democrats Howard McGrath and general chair Christopher Dodd.

Apart from Congress, the national-level political office with which the most chairs have been associated has been that of postmaster general, a position abolished when the U.S. Postal Service was created in 1971. The list of chairs who had served previously, subsequently, or simultaneously as head of the former Post Office Department consists of Democrats James A. Farley, Frank C. Walker, Robert Hannegan, and Lawrence F. O'Brien, and Republicans Marshall Jewell, Henry C. Payne, George B. Cortelyou, Harry S. New, Frank H. Hitchcock, Will Hays, and Arthur E. Summerfield.

Gubernatorial linkages, not uncommon in the nineteenth and early twentieth century, are now relatively rare. In the post–World War II period, three former governors held the na-

tional chairmanship of the in-party: Republican Paul Laxalt; and Democrats Howard McGrath and Kenneth Curtis.

Recruits of recent years from preconvention campaign organizations included Republican Lee Atwater and Democrat David Wilhelm. Both also belonged to the category of professional political consultants. These new players in electoral politics have increasingly superseded traditional party managers in the conduct of election campaigns.

The early chairs were often men of considerable wealth. Although sizable personal fortunes have not been a disqualification in recent years, they are no longer quite so common. Until the 1970s the party chair was exclusively the province of white males. Democrat Jean Westwood broke this pattern in 1972, followed by Republican Mary Louise Smith in 1974. The Democrats also shattered precedent in 1989 and chose an African American, Ronald H. Brown, as chair. Only Smith chaired the incumbent president's party.

The average tenure for post–World War II national chairs of the party controlling the White House is approximately two and one-half years. Thus, virtually all presidents have the opportunity to interact with the national party in selecting the national chair. Among modern presidents, only Lyndon B. Johnson never chose a party chair. (See "Lyndon B. Johnson," p. 78.)

Customarily, when a vacancy exists, perhaps at the instigation of the president, the national committee sends a delegation of its members to call on the president at the White House to be informed of the president's choice. Trial balloons will no doubt have been floated and reacted to prior to the official visit. The national committee then convenes to elect that person. Having done so, the national committee's subsequent interaction with the president typically is limited to occasional presidential addresses and receptions scheduled in conjunction with regular meetings of the committee.

As the top leadership position in the party organization hierarchy, the position of party chair unquestionably has high symbolic value, especially to the activists who make up the party organization at all levels. Its high visibility makes it something of a plum for persons and factions within the party. Its substantive significance varies considerably according to the expectations of the nominee or president and the orientations of the designated chair.

Patterns in Recruitment. In examining patterns in the recruitment of national party chairs, the paramount considerations pertain to the timing of the selection and whether the party controls the White House. Historically, most party chairs have been chosen in the wake of the nominating conventions. Alternatively, frequent between-convention vacancies have required replacements. The recent realignment of the terms of the national party chairs, beginning in January following the November presidential election and lasting two years for the Republicans and four for the Democrats, introduces a new structure for recruiting party chairs.

Within the party controlling the White House, the president typically dominates the process, unless that incumbent is a lame duck whose successor as party nominee has already been designated. In that case the nominee assumes leadership in selecting the chair, and nominees of both parties have done so. The national committee, nominally authorized to choose its chair, actually does so only when the vacancy occurs between conventions when the party does not control the White House.

Party chairs chosen by nonincumbent presidential nominees soon after the convention tended to be chosen for reasons directly related to the presidential campaign. Typically, they fell into two broad and potentially overlapping categories: personal loyalists from the preconvention campaign organizations or state organization leaders who had delivered crucial delegate support to the nominee. In recruiting a personal loyalist, the nominee rewarded a trusted associate while taking steps to ensure the responsiveness of the party machinery and stamping a personal imprint on it. For state party leaders, the position of national chair often served as a bargaining gambit, offered as a reward for assistance in securing a hotly contested nomination.

Franklin Roosevelt's 1932 selection of James Farley embodies both patterns. Farley was simultaneously Roosevelt's preconvention campaign manager and the leader of the powerful New York state Democratic Party organization.

Nominees traditionally used the prerogative of naming the party chair to cultivate or mollify important party or electoral constituencies. Several demographic variables such as region, ethnicity, religion, and gender came into play here. Nominees sometimes saw in the naming of the party chair an opportunity or a responsibility to recognize and represent a regional center of party power.

For more than three decades in the middle of the twentieth century, every chair of the Democratic Party was an Irish Catholic. This pattern rewarded that powerful constituency within the party organization. Also, it compensated for the absence of a Roman Catholic on the party's presidential ticket between the nominations of Al Smith in 1928 and John Kennedy in 1960.

Democratic nominee George S. McGovern's 1972 selection of Jean Westwood, the first woman to chair a national party committee, reflected two important developments in presidential nominating politics that had relevance for the position of party chair. The first was the growing influence of women in party affairs. The second was the emergence of new bargaining units at the convention transcending the state party delegations— namely, caucuses that represented pressure groups in the larger political order.

On occasion, similar symbolic considerations encouraged nominees to view the party chair as a potential consolation prize for an unsuccessful aspirant for a spot on the presidential ticket. Kennedy's choice of Henry Jackson in 1960 illustrates this pattern.

Long before the recent rescheduling of the term of the chair, distancing it from the national convention, presidential nominees frequently put aside their prerogative of designating the party chair in favor of retaining the incumbent. In fulfilling their responsibilities, party chairs such as Paul Butler (D, 1956), Thruston Morton (R, 1960), Ray Bliss (R, 1968), Robert Strauss (D, 1966), William Brock (R, 1980), and Charles Manatt (D, 1984) developed strong and vocal personal followings, which provided pressures and incentives for their retention, in recognition of jobs well done and in the interests of party unity.

A final consideration taken into account by the nominee in the selection of the party chair was the primary role anticipated for the chair in the upcoming general election campaign. The traditional role was one of management, concentrating energies and talents on problems of campaign organization and strategy. Subsequently, the role became one of spokesperson, highly visible but largely separated from the centers of campaign decision making.

Presidents-elect and incumbents have tended to make their designations of party chairs for reasons less immediately connected to the presidential campaign. Again, the expectations regarding the role of the party chair greatly affect recruitment. A general distinction can be drawn between chairs recruited primarily as party builders versus those assigned the role of party spokesperson.

Chairs have come from diverse political backgrounds, with state organization leaders and incumbent national legislators predominating. Generally, the state organization leaders have dominated the party-builder category, while the national legislators have acted as party spokespersons. Although these chairs typically have been identified with the political causes and campaigns of their presidents, few qualify as close personal associates.

The aforementioned demographic considerations of region, religion, and gender that were present in postconvention selections are often present in these decisions also. For example, in the years since World War II, a regional background has been common between the president and the party chair about half of the time. Most of the Democratic chairs have been Roman Catholics, while Methodists and Episcopalians have predominated among Republicans. Their average age at election has approached fifty. Gerald Ford chose the only woman, Mary Louise Smith (1974).

Within-term vacancies have occurred for a variety of reasons. On several occasions, presidential promotions of chairs to high-level government positions have created openings. Truman named Sen. Howard McGrath attorney general; Nixon chose Rep. Rogers Morton to lead the Interior Department; and Ford sent George Bush to the People's Republic of China to head the United States Liaison Office.

Most chairs have left for personal reasons or to pursue their own political interests. On a handful of occasions, presidential dissatisfaction with the performance of the party chair has figured in press speculation, most recently in the 1994 resignation of David Wilhelm as Democratic national chair; and scandal tainted the resignations of both Democrat William Boyle (1951) and Republican Wesley Roberts (1953).

Changing Role of the Party Chair

The role of the in-party chair has undergone major changes during the past fifty years. Once, the national chair was a central actor in presidential politics. By and large, this is no longer the case. Chairs of both the in-party and the out-party today are far more involved in directing ongoing party-building endeavors—national, state, and local—than was previously typical. This has come about because of changes in both the presidency and the political parties.

In the past the national chair customarily directed the party campaign, of which the presidential race was the central feature. The expectation of tying together the overall party effort and the specifically presidential campaign underlay the development of the custom whereby the national committee solicits the presidential nominee's recommendation for its chair. Operating out of party headquarters, the president's choice would direct the campaign.

More recently, the presidential nominees have instead developed and relied on personal campaign organizations. The reasons include strategic considerations related to declining party identification in the electorate, federal election laws effectively mandating the establishment of separate organizations, and, most important, changes in the nature of nominating campaigns.

Years ago, nominating campaigns were low-key efforts designed to elicit the support of a relative handful of party chieftains, who in turn controlled state delegations at the convention. With the advent of primary contests to select delegates, prospective nominees must develop full-scale campaign organizations well in advance of the convention.

The road to the convention nomination now proceeds through delegate-selection primaries in well over thirty states, where campaign organizations are tried and tested. The eventual winner normally will be inclined to continue to operate through that organizational vehicle in the general election campaign that follows.

This development relegates the national organization to the periphery of the campaign effort. It similarly places the chair outside the inner circle of campaign decision makers. Thus a major role traditionally performed by the party chair has been rendered negligible.

At the outset, national chairs had important patronage responsibilities. The chair claimed the spoils of electoral victory for the party loyalists. The traditional association between the chair and the postmaster generalship pertained directly to this task, because the Post Office Department provided an abundance of government jobs to be distributed among the party faithful. By the time of the Nixon administration, the Post Office's patronage position had long since been decimated by civil service expansion. In 1971 the department was restructured as the Postal Service, a government corporation, removing it from both the cabinet and party politics.

Throughout the government, the establishment and expansion of the merit system of federal hiring has drastically reduced the available patronage. Moreover, the types of positions now available tend to be less appropriate for party organization claimants. The role of the party chair as patronage dispenser has become passé.

Party chairs in days gone by also served their presidents as key political advisers. They kept chief executives in touch with the perspectives of their counterparts in statehouses and city halls.

Modern presidents have perceived much less need for such advice. They now have a sizable personal staff of aides they can rely on as advisers and intermediaries with other political leaders. Polling organizations provide presidents with an abundance of data about the public pulse. Here again, the traditional role of the chair has been supplanted.

Developments within the party organization also have worked to distance the chair from the presidential inner circle. Party chairs have always operated under a norm of neutrality toward competing candidacies for the presidential nomination. Usually, this norm was conveniently ignored by chairs of the party in power, who were serving as presidential appointees and pursuing the interests of their sponsors. As the parties have become more bureaucratic and institutional, the expectations regarding neutrality are growing stronger. Federal election laws reinforce the pressure for the chair to remain impartial.[16] As a result, modern party chairs are less likely to occupy the role of key presidential adviser.

Another of the chair's traditional roles—that of fund raiser—endures today, but in vastly altered form and more removed from presidential politics. Nineteenth-century chairs tended to be wealthy individuals who made major personal contributions to the presidential campaign, bankrolled a limited party operation that supplemented the campaign, and prevailed upon their similarly disposed friends and associates to do likewise.

The growing costs of presidential campaigns have placed their financing beyond the means of a relative handful of individuals, even those of immense personal wealth. Further, federal election laws limit the financial contributions of individuals. Federal law also provides for public funding of presidential campaigns.

National party headquarters operations have also grown beyond the capacity of the chair personally to subsidize them. While contemporary chairs continue to perform a significant fund-raising function, they do so in an altered fashion that is oriented toward party building and somewhat distanced from the presidential arena.

Both national committees have for many years established finance committees and designated individuals to chair them. The Republicans began doing so in the 1930s, and the Democrats followed suit some two decades later. These individuals, while under the authority of the national chair, nevertheless operate separately, relieving the chair of many traditional fund-raising responsibilities.

As these traditional roles have diminished in importance, other time-honored functions have attained heightened significance. Three such roles identified by political scientists Cornelius Cotter and Bernard Hennessy are those of *image-maker, hell-raiser,* and *administrator.*[17]

• Image-Maker. Public relations has always been a major responsibility of the party chair. In the nineteenth century many national chairs came from newspaper backgrounds. Although this has been much less the case since World War I, a sensitivity to and a flair for public relations continue to be expected of the chair.

The chair seeks to promote a positive public image for the party, to position its actions and objectives in the best possible light. This can be done by personally assuming the role of party spokesperson. Such a chair will regularly make the rounds of the network television interview shows such as *Meet the Press* and *Face the Nation,* along with the proliferating cable television presentations like *Capital Gang* and *Crossfire,* while remaining readily available for interviews and comments to print reporters. In addition, the chair acts as a goodwill ambassador for party unity and expansion. Chairs uncomfortable with personal appearances will nonetheless sponsor similar efforts by other voices for the party.

• Hell-Raiser. The chair as hell-raiser is the partisan's partisan. Such a figure will seek to satisfy the expectations of the party faithful by flailing away at the opposition party and right-

eously defending the party against detractors' assaults. Presidents often rely on their party chairs to emphasize this party leadership role. Doing so enables presidents to appear above partisan battles. Senator Dole enthusiastically took on this task for President Nixon in his 1972 campaign against Democratic challenger George McGovern.

• Administrator. As administrators, party chairs supervise the activities of the national headquarters—a role that has grown with the headquarters' expansion. The current requirement that the chair's position be full time and salaried also serves to emphasize the administrative aspects of the job.

Opportunities for Interaction with the White House

Installed in office by the president, and serving at the president's pleasure, national chairs encounter their party leaders in circumstances that vary considerably in both frequency and substantive significance. The tendency is toward infrequent meetings in rather formal, ceremonial settings. To be sure, President Truman had a standing appointment every Wednesday afternoon with the Democratic national chair to discuss party politics. Somewhat similarly, President Eisenhower genuinely expected his party chair to be the "political expert" in his delegation of administrative responsibilities.

Still, a facetious anecdote shared by Senator Dole about his tenure as party chair captures well the contemporary character of the relationship. Dole tells of receiving a telephone call from the White House, informing him that his long-standing request to see President Nixon was about to be granted. All he had to do was to turn his television set to the proper channel to receive the president's scheduled campaign address.[18]

Cabinet Meetings. Although no one has served simultaneously as party chair and as a cabinet secretary since 1947, several party chairs have made individual arrangements to attend cabinet meetings either regularly or intermittently. At these sessions, party chairs can be kept informed of the administration's public policy proposals, can assess their partisan ramifications, and can seek to present the party's perspective on them. In addition, cabinet meetings can provide the chair with opportunities to request and establish clearance procedures for political appointments. In general, although the party chair's physical presence at cabinet meetings undoubtedly affords an avenue of access to the president, the value is more symbolic than substantive.

White House Staff Meetings. Some recent party chairs have requested and been invited to be present at regular meetings between the president and top-level White House staff assistants. This action reflects the chair's recognition that the White House Office has become the epicenter of presidential party leadership. In addition, party chairs often journey to the White House for regular sessions with presidential staff in the absence of the president. On such occasions, the presidential staff's intermediary role between the president and the party chair is heightened.

Congressional Leadership Meetings. The inclination of some modern presidents to name incumbent legislators as party chair has introduced a new arena for interaction—the weekly con-

President Lyndon Johnson talks with Democratic Party chair John Bailey in the Oval Office in 1968. Serving for seven and one-half years, Bailey had the longest tenure among the post–World War II national party chairs.

gressional leadership meetings. Although none of these chairs has been a ranking member of the party congressional hierarchy, several of them (along with chairs who are not members of Congress) have requested permission to attend sessions where legislative strategy is planned and progress is monitored. Here, the presence of the party chair enables coordination of legislative activities with the party's organs of party policy and publicity and provides a forum to bring the chair's point of view directly to the president.

Headquarters Management. Another form of interaction between the White House and the national party is the management of the national party headquarters. Ostensibly, headquarters management would appear to be the primary responsibility of the chair, but few chairs have devoted much personal attention to this task. Other responsibilities with higher priority and other institutional and professional affiliations typically conflict with that of administrator. The accepted procedure is for the chair to exercise discretion in delegating managerial authority to a chosen subordinate. The chair then remains free in varying degrees to engage in other activities.

On several occasions in recent years, the president or White House aides have deployed at party headquarters a presidential agent with managerial authority. Typically, these instances have occurred when a legislator has been named chair and by definition serves part time. Such a situation developed during the Truman presidency with the assignment of Truman's old Missouri political assistant William Boyle to a management position at the Democratic National Committee then headed by Sen. Howard McGrath.

In his first months in office, Nixon sought to establish an analogous arrangement at the Republican National Committee. According to journalists Rowland Evans and Robert Novak, he promised a position there to longtime associate Murray Chotiner. The apparent understanding was that Chotiner would have responsibility for running the headquarters operation with an appropriate title under a figurehead chair. When the designated chair, Rep. Rogers Morton, refused to go along with the plan, it fell through. Subsequently, however, Nixon succeeded with a similar arrangement, using Thomas Evans at the outset of the tenure of Morton's successor, Senator Dole.[19]

Some chairs who were not members of Congress have likewise received this treatment. While retaining Kennedy-designate John Bailey as party chair, President Lyndon Johnson sent his Texas operative Clifton Carter to the Democratic National Committee headquarters to represent the president's interests there. President Jimmy Carter originally though briefly installed fellow-Georgian Phil Wise as Chairman Ken Curtis's executive director.

President Bill Clinton made two noteworthy moves in this direction of installing a manager at committee headquarters. At the outset of his presidency, he placed longtime Arkansas personal associate Craig Smith at the DNC as political director under David Wilhelm. Later, following Smith's eventual departure, the White House responded to rumblings from congressional Democrats about Wilhelm's performance by orchestrating the appointment of former representative Tony Coelho as senior adviser to the party chair. Wilhelm's resignation announcement followed shortly.

Financial and Organizational Collaboration

The national party organization engages in a great deal of congenial accommodation in behalf of the White House. Routinely, the White House relies on the financial and organizational structures of the national committee to sponsor what are really White House programs. For example, the White House bills the national committee for travel and living expenses incurred by the president while attending to party leadership responsibilities. Such situations include personal campaigning, campaigning for other party candidates, and appearances at party-sponsored affairs such as fund-raisers, rallies, and the national convention. Occasionally, the national committee can be prevailed upon to carry on its payroll individuals who actually work at the White House.

The national committee staff and the White House also interact in the preparation of publications that serve as public relations tools for the administration. The White House staff is in a position to furnish the party headquarters with data and inside information to make the publication attractive, relevant, and substantive. Typically, the party headquarters seeks and welcomes such assistance.

During the Clinton presidency, the DNC energetically and very visibly solicited public support for presidential policy initiatives. It established a "war room" to provide assistance during the budget battles that dominated Clinton's first year in office, and it similarly, though less successfully, mobilized support for his health care initiative during the second year.

Convention Arrangements and Management

An impending national nominating convention provides the setting for a great deal of interaction between the White House and the national party organization. Although the national committee has responsibility for arranging and conducting the convention, it does so under the close supervision of the president, even when the incumbent is not a candidate for reelection.

When the party is out of power, the national committee is supposed to be neutral toward competing candidacies for the nomination. When an incumbent president is seeking the nomination, however, the party headquarters usually strongly supports that candidacy.

Even when the incumbent is not a candidate, White House concern and interest about the party's choice abound. Typically, the retiring president's aides will monitor convention arrangements and become deeply involved in maneuvers during the proceedings. In past years, these agents have afforded outgoing presidents considerable influence at the convention.

The national committee formally establishes the site of the convention, but the president's preference, if not volunteered, is routinely solicited and accepted. According to Nixon campaign aide Jeb Stuart Magruder, for personal and political reasons Nixon insisted that the 1972 Republican national convention meet in San Diego, California. The White House sent Magruder, an official at the Committee for the Reelection of the President, to Denver, Colorado, in July 1971, to monitor the meeting of the Republican national committee's site selection committee. The committee was not inclined to choose San Diego, but party chair Dole informed the members that "if the president wanted

the convention in San Diego, it would just have to be in San Diego."[20] Although the committee obediently selected San Diego, the convention site subsequently had to be shifted to Miami Beach, Florida. The change took place amid concerns about inadequate hotel facilities in San Diego and fears that security arrangements there would be inadequate to deal with the expected onslaught of anti–Vietnam War demonstrators at the convention site.

Similarly, the convention date can be manipulated to the benefit of the incumbent. It is surely no coincidence that modern conventions expected to nominate incumbent presidents all have been scheduled relatively late in the summer, after those of the opposition party. For a unified party led by an incumbent president, a late convention builds momentum for the upcoming general election campaign.

When the president is a candidate, considerable White House effort is usually evident in the preparation of the party platform. Such participation ensures that the president's policies receive party endorsement, equates the party's stance on issues with that of the president, and precludes significant divergence toward an independent position.

Even when the president is not a candidate, the presidential presence is likely to hover over platform deliberations. Beyond party policy, recent presidents and White House staffs have concerned themselves with administrative details of convention management, to the point of preparing minute-by-minute scenarios.

Traditionally, the national party has convened only in connection with the nomination of the presidential ticket. In 1974, however, the out-of-power Democrats met in Kansas City for an issues conference midway through the presidential term. Four years later, with Democrat Jimmy Carter in the White House, a similar conference was held in Memphis, which provided an unprecedented opportunity for interaction between the White House and the national party. On this occasion, encountering substantial anti-Carter sentiment in the ranks of the delegates, the White House and presidential agents at the national party headquarters designed and controlled the agenda. They mounted a monitoring operation on the conference floor to ensure that the administration's positions would prevail against intraparty challenges. The effort duplicated the typical pattern of White House surveillance and supervision repeatedly demonstrated at the nominating conventions. The Democrats have not held a midterm convention since 1982.

Presidential exercises of convention leadership have produced a long string of successes for presidents who wanted to be renominated. Not since Chester A. Arthur in 1884 has an incumbent president who sought his party's nomination been denied it, and not since Franklin Pierce in 1856 has an elected incumbent been denied.[21] Indeed, most of Arthur's successors have been nominated with ease. Although both Truman and Johnson were constitutionally eligible to seek a second elected presidential term, both chose not to in the face of growing opposition.

In 1976, 1980, and 1992, serious nomination challenges were

mounted against the incumbents. Ronald Reagan's contest against President Ford, Sen. Edward M. Kennedy's against President Carter, and Patrick Buchanan's against President Bush suggest that post-1968 reforms in the methods of selecting convention delegates may offset partially the incumbent's traditional advantages. These reforms drastically reduced the state party organizations' control over delegate selection and increased popular participation in that process. Customarily, an incumbent president seeking the nomination could count on the support of the state party leaders. They had been the beneficiaries of presidential favors and attention and would fear presidential reprisal should support be withheld. Thus, even an unpopular president could be quite secure in the face of a nomination challenge. Recent reforms deprive modern presidents of this bulwark of potential support, however, leaving them potentially more vulnerable to intraparty challengers able to capitalize on popular disenchantment.

Even before the rules changes of the 1980s, which moved the selection of party chair from after the convention to after the general election, incumbent presidents were less inclined than nonincumbent nominees to replace the national chairs. They usually retained the current chair at least through the general election. Put differently, incumbent presidents expecting renomination installed their choices as party chairs well in advance of the nominating convention and retained them in its successful wake.

Presidential Election Campaigns

Journalist Theodore H. White observed that a presidential campaign "starts with a candidate, a handful of men, a theme and a plan. By November of election year it has enlisted hundreds of thousands of volunteers, politicians, state staffs, national staffs, media specialists and has become an enterprise."[22] A key question is, what is the relationship of the national party organization to the presidential campaign?

Traditionally, that role was central. National party committees came into being in the midnineteenth century to provide direction to the presidential campaign. Party chairs customarily served as campaign managers. Indeed, the practice of allowing the presidential nominee to name the party chair developed to facilitate integration of the presidential campaign with the party effort.

The campaign manager and a handful of key associates would set up shop at the headquarters of the national party. The party organization provided the nominee with the potent party symbol legitimizing the candidacy. Further, it made available the personnel necessary for the labor-intensive campaign that had to be waged.

More recently, however, presidential nominees have tended instead to establish autonomous campaign organizations, headquartered separately from the national party. A number of factors account for this development. Strategic considerations can turn a campaign away from the party organizations. A nominee representing the minority party in the electorate, for example,

might prefer to maintain some distance between the candidacy and the party effort in hopes of attracting broader support. Republican Richard Nixon's 1960 and 1968 campaigns took this approach.

On the Democratic side, the relative autonomy of Adlai E. Stevenson's 1952 campaign resulted in part from his ongoing status as governor of Illinois, necessitating the establishment of campaign headquarters in Springfield, the state capital. The Stevenson campaign also wanted to distance itself symbolically from the "mess in Washington," the home base of Democratic president Harry Truman and the national party headquarters.

Democrat Bill Clinton, facing a somewhat similar situation in 1992, responded in like fashion. His status as the incumbent governor of Arkansas enabled him to promote his "outsider" candidacy by setting up campaign headquarters in Little Rock.

Modern presidential nominees seek to appeal to an electorate that is decreasingly dependent on partisan sources and structures for political information, economic employment, and social services. As a result, the electorate appears decreasingly inclined to make durable partisan attachments. Thus the nominees are wary and disinclined to rely primarily on the party organization to carry them to victory.

Modern communications and transportation also have altered the character of election campaigns. Television brings a candidate into living rooms throughout the country. Jet airplanes allow an office seeker to cross the country both rapidly and comfortably. Candidates now can wage far more individualistic efforts than they could previously, and with far less need to rely on the party.

From a different standpoint, changes in the rules governing presidential nominations and elections have contributed to this shift toward more autonomous campaigns. The expansion of presidential primaries has made the coveted presidential nomination increasingly attainable through an appeal to the party electorate rather than the party organization. Indeed, recent nominating conventions have served less as decision-making bodies than as coronations for the party's nominee, already chosen in the fragmented and decentralized delegate selection contests.

This development contributes to autonomy in the campaign organization, since candidates must assemble an effective campaign staff well before the nominating convention in order to run in the primaries. During the preconvention period, unless an incumbent president is seeking the nomination, the party organization is expected to be neutral toward competing candidacies, which precludes integration of the party and the campaign staffs. Yet after the convention the tested campaign vehicle of the victor remains intact. This both complicates integration and makes it relatively unnecessary.

Finally, federal election laws enacted in the 1970s require a separate campaign organization for a candidate to qualify for public funds. Thus the contemporary likelihood of the traditional sort of integrated campaign, conducted under the auspices of the party apparatus, is virtually nil. Current provisions allow party committees to receive contributions (soft money) that can be spent in the presidential campaign. As a result, the reinvigorated party organization can play a significant, but nevertheless peripheral, campaign role.

All in all, no longer does the presidential campaign provide the context for interaction initiating the president-to-be's leadership relationship with the national party organization. The other traditions on which the relationship was based—political operations and patronage—also have eroded. The national party organization has become increasingly superfluous in presidential politics.

STATE AND LOCAL PARTY ORGANIZATIONS

Substantial variations exist among the fifty state and countless county and subcounty units of the political parties. Statewide, the structural components typically replicate the national pattern: convention, committee, chair, and, in recent years, headquarters staff.[23] At the lower levels, the pattern persists, though usually with the omission of headquarters staffs.

State Conventions

State conventions ordinarily meet once every two years, preceding the scheduled elections. They bring together representatives of the lower-level party units and vary in size. Most draw fewer than a thousand delegates, but several exceed this total. In 1994 more than 14,000 delegates assembled for the Virginia Republican convention.

The advent and acceptance of the direct primary in this century has almost completely taken from these bodies what was originally one of their primary responsibilities—nominating candidates for statewide offices. Contemporary conventions may elect party officers and adopt a party platform. During presidential election years, the state conventions traditionally played an important role in the selection of the state parties' delegates to the nominating convention. Party reforms have substantially reduced this role.

State Committees

State party committees also vary in size, from under fifty to more than five hundred. California, the biggest, assembles more than eight hundred members. As is the case at the national level, the state committees are charged with leadership selection and guiding the party's fortunes between conventions. By and large, these tasks are delegated to chairs and headquarters staffs. Many state party committees also designate executive committees to act for them.

State Chairs

State party chairs can be categorized into in-party and out-party groups, depending on whether the party's nominee holds the governorship. In-party chairs can be further subdivided into those who act as political agents of their governors and those who act independently. In many state parties, the convention or the committee defers in selecting a chair to the wishes of the governor or the gubernatorial nominee. Party building is a primary concern of state party chairs, who also are involved in fund-raising and campaign-related activities.

State Headquarters

Contemporary state party chairs usually operate out of year-round party headquarters occupied by small but full-time, paid staff. This development is relatively recent, dating to the early 1960s. Political scientist Robert Huckshorn attributes this phenomenon to four factors. One is the increase in party competition at the state level, especially in the South. Another is the growth of technology that has inspired state parties to take advantage of new methods and approaches in electoral politics.

A third factor is pressure from the national parties and government. Reforms in the selection of delegates to the national convention have imposed procedural guidelines on the state parties that require considerable attention to detail. Federal campaign finance legislation also has imposed stringent reporting guidelines.

Finally, Huckshorn contends that increased communication among the state chairs in recent years, taking the form of meetings under formal organizational auspices, has encouraged chairs lacking headquarters facilities to emulate those who do by setting up an office and operating in a businesslike manner. The result is an increased bureaucratization of the state parties.

Local Party Organization

At the local level, the components of convention, committee, and chair exist amid vast variations. The legendary urban party machines are essentially extinct. Nevertheless, some retain a residual and relative strength. In Chicago, for example, remnants of the once-powerful Daley organization linger. Elsewhere, some local parties are but organizational shells, with positions unoccupied and handfuls of officials quietly tending to procedural regularities. Here as at the other levels, election campaigns provide the primary arena for party activity. A comparative study a decade ago found few signs of organizational decline among local parties.[24]

State and Local Parties and Presidential Politics

The traditional relationship between state and local party organizations and the presidency centered on presidential selection. Changes in the presidential selection process have substantially disengaged connections between the two.

After the national convention became the nominating vehicle in the 1830s, and until recently, state and local party leaders tightly controlled the selection of convention delegates and effectively instructed their delegations in voting on nominees. Astute presidential candidates sought the support of these grassroots political leaders.

The preconvention presidential campaign typically consisted of relatively low-key efforts by candidates and managers to line up commitments from the party bosses. In turn, the bosses had options such as jumping aboard a bandwagon, backing favorite sons, or remaining uncommitted in hopes of ultimately tipping the balance at a divided convention.

Conventions in those days featured "smoke-filled rooms" where the party leaders gathered to wheel and deal for the presidential nomination. The victor would be beholden to the bosses who had authorized the outcome. Around the turn of the century, Ohio's Mark Hanna epitomized power brokers of this type.

In the years immediately preceding World War II, Frank Hague of New Jersey and "Boss" Crump of Memphis, Tennessee, represented the breed. As late as the 1960s, Mayor Richard J. Daley of Chicago still embodied the traditional pattern.

In campaigns of this era, the presidential nominee relied heavily on personnel resources that the state party leaders could mobilize. Old-time campaigns were much more labor-intensive than they are today. Until about 1960 the state party leaders were able to provide the necessary campaign workers.

Following the campaign, the victorious party's bosses would claim the federal patronage as a reward for their workers. Through the spoils system, the presidential-selection process clearly linked the state and local parties with the presidency.

Party reforms, beginning in the Progressive Era around 1900 and picking up steam after 1968, have drastically diminished the role of state party leaders in designating and controlling delegations to the national convention. Delegates formerly handpicked by party leaders now are mostly chosen through primaries and, less frequently, participatory caucuses.

In presidential primaries, party voters sometimes vote directly for convention delegates. In many states, they do so in conjunction with a vote for the presidential candidate of their choice. Convention delegate slots usually go to supporters of the various presidential candidates in proportion to their electoral support.

In the caucuses, local party activists gather at specified locations in voting precincts to register their support for particular presidential candidates. Each precinct will send representatives to a county-level assembly in proportion to the initial division of support for the various contenders.

At the county level, candidate supporters will be selected, again proportionally, to attend congressional district and finally state conventions. There the national convention delegates will be chosen from among the survivors of the earlier trials. The state parties also provide for at-large representatives to be chosen at the state level.

Although modern presidential candidates still court state party leaders' support, they are considerably less dependent on it than were their predecessors. Instead, they will emphasize appeals to pressure group leaders and party activists in the electorate who, through presidential primaries and participatory caucuses, have the controlling say in delegate selection. The delegations so chosen will be more under the direction of candidate and pressure group organizations, lessening the state party leaders' influence on the convention's choice.

Modern presidential campaigns are capital and technology intensive. Where once party workers rang doorbells to solicit support, today through television candidates themselves appear in living rooms throughout the land.

The expansion of civil service and consequent reduction of patronage resources also have helped to disengage state and party leaders from the presidency. This is not to say that the state and local parties have declined organizationally. Indeed, there is considerable evidence to the contrary.[25] But their organizational activity no longer relates so clearly to the presidency as it once did.

NATIONAL-STATE PARTY RELATIONS

National parties of the past were weak and lacking in resources compared with the state and local political organizations, primarily because the federal system decentralized political power in general and party power in particular.[26] In recent years, a dramatic "nationalization" has taken place as the national parties expanded authority and influence over their state counterparts. The two parties have taken different paths to similar ends. The Democrats have reformed party rules that primarily address delegate-selection procedures for the national convention. The Republican approach has been less legalistic, concentrating instead on making the state parties more reliant on the national party for needed services.[27]

The Democrats' altered course began in the late 1940s in the context of uncertainty about the loyalty of certain southern state parties toward the national ticket and platform. Twice in a twenty-year period, sizable elements of the southern Democratic Party bolted to follow a regional favorite son.

In 1948 several southern delegations walked out of the national convention following the passage of a controversial platform plank supporting civil rights. After the convention, several southern state parties held a rump assembly and nominated South Carolina governor J. Strom Thurmond to head a "Dixiecrat" ticket in the presidential election. Thurmond won four states and thirty-nine electoral votes.

In 1968 Alabama governor George C. Wallace mounted a presidential bid under the American Independent Party label. He carried five states and won forty-six electoral votes.

During the two decades of conflict over the loyalty issue, the national party demanded that the state units guarantee support for the convention's decisions. To put teeth in this demand it threatened not to seat noncomplying state delegations at subsequent conventions.

Initially, this controversy was closely associated with the issue of civil rights. The 1964 Democratic national convention resolved to prohibit racial discrimination in delegate selection to the 1968 convention. This constituted a historic assertion of national authority over what had previously been the state parties' exclusive prerogative. It also authorized the national chair to appoint a committee to assist the state parties in complying with this new guideline.

This committee and the 1968 convention, along with a new

group established by the latter, the Commission on Party Structure and Delegate Selection, broadened the issue beyond that of civil rights to embrace more generally popular participation in delegate selection and other party activities. These various proposals were accepted by the Democratic National Committee and the party's 1972 convention. They culminated at the 1974 midterm convention in the adoption of a charter that clearly subordinates the state parties to their national counterpart. As amended, this charter and accompanying bylaws remain in force as the party's "constitution."

The nationalization of the Republican Party has placed much less emphasis on formal rules. Where the national Democrats have mandated reform in delegate selection, the Republicans have merely recommended it. In practice, however, many of the Democratic Party guidelines have been incorporated by state legislatures into laws, so that they are similarly binding on the state Republican parties.

The national Republican Party has amassed a formidable financial foundation that allows it to bestow "favors," such as monetary assistance and campaign and party-building expertise, that bind state and local parties to the national organization. Therefore, although the Republicans have not formally altered their party structure, they too have positioned the national organization in the dominant position.

Presidential Party Leadership within the Executive Branch

President-party relations within the executive branch have undergone dramatic structural changes since the 1930s. White House aides have taken over party-management responsibilities once assigned to members of the cabinet, particularly the postmaster general. Appointments once provided the president as party chief with party-building resources, but the decline in the quantity and elevation in the quality of presidential patronage have diminished drastically this party leadership consideration. Although partisanship is still a vital part of presidential appointments, it remains significant primarily as an indicator of policy responsiveness and has become largely divorced from party-building concerns.

The Constitution authorizes the president to act as chief executive, that is, as head of the executive branch. Party leadership augments executive authority in presidential relations with the administration and the bureaucracy.

In the context of party relations in the executive, three conceptual distinctions should be made. First, the word *presidency* refers to the office of the president, those elements within the executive branch most directly under the control of the chief executive. They would include the White House Office, support agencies reporting to the president (such as the National Security Council and the Office of Management and Budget), and the people who operate the White House as the president's residence. Second, *administration* is a less precise term that applies to a particular president and the surrounding team of appoint-

ed aides, advisers, and managers within the upper echelons of the executive branch. Team members could include the vice president, the president's spouse, cabinet members, the press secretary, and others who derive their authority from their official or de facto association with the current president. Third, the *bureaucracy* is the permanent government, the men and women who are essentially full-time governmental employees more removed from the president's direct supervision.

PARTY MANAGEMENT IN THE EXECUTIVE BRANCH

The president's exercise of party leadership has long featured the establishment of organizational bases within the executive branch for oversight of party affairs. Traditionally, the president's cabinet, composed of the executive department heads, included one or more key political advisers who were deeply involved in party management.

The Post Office and Party Politics

For more than a century, the post office provided the customary haven for a political adviser and party manager. Since it was established as a cabinet office during President Andrew Jackson's administration, the position of postmaster general often went to a leading party strategist. Before the Civil War new presidents frequently named their campaign managers as postmasters general. In that position, this person's political acumen could be put to fruitful use. The primary task was to allocate the considerable resources of federal patronage available through the post office.

With the strengthening of party organization in the latter half of the nineteenth century, the postmaster generalship regularly went to a prominent party politician. After the turn of the century, it became established practice to place the national party chair in that position.

George Cortelyou (R, appointed in 1905), Frank Hitchcock (R, 1909), Will Hays (R, 1921), James Farley (D, 1933), Robert Hannegan (D, 1945), and Arthur Summerfield (R, 1953) were all incumbent party chairs who became postmasters general. Democrat Frank Walker (D, 1943) reversed the process when, while serving as postmaster general, he became the party chair in 1943. Hitchcock and Summerfield resigned their position as party chair on assuming their responsibilities at the post office; the others held the two positions simultaneously, at least for a time.

The alliance was one of convenience, and the keystone was government patronage, dispensed by the post office to recipients authorized by the party organization. This practice also gave relatively formal representation to the party organization in the inner circles of presidential politics. Thus President Truman could refer to Hannegan as the "political representative of the Democratic party in the cabinet of the president."[28] No party chair since Hannegan, however, has held the two offices at the same time; and no party chair since Summerfield has been named to head the post office or its successor, the Postal Service.

Nevertheless, through the 1960s, the head of the post office

Robert Hannegan simultaneously served as postmaster general and Democratic Party chair. His good friend President Harry Truman referred to Hannegan as the "political representative of the Democratic Party in the cabinet of the president."

continued to be associated with party politics and political operations. Lyndon Johnson named White House political aide Lawrence O'Brien postmaster general in 1965. O'Brien went on to chair the Democratic National Committee on two occasions, 1968–1969 and 1970–1972. After O'Brien resigned as postmaster general in 1968 to direct Sen. Robert F. Kennedy's presidential campaign, Johnson appointed another White House political assistant, appointments secretary Marvin Watson, a former Texas state Democratic Party chair, as postmaster general. Richard Nixon's choice for that position was Winton Blount, an Alabaman prominent in the growth of the Republican Party in the South and a visible symbol of Nixon's southern strategy, an effort to expand his personal and partisan base in that region.

During the Nixon presidency, administrative reform changed the structure of the post office, removing it from the cabinet and reconstituting it as a government corporation, the U.S. Postal Service. This development ended the historic connection between the post office, party management, and the party chair.

Three important factors brought about this change. First, after World War II the post office had severe financial problems that required the exercise of active and effective management at the top. The traditional assumption that the department essentially would run itself, leaving the postmaster general free to tend to partisan politics, had to be discarded. So began a trend toward placing business and public administration executives in this traditional sanctuary of party managers.

Second, presidents began to realize that the major justification for placing a party manager in the post office no longer applied. Even before World War II, the increasing proportion of executive branch positions under civil service protection had greatly depreciated the value of the post office as a strategic operating base for dispensing federal patronage. The civil service

classification of the positions of postmasters, the basic patronage commodity, was virtually complete by 1938, although a residual degree of discretion lingered. Moreover, the Hatch Act of 1939 prohibited overtly partisan political activity by government employees. This law thereby restricted the maintenance of an ongoing political organization through a network of post office activists.

In her 1943 study of the political significance of the postmaster generalship, Dorothy G. Fowler made a prediction that became an epitaph: "Shorn of his patronage weapon, his employees forbidden to participate in party management or be assessed for campaign funds, the postmaster general may become, like his British counterpart, merely the head of a large business organization rather than the political adviser of the president."[29]

Finally, considerations of "good government," rooted in the Progressive Era, contributed to the separation of the post office from party politics. In the years immediately following World War II, influential public administration specialists decried the official coupling of the political and administrative responsibilities. The Hoover Commission officially recommended that the postmaster general "should not be an official of a political party, such as chairman of a national committee."[30]

Presidents often find it politically expedient and beneficial to appear nonpartisan. The separation of the post office from party politics provided an appropriate opportunity to do so.

The Justice Department and Party Politics

In a 1959 study of the president's cabinet, political scientist Richard Fenno observed, "If a party politician lands in the cabinet at some other position [than postmaster general], it is likely to be that of attorney general."[31] Warren G. Harding appointed his 1920 presidential campaign manager, Harry Daugherty, to that position. Homer Cummings, a former chair of the Democratic National Committee, became Franklin Roosevelt's first attorney general in 1933.

Soon after election in his own right in 1948, Truman moved campaign party chair Howard McGrath over to head the Justice Department. Similarly, in 1953 Dwight Eisenhower named former GOP national chair and key campaign strategist Herbert Brownell Jr. to this position.

Subsequently, John F. Kennedy appointed his 1960 presidential campaign manager, brother Robert Kennedy, attorney general. Nixon did the same for his 1968 campaign manager, John N. Mitchell. When Mitchell resigned early in 1972 to head up Nixon's reelection effort, his successor was his deputy, Richard G. Kleindienst, an old hand in Republican presidential campaigns.

By the early 1970s the designation of a leading campaign official as attorney general had become a standard feature of the twentieth century presidency. When the Watergate scandal enveloped both Mitchell and Kleindienst in criminal prosecutions that resulted in convictions, this particular recruitment pattern came under serious attack.

Presidential candidate Jimmy Carter was one of the leading

critics of the modern tendency to politicize the Justice Department. Nevertheless, his attorney general, Griffin B. Bell, was an old political ally, adviser, and friend. Indeed, Bell was the only figure with such a background to be named to the cabinet. In the Reagan administration, the attorney generalship went first to the president's California associate William French Smith. Following Smith's resignation, Edwin Meese III, an even closer political aide and adviser, took over the office.

The Justice Department always has been politically sensitive and significant. Presidents have long recognized that the office of attorney general is one that can occupy profitably the talents of a key political adviser.

Several prestigious political appointments are channeled through the Justice Department, including U.S. attorneys, assistant U.S. attorneys, and federal marshals. The department also makes important recommendations about presidential nominations of federal judges, including justices of the Supreme Court.

The increasing tendency of interest groups to resort to litigation as a means of achieving their objectives has heightened the political sensitivity of the Justice Department. Increased government regulation of the economy has placed the Justice Department in the midst of significant government decisions about benefits and penalties. Key political constituencies can be cultivated and managed by lending support and by exercising discretionary aspects of its law enforcement and prosecutorial powers.

It obviously behooves a president to place a politically astute ally in this crucial post. Moreover, the position itself is a very attractive one, part of the "inner cabinet" made up of the men and women who head the largest and most essential federal departments. Compared with the position of postmaster general, the attorney generalship is more prestigious and substantive. For a lawyer, being chosen to head the Justice Department is a distinct professional as well as political honor. It has often been a steppingstone to a seat on the Supreme Court.

After World War II the attorney generalship supplanted the position of postmaster general as the office within the cabinet to be occupied by a key political adviser. Still, the attorney general was less affected by explicit party politics than was the postmaster general. The party thus lost institutional representation within the cabinet. Subsequent political pressures to depoliticize the Justice Department have left the White House Office without an institutional alternative within the government for the management of political operations.

White House Office

Without a cabinet-based alternative, White House staff assistants today have the major responsibility for the conduct of political operations and the management of party affairs. The White House Office was established in 1939 during Franklin Roosevelt's administration. Previous presidents had received clerical support from a handful of secretaries and personal aides, but the growing size of and demands on the federal government in the New Deal era led a 1937 presidential commission on administrative management to report that "the president needs help."[32] Congress responded by passing a governmental reorganization act creating the White House Office as part of the Executive Office of the President and authorizing the president to hire additional administrative assistants. Since then, White House staff has expanded tremendously. In 1996, during the Clinton presidency, the *U.S. Government Manual* listed 116 titled assistants under the heading "White House Office."

These aides usually have come from the campaign organizations of incoming presidents. They typically exhibit a strong personal loyalty to the president and an organizational responsibility to the presidential office. Although recruits almost always come from the president's political party, their political experience often is limited to efforts in behalf of their candidate. Only a very few former elected officials and party warhorses appear on the rosters of the White House staff. The president's political interests dominate the personal and organizational perspectives of White House aides.

With this enlarged staff, Truman and all subsequent presidents have chosen to set up political operations inside the White House. Staff assistants now handle many of the political chores once assigned to the national party organization. Further, such assistants have become the principal instruments through which the president exercises party leadership.

Two ongoing practices have produced this turn of events. The first is the designation of staff assistants as the president's personal contacts with party and political leaders throughout the country, including the national party organization and the congressional party. The second is the employment of personnel and the establishment of an apparatus at the White House for handling political appointments.

As liaison, a presidential staff assistant ostensibly serves merely as a conduit in a two-way flow of advice and information, requests and demands, between the president and representatives of the political party. In speaking and acting for the president in party matters, however, a White House aide inevitably supersedes and supplants the party chair in that central linkage role.

To be sure, the president's primacy as party leader has always made the White House the focus of attention for party representatives. Still, the establishment of a sizable White House staff, sufficient and willing to meet expectations, has enhanced this tendency greatly. In the process of conveying messages, power gravitates to the conveyer, at the expense of those who once dealt with the president directly and now do so through a presidential assistant.

Every White House staff since Truman's has included at least one such figure. This modern pattern of White House staff management of president-party relations first emerged in the deployment of Matthew Connelly, Truman's appointments secretary. During most of the Eisenhower years, chief of staff Sherman Adams filled this role. For Kennedy, it was Kenneth O'Donnell. Walter Jenkins and then Marvin Watson served Johnson in this crucial capacity.

The increasing size of the White House staff has resulted in a specialization of function, with a political affairs office usually established under the direction of the chief of staff. Nixon used H. R. "Bob" Haldeman to direct a team of political operators. Ford relied on Donald Rumsfeld and later Richard Cheney. Hamilton Jordan was Carter's chief political agent. During the Reagan years, the White House chief of staff had overall responsibility for political operations, while subordinates Lyn Nofziger and later Edward Rollins and Mitchell Daniels were primarily in charge of Reagan's interaction with the Republican Party. In the Bush White House, chiefs of staff John Sununu and later Samuel Skinner supervised the political operations office. Similarly, the Clinton White House designated a midlevel staff member as political director, under supervision of the chief of staff. During the first two years of Clinton's presidency, Rahm Emanuel and Joan Baggett occupied the former role, and Thomas M. "Mack" McLarty and his successor, Leon Panetta, the latter. From 1994 to 1996 deputy chief of staff Harold Ickes Jr. was the major force for political operations in the Clinton White House.

In recommending the establishment of the White House office, FDR's Commission on Administrative Management envisioned presidential assistants operating with a "passion for anonymity." Instead, these political operators have become very visible and powerful presidential party managers.

In the White House, as in any other office, expansion in size has been accompanied by increased division of labor and specialization. Another characteristic has been the assignment of a presidential assistant to operate an in-house personnel office managing presidential appointments. In the late 1940s Truman administrative assistant Donald Dawson set up such an office as a clearinghouse for information on jobs available and potential candidates to fill them. In subsequent administrations, this administrative apparatus and function has been maintained and has become institutionalized.

This organizational development has placed White House aides at the center of what was once a major responsibility of the national party organization. Because partisanship continues to be a major factor in presidential appointments, this element within the White House Office also serves as a major component of presidential party management.[33]

PARTISANSHIP AND POLITICAL APPOINTMENTS

Political appointments constitute a chief means by which presidents exercise leadership within the executive branch. The Constitution confers on the president a broad appointing power. Article II, section 2, provides that the president "shall nominate, and by and with the Advice and Consent of the Senate, shall appoint . . . Officers of the United States, whose Appointments are not herein otherwise provided for, and which shall be established by Law." In addition, it authorizes the houses of Congress to "vest the Appointment of such inferior Officers, as they think proper, in the President alone."

What is the significance of partisanship in presidential appointments and the influence of party in the making of those appointments? Generally, the president's primary concern in making executive appointments is policy responsiveness. Partisanship and party influence are less ends in themselves than instruments for achieving that purpose.

Development of the Spoils System

As the first president, George Washington had the initial responsibility of filling subordinate positions within the executive branch. Ostensibly, partisanship played no role in his decisions; for at the outset of his administration, political parties had yet to appear on the scene. Washington deplored even the idea of partisan division and put forward instead the criterion of fitness of character for consideration as a presidential appointee. Nevertheless, the great majority of the fit characters receiving presidential appointments during his and John Adams's administrations turned out to be followers of the policies advocated by Alexander Hamilton.

Thus, by the time Thomas Jefferson entered the presidential office in 1801, the executive branch was filled with his partisan adversaries. For the most part, Jefferson did not so much clean house as make new and replacement appointments with partisan considerations in mind. Andrew Jackson, the seventh president, joyfully embraced what came to be called the *spoils system* (from the Roman adage, "to the victor belong the spoils"). Under the spoils system appointive positions were viewed as rewards of electoral victory, to be doled out to the party of the winning presidential candidate. Thus, after a half-century under the Constitution, the principle of partisanship as a criterion for a presidential appointment had become well established.

Presidents needed assistance in making the appointments available. If partisanship was to be a major expectation, who better than the party could provide that help? The emerging national party organizations of the post–Jacksonian era quickly asserted claims on the distribution of federal patronage. They had assembled and directed the campaign support essential to electoral victory, and patronage was the means by which they could reward the party faithful. Within the federal government, the post office offered a harvest of available jobs, establishing the long-standing connection between the post office and party politics detailed earlier. Presidents usually retained personal control over the high-level appointments in the executive branch, but they customarily delegated responsibility for the vast number of lower-level appointments to the party managers.

The operation of the spoils system in the midnineteenth century produced extensive partisanship and party control over presidential appointments. Further, it enhanced policy responsiveness within the executive branch. It also was associated, however, with allegations of incompetence and scandal. Increasingly, reformers called for its abolition in favor of a system of civil service based on merit.

Rise of the Merit Principle

The 1881 assassination of President James A. Garfield by Charles Guiteau, who was angry at not being appointed U.S.

consul to Paris, led Congress in 1883 to pass the Pendleton Act, also known as the Civil Service Reform Act. This landmark legislation sought to replace partisanship with merit as the essential standard for lower-level positions within the executive branch. It established a nonpartisan Civil Service Commission with authority over certain classes of executive positions.

Initially, only a small minority, about 10 percent, of the total number of executive branch positions came under the coverage of the Civil Service Commission. The majority remained in the hands of the president and continued to be allocated through the party as spoils. Gradually, however, the number and proportion of civil service positions increased. By the beginning of the twentieth century, more than 40 percent were classified. Under President Theodore Roosevelt (1901–1909), a reformer and former Civil Service commissioner, the merit system covered more than 50 percent of the positions within the executive branch.

In the 1910s civil service classification was extended to 60 and then 70 percent of the positions and the figure hovered around 80 percent by 1930. The percentage declined to 67 percent during the presidency of Franklin Roosevelt, when the numbers of federal positions increased dramatically as the federal government responded to the crises of the Great Depression and World War II. The percentage rose into the mid-80s shortly after the war and remained relatively constant at that level for more than two decades.[34] Since the 1970s it has hovered around 90 percent, a rough reversal of the percentage distribution at the outset of the civil service system more than a century earlier.

Partisan considerations dominated this expansion of civil service coverage. Under the "good government" guise of civil service reform, presidents would extend classification to large groups of their appointees, who had been awarded jobs because of their party affiliations. In turn, subsequent presidents would find their discretion in making appointments severely limited by the actions of their predecessors.

Establishment of the White House personnel offices further changed the procedures for allocating presidential appointments. Partisanship remained important, but the role of the party organization was reduced.

Critical Developments: Roosevelt to Eisenhower

Several critical developments encompassing the presidencies of Franklin Roosevelt and Dwight Eisenhower illustrate these patterns. After Roosevelt's election in 1932, national party chairman Jim Farley took on the assignment of patronage distribution. Besieged by job seekers during the depression-ridden early days of the New Deal, Farley allocated government positions by the thousands to "deserving Democrats." According to his own testimony, he gave special favor to those members of the FRBC club (For Roosevelt Before Chicago, the site of the 1932 nominating convention). Farley discussed major appointments directly with the president and other high government figures, but he had considerable leeway in making the lower-level appointments. He intended to deal with applicants at national party headquarters. He soon found their numbers so great, however,

National party chair James A. Farley, right, speaks to President Franklin Roosevelt. Using new executive organizations created by New Deal legislation, they collaborated to award jobs to loyal Democrats.

that he moved to the more spacious post office building. Serving as both party chairman and postmaster general, Farley easily could make this shift.[35]

In making political appointments, Roosevelt and Farley benefited from New Deal legislation creating several new executive organizations to administer the expansive New Deal social and economic programs. Initially, positions in these new entities were not covered by the civil service. Thus, they could be and indeed were awarded to loyal Democrats. Presidents Roosevelt and Truman later extended civil service protection to many of the positions.

Recognizing the partisan character of the executive branch under Roosevelt, Congress passed another landmark law affecting the civil service, the Hatch Act of 1939. It prohibited partisan political activity by federal government workers. A second Hatch Act a year later extended this prohibition to state and local government employees engaged in programs supported by federal funds. Political scientist Herbert Kaufman has observed, "While the Civil Service Act sought to keep political workers out of the government service, the Hatch Acts operated to keep government workers out of the parties."[36]

Meanwhile, within the Roosevelt administration, Farley's stature diminished considerably after the 1936 reelection campaign. In retirement some years later, Farley attempted to analyze the circumstances surrounding his fall from grace.

Almost before I knew it, I was no longer called to the White House for morning bedside conferences. My phone no longer brought the familiar voice in mellifluous tones. Months dragged by between White House luncheon conferences. Soon I found I was no longer being consulted on appointments, even in my own state. White House confidence on politics and policy went to a small band of zealots, who mocked at party loyalty and knew no devotion except unswerving obedience to their leader.[37]

Farley's fate reflects institutional as well as personal considerations. The emerging White House Office was beginning to have an influence on presidential politics, to the detriment of the traditional party organization representatives. As noted earlier, during the Truman administration White House aide Donald Dawson set up a personnel office to serve as a clearinghouse for information on jobs available and potential candidates to fill them.

Dawson toiled in relative obscurity at the White House, while the public spotlight continued to focus on the party chair as the administration's patronage dispenser. Indeed, the party headquarters continued to play a significant patronage role. It was by no means ignored or completely supplanted by the White House personnel office. Yet an administrative structure, inside the White House and apart from the party, had begun to handle presidential appointments.

During the Eisenhower years, the changing patterns of patronage availability and allocation came sharply into focus. The 1952 presidential election returned the presidency to the Republicans for the first time in twenty years. The hopes of party regulars clamoring for jobs climbed then quickly plummeted into disillusionment as they discovered to their dismay that patronage of the variety they remembered and expected simply no longer existed. Indeed, the expansion of civil service coverage had the effect of classifying jobs held by Democratic partisans.

Moreover, their standard-bearer was neither attuned nor sympathetic to the idea of using patronage as a tool for party building. Within the White House, Eisenhower assigned responsibilities for managing political appointments to Charles Willis, one of Chief of Staff Sherman Adams's assistants. An energetic young businessman, Willis was an amateur in politics who had cofounded and directed Citizens for Eisenhower, an amalgamation of independents and "discerning" Democrats, enthusiastically committed to the Eisenhower presidential candidacy but distinctly uncomfortable with the regular Republican Party organization. The selection of Willis at the outset reflected the new president's organizational and philosophical disposition to keep presidential appointments out of the realm of party politics.

The Republican national organization, under the capable direction of party chair Leonard Hall, sought to assert its traditional prerogatives in the appointment process. Hall was able to institute a procedure whereby the party headquarters was informed of any job openings and was entitled to make recommendations.

For a time Willis formally routed employment applications through the Republican National Committee. When press reports publicly exposed this program a few months after its inception, however, considerable criticism ensued from proponents of a depoliticized civil service; the Eisenhower administration quietly abandoned it.

Thus, over the years, two clear patterns had developed. The first was the reduction in the number of political appointments available to the president. The second was the shift of influence over the appointment-making process from the national party organization to the White House. These patterns continued in subsequent presidencies.

Diminishing Patronage Categories and Party Role

The decline in patronage has coincided with a significant alteration in the general categories of available patronage. The classification process over time virtually "blanketed in" the types of jobs, such as postmaster, that the political party was best able to fill from the ranks of its qualified activists. Since the New Deal era, low-level jobs for deserving partisans have been in exceedingly short supply; and the old-style patronage, associated with party chairs such as Jim Farley, is nearly obsolete.

Today, executive branch presidential patronage applies primarily to the relatively small number of political appointments to upper-level, executive positions in the departments and agencies that the president is authorized to fill. To be sure, party affiliation continues to be an important consideration in presidential appointments. Democratic presidents tend to appoint Democratic partisans; Republican presidents appoint Republicans. But the shift in primary organizational responsibility for handling presidential appointments from the national party to the White House means that patronage has become much less oriented toward party building than was true in the past. The party organization's role has become peripheral. Although it may be called on to make recommendations or to provide political clearances, these requests occur at the discretion of the White House.

Policy responsiveness has always been a primary presidential objective in presidential appointments. In years past, however, it usually went hand in hand with party building. Consider the case of a Democratic president doling out jobs to deserving partisans. The very act of placing party loyalists in positions charged with enforcing policies provided (1) the expectation that implementation would occur according to the president's designs, and (2) a significant reward for services rendered to the party. Prospects of such rewards constituted important incentives for partisan involvement. Further, the holders of these positions could be expected to look out for the interests of the party from their strategic vantage points. This has become much less the case in the post–World War II era. The two have become separated.

The staffing practices developed by the Reagan White House illustrate well this altered emphasis in managing presidential appointments. Control over appointments was centralized tightly in the White House, under the supervision of personnel officer E. Pendleton James. Ideological compatibility with the president emerged as the chief standard in making appointments. Indeed, for this reason President Reagan, compared with his predecessors, was able to effect noteworthy success in ensuring responsiveness from his appointees in the executive branch.

Neither of his successors to date—George Bush or Bill Clinton—was so attentive to ideological considerations, although Clinton emphasized demographic criteria in keeping with his pledge to form a cabinet that "looked like America."

Civil Service Classification and Policy Responsiveness

The extension of civil service classification has generated new problems for policy responsiveness. A bureaucracy designed to enhance expertise may well sacrifice accountability in the process. Modern presidents have grown increasingly frustrated with the perceived unresponsiveness of the permanent bureaucracy.

In 1978 President Carter promoted the cause of civil service reform to increase presidential control. In that year, Congress enacted the Civil Service Reform Act, which had two important features.

First, the act created the Senior Executive Service (SES), a group comprising mostly high-level career civil servants. From the president's perspective, this innovation was designed to give the White House more flexibility in dealing with the upper echelons of the bureaucracy and to increase the bureaucracy's responsiveness to the White House. According to political scientist Terry Moe, President Reagan systematically politicized the SES. He ousted career officials from important positions in the bureaucracy, replacing them with partisans.[38] Reagan's successors have taken less aggressive advantage of this opportunity, and bureaucratic responsiveness remains a problem for modern presidents.

Second, the 1978 Civil Service Reform Act abolished the Civil Service Commission, the bipartisan body created in 1883 to oversee the establishment of the merit principle in the federal bureaucracy. In the commission's stead Congress created the Office of Personnel Management (OPM). Headed by a single presidential appointee, OPM seeks to increase presidential direction of the civil service. Still, even though the president wants a responsive bureaucracy, OPM's concerns are not specifically partisan, thus widening the breech between policy responsiveness and party building.

Presidential Party Leadership in Congress

Presidential party leadership within the executive branch augments the executive authority the Constitution provides for the president. Such constitutional authority is largely lacking when the chief executive confronts Congress. Rather, the constitutional principle of separation of powers positions the president as an outsider in dealing with the legislature. Moreover, legislative leadership is not an explicit constitutional responsibility. Rather, it emerges out of presidents' ambitions and the expectations of their followers.

Presidents seeking to lead Congress in the enactment of presidential initiatives must do so without formal command authority. Persuasion becomes the key.

With the conspicuous exceptions of Thomas Jefferson and, to a lesser extent, Andrew Jackson, nineteenth-century presidents did not seek much in the way of legislative initiatives; nor was Congress disposed to look to the president for legislative direction. In the first half of the twentieth century, however, pivotal presidents such as Theodore Roosevelt, Woodrow Wilson, and Franklin Roosevelt, by dint of their expansive conceptions of the presidential office and in response to new situations and demands, succeeded in altering the political environment, placing the presidency in a much more activist legislative posture.

In the separated institutional environment, party emerges as a potentially important unifying force. Presidents can employ their standing as party leaders to secure cooperation from party members in Congress. In principle, the idea and the organization of party can bridge the constitutionally separated institutions under the leadership of the president. Thus, from the presidential perspective, party leadership provides the foundation for legislative leadership.

Such leadership is, however, extremely problematic. Its success is dependent on numerous structural and stylistic factors. Indeed, relatively few presidents have been able to unlock the party key to legislative leadership.

THE CONGRESSIONAL PARTY

Political parties had no formal standing in 1787 when the Constitution organized and defined the powers of Congress. But today one speaks of the congressional party, or the party in Congress, a concept founded on the fact that for a long time virtually all members of Congress have been elected as nominees of the major political parties. Thus today there are four congressional parties: House Democrats, House Republicans, Senate Democrats, and Senate Republicans.

Further, partisanship provides the basis for the leadership and organization of Congress. A central purpose of congressional party leaders and organizations is to heighten the significance of the party cue in congressional behavior. In each chamber, House and Senate, the members of the congressional parties constitute the party caucuses, or, as the Republicans prefer to style themselves, the party conferences. At the outset of each session of Congress, the party caucuses meet to select their party leaders.

Party Leaders

Congressional party leadership includes the constitutional leadership positions within Congress: the Speaker of the House and the president pro tempore of the Senate. These positions are held by the majority party, but the majority and minority parties elect other leaders as well.

When Congress formally convenes, each party caucus in the House chooses a leader. Both leaders are nominated for Speaker, who is elected by the full House under party lines, with the majority party's victorious candidate becoming Speaker and the loser becoming minority leader. The majority caucus also designates a deputy to fill the position of majority leader under the

Speaker. The majority and minority leaders are also called "floor leaders."

In addition, both party caucuses select party whips to assist their leaders in maintaining two-way communication with the party members, especially about party positions and expectations on pending legislation. Both parties have established elaborate yet flexible whip organizations, consisting of deputy whips. The whips extend the congressional party leadership well into the rank and file.

The Senate has no direct counterpart to the House Speaker, who serves both as presiding officer and majority leader. The Constitution names the vice president of the United States as the president of the Senate, or presiding officer, who votes only to break a tie. The Constitution also authorizes the designation of a president pro tempore to preside in the absence of the vice president.

The president pro tempore, like the House Speaker, is elected on party lines. The incumbent president pro tempore does not stand for reelection at the outset of each Congress, however, as does the Speaker. Rather, the incumbent remains in office as long as the party retains its majority. A change will occur only with (1) the departure of the incumbent from the Senate or (2) a change in party power.

In the nineteenth century, vice presidents routinely attended to their presiding responsibilities. In their occasional absences, presidents pro tempore were elected ad hoc to serve until the return of the vice president. Beginning in 1890, the position of president pro tempore (usually shortened to president pro tem) became much more stable, with the incumbent now serving until the Senate otherwise orders. Twentieth-century vice presidents have virtually abandoned their senatorial presiding duties, so opportunities for the president pro tempore have increased. Since 1945, the position of president pro tempore customarily has gone to the member of the majority party who has served the longest. Junior members of the majority typically assume much of the daily burdens of presiding.

Despite its constitutional authorization and the status of its incumbent as the senior majority party member, the position of president pro tempore has not emerged as a significant party leadership position as has that of House Speaker. Rather, it is much more an honorific office.

The main party leaders in the Senate are the majority and minority leaders, chosen by the party caucuses. As in the House, each floor leader is assisted by a whip. Because of the smaller size and less formal operating procedures that differentiate the Senate from the House, however, much less elaborate whip organizations have evolved in the upper chamber.

Party Organizations

House and Senate party leadership positions operate within the context of partisan organizations. Traditionally, caucus responsibilities have been limited to presession preparation, but they have occasionally maintained a presence throughout the session.

In the Jeffersonian era, the Democratic-Republican caucus reportedly met frequently during congressional sessions. More recently, among House Democrats, noteworthy instances of ongoing caucus meetings occurred during the early years of the presidencies of both Woodrow Wilson and Franklin Roosevelt, and again in the mid-1970s when Republicans Richard Nixon and Gerald R. Ford occupied the White House. For House Republicans, regular meetings of the conference were a standard feature in the 1940s and 1950s. With the return of House Republicans to majority status in the midterm 1994 elections, a revitalized conference provided a regular, lively forum for discussion, if not direction, of party politics and policy.

In addition, in recent times, both congressional parties established "steering" and "policy" committees to work with the leadership on scheduling and strategy. Both also created ad hoc groups to recommend committee assignments. These various tasks have frequently been combined in single bodies.

The congressional parties play central roles in the committees of Congress. The party caucuses authorize procedures and ratify decisions for the assignments of party members to the committees. Further, the majority party in each chamber controls the chairs of all the committees in that chamber, with positions on all committees distributed roughly proportionally between the parties: the larger a party's majority within the chamber that term, the larger its majority on each committee.

For example, in the Democratic-controlled 103d Congress (1993–1995) (258 D, 176 R, 1 I), the fifty-nine-seat House Appropriations Committee had thirty-seven Democrats and twenty-two Republicans. At the outset of the Republican-controlled 104th Congress (1995–1997) (231 R, 203 D, 1 I), membership on the same committee was reduced to fifty-six, with the majority GOP claiming thirty-two seats, leaving twenty-four for the minority Democrats.

Within the congressional committees, leadership typically has been established and maintained according to the "seniority system," whereby the position of committee chair goes to the member of the majority party with the most years of continuous service on the committee. However, this custom has been by no means absolute. In the 1970s House Democrats in caucus deposed a handful of senior members from their committee chairs. In the 104th Congress, Republican Speaker Newt Gingrich received conference support for his decisions to abandon seniority in designating committee chairs in several instances.

Additional party organizations in Congress are among the diverse array of special interest caucuses (technically known as legislative service organizations or LSOs) that have proliferated in recent years. These LSOs typically are based on the members' ideology, region, or entry "class" (the election or Congress in which the members initially took office). Examples of partisan LSOs include the Democratic Study Group, the Republican Study Committee, the California Democratic Congressional Delegation, and the Ninety-ninth New Members Caucus (Democratic). In the 104th Congress (1995–1997), federal funding for such caucuses was slashed drastically. Most lost their federal funding entirely but continued to function in limited fashion with support from the political parties or private contributors.

Finally, since the Civil War, congressional parties have maintained their own campaign committees. These committees assist the election campaigns of party candidates to Congress. Thus the congressional party as a concept embraces a wide variety of specific groups and organizations.

THE PRESIDENT AND THE CONGRESSIONAL PARTY

How does the president as party leader exert influence in the congressional party? Thomas Jefferson's pioneering exercise of presidential party leadership extended to designating floor leaders and even, according to contemporaneous although inadequately substantiated Federalist reports, meeting with and presiding over the caucus.

Jefferson's successors have fallen far short of these alleged accomplishments. By and large, the congressional party organizes itself and selects its leadership without direct regard to the president's needs and interests. It does so in keeping with the principle of separation of powers and with the institutional need to protect itself against outside, presidential domination.

No direct presidential participation in the congressional party caucuses has even been suggested in the post–Jeffersonian era. More recent activist presidents such as Woodrow Wilson, Franklin Roosevelt, and Bill Clinton, however, have personally conveyed messages to the caucuses informing the members of presidential concerns.

Congressional Party

Respectful of congressional sentiments, wary of the consequences of unsuccessful initiatives, and aware that hierarchical succession is often the norm, presidents usually are loath to intervene in congressional party leadership contests. A noteworthy exception occurred in 1937 when, following the death of Senate Democratic majority leader Joseph T. Robinson, President Roosevelt did not hide his clear preference that the successor be Alben W. Barkley of Kentucky rather than B. Patton "Pat" Harrison of Mississippi. Barkley won a narrow victory.

Much more typically, presidents view the party leadership contests as internal congressional matters and are content to work with the leaders thus chosen. Similarly, in the committees, the seniority system insulates leadership positions from presidential influence.

This hands-off approach can invest congressional party leadership in individuals antagonistic to the president and presidential objectives. The death of Senate Republican majority leader Robert A. Taft in 1953, early in President Eisenhower's first term, resulted in the elevation of Republican senator William F. Knowland of California. Knowland frequently opposed Eisenhower's legislative objectives. Democratic representative John W. McCormack, who succeeded Sam Rayburn in the Speaker's chair after Rayburn's death in 1961, represented a faction in Massachusetts politics that sometimes conflicted with that of the president, John Kennedy. In neither case, however, did the president exercise effective influence in the determination of the congressional party.

Franklin Roosevelt and the presidents who succeeded him have set up regular meetings with the congressional party leadership. Typically, these sessions have occurred on a weekly basis when Congress is in session. They provide regular opportunities to trace the course of the president's program in Congress, to establish priorities, and to develop and coordinate strategies and tactics.

Depending on the president's style and schedule, these sessions may take place in the early morning over coffee and doughnuts or perhaps in the late afternoon accompanied by bourbon and branch water. Should the president's party be in the minority in a congressional chamber, as has been the case more often than not since World War II, then the opposition party leadership may well be invited to participate in some such sessions.

In addition to regular meetings with the party leadership, presidents can and do meet with committee chieftains and individual members and groups of the party rank and file in pursuit of their legislative objectives. The frequency with which a president holds such meetings depends very much on considerations of personal style. Lyndon Johnson did so often; Jimmy Carter, less so. Bill Clinton was much more inclined to do so than his predecessors, Ronald Reagan and George Bush.

White House Legislative Liaison

The determination of the Brownlow Commission in 1937 that "the president needs help" has had an institutional influence on the presidential conduct of legislative leadership. With the expansion of the White House Office, aides received specific presidential responsibilities for congressional relations.

During the Eisenhower administration, the structure of a legislative liaison office took formal shape under Wilton B. "Jerry" Persons, a deputy to Chief of Staff Sherman Adams. When Persons replaced Adams as chief of staff in 1958, Bryce Harlow took charge of the liaison office. These staffers and a handful of associates had the task of establishing and maintaining a presidential presence on Capitol Hill. In a word, they became the president's official lobbyists.

In the ensuing years, this office has grown in size and stature. It has become a vital part of the president's conduct of legislative leadership. It has partisan significance in that it naturally is staffed by members of the president's party and it normally works more closely and effectively with the leaders and members of the president's party than with the opposition.

Presidential Appeals and Methods of Persuasion. Personally, and with the assistance of legislative liaison assistants, presidents put forward a variety of appeals to their fellow partisans in encouraging them to support the president's legislative initiatives. In many respects, they merely overlap with and build upon the foundations established at the outset by Thomas Jefferson. In a study of presidential influence in Congress that casts

President Ronald Reagan meets with Republican members of Congress in front of the White House in 1984.

doubt on the ultimate value of these appeals, political scientist George C. Edwards III details a number of diverse approaches.[39]

Appeals may be purely partisan, focusing on the centrality of the measure in question to the party program, and calling for support on the basis of party loyalty. Oftentimes, this invocation is sufficient. Themselves elected on the party ticket, members of the president's party typically are sympathetic to appeals that call forth their own emotional commitments to the party, its programs, and its leader, particularly if they face a unified partisan opposition. In his first year in the White House, Bill Clinton faced unanimous Republican opposition to his budget proposals. He narrowly prevailed in both House and Senate by evoking extraordinary party support from his fellow Democrats, making the powerful argument that the votes were a test of the Democratic Party's capacity to govern. Vice President Al Gore's vote was needed in the Senate to break the 50–50 tie on the bill.

More specific approaches aimed primarily at the partisan audience include patronage and campaign assistance. As noted earlier, the number of political appointments the president can bestow declined markedly in the twentieth century, but party is an important consideration for presidents in making such appointments as remain. These can be used to entice or reward supportive members of Congress—who tend to be vitally interested in presidential appointments in their states and districts—by designating individuals recommended by the members. At the outset of the Kennedy administration, the White House staff functions of patronage distribution and legislative liaison were combined in a single office under the direction of Lawrence O'Brien. This ensured that the congressional party interest in patronage would be addressed. Although subsequent administrations separated these staff functions, the potential linkage endures.

Another service the president as party leader can provide for fellow partisans in the legislature is campaign assistance. The president can agree to campaign for members running a close race, honoring them and their constituencies with the presidential presence and establishing a credit balance for future dealings. The president also may influence the national party organization in deciding whether to offer its financial and organizational resources to a particular legislator's campaign.

Supplementing partisan appeals are those directed at members without regard to partisan affiliation. Among these bipartisan efforts are some of a more personal nature, in which presidents solicit backing as a personal favor. Lyndon Johnson could call on congressional and senatorial colleagues of decades-long standing, pleading with them on the basis of friendship to support him on a critical issue. Ronald Reagan lacked congressional experience and familiarity with congressional personages. Nevertheless, he would resort to his experience as a Hollywood actor, imploring members of Congress to "win one for the Gipper."

Alternatively, the bipartisan appeal may be based on principle. This was the case for Bill Clinton in seeking congressional support for two controversial foreign trade initiatives, NAFTA and GATT. Confronted with significant opposition among his fellow Democrats, he nevertheless secured enactment of both agreements by appealing to Republicans on the basis of mutual commitment to free-trade principles.

Members of Congress are often quite susceptible to presidential entreaties, for they invoke the prestige of the presidential office and entail direct access to the president, either over the telephone or in person. Further, such appeals are typically linked with an overarching national interest transcending the party one. Among recent presidents, Lyndon Johnson was particularly prone to invoke nationalistic themes in appealing for congressional support. Although he clearly did so in a calculating fashion, he was also unquestionably sincere and emotional in his personal patriotism.

Similarly, presidents can use the numerous amenities at their disposal to curry favor with members of Congress and thus reinforce these personal appeals. The amenities include visits to the White House or the presidential retreat at Camp David, photo opportunities with the president, flights on *Air Force One*, and the like. The president's desk in the Oval Office is filled with souvenirs bearing the presidential seal, such as cuff links, matches, ash trays, and golf balls. Visitors to Camp David are provided with windbreakers similarly labeled. Members of Congress are not immune to such blandishments.

Conversely, presidents can make themselves available to members of Congress at the members' initiative. Lyndon Johnson and Gerald Ford took care to return promptly telephone calls from members of Congress. Richard Nixon and Jimmy Carter were much less attentive. The accessibility of the president looms large in congressional responses to and evaluations of presidential legislative leadership.

Presidents also can resort to bargaining in pursuit of their legislative objectives. Here, presidents provide favors to members of Congress in return for legislative support. In the congressional vernacular, this is called "logrolling"—you scratch my back and I'll scratch yours.

Edwards has documented several examples of presidential logrolling. He reported that President Kennedy was attempting with little success to persuade Sen. Robert Kerr of Oklahoma, an influential member of the Finance Committee, to support an investment tax credit bill that was languishing in committee. In turn, Kerr expressed his dissatisfaction with the administration's unwillingness to back an Arkansas River project he was pushing. Kerr proposed a trade, to which Kennedy responded, "You know, Bob, I never really understood that Arkansas River bill before today." Thus the deal was done, to the mutual satisfaction of president and senator.[40] Although the president or presidential aides occasionally may initiate bargaining, members of Congress are perhaps more likely to do so, as this anecdote suggests, in response to a presidential request for help. Bill Clinton's dependency on unified party support in the first two years of his presidency emboldened Democratic members of Congress to extract their pounds of flesh in the form of presidential support for pet ideas and projects in return for crucial votes.

Presidents have at their disposal a variety of services that can be useful to members of Congress. Making these services available builds goodwill and potential support. Although job-related patronage went into decline a century ago, another brand of patronage—pork barrel patronage, the allocation of federal programs and projects among the states and congressional districts—rose to new heights in the twentieth century with the expansion of the national government. As Senator Kerr's behavior indicates, pork barrel patronage provides the president with a potential device to encourage cooperation on the part of members. Since the 1980s, however, an economic climate featuring massive federal budget deficits has generated pressure for down-

sizing the federal government, thus reducing both the availability and attraction of pork barrel patronage.

As head of the executive branch, the president is in a position to make available the resources and assistance of the executive branch in behalf of a member's special legislative interests. An overriding concern of most members is winning reelection, and here the president can help raise money for the incumbent's campaign by appearing at a fund-raising event. The president also can provide assistance to a member's constituents as an incentive for legislative support. Presidents Kennedy and Johnson instructed their legislative liaison offices to solicit from members of Congress such opportunities to provide assistance.

All of the above are carrots offered by the president or presidential agents as incentives for support. In contrast, the president has relatively few sticks available to use if Congress chooses not to cooperate. About all the president alone can do is to threaten to withhold the available incentives. This can be effective for members of Congress who are accustomed to them and reliant on them. For more independent members who are willing and able to do without presidential support, the president's threats often can be disregarded.

During the Johnson presidency, Sen. J. William Fulbright, an Arkansas Democrat, chaired the powerful Senate Foreign Relations Committee. After Fulbright began expressing reservations about the administration's Vietnam War policies, he found that his once warm relationship with the president began to cool noticeably. Indeed, where invitations to White House state dinners for visiting foreign dignitaries had once been common, befitting Fulbright's leadership position, they were no longer forthcoming. Fulbright ignored the obvious slights and continued his opposition.

Alternatively, presidents can seek to pressure members of Congress through the use of outside strategies, employing and relying on interest groups and public opinion to encourage or intimidate members to support presidential initiatives. This approach is akin to a bank shot in billiards. The president appeals directly to interest groups and the public, and they in turn exert pressure on the members of Congress. *(See Chapter 5, The Presidency and Interest Groups.)*

For example, a president seeking to influence members of Congress from industrial states to support a presidential program might encourage allies in the labor unions to lobby those members in behalf of the president. Or, in reaching out to members from farming states, the president could deploy supporters from among agricultural interest groups. In the television age the president has the opportunity to go public with pleas to citizens across the nation to write, call, fax, or e-mail their representatives and senators.

Shifting the perspective from individual members to Congress as a whole, the Constitution does authorize a presidential veto of legislation unacceptable to the chief executive. Its use is thus indicative of unsuccessful legislative leadership. In this fashion, the veto stands as a dramatic negative form of legislative leadership. Interestingly, the president who resorted most often to the veto was Franklin Roosevelt, routinely acknowledged as a masterful legislative party leader. He did so on more than six hundred occasions. Recent presidents have used the veto, on average, about ten times a year. Bill Clinton, however, went through the entire 103d Congress without vetoing a single piece of legislation. He cast his first vetoes in the Republican-controlled 104th Congress—issuing seventeen vetoes from 1995 to 1996.

Congressional Party Voting and Presidential Support

Empirical research on congressional behavior shows that party is the major influence on roll-call voting and that party is the foundation of presidential support in Congress. Yet other factors also affect members' voting decisions. It is therefore difficult to know exactly how much influence the parties have.

It is entirely correct to observe, for example, that Democrats tend to vote with other Democrats, and Republicans with other Republicans. Similarly, presidents receive stronger support from their fellow partisans in Congress than from the opposition. Yet disquieting questions emerge when one tries to draw conclusions from these findings. Do Democrats vote with other Democrats simply because they belong to the same party? Common policy preferences, constituency pressures, or the personal influence of other members may be the reasons; party affiliation may be merely coincidental. Similar questions surround ostensibly partisan support for presidential initiatives.

Still, these questions notwithstanding, party remains a key to presidential support in Congress. The president's challenge as party leader is to mobilize this base of support by heightening the significance of the party cue. (See Table 2-4 and Table 2-5, p. 66.)

LIMITATIONS ON PRESIDENTIAL PARTY LEADERSHIP IN CONGRESS

For generations, political scientists have spoken appreciatively of a government model operated by a responsible party. This model contains several components. Initially, parties develop programs to which they commit themselves. Then, they nominate candidates for public office who share those programmatic commitments. Competing parties provide voters with clear policy alternatives. Voters choose between or among the competing parties and authorize one to govern. Then, the elected representatives of the party demonstrate sufficient discipline and cohesion to enact the party's promises as public policies, responsibly fulfilling its commitments to the voters.

The British party system has long been viewed as an excellent working illustration of responsible parties. American parties, however, have been roundly criticized for falling well short of the mark, particularly with regard to the behavior of the party in the government.

As noted earlier, party does provide the central cue for congressional voting behavior and the primary foundation for presidential support. Moreover, party unity is clearly on the rise in recent Congresses. Still, the members of the congressional party

normally exhibit an independence from the party program and leadership in both Congress and the White House. That independence is striking when compared with Congress's European counterparts. Why are the party leaders and members in Congress often disinclined to respond positively to presidential leadership? The initial answers can be found in the Constitution.

Separation of Powers

The Constitution does not provide for political parties, nor does it authorize party leadership. However, its separation-of-powers principle places the president largely outside the legislative arena. This is in distinct contrast to a British-style parliamentary model that officially combines executive and legislative authority, establishing the leader of the majority party in the legislature as the chief executive.

The presence of party competition within the context of separation of powers makes possible divided party government, again impossible under the classic parliamentary system. Should the president encounter an entire Congress or a chamber controlled by the opposition party, the limitations of party leadership are obvious. A president hardly can be expected to pursue legislative objectives primarily in a partisan fashion when the party constitutes a legislative minority. In such circumstances, legislative leadership by definition demands a bipartisan approach.

Significantly, divided government has been the norm in the post–World War II era. All the Republican presidents have confronted it. Eisenhower had to deal with Democratic majorities in both houses for six of his eight years in office. Nixon and Ford faced opposition party control throughout their presidencies. During the Reagan years, the Democrats prevailed throughout in the House and for the last two years in the Senate. Bush encountered a Democratic Congress throughout his term.

Only two modern Democrats have had to deal with Republican control of Congress. Harry Truman experienced it in the wake of the midterm 1946 elections until his own successful election effort in 1948. Bill Clinton presided over the 1994 midterm elections that saw the Republicans retake the Senate and House for the first time since 1986 and 1954, respectively.

Only two modern presidents, Democrats Johnson and Carter, have had the benefit of unified party control of the executive and legislative branches of government for a full four-year term. In contrast, four Republicans, Nixon, Ford, Reagan, and Bush, experienced nothing but divided government. Three presidents, Truman (D), Eisenhower (R), and Clinton (D), had periods of both unified and divided party government.

Scholars and journalists disagree on the implications and repercussions of divided party government for the process and substance of policy making. There is no doubt, however, that divided government undermines presidential party leadership in the legislative arena.

As an offshoot of separation of powers, the constitutional principle of checks and balances consciously breeds antagonism

TABLE 2-4 Presidential Support by Party, House of Representatives, 1953–1996 *(percentages)*

President	Year	Democrats	Republicans
Eisenhower (R)	1953	49	74
	1954	45	71
	1955	53	60
	1956	52	72
	1957	50	54
	1958	55	58
	1959	40	68
	1960	44	59
	AVERAGE	49	65
Kennedy (D)	1961	73	37
	1962	72	42
	1963	73	32
	AVERAGE	73	37
Johnson (D)	1964	74	38
	1965	74	42
	1966	64	38
	1967	69	46
	1968	64	51
	AVERAGE	69	43
Nixon (R)	1969	48	57
	1970	53	66
	1971	47	72
	1972	47	64
	1973	36	61
Nixon/Ford (R)	1974	44	57
	AVERAGE	46	63
Ford (R)	1975	38	63
	1976	32	63
	AVERAGE	35	63
Carter (D)	1977	63	42
	1978	60	36
	1979	64	34
	1980	63	40
	AVERAGE	63	38
Reagan (R)	1981	42	68
	1982	39	64
	1983	28	70
	1984	34	60
	1985	30	67
	1986	25	65
	1987	24	62
	1988	25	57
	AVERAGE	31	64
Bush (R)	1989	36	69
	1990	25	63
	1991	34	72
	1992	25	71
	AVERAGE	30	69
Clinton (D)	1993	77	39
	1994	75	47
	1995	75	22
	1996	74	38
	AVERAGE	75	37

SOURCES: *Congressional Quarterly Almanac,* various years, and *Congressional Quarterly Weekly Report,* December 21, 1996, 3455.
NOTE: Congressional Quarterly determines presidential positions on congressional votes by examining the statements made by the president or the president's authorized spokespersons. As defined by Congressional Quarterly, *support* measures the percentage of the time members voted in accord with the position of the president. *Opposition* measures the percentage of the time members voted against the president's position.

TABLE 2-5 Presidential Support by Party, Senate, 1953–1996 *(percentages)*

President	Year	Democrats	Republicans
Eisenhower (R)	1953	47	67
	1954	40	71
	1955	56	72
	1956	39	72
	1957	52	69
	1958	45	67
	1959	38	72
	1960	42	65
	AVERAGE	45	69
Kennedy (D)	1961	65	37
	1962	63	40
	1963	73	44
	AVERAGE	67	40
Johnson (D)	1964	62	45
	1965	65	48
	1966	57	43
	1967	61	53
	1968	48	47
	AVERAGE	59	47
Nixon (R)	1969	47	66
	1970	45	62
	1971	41	65
	1972	44	67
	1973	37	61
Nixon/Ford (R)	1974	39	56
	AVERAGE	42	63
Ford (R)	1975	47	68
	1976	39	63
	AVERAGE	43	66
Carter (D)	1977	70	52
	1978	66	41
	1979	68	47
	1980	62	45
	AVERAGE	67	46
Reagan (R)	1981	49	80
	1982	43	74
	1983	42	73
	1984	41	76
	1985	35	75
	1986	37	78
	1987	36	64
	1988	47	68
	AVERAGE	41	73
Bush (R)	1989	55	82
	1990	38	70
	1991	41	83
	1992	32	73
	AVERAGE	42	77
Clinton (D)	1993	87	29
	1994	86	42
	1995	81	29
	1996	83	37
	AVERAGE	84	34

SOURCES: *Congressional Quarterly Almanac,* various years, and *Congressional Quarterly Weekly Report,* December 21, 1996, 3455.
NOTE: Congressional Quarterly determines presidential positions on congressional votes by examining the statements made by the president or the president's authorized spokespersons. As defined by Congressional Quarterly, *support* measures the percentage of the time members voted in accord with the position of the president. *Opposition* measures the percentage of the time members voted against the president's position.

President Bill Clinton shakes hands with House Democratic leaders at the White House the morning after the House passed the administration's 1993 budget proposal.

between the two separated branches. In James Madison's view, protection against concentration of power, leading toward tyranny, necessitated not merely separating the executive and the legislature, but also pitting the two against each other, providing "constitutional means and personal motives to resist encroachments. . . . Ambition must be made to counteract ambition."[41]

Bicameralism further divides the congressional party into House and Senate bodies. Institutionally, the members of each chamber are conditioned to preserve and protect their particular prerogatives, against each other as well as the president.

Federalism

Federalism, the division of governmental power between the central government and the states, inhibits the president's party leadership in Congress in several ways. First, it works to decentralize party organization in the United States. Party organization parallels government organization at each level: national, state, and local, separating national parties from their state and local counterparts.

Party nominating power for congressional offices clearly rests with the local party organizations. Further, the advent of the direct primary method of party nomination places control over the nominations in the hands of party voters in the states and districts, far removed from the president's party leadership. The national party and the president as party leader have minimal say over who receives party nominations for seats in the legislature. Indeed, those nominations could go even to individuals openly antagonistic to the president and the party program.

Second, the federal principle provides for different electoral constituencies—national for the president, state and local for senators and representatives. Diverse constituencies undermine the unifying potential of party. In the heterogeneous American society, regional variations persist. Massachusetts Democrats and Arkansas Democrats can be two distinctive breeds, as can Pennsylvania and California Republicans.

Staggered Elections

In addition, the Constitution staggers electoral terms and schedules. Presidents serve four-year terms, representatives two, and senators six. In the context of a presidential election, all the representatives and one-third of the senators will be elected simultaneously. Two years later, however, all the representatives and another third of the senators will be elected apart from the president. These disjointed elections undermine the unity that party can bring to the political order by partially separating presidential and congressional elections.

Moreover, the midterm congressional elections almost invariably produce a decline in the numbers of the president's party in Congress. This development weakens the president's influence on the legislature. It undermines the base of party support and encourages the partisan opposition. In the November 1994 congressional elections, the Democratic Party suffered massive losses that reduced it to minority status in both the House and the Senate, shifting control of the legislative agenda to the Republicans and immensely complicating President Clinton's exercise of legislative leadership.

In large measure because of these constitutional features of separation of powers, federalism, and staggered elections, political parties in the United States have not developed the discipline and responsibility demonstrated by their counterparts in parliamentary systems. Many of the limitations on party leadership by the president also hold true for the congressional party leadership. Take, for example, regional differences enhanced by the federal system. Democratic president Carter, a Georgia native, lacked rapport with many northern liberals in the congressional party; some southern conservative Democrats viewed House Speaker Thomas P. "Tip" O'Neill Jr. with suspicion because of his Massachusetts background. Neither Carter nor O'Neill, both representing central, national party leadership, had much say over whom the voters in the 435 congressional districts and the fifty states sent to Congress. Of course, should congressional party leaders be antagonistic toward the president, presidential problems intensify.

Political Culture

The political culture in the United States—that is, the widely held attitudes and beliefs about politics and the political order—is another limitation on presidential party leadership in Congress. In the United States the general public has long viewed political parties with considerable disfavor. In part this negative view can be traced to the antiparty position of the Framers in the late eighteenth century. It was reinforced about a century later by the progressive reformers' intellectual assault on parties.

Further, the U.S. political culture is individualistic. Americans expect their political representatives to look out for them and not to subordinate their needs and interests to the party's. The public effectively discourages members of Congress from acting out of a fundamental commitment to party loyalty.

PRESIDENTIAL INFLUENCE ON CONGRESSIONAL ELECTIONS

All these specific and general limitations notwithstanding, the fact remains that members of the president's party in Congress are more inclined to support presidential legislative initiatives than are the partisan opposition. Therefore, among the most potentially effective exercises of presidential party leadership are those that influence the election of fellow partisans to Congress. Presidential coattails, midterm campaigning, and party purges are three ways presidents have tried to affect the partisan composition of Congress.

Presidential Coattails

"Presidential coattails" is the voting phenomenon by which voters attracted to a presidential candidacy tend to cast their ballots in congressional elections for the nominees of the president's party. In turn, the coattails effect presumably translates into increased presidential support in Congress. Since shared party affiliation produces a predisposition to support the president, a swelling of the ranks of the congressional partisans should increase presidential support. Further, the members who have ridden into office on the president's coattails should be particularly grateful to their benefactor and thus inclined to be particularly supportive.

This theory of presidential coattails as an influence on Congress is, however, both riddled with holes and difficult to test. In the first place, not all presidents have "coattails." In the post–World War II presidential elections, several presidents appear to have been associated with minimal changes in the size of the congressional parties. Moreover, there is also the possibility of reverse coattails. Note that on four occasions—1956, 1960, 1988, and 1992—the elected president's party actually lost seats in the House, while in 1972, 1984, 1988, and 1996, it lost seats in the Senate.

It is not uncommon for the presidential nominee to run behind the congressional party nominees in their states and districts. For example, in 1960 Democratic presidential nominee John Kennedy, a Massachusetts Catholic, ran behind the party's congressional and senatorial nominees throughout the South. Conversely, in 1976, the party's presidential nominee, Jimmy Carter of Georgia, trailed the party ticket in many northern states and districts. Harry Truman and Bill Clinton (twice) were elected president without popular vote majorities. Their victorious congressional party counterparts, typically facing only one opponent, clearly outpolled them.

The Democratic Party's domination of Congress in the post–World War II era also complicates the theory of a coattails effect. The Democrats seized control of both houses of Congress in the election of 1948, when Truman won by a narrow margin. They relinquished it in 1952 when Eisenhower won the presidency. Only two years later, however, the Democrats reestablished majority control that they maintained for forty years, finally losing it in the 1994 midterm elections. After a twenty-six year drought, the Republicans gained control of the Senate in 1980 when Reagan won the presidency. Six years later, the Democrats returned to power in the Senate, once again giving them majorities in both chambers. The Democrats also lost control of the Senate in 1994.

Only the elections of Presidents Truman and Eisenhower coincided with shifting party control of both chambers; Reagan's coincided with shifting party control of only one. The gains and losses of the president's party in the remaining presidential elections affected the size of existing party majorities, to be sure, but not the majorities themselves. From an empirical examination of the coattails effect in the House, political scientist George Edwards identified specific coattail victories in elections from 1952 through 1980. He credited Johnson in 1964 with the most, seventeen, and Carter in 1980 with the fewest, four.[42] Edwards concluded that "the coattail effect on congressional elections has been minimal for some time" and attributed this result primarily to decreasing competitiveness of congressional districts.[43] In other words, safe seats have become pervasive in Congress and they severely reduce presidential opportunities to influence electoral outcomes. He finds the explanation for this phenomenon in the heightened congressional responsiveness to the voters. Subsequent developments that have called into question the conventional wisdom regarding safe seats have not increased the likelihood of presidential coattails.

The decline of the coattails effect hinders the president's ability to exercise party leadership in Congress. If presidents are unable to carry partisan supporters into office, they have lost a key incentive in winning congressional support.

Midterm Campaigning

The Constitution mandates that midway through the president's term elections be held for the entire House and one-third of the Senate. By campaigning for party nominees, the president may influence the partisan composition of Congress.

Midterm campaigning is one of the most visible manifestations of presidential party leadership. Here the president departs from an above-partisanship stance to assume openly the mantle of party chief. Among the forms this activity can take are public speeches, statements and gestures of support for the party ticket, appearances throughout the country in behalf of selected party congressional nominees, mobilization and deployment of administrative personnel such as cabinet members, access to the national party's organizational resources, and fund raising.

Of those activities, presidential fund raising has taken on particularly heightened significance in recent years. Political scientist James Davis reports that in 1990 President Bush raised an unprecedented $80 million for the party ticket.[44] Immediately on his accession to the presidency, Bill Clinton took the lead in fund raising for the national party in anticipation of the 1994 midterm elections. His early efforts were extraordinarily successful, generating a record $41 million in "soft money" before the campaigns got formally under way.[45]

As a dimension of presidential party leadership, midterm campaigning has emerged relatively recently. Political scientist Roger Brown points to President Woodrow Wilson as the inaugurator of the practice in 1918.[46] In that year Wilson put forward an unprecedented plea to the electorate to vote Democratic to demonstrate support for and to protect the integrity of his foreign policy objectives.

More recently, the allegedly nonpolitical Dwight Eisenhower has been credited with extending presidential involvement in midterm campaigns. Indeed, his participation in the 1954 campaign went well beyond the precedents already established. According to Eisenhower biographer Stephen E. Ambrose, the president initially expressed an unwillingness to participate in the midterm campaign. He viewed such participation as improper, unlikely to succeed, and threatening to his health. In mid-October, with clear indications that party fortunes were in peril, he belatedly responded to the pleas of party leaders. He embarked on a tour of the states east of the Mississippi River that covered more than ten thousand miles and required nearly forty speeches.[47]

In 1962 President John Kennedy exceeded his predecessor's pace. In the ensuing years, presidential midterm campaigning has become an important component of the expectations and responsibilities of presidential party leadership.

These exercises of presidential party leadership cannot be associated with conspicuous success. Indeed, one of the abiding truisms of electoral politics in the United States is that the president's party loses seats in the House at the midterm elections.[48] The record in the Senate is less clear, but significant gains have not been the norm.

The 1994 election campaign presents an extreme example of this phenomenon of midterm in-party losses in Congress. President Clinton, despite his low popularity ratings, was extraordinarily energetic in his campaign for Democratic nominees. He contributed to a heightened nationalization of the congressional elections, presenting them as a referendum pitting his leadership and policies against those of his Republican predecessors. The elections resulted in an overwhelming rejection of Democratic nominees, transferring majority control of both houses of Congress to the Republicans.

Efforts to explain the consistent pattern of midterm losses for the president's party point in a variety of directions. Although some analysts view the president as a central actor in accounting for election outcomes, others focus attention elsewhere, alternatively contending that different electorates are present in presidential and midterm elections, that economic conditions have significant influence, or that incumbency is the critical variable.

Whatever the explanation, midterm campaigning appears more an effort to minimize losses than to maximize gains. One of the most visible exercises of presidential party leadership therefore appears, at least on the surface, to be one of the least productive.

When one party controls the presidency and another controls at least one chamber of Congress, midterm campaigning carries potentially severe disadvantages for presidential legislative leadership. It can inflame partisan opposition, making the president's subsequent bipartisan appeals less effective. Further, some presidents have found members of the opposition party to be more consistently supportive than their own partisans. They have therefore been reluctant to campaign against those members.

For this and other reasons, presidents occasionally delegate certain of their midterm campaign chores to their vice presidents. Most notably, President Eisenhower asked Nixon to campaign in 1954 and 1958, and President Nixon assigned campaign tasks to Spiro Agnew in 1970. In the 1958 and 1970 elections, a Republican president confronted a Congress controlled by Democratic majorities.

The presidential placement of the vice president in the forefront of the party effort in midterm congressional campaigns can be interpreted as an attempt to fulfill party leadership responsibilities while avoiding direct personal involvement that might antagonize the leaders and members of the opposition party and impair presidential stakes in the upcoming Congress.

Party Purges

In the decentralized parties, presidents usually are far removed from the selection of party senatorial and congressional nominees. This is the task of the voters in party primaries in the states and districts. Further, one of the fundamental norms of U.S. party politics is that the party organization should be neutral toward competing candidacies for a nomination, and then it should willingly support whoever secures that nomination. Departures from this norm, when they do occur, are to shore up incumbents against intraparty challengers.

Nevertheless, on rare occasions, presidents have tried to bring about the defeat in primary elections of party members in Congress who consistently oppose them and their policy initiatives. The most well known and widespread of these efforts occurred in 1938 when President Roosevelt openly sought the defeat of several congressional party incumbents who had voted against New Deal legislation. According to political scientist Sidney Milkis, "In the dozen states within which the president acted against entrenched incumbents, he was successful in only two of them."[49] The blatant purge effort must be judged a failure.

In the 1970 general election, the Nixon administration undertook to purge a single Republican senator (in New York) by supporting the candidacy of Conservative Party nominee James L. Buckley over the incumbent Republican Charles E. Goodell. Although President Nixon stopped short of an endorsement of Buckley, confining himself to a statement of appreciation, Vice

President Agnew was openly critical of Goodell as a betrayer of party interests. Aided by administration support, Buckley succeeded in his campaign to unseat Goodell.

This incident notwithstanding, presidents are unlikely to exercise party leadership by seeking the removal from Congress of antagonistic partisans. When attempted, party purges are rarely successful and therefore are not a very realistic option available to the president.

President, Party, and Judiciary

The federal judiciary consists of the Supreme Court of the United States, explicitly provided for in the Constitution, and inferior courts, established by Congress under constitutional authorization. The system of inferior federal courts consists of district courts and courts of appeals, or circuit courts.

The constitutional principles of separation of powers and checks and balances frame the relationship between the executive and judicial branches. The chief executive check is the president's responsibility for nominating federal judges. The judiciary's check on the presidency is its capacity to exercise judicial review, which holds the president's actions accountable to the Supreme Court's interpretation of presidential power under the Constitution.

Partisan considerations rarely surface directly in analyses of the federal judiciary. Unlike the chief executive and members of Congress, federal judges are not elected in the wake of party nominations. Rather, they are appointed. Moreover, unlike the legislature, the judiciary is not organized along partisan lines, with majority and minority institutions. Judges do not take action as overt partisans. Indeed, the judicial role ostensibly requires a nonpartisan stance.

One should not assume, however, that partisan considerations and presidential party leadership have no relevance in the federal judiciary. They do, but in an indirect and often shrouded fashion. In the judicial arena, partisanship manifests itself perhaps most clearly in the appointment of judges.

Appointment in turn is a two-stage process consisting of nomination and confirmation. Article III of the Constitution specifically empowers the president to nominate justices of the Supreme Court. The appointment occurs by and with the advice and consent, or confirmation, of the Senate to the president's nomination. The appointment process for lower federal judges also consists of presidential nomination and senatorial confirmation.

PARTISANSHIP AND SUPREME COURT APPOINTMENTS

According to the Constitution, Congress determines the size of the Supreme Court. Over the years, the number of justices has fluctuated between five and ten. Since 1869 the number has been set at nine.

In making nominations to the Supreme Court when vacancies occur, the president normally considers several factors. Par-

tisanship looms large among these. Certainly, the record of appointments to date indicates that presidents are strongly inclined to name persons who share their party affiliation. Political scientist Henry Abraham found that presidents do so approximately 85 percent of the time. From his examination of the 110 presidential appointees who actually served on the Court between 1789 and 1992, Abraham was able to identify only fourteen instances when a president crossed partisan lines in the appointment process.[50] *(See Table 2-6.)* In 1993 and 1994 Democratic President Bill Clinton raised the percentage of party-based nominations by presenting two fellow Democrats, Ruth Bader Ginsburg and Stephen G. Breyer, for senatorial advice and consent.

Thus the question is not whether partisanship is associated with presidential nominations to the Supreme Court, but why partisanship is important. Do Supreme Court nominations constitute a presidential party leadership opportunity?

The answer is a qualified yes. In the words of President Theodore Roosevelt,

In the ordinary and low sense which we attach to the words "partisan" and "politician," a judge of the Supreme Court should be neither. But in the highest sense, in the proper sense, he is not in my judgment fitted for the position unless he is a party man, a constructive statesman constantly keeping in mind his adherence to the principles and policies under which this nation has been built up and in accordance with which it must go on.[51]

Supreme Court nominations are probably the highest form of presidential patronage. They can be used to reward persons for previous services rendered to the president and the party. Several presidents, for example, have elevated members of their cabinets to the Court, with the attorney generalship in particular being a steppingstone. In the twentieth century, five attorneys general were named to the high court: James C.

TABLE 2-6 Nonpartisan Presidential Supreme Court Nominations

Year	President	President's party	Nominee	Nominee's party
1845	Tyler	Whig	Samuel Nelson	Dem.
1863	Lincoln	Rep.	Stephen J. Field	Dem.
1893	B. Harrison	Rep.	Howell E. Jackson	Dem.
1909	Taft	Rep.	Horace H. Lurton	Dem.
1910			Edward D. White[a]	Dem.
1910			Joseph R. Lamar	Dem.
1916	Wilson	Dem.	Louis D. Brandeis	Rep.
1922	Harding	Rep.	Pierce Butler	Dem.
1932	Hoover	Rep.	Benjamin Cardozo	Dem.
1939	F. Roosevelt	Dem.	Felix Frankfurter	Ind.
1941			Harlan F. Stone[a]	Rep.
1945	Truman	Dem.	Harold D. Burton	Rep.
1956	Eisenhower	Rep.	William Brennan	Dem.
1971	Nixon	Rep.	Lewis F. Powell	Dem.

SOURCE: Henry J. Abraham, *The Judicial Process*, 5th ed. (New York: Oxford University Press, 1986), 68.
NOTE: a. Elevated from associate justice to chief justice.

McReynolds (1914), Harlan Fiske Stone (1925), Frank Murphy (1940), Robert H. Jackson (1941), and Thomas C. Clark (1949).

From a slightly different and more symbolic perspective, Supreme Court nominations provide presidents as party leaders with opportunities to reward supportive groups or to broaden the party coalition by reaching out to new groups within the electorate. Here persons appointed can be identified with larger groups of which they are a part. Consider the long-standing customs of maintaining geographical, Catholic, and Jewish seats on the Court, along with the more recent appointments of African Americans and women.

In 1967, in an era featuring dramatic advances in federal civil rights policies, President Johnson nominated noted African American civil rights advocate Thurgood Marshall to a Court seat. In 1981, with women's groups becoming increasingly visible and assertive in the political process, President Reagan named Sandra Day O'Connor to the Court, fulfilling a campaign promise to choose a woman if the opportunity arose. In each instance, the president recognized an important political constituency and achieved a historic first by choosing a member of a previously unrepresented group.

Both these precedents subsequently received reinforcement, providing them with staying power. In 1991, following Marshall's resignation, President Bush nominated Clarence Thomas, an African American conservative Bush previously had named to a seat on a federal circuit court. Bush thus maintained the Johnson precedent and also sought to make Republican inroads in the Democratic hold on black voters established in the New Deal era and solidified in the 1960s. President Clinton awarded his first Supreme Court nomination to a female federal judge, Ruth Ginsburg. This action, which doubled the number of women on the Court, fulfilled Clinton's expressed commitment to greater gender diversity in the federal government and recognized the importance of women voters to his recent election and his prospective reelection.

Notwithstanding presidential initiatives, organized interests can and do put pressure on the president for representation on the Court. Similarly, party managers encourage the president to be attentive to party interests in making Supreme Court nominations. In 1969, with two vacancies to be filled by President Nixon, national party chairman Rogers Morton encouraged the president to "think Republican." He added, "That's the name of the game. This is our opportunity and we ought to take it."[52]

Party leadership considerations, however, are not the primary motivations underlying Supreme Court nominations. Rather, as in executive branch appointments, presidents first seek policy responsiveness. The stakes are much higher in naming Supreme Court nominees because of their tenure. Executive appointees serve at the pleasure of the president, but justices, according to the Constitution, hold office during good behavior, which is tantamount to a lifetime term. Thus presidential nominees on the Court can influence the course of public policy long after the departure of the president.

From this vantage point, partisanship takes on significance mostly as an indicator of policy orientation. Ideological compatibility emerges as the overriding presidential expectation, with party-building considerations occupying a slot of secondary importance. In the Clarence Thomas nomination, certainly President Bush was more sure of Thomas's ideological conservatism than of the prospect of attracting black voters to the Republican banner. Thus the Thomas nomination can be properly interpreted as an effort by Bush to solidify his own vulnerable standing among Republican conservative activists.

Republican president Theodore Roosevelt illustrated his endorsement of this partisan-ideological distinction in an observation to Henry Cabot Lodge about the prospect of nominating Democrat Horace H. Lurton: "The nominal politics of the man has nothing to do with his actions on the bench. His real politics are all important."[53]

Partisan considerations can reinforce ideological ones in the senatorial confirmation process. Divided party government introduces a possible complication. In 1969–1970 the Democratic-controlled Senate rejected two of Republican president Nixon's nominations. More recently, the return of the Democrats to majority status in the Senate in the 1986 elections set the stage for the Senate's 1987 rejection of Republican president Reagan's nominee Robert H. Bork.

PARTISANSHIP AND LOWER FEDERAL COURT APPOINTMENTS

As of 1996, the lower federal court system comprised ninety-four U.S. district courts, with 636 judges, and thirteen U.S. courts of appeals, with 179 judges.[54] The formal appointments process for judges on lower federal courts is the same as for justices of the Supreme Court: presidential nomination and senatorial approval. The president tends to be much less involved, however, owing to the larger number of appointments. Typically, the attorney general and Justice Department associates play a critical role in the recruitment process, as well as White House staff.

The long-standing practice known as senatorial courtesy also comes into play in lower-court nominations. Under this tradition, senators of the president's party from the state in which the nominee is to serve have effective veto power over that nomination. Thus presidents or their agents usually consult the relevant senators before making the nomination.

Further, presidents may well encourage recommendations from these senators, or the senators may volunteer candidates. In practice, senators' recommendations for district court judges carry more weight than those for the appeals courts.

Should a judicial vacancy occur in a state where the president's party is not represented in the Senate, the senatorial role remains important. The opposition senators normally are at least consulted. In this case, bipartisan consensus or perhaps allocation of nominations between the senators and the president may occur.

State and local party leaders can play significant roles in such nominations. In addition, members of the state delegation in

TABLE 2–7 Federal Judicial Appointments of Persons Belonging to the Same Political Party as the President, 1884–1992 (percentages)

President	Party	Percentage
Cleveland	Democratic	97.3
B. Harrison	Republican	87.9
McKinley	Republican	95.7
T. Roosevelt	Republican	95.8
Taft	Republican	82.2
Wilson	Democratic	98.6
Harding	Republican	97.7
Coolidge	Republican	94.1
Hoover	Republican	85.7
F. Roosevelt	Democratic	96.4
Truman	Democratic	93.1
Eisenhower	Republican	95.1
Kennedy	Democratic	90.9
L. Johnson	Democratic	95.2
Nixon	Republican	93.7
Ford	Republican	81.2
Carter	Democratic	98.4
Reagan	Republican	94.4
Bush[a]	Republican	93.5

SOURCE: Henry J. Abraham, The Judicial Process, 6th ed. (New York: Oxford University Press, 1993), 72.

NOTE: a. As of mid-1992.

the House of Representatives who share the president's party affiliation may assume and assert influence over presidential nominations. Their participation is not institutionalized in the fashion of senatorial courtesy; there is no guarantee they will be consulted. Rather, their influence depends on such considerations as power relationships, friendships, and favors owed and claimed. State party leaders sometimes mediate disagreements within the state's senatorial delegation over judicial appointments. Alternatively, if the state delegation in the Congress does not include a member of the president's party, the state party leader may play a more assertive role.

Other persons and groups who may influence judicial nominations include the American Bar Association, sitting judges, and interest groups. In these cases, partisan and party leadership considerations recede in importance.

Lower federal court judges share the president's party affiliation in even higher percentages than do Supreme Court justices—about 90 percent according to Abraham's study. (See Table 2-7.) As with Supreme Court nominations, policy responsiveness has become the overriding consideration. Ideological compatibility may even transcend partisanship. Party leadership considerations arguably receive greater weight in staffing the lower federal courts than in filling Supreme Court vacancies, however, simply because of the vast number of positions, the key role of the senatorial party, and the pressure from state party leaders.

Because members of the Senate are more directly involved in the recruitment of lower-court judges, the confirmation process itself is rarely controversial or overtly partisan. The Judiciary Committee receives the nomination, typically holds brief hear-

ings, and then recommends the nomination to the entire Senate. On the Senate floor, lower federal court nominations ordinarily pass by voice votes. Still, as in the case of Supreme Court nominations, the presence of divided party government can complicate the presidential nomination of lower court judges, making senatorial confirmation potentially more problematic. In such cases the president is likely to designate noncontroversial nominees rather than risk senatorial rejection.

President, Party, and the Electorate

For parties there is strength in numbers. Like its rivals, the president's party is in constant competition to attract more adherents and maintain good relations with them as well as with the party faithful. Thus the party in the electorate forms a crucial part of the president's core constituency. The concept of the party in the electorate refers to people who are qualified to vote and who identify with the party, its causes, and its candidates.

PARTY IDENTIFICATION IN THE U.S. ELECTORATE

Party identification is an attachment a person feels toward a political party. It is ascertained by self-classification and manifests itself most significantly in voting behavior.

Survey research during the past half-century indicates that most Americans develop partisan attachments that are relatively persistent for individual voters and, in the aggregate, are stable over time. A Gallup Poll Monthly report on trends in party identification from 1937 through mid-1995 indicates that the percentage of self-proclaimed Republican identifiers within the population stood at 34 percent in 1937 and at 29 percent in 1995. It varied between a high of 40 percent (1946) and a low of 22 percent (1975, 1979). For the Democrats, the percentage of identifiers was 50 percent in 1937 and 38 percent in 1995. The fluctuation ranged from 53 percent (1964) to 38 percent (1985, 1995).[55]

Party identification develops through political socialization—the acquisition of political information and attitudes. Students of political socialization have learned that party loyalties often emerge relatively early in a person's life; they are usually in place by the elementary school years. This finding points to the family as a primary agent for determining a person's party identity. Further, surveys of elementary school children indicate that although they may know little else about politics, children are fully aware of the identity of the president and generally associate the president with a political party.[56]

The president's extremely high public visibility combines with the public's awareness of the president's political party to make the chief executive's status as party leader perhaps most clear from the perspective of the party in the electorate. Here, there is no real appreciation for the conflicts, rivalries, and tensions that can beset exercises of presidential party leadership of the party organization or the congressional party. Rather, the president's party leadership is readily and uncritically acknowledged.

PARTISANSHIP AND PRESIDENTIAL SUPPORT

Partisanship in the electorate influences evaluations of the president by providing filters or screens through which people see the chief executive. As Gallup poll surveys show, voters who identify with the president's party are inclined to be supportive, while opposition party identifiers invariably are less so inclined. *(See Table 2-8.)* In addition, evidence indicates that members of the president's party think of themselves and the president as having similar policy positions. On the one hand, they tend to believe the president shares their stances. On the other, they may alter theirs to conform to the president's.[57]

This link between the president and the party in the electorate emerged during the presidency of Andrew Jackson. It was not a part of Thomas Jefferson's pioneering presidential party leadership. In Jefferson's day, voter eligibility was restricted by state law to Christian, white, male property holders.

Moreover, the Constitution had placed presidential selection in the hands of electors, themselves chosen by methods determined by the state legislatures. At the outset, the state legislatures divided between those making the choice of electors themselves and those authorizing the popular vote to do so. More opted for the former than the latter.

Gradually, however, more democratic norms and practices began to prevail. During the next three decades, revised state constitutions eliminated religious tests and property requirements for voting, and the constitutions of the new states entering the Union omitted them. Also, the state legislatures that initially had retained control over selection of presidential electors passed that power to the voters. By the time of the Jackson presidency in 1828, the country was more democratic than it had been at the founding. A connection between president and the party in the electorate had been established.

In turn, Jackson was a popular hero who seized this opportunity unavailable to his predecessors to fashion the public link. In doing so, he dramatically increased the political power of the president. Henceforth, the president could claim to have been chosen by the people and derive power from their sovereignty.

Twentieth-century innovations in the realm of communications technology enhanced this popular connection. First radio and then television brought the president into the living rooms of partisan supporters throughout the nation, heightening the sense of identification. In this fashion, the president emerged as the embodiment of the party in the eyes of the voters.

An intriguing question arises about a president's capacity to influence and even induce party identification within the electorate. Most studies of the distribution of party loyalties point toward social class, region, religion, race, and sex as controlling factors. They see the appeal of individual politicians' personalities, and issues also, as having short-term importance in explaining departures from party loyalty.

In the 1950s millions of Americans could like Ike (Dwight Eisenhower) without abandoning their traditional Democratic

TABLE 2–8 Partisanship and Public Approval of the President, 1953–1995 *(percentages)*

President	Year	Democrats	Republicans	Independents
Eisenhower (R)	1953	56	87	67
	1954	49	87	69
	1955	56	91	74
	1956	56	93	75
	1957	47	86	66
	1958	36	82	56
	1959	48	88	66
	1960	44	87	64
Kennedy (D)	1961	87	58	72
	1962	86	49	69
	1963	79	44	62
Johnson (D)	1964	84	62	69
	1965	79	49	69
	1966	65	31	64
	1967	59	26	38
	1968	58	27	36
Nixon (R)	1969	50	83	61
	1970	42	83	57
	1971	36	79	49
	1972	41	86	67
	1973	26	71	43
Nixon/Ford (R)	1974	25	60	35
Ford (R)	1975	33	66	45
	1976	36	71	51
Carter (D)	1977	73	46	60
	1978	56	28	42
	1979	47	25	35
	1980	54	26	36
Reagan (R)	1981	38	83	57
	1982	24	79	46
	1983	28	80	49
	1984	32	88	59
	1985	35	89	62
	1986	40	86	60
	1987	26	79	50
	1988	30	85	53
Bush (R)	1989	46	82	53
	1990	53	86	63
	1991	58	89	70
	1992	18	65	36
Clinton (D)	1993	70	22	42
	1994	75	21	46
	1995	76	20	47

SOURCES: Gallup poll; George C. Edwards III, *The Public Presidency* (New York: St. Martin's, 1983), 214; updated by author from *Gallup Poll Monthly*, various issues, 1981–1995.

loyalties. Similarly in the 1980s, even though the Democrats continued to hold the professed allegiance of more voters than did the Republicans, Ronald Reagan could attract droves of Democratic voters in his sweeping electoral victories.

Still, fundamental realignments of party loyalties have taken place in years past and have elevated new parties into positions of dominance. Environmental factors, especially economic ones producing depressions, remain an important explanation of these phenomena. But the potential contribution of presidential party leadership cannot be ignored.

One of the president's major challenges is to establish or maintain the party in the dominant position. By this standard, Franklin Roosevelt was eminently successful, while Dwight Eisenhower fell short.

Party identification in the electorate has declined in recent years.[58] This decline can been seen first in a weakening of the commitments of the professed party identifiers and second in the corresponding rise in split-ticket voting. Third, the number of declared independents is on the rise. This trend will likely reduce the significance of party and of party leadership in presidential relationships with the electorate.

GROUP BASES OF PARTY ELECTORAL COALITIONS

To speak of the party in the electorate is to recognize that the electorate is divided into many different groups. Parties seek to enlist the support of these groups in behalf of their nominees. In turn, appealing nominees can point voters in these groups toward their parties. In the electorate, a president's personal and party leadership interests converge in an effort to maintain and expand the party's electoral coalition.

In the context of presidential campaigns, candidates make specific overtures to various groups in seeking their support. The most common approach takes the form of an issue or policy stance proposed to gain favor with the group. A candidate seeking to appeal to Jewish voters, for example, might emphasize a commitment to aid for Israel. In 1980 Ronald Reagan solidified traditional business support for the Republican Party with a strong advocacy of deregulation.

Political parties assemble platforms, or wide-ranging statements of issue positions, and present them to voters as promises in return for support. The party's presidential nominee usually has a significant role in the development of the platform. The positions that presidential nominees and incumbent presidents take inevitably are attributed to the nominating party.

PRESIDENTIAL PATRONAGE

Patronage provides presidents with opportunities to develop and maintain support from interest groups. Appointments to positions in the executive and judicial branches, particularly those with high visibility, enable the president to recognize and to reward representatives of key interest groups in the electoral coalition. Also, presidents can reach out to new constituencies through an astute use of the appointing power.

As mentioned earlier, President Lyndon Johnson's 1967 nomination of Thurgood Marshall, an African American, to a seat on the Supreme Court had immense symbolic and substantive value. It recognized the contribution of black voters to the electoral successes of the president and the Democratic Party. Further, it demonstrated the abiding commitment of the Johnson administration to the cause of civil rights.

Political scientist Nelson Polsby identifies "clientele representation" as one of three strategies presidents use in forming cabinets. Presidents acknowledge that many federal departments serve as advocates for major interests, and they appoint as departmental secretaries leaders who reflect these interests.[59] Recent examples of cabinet appointments that fit this pattern include Bush's designation of Clayton Yeutter as secretary of agriculture and Clinton's decision to name Bruce Babbitt secretary of the interior. Yeutter had a lifelong background in agriculture concerns, while Babbitt maintained close ties with environmental groups.

PUBLIC LIAISON

In addition to electoral and symbolic appeals to distinct groups, presidents since Franklin Roosevelt have made the White House a point of direct access for representatives of supportive interest groups. Previous presidents, of course, had to be attentive to the groups that composed the party coalitions. The modern presidency, however, developed an organizational unit, the White House Office of Public Liaison, to work with a variety of interests.

As with any organization, the expansion of the White House Office has been accompanied by division of labor and specialization. Early on, in the Truman White House, one task of presidential assistant David Niles was to maintain relations with representatives of minority groups. Subsequent presidents built on this foundation and broadened it by designating specific aides as liaisons with specific interest groups. For example, in the Eisenhower administration, Frederick Morrow, the first African American ever appointed to the White House staff, served as a contact point for the black community on issues pertaining to civil rights. Through designated staff assistants, Lyndon Johnson reached out to Catholics and Jews.

During the Nixon years, plans to organize and give more official standing to this activity took shape. Ford established the Office of Public Liaison, with a director and a staff, in the White House. The institution has continued under Ford's successors, and it is now established firmly as part of the White House Office.

Public liaison aides play an intermediary role. On the one hand, they communicate to the president the needs and interests of the various groups. On the other, they seek to build support for the president and presidential policies within and among the groups.

In institutionalizing this liaison function in the White House Office, in one sense presidents have advanced the cause of presidential party leadership. Because of the clear identification in the public mind between president and party, the party can benefit from the president's successful efforts to call forth support from interest groups.

Alternatively, however, this establishment of direct presidential communications with interest groups can work to the detriment of the political party. Historically, parties served as intermediary associations connecting the electorate, including groups, with the government. The development and maintenance of direct ties between interest groups and the presidency largely bypass the party as an intermediary. To the extent that the president can assemble interest groups into a coalition of supporters, they constitute themselves as a presidential party, in a manner of speaking.

This aggregation must then be linked up in an enduring fashion with the existing party organization. The capacity to do so constitutes a measure of considerable success in presidential party leadership. Failure, in turn, intensifies separation between president and party and can contribute to antagonism in president-party relations.

FDR to Clinton: Party Leadership Portraits

Presidential style is an elusive concept. As used in this section, it refers to the distinctive behavior of the president as party leader. The presidency is an extremely personal office that takes on the character of its immediate occupant. In a study of presidential character, political scientist James David Barber focuses attention on the significance of the personal dimensions of the presidency.[60]

Presidents exercise leadership within a structural framework that provides opportunities in some situations and constraints in others. A critical assessment of individual presidents as party leaders therefore must consider both personal and structural factors.

The background and experiences of the president, particularly as they pertain to party politics, are highly relevant. Structurally balancing these characteristics are (1) the distribution and significance of partisanship in both the electorate and Congress during the president's tenure, along with (2) the vitality of the party organization. Linking the two are the assistance the party is able to provide toward the achievement of the president's political objectives and the personal contributions of the president to the structure of party competition. What follows are brief biographical characterizations of recent presidents as party leaders.

FRANKLIN D. ROOSEVELT

Franklin D. Roosevelt was a transformative figure in American government history, presiding over the emergence of the modern presidency. His actions as party leader set in motion some developments and patterns that have become standard features for his successors. Roosevelt was an enthusiastic partisan who was instrumental in remaking the Democratic Party.

Roosevelt came from a distinguished New York family. His branch of Roosevelts settled in Hyde Park, where they were known as the Democratic Roosevelts. This label distinguished them from their Oyster Bay cousins, led by Theodore, who were Republican to the core.

While still in his twenties, Franklin Roosevelt entered party politics and ran successfully for a seat in the New York state senate. He supported Woodrow Wilson's presidential candidacy in 1912. After Wilson was elected, he named Roosevelt assistant sec-

Two political campaign buttons of the 1930s promote Franklin D. Roosevelt and the Democratic Party as the remedy to the Great Depression.

retary of the navy. Roosevelt held this position until the end of the Wilson administration. The Democratic Party nominated him for the vice presidency and James M. Cox for the presidency in 1920.

Unsuccessful in that quest, Roosevelt retired to private life and underwent a debilitating bout with polio. He labored in behalf of fellow Democrat Al Smith in Smith's campaigns for the Democratic presidential nomination in 1924 and 1928. Following Smith's nomination in 1928, Roosevelt received the state party nomination to succeed Smith as governor. Elected in 1928 and reelected in 1930, he sought his party's presidential nomination in 1932 with a clear and long-standing identity as a Democrat.

Roosevelt's successful nomination campaign was spearheaded by party chieftain James Farley, who traveled the country lining up support among key party activists. For the general election campaign, he named Farley as party chair and emphasized his party affiliation. His electoral victory accompanied Democratic successes in the congressional elections.

Thus Roosevelt entered the White House as an unabashed partisan with comfortable party majorities in Congress. Not surprisingly, he openly grasped the mantle of party leadership. The Democrats in Congress responded by enacting a broad social and economic program called the "New Deal."

Roosevelt's relations with congressional Democrats also featured considerable conflict, however. Not only did the president fail dramatically in his effort to gain legislative approval to add justices to the Supreme Court (the "court-packing" plan), he also vetoed a record number of congressional bills.

Both inside and outside Congress, Roosevelt sought to remake the Democratic Party in a modified image that would alter its structure and its ideological orientation. This effort entailed bringing new groups and forces into the Democratic electoral coalition. It also meant moving the party in a more liberal direction ideologically. This required extraordinary efforts to influence the composition of the party in office by openly campaigning against recalcitrant incumbents in congressional party primaries.

Finally, Roosevelt sought to relocate control within the party away from the traditional bosses in the states and localities, replacing them as leaders with his agents in positions of responsibility within the federal government. It was partly this development that led to a widely publicized falling out between Roosevelt and party chairman Farley.

Although he fell short of fully achieving these ambitious objectives, Roosevelt otherwise enjoyed conspicuous success in his exercise of presidential party leadership. Further, his extraordinarily long tenure, spanning both the Great Depression and World War II, established him as the exemplar of the modern presidency. Roosevelt provides the benchmark for evaluating subsequent presidents as party leaders.

HARRY S. TRUMAN

On Roosevelt's death in 1945, Harry Truman succeeded to the presidency. In his rise to the vice presidency, Truman had developed an intimate association with Democratic Party politics. Indeed, he began his political career in the Kansas City area of his native Missouri toiling for the Pendergast machine, renowned for its strength and its corruption. He served as county judge and received the party nomination for the United States Senate in return for his loyalty to and services in behalf of the party organization. Party loyalty marked his senatorial career, placing him in position to receive the vice-presidential nomination in 1944. He held that office less than three months before Roosevelt's death.

A vice president elevated to the presidency through a vacancy inherits certain constitutionally based roles and responsibilities. The presidential role of party leader, however, operates outside the specific constitutional framework. Truman's exercise of party leadership as an accidental president illustrates a variation from the normal pattern in which the party's presidential nomination initially confers leadership status that is confirmed by the victory in the general election.

Truman became party leader without the legitimacy of nomination and election. Nevertheless, he benefited from Robert Hannegan's presence in the national party chair. Hannegan was an old Missouri political ally who held that position in part because of Senator Truman's earlier recommendation. In turn, Hannegan had been instrumental in pushing for Truman's selection as Roosevelt's vice-presidential running mate in 1944.

Thus the relationship between President Truman and the party organization began on a positive note. Following Hannegan's departure, Truman did not hesitate to exercise his presidential prerogative in recommending a successor to the national committee. His choice, Sen. J. Howard McGrath of Rhode Island, quickly received committee approval.

Truman began his presidential tenure with Democratic Party majorities in both houses of Congress. The foreign and defense policy tasks of concluding World War II and preparing for peace in the postwar world precluded, however, any major domestic policy initiatives at the outset. In the 1946 midterm congressional elections, the Republicans won majorities in both houses. The president pursued a combative strategy in dealing with the Republican congressional leadership in domestic affairs for the next two years.

In 1948 Truman won an upset victory over his Republican challenger, Gov. Thomas E. Dewey of New York. The Democrats also regained control of Congress and maintained it for the duration of Truman's presidency. During these years, Truman sought without noteworthy success to secure the enactment of his domestic policy agenda, the Fair Deal.

Developing strains in the Democratic Party coalition posed a serious problem for Truman. A major controversy over the party's commitment to civil rights split the 1948 national convention, resulting in a walkout by several southern delegations and the subsequent formation of the States' Rights or Dixiecrat Party for the general election. The Democrats also experienced ideological conflict that led the same year to the departure of a portion of the party's left wing under the banner of former vice president Henry Wallace and the Progressive Party.

In sum, Truman followed Roosevelt in openly and enthusiastically embracing partisanship. He was a Democrat to the core, fully comfortable with the mantle of party leadership in spite of the extraordinary conditions surrounding his accession. Yet his presidential party leadership did not demonstrate the transformational character of his predecessor's.

DWIGHT D. EISENHOWER

Dwight Eisenhower entered national politics at the presidential level following his distinguished military career. He lacked any background or experience in party politics. Courted by representatives of both major parties, he cast his lot with the Republicans at a time when they had not won a presidential election in more than two decades and when they held the allegiance of a distinct minority of the electorate.

Eisenhower's presidential candidacy attracted an abundance of enthusiastic amateurs under the organizational umbrella Citizens for Eisenhower. In the years to come, the president labored without noteworthy success to integrate this element into the regular party organization. In that effort, he encountered resistance from amateurs and party regulars alike.

As president, Eisenhower exhibited a leadership style that political scientist Fred Greenstein has characterized as "hidden hand."[61] He self-consciously and systematically sought to obscure his political activities. Although all presidents are aware of the political benefits to be derived from a nonpolitical posture, Eisenhower appreciated this reality more than most.

He was acutely aware of his lack of formal authority over the Republican Party. This is clearly evident in his comments at two press conferences about midway through his tenure. In the first, weeks away from his 1956 reelection victory, he observed:

Now, let's remember, there are no national parties in the United States. There are forty-eight state parties, then they are the ones that determine the people that belong to those parties.

There is nothing I can do to say that one is not a Republican. The most I can say is that in many things they do not agree with me. We have got to remember that these are state organizations, and there is nothing I can do to say so-and-so is a Republican and so-and-so is not a Republican.[62]

In the second statement, less than six months into his second term, Eisenhower noted: "He, the president, is the leader not of the, you might say, hierarchy of control in any political party. What he is is the leader who translates the platform into a legislative program in collaboration with his own executive departments and with the legislative leaders."[63]

Eisenhower regularly bemoaned his inability to move the party in the direction of the "modern Republicanism" he espoused. In turn, party activists often viewed him as inattentive to their interests. Certainly, he demonstrated little concern with or enthusiasm for the exercise of patronage power as a party-building device.

His administrative style featured extensive delegation of authority, and he tended to view "politics" as the special province of the party chair. The party chairs who served during his presidency found themselves more within the presidential circle than has been typical since World War II. His 1956 reelection campaign, under the general direction of party chairman Leonard Hall, featured extensive integration with the national party effort.

In Congress, the Republican Party gained a majority of the seats in both houses in the 1952 elections that brought Eisenhower to the White House. The party lost control of Congress in the midterm 1954 elections, however, and remained in the minority for the remainder of his presidency. This development forced Eisenhower to look beyond the party ranks in seeking support for his policy initiatives and further muted his partisanship.

For Eisenhower, personal and structural factors combined to diminish the emphasis on presidential partisanship in comparison with the Roosevelt and Truman years. He was not personally comfortable with its exercise. Neither did the political climate encourage presidential partisanship. Indeed, Eisenhower perceived political benefits in denying it. Further, such efforts as he made to reshape the Republican Party and make it over as a majority party failed. Still, he remained a revered and unifying figure in the eyes of most of his fellow Republicans.

JOHN F. KENNEDY

In contrast with his predecessor, John Kennedy ardently embraced partisanship. His family was closely identified with the Democratic Party, and successful congressional and senatorial contests under the party banner had preceded his race for the presidency. In the early days of that candidacy, he proclaimed his leadership responsibilities in the party arena.

No president, it seems to me, can escape politics. He has not only been chosen by the nation—he has been chosen by his party. And if he insists that he is "president of all the people" and should, therefore,

Presidential candidate John F. Kennedy and running mate Lyndon B. Johnson talk with Eleanor Roosevelt at a Democratic Party rally in New York City on November 5, 1960.

offend none of them—if he blurs the issues and differences between the parties—if he neglects the party machinery and avoids his party's leadership—then he has not only weakened the political party . . . he has dealt a blow to the democratic process itself.[64]

Kennedy installed his long-time political ally, Connecticut party chairman John Bailey, as the national party chair. There, Bailey lacked direct access to the president. White House appointments secretary Kenneth P. O'Donnell provided primary liaison between the party organization and the president.

In Congress, Democratic majorities controlled both chambers during the Kennedy administration, but a large portion of the party and committee leadership consisted of southern conservatives who were not keen on some of his policy initiatives and were adamantly opposed to others. As a result, the Kennedy administration had failed to achieve noteworthy legislative successes at the time of the president's assassination.

As party leader, President Kennedy reverted to the Roosevelt-Truman pattern of unabashed partisanship in his rhetoric. His substantive accomplishments in this realm were not particularly noteworthy. Any evaluation of his presidency must take into account, however, his short tenure in office.

LYNDON B. JOHNSON

Although clearly identified as a Democrat, Lyndon Johnson sought consensus throughout his political career. He came to Washington from a background in the one-party politics of his native Texas, where party organization was notoriously weak. In his rise to the presidency he served consecutively as congressional assistant, New Deal bureaucrat, representative, senator, and vice president.

On assuming the presidency following the assassination of John Kennedy, Johnson inherited the party management team assembled by his predecessor. He retained the members in the interest of party unity and also because he needed their expertise in his upcoming quest for a presidential term on his own. Still, he felt he could not fully trust the Kennedy loyalists to act in his behalf.

Johnson interspersed his own trusted associates amid the Kennedy holdovers. In the realm of party relations, the main responsibilities initially were assigned to Walter Jenkins at the White House and Clifton Carter, who went to the national committee as the president's untitled representative. Subsequently, Marvin Watson took over the White House end, and John Criswell succeeded Carter at the national headquarters. Having established this structure, Johnson generally was inattentive and occasionally even antagonistic to the needs and interests of the party organization.

In Johnson's 1964 campaign for president, his agents supervised the convention proceedings closely. The national party headquarters, however, was much less visible within the campaign organization than its counterpart had been during President Eisenhower's 1956 reelection campaign. After the Republicans nominated Barry Goldwater, a strong ideological conservative, Johnson was able to draw support from disaffected Republicans. In doing so, he blurred his own partisanship and undertook a nonpartisan effort. The result was a landslide victory of historic proportions.

The 1964 elections also brought impressive Democratic majorities to both houses of Congress, giving Johnson a strengthened partisan base on which to seek the enactment of his party's legislative program. He was much more successful than Kennedy not only because of the improved arithmetic, but also because of his considerable skill as a legislative leader. He clearly appealed to party loyalty and unity, but he also worked closely and cooperatively with the opposition leadership, particularly on civil rights legislation, to offset southern Democratic opposition and to promote national unity.

As his term wore on, Johnson faced increasing opposition within his own party to both his domestic initiatives and his foreign policies. The Vietnam War was especially divisive. At the beginning of the 1968 presidential campaign season, Sen. Eugene McCarthy of Minnesota announced his challenge to Johnson's expected renomination. McCarthy's impressive early showing in the New Hampshire primary encouraged Sen. Robert F. Kennedy of New York to join the race. In a dramatic nationally televised address on March 31, 1968, President Johnson announced that he would neither seek nor accept the party's presidential nomination. For the remainder of his term, Johnson affected a nonpartisan stance, although his agents were very visible at that summer's Democratic national convention.

President Johnson never appeared fully comfortable in his role as party leader. His consensus style did not allow the exclusion of significant elements of Congress or the electorate from his domain.

During his retirement years, the vehement opposition Johnson had engendered within the party lingered, precluding his assumption of a role as party elder statesman. Indeed, at the 1972 national convention, he received none of the accolades customarily accorded a former nominee and president. He died in 1973.

RICHARD NIXON

Richard Nixon began his campaign for the White House in 1968 with a well-deserved reputation as a slashing Republican partisan. He had earned this designation during his years as a member of the U.S. House and Senate from 1947 to 1953. He reinforced it as Eisenhower's vice president from 1953 to 1961. As vice president he assumed many of the responsibilities of party leadership with which Eisenhower was uncomfortable. He gained the enduring gratitude of Republican activists for his extensive party-building efforts. His scathing attacks on Democratic personalities and programs simultaneously generated emotional public support and antagonism. In his successful 1968 presidential campaign, however, Nixon labored to appear above partisanship and called for a lowering of voices and an end to divisiveness.

In the Oval Office, President Nixon frequently disappointed party regulars with his general disregard and occasional animosity toward the party organization. He assembled a team of personal loyalists who demonstrated a low regard for the needs and interests of the party organization. Three national party chairs—Rep. Rogers Morton, Sen. Robert Dole, and George Bush—found themselves largely excluded from the conduct of presidential party leadership.

In Congress, Nixon encountered Democratic Party majorities in both houses. This reality forced on him a nominal posture of bipartisanship, although the opposition Democrats were not inclined to support his policy initiatives.

In organizing his 1972 reelection effort, Nixon chose virtually to ignore the Republican National Committee in favor of the Committee to Re-elect the President, a personal electoral vehicle. The presidential effort went forward with little attention to the needs of other Republicans on the party ticket. In seeking reelection, Nixon gave only rhetorical support to the concept of a "new American majority" that would realign the party coalitions with greater ideological consistency.

In June 1972 agents of the president's campaign organization were arrested on charges of breaking and entering the headquarters of the Democratic National Committee at the Watergate office building. The scandal that ensued, known as "Watergate," had little effect on the election. President Nixon won an overwhelming victory that portended a new era of Republican domination in presidential elections.

Eventually, however, Watergate and related scandals drove the president from office. By the time Nixon resigned on August 9, 1974, he had lost the support of large numbers of party activists and officeholders whom he had treated so cavalierly throughout his presidency. Further, the Republican Party was tainted by the scandal.

Like his predecessor Lyndon Johnson, Nixon was viewed as a pariah in party circles in the years immediately following his departure, although he regained considerable measures of respect and status in the latter years of his lengthy retirement. His death in 1994 was accompanied by accolades of appreciation for his insights and abilities as a political strategist and party coalition builder.

GERALD R. FORD

Gerald Ford became president after Nixon resigned on August 9, 1974. Ford's background was in Congress, where he had toiled from 1949 until 1973 in behalf of the Republican Party. He served as minority leader from 1965 until his elevation to the vice presidency in 1973.

The unique circumstances that produced Ford's accession, and his struggle to maintain his incumbency in the face of vigorous nomination and general election challenges, elevated the significance of party leadership considerations. Ford was not only the first president to come to office via the resignation of his predecessor; he was also the first person to become vice president through the procedures of the Twenty-fifth Amendment—nomination by the president and confirmation by majority vote of both houses of Congress. In no way had the national party legitimized his incumbency.

In certain respects, the pattern of Ford's dealings with the national party organization did not differ significantly from Nixon's. A vacancy in the party chair occurred when Ford sent George Bush to head the U.S. Liaison Office in China. The incumbent vice chair, Mary Louise Smith, received the president's blessing as Bush's successor. She became the first woman to chair the Republican National Committee. Meanwhile, White House political advisers provided liaison with the party headquarters.

The initial expectation that Ford might be a caretaker president and not seek the 1976 presidential nomination for himself, and the subsequent prospect and presence of a serious nomination challenge from Ronald Reagan, produced an unusual relationship between the party chair and the president. Although Smith publicly supported Ford, she did not overtly forestall or hinder the Reagan challenge in a manner comparable to previous party chairs favoring incumbent presidents.

Ford's postnomination choice of Kansas Senator Robert J. Dole as his vice-presidential running mate signaled his intention to assume an above-the-battle, presidential stance in the upcoming general election campaign. A former party chair, Dole spiritedly took on the tasks of partisan attacks on the Democratic opposition.

Ford's dealings with the Democratic-controlled Congress were more congenial (if no less partisan) than Nixon's had been during the latter years of his presidency. During Ford's long years of service in the House of Representatives, he had established comfortable social and working relationships with the Democratic Party leaders in Congress. Executive-legislative relations during his presidency, however, suffered not only from conflicts over policy and ideology but also from the legislators' institutional desires to assert themselves against a presidency weakened by the ravages of Vietnam and Watergate.

As party leader, President Ford openly and willingly embraced his party. He asserted his presidential prerogatives in party affairs despite his unique status as an accidental president. He strove with some success to restore the party's credibility in the aftermath of Watergate. As is true of John Kennedy, his brief tenure as president makes evaluation inconclusive.

JIMMY CARTER

In 1976 former Georgia governor Jimmy Carter came out of obscurity to win the Democratic presidential nomination and then to defeat President Ford in the general election. He assumed the reins of party leadership as an outsider unfamiliar with national party politics.

In his dealings with the national party organization, Carter followed closely in the pattern of his recent predecessors. After receiving the party nomination, he retained the incumbent party chair, Robert Strauss, while keeping intact and relying on his personal campaign organization for the conduct of the general election campaign. After the election, he brought Strauss into the administration and designated former Maine governor Ken Curtis as the party chair.

But the White House controlled political operations, which did not set well with the party regulars. Indeed, the national committee became so outraged by the White House's unwillingness to address the needs and interests of the party organization, especially in the realm of patronage, that it formally rebuked the president for his neglect. Carter set up an apparatus and process for conducting political operations and supervising those of the national party organization. Similarly, the White House personnel office established a recruitment and management program for presidential nominations that largely ignored the patronage claims of state party leaders. When the Democratic National Committee convened in April 1977, it showed its displeasure by directing a formal rebuke to the White House.[65]

One year into his presidency, Carter attempted to make amends. He replaced Curtis as party chair with Texas politico John C. White and pledged increased accommodation and sensitivity in the future. For the remainder of his presidency, the national committee supported the president without incident. This support was an important factor in the president's success in thwarting the major challenge to his renomination mounted by Massachusetts senator Edward M. Kennedy.

In dealing with Congress, Carter had the benefit of comfortable party majorities in both houses. Still, he achieved little success for his legislative initiatives. His difficulties stemmed from several sources. First, his electoral victory had been narrow, and he had run behind Democratic senatorial and congressional victors in most districts and states. He therefore could not claim that his coattails had secured the positions of many legislators. Second, his ideological leanings were moderate, placing him at odds with many of his fellow partisans of a more liberal bent. As an outsider, he was unfamiliar with the norms and procedures of Congress. Finally, he appeared uncomfortable with expectations of many legislators that presidents seeking their support shower them with personal attention and engage in lengthy bargaining sessions.

President Carter was never comfortable with the cloak of party leadership. His approach to presidential leadership was more administrative and technical than political and partisan. His antiestablishment campaign placed him at odds with both the party organization and the congressional party.

RONALD REAGAN

Ronald Reagan came to Republican Party politics relatively late in life. After a lengthy career as a Hollywood actor, during most of which he claimed a Democratic Party affiliation, he gradually shifted allegiance during the 1950s. In 1960 he openly supported Nixon's presidential candidacy; and in 1964, he was highly visible in behalf of Barry Goldwater. By this time, Reagan clearly identified with the ideological conservatives of the Republican Party's right wing and served as one of that faction's chief public voices.

Reagan successfully sought the Republican nomination for the governorship of California in 1966, and he went on to win in the general election. In 1968 he conducted a late and very tentative campaign for the GOP presidential nomination that failed to ignite. He won reelection as governor in 1970, retiring at the end of his second term in 1974. In 1976 he challenged incumbent president Gerald Ford for the party's presidential nomination and came close to success. In 1980 he won a comfortable nomination victory, followed by his election in November over President Jimmy Carter.

Although late blooming, Reagan's Republican Party loyalty had become extremely strong during the previous two decades. He willingly accepted the responsibilities of party leadership. Structurally, the relationship between Reagan and the Republican National Committee developed along the lines of his presidential predecessors', with White House aides assuming responsibility for political operations, including party liaison. Rumors of White House dissatisfaction with Richard Richards's performance accompanied his resignation as national party chair after two years in office.

Nevertheless, the spirit of the relationship between the party chair and the White House was much more positive than it had been during the Johnson, Nixon, and Carter presidencies. Cooperation and goodwill prevailed as President Reagan provided strong support and encouragement for the party-building efforts undertaken by the national headquarters. In staffing his administration, Reagan demanded unprecedented ideological loyalty that identified the Republican Party more clearly with conservatism.

In dealing with Congress, Reagan benefited from the 1980 senatorial elections that placed the Republican Party in a majority position for the first time in a quarter-century. He worked closely and cooperatively with the congressional party leadership in pursuit of economic policy objectives.

Reagan's relations with the House of Representatives, still controlled by the Democrats, were more antagonistic. He tried to expand the boundaries of his secure party base by enlisting the support of conservative House Democrats. In that respect, he emphasized ideology over partisanship.

In 1984 Reagan won a massive reelection victory over Democratic challenger Walter F. Mondale. The party majorities in the House and Senate remained stable. In 1986, however, the Democrats recaptured control of the Senate, preventing the president from relying primarily on the party symbol in pursuing his policy objectives there. Increasingly, he resorted to threats of presidential vetoes in congressional relations.

Reagan's record of party leadership may be regarded as among the most successful in the modern era. He was a committed partisan who established and maintained congenial relations with the congressional party and the party organization.

Moreover, Reagan's electoral successes attracted new groups of voters to the Republican ranks. Whether this portended a significant partisan realignment transforming the Republicans into enduring majority status remains unclear.

Significantly, the 1988 electoral victory of Reagan's anointed successor, Vice President George Bush, was the first by a nonincumbent nominee of the party controlling the presidency since

Herbert Hoover succeeded Calvin Coolidge in 1928, and the first by an incumbent vice president since Martin Van Buren succeeded Andrew Jackson in 1828. Clearly, Ronald Reagan restored a positive aura to the presidential role of party leader following a sequence of negative experiences.

GEORGE BUSH

With regard to background and experiences, George Bush had unmatched preparation for assuming the mantle of presidential party leadership. As the son of a Republican U.S. senator, he brought to the role a noteworthy familial heritage of party identity and accomplishment, complemented by his impressive record of party organization leadership at the county and national levels, high-level executive branch appointments, and party nominations and elections to positions in both Congress and the executive.

In the 1988 presidential campaign, the national party organization, under the leadership of holdover chair Frank Fahrenkopf, played its now customary peripheral role, with central direction coming from the personal campaign organization headed by Lee Atwater. Atwater, an astute and creative electoral strategist, had played a key role in building the modern South Carolina Republican Party before coming on the national scene. The relationship between the personal campaign organization and the national party was quite amicable. The party's main contributions to Bush's victory came in the areas of fund raising and generic advertising.

After the election, when Fahrenkopf's term expired, Bush named Atwater to head the national committee. The selection of a highly visible presidential insider, along with the belief that

Of all presidents to date, only George Bush, chair of the Republican Party from 1973 to 1974, has held the position of chair of his national party.

Bush as a former national chair would be especially attentive to the party's needs and interests, promised to elevate the prestige of the office of national chair and restore it to its traditional role as the political arm of the administration.

Although optimism initially prevailed, some fourteen months later, in the wake of controversies that had already forced him to assume a lower public profile, Atwater became incapacitated by a brain tumor. While continuing to occupy the chair for the remainder of his two-year term, Atwater's attention shifted from partisan responsibilities to his fight for life.

The national party's hopes for a central role in presidential politics became a casualty of Atwater's illness, as White House aides led by chief of staff John Sununu came to dominate the conduct of presidential politics in a manner now typical of the modern presidency. To succeed Atwater as national chair, Bush called on Agriculture Secretary Clayton Yeutter, who lacked Atwater's forceful presence and was disinclined to challenge the preeminence of the White House staff in the conduct of partisan political operations.

Although he claimed to be the heir to the Reagan legacy, President Bush was more pragmatic than ideological in style. Less insistent than Reagan on ideological conformity, Bush tolerated among some principal appointees moderate views that generated sustained criticism from party conservatives. More generally, this group expressed increasing disenchantment with Bush for his perceived lack of vision and direction, particularly in domestic policy.

In his relations with the Republican Party in Congress, Bush was well served by his previous membership in those ranks. He worked comfortably with old congressional colleagues, and he clearly understood, appreciated, and embraced the traditional congressional norms of compromise and accommodation.

However, the minority status of the Republican Party in Congress throughout Bush's presidency created noteworthy tensions for his party leadership, particularly among Republican right-wingers on Capitol Hill who bemoaned the apparent lack of ideological vision and commitment manifested in his willingness to seek necessary bipartisan support for legislative initiatives.

Public approval of the Bush presidency skyrocketed in early 1991, in the context of the Persian Gulf War, reaching an unprecedented high near 90 percent. After the war, however, with the economy in recession, Bush's popularity with the electorate plummeted. Once considered a shoo-in for reelection, the president appeared suddenly vulnerable by the fall of 1991.

Patrick Buchanan, a conservative political commentator, mounted a challenge to Bush's party renomination. Bush rather easily defeated Buchanan in the spring primaries, successfully relying on his base of support in the party organization, now headed by his old deputy, Richard Bond. Disaffection with Bush from party conservatives was increasingly apparent, however, as was his declining level of support among middle-class voters, many of whom deserted him in favor of either Democratic nominee Bill Clinton or independent candidate Ross Perot.

In the November balloting, Bush suffered an electoral repudiation, winning only 38 percent of the popular vote and eighteen states with 168 electoral votes. His convincing electoral defeat left his initially promising presidential party leadership in tatters.

BILL CLINTON

Prior to his successful 1992 bid for the presidency, Bill Clinton had spent virtually his entire adult life in electoral politics in his native state of Arkansas. The traditional dominance of the state's Democratic Party had persisted for the most part, although the Republican Party was making strong inroads elsewhere in the South. In this hospitable arena, Clinton usually prospered under the Democratic banner, winning election to a single term as attorney general and five terms as governor, while suffering two general election defeats: in 1974, for the Third District congressional seat; and 1980, for reelection as governor.

Clinton unequivocally embraced the Democratic Party label. However, he shared with Presidents Johnson and Carter an identification with the "no-party politics" of the traditionally Democratic South. As governor, in his dealings with the Arkansas legislature, he never had to worry about a Republican opposition spearheading and energizing a coalition capable of defeating his policy initiatives. On the other hand, Clinton's adherence to no-party politics meant that neither was party loyalty available to him as an effective cue to generate legislative support.

As governor, Clinton made his presence felt on the national party scene. He was a leader in the formation and development of the centrist Democratic Leadership Council (DLC), chairing the body in 1990–1991. Campaigning for the Democratic presidential nomination, Clinton effectively used his DLC affiliation to promote himself as a "New Democrat," one who could lead his party away from its perceived liberal leanings back toward the center.

At the outset of his presidency, Clinton confronted a complex and contradictory political environment for party leadership. On the one hand, he started out with comfortable party majorities in both houses of Congress, the first president since Carter to so benefit. However, his political base was weak, since he had been elected with only a 43 percent plurality in a three-candidate race that featured the best popular vote showing by an independent candidate, Ross Perot, since Theodore Roosevelt in 1912. Perot's performance suggested deepening strains in the enduring commitment of American voters to the two major parties, with distressing implications for presidential party leadership.

As president, Clinton put forward an ambitious policy agenda, seeking legislative enactment of several high-profile, controversial measures. In his first year in office, he achieved narrow but noteworthy successes relying on two distinct leadership strategies.

In the first instance, Clinton's budget proposal passed without the vote of a single Republican member of Congress. His impressive effort to mobilize party support was costly, as emboldened Capitol Hill Democrats advanced their own special interests in negotiations with the White House in return for their necessary support. In contrast, the Clinton-supported North American Free Trade Agreement (NAFTA) passed Congress despite substantial Democratic defections because Clinton was able to enlist strong support from the Republicans.

Congressional relations took a distinct turn for the worse in Clinton's second year. He failed to marshal either partisan or bipartisan backing for the centerpiece of his legislative agenda, his heralded health care initiative.

Clinton's Capitol Hill problems were attributable in considerable measure to his inability to generate sustained public support for himself, his policy proposals, or his party. The midterm 1994 congressional elections produced a historic landslide victory for the opposition Republicans that placed them in control of both chambers. Clinton became the first Democratic president since Truman to face a Congress dominated by Republicans.

A casualty of this deteriorating political environment was Clinton's national party chair, David Wilhelm, who had served with distinction as his 1992 campaign manager. Wilhelm had labored to develop the capacity of the national party headquarters to mobilize public support for the president's policy initiatives. The party's energetic efforts fell short of success. Well in advance of the midterm elections, amid rumbling discontent from Democrats in Congress and the states, as well as rumored dissatisfaction on the part of the White House, Wilhelm announced his decision to resign after the elections.

Clinton used this opportunity to position the party to deal with the rising Republican tide by enlisting a dual leadership structure. He secured the selection of U.S. senator Christopher Dodd of Connecticut as general chair and party spokesperson, while anointing Donald Fowler, a South Carolina party leader, as the national chair and party manager.

Midway through his term, Clinton's party leadership was imperiled. The electoral fortunes of the party he led were in decline, attributable in considerable measure to public disenchantment with him and his policies. His formidable challenge was to enhance his popular standing and elevate that of his party in the process. In turn, his ability to lead his party was complicated by his own inability to date to sustain his campaign image as a "New Democrat."

In 1995, however, Clinton's political fortunes began to revive. He successfully pursued a policy of "triangulation" that centrally positioned him between the extremes represented in Congress by the Republican majority and the Democratic minority. Clinton's protracted 1995–1996 budget battle with congressional Republicans increased his popular support as a majority of Americans favored his budget priorities. Later in 1996 Clinton signed sweeping legislation to reform welfare—despite opposition from the liberal wing of his party. Although Clinton's move to the center contributed to his convincing reelection in 1996, the policy called into question his understanding of and commitment to presidential party leadership.

COMPARING THE PRESIDENTS AS PARTY LEADERS

The experiences of the modern presidents as party leaders have differed in numerous and significant ways, yet they were similar in some respects. The variations appear to be threefold. They pertain first to the presidents' personal orientations toward partisanship, generally positive or negative; second to the tone of president-party relations, relatively congenial or hostile; and third to the political circumstances confronted by the incumbents, either favorable or unfavorable for the exercise of party leadership. These factors can either reinforce one another or diverge for particular presidents.

Among modern presidents, Roosevelt, Truman, Kennedy, Ford, Reagan, Bush, and Clinton viewed partisanship in a generally positive fashion. Eisenhower, Johnson, Nixon, and Carter were less affirmatively disposed. Party relations were relatively congenial for presidents Roosevelt, Truman, Eisenhower, Kennedy, and Reagan, but they were more hostile for presidents Johnson, Nixon, and Carter. Ford, Bush, and Clinton occupy intermediate positions on this continuum.

Political circumstances relate primarily to party competition in the electorate and in the government. Since the Great Depression, the Democratic Party has consistently claimed more professed loyalists than its Republican opposition, measured by public opinion surveys and voter registration totals. Since the Reagan years, however, the gap between the two parties has narrowed considerably.

Further, the Democratic Party has controlled Congress the great majority of the time. The only exceptions have been 1947–1949, 1953–1955, 1981–1987, and 1995 to date. On the first two and last occasions, the GOP held both houses; on the third, only the Senate came under Republican domination. In general, for the time period considered, Democratic presidents would appear to have been better positioned to exercise party leadership in the political arena than their Republican counter-parts.

Roosevelt, Eisenhower, Johnson, Nixon (1972), Reagan, and Bush all won comfortable, if not landslide, electoral victories. Truman, Kennedy, Nixon (1968), Carter, and Clinton had much narrower winning margins. Ford was an unelected president throughout his brief tenure. The general expectation is that a generous margin of electoral victory should enhance the prospects for presidential party leadership.

Taking these factors together, Roosevelt most clearly combined personal partisan commitment, positive party relations, and a favorable political context for the exercise of presidential party leadership. Truman, Kennedy, Ford, Reagan, Bush, and Clinton generally shared his positive orientations and congenial relations amid less favorable political circumstances.

Alternatively, although Eisenhower's party relations were relatively congenial, he lacked partisan commitment and confronted a political setting that inhibited party leadership. Johnson, Nixon, and Carter faced very different political circumstances—positive in Johnson's case and less so in the others' cases. They not only appeared personally uncomfortable with party leadership, but also they experienced and contributed to generally antagonistic relations with the parties they nominally led.

Party Leadership and Presidential Power

In a constitutional sense, party leadership conveys no power. The president derives no legal power from the role, and within the party the president lacks command authority. Rather, party leadership operates within the transactional domains of bargaining and negotiation.

Party leadership ordinarily is intertwined with other leadership roles and responsibilities. The reason other elements in the party—elected and appointed public officials, party organization officials and activists, and party supporters in the electorate—look to the president for leadership has less to do with party power per se than with power coming from other sources, such as the Constitution and the laws, or public support.

The exercise of party leadership often enables the president to perform successfully in other roles. Policy responsiveness is an important presidential expectation in making executive appointments. Although partisanship is not an absolute requirement for policy responsiveness, it serves as a convenient indicator. Presidents' effectiveness as chief executive turns in part on their success as party leader.

Similarly, by acting as party leader the president can be an effective legislative leader, another presidential role that has no constitutional authority. The party connection can unite the separated executive and legislative branches under presidential leadership. In a situation of divided party government, however, where opposing parties control the White House and Congress, presidential party leadership can become less an opportunity than an obstacle.

Party leadership is relevant to the president's powers and responsibilities as chief economic manager because the general public identifies the president with the party. The president's success in controlling the economy can influence the electoral fortunes of the party's nominees, including the president.

Further, presidential approaches to economic management can reflect ideological positions associated with the party. For example, the more ideologically conservative Republican presidents have tended to view monetary policy (dealing with the supply and circulation of money) as a more appropriate response than fiscal policy (on taxing and spending). The more liberal Democratic presidents have tended to prefer fiscal to monetary policy.

Presidential party leadership has less obvious relevance for the president's responsibilities in the diplomatic and military aspects of foreign affairs. The United States has a long heritage of foreign policy bipartisanship. Nevertheless, the electoral and ideological considerations mentioned above can come into play here also, along with those elements of partisanship associated with political appointments. For example, the Democratic Senate rejected President Bush's 1989 nomination of John Tower to serve as secretary of defense. Similarly, the shift to Republican control of the Senate in 1995, with the attendant confirmation difficulties, may have precluded Secretary of State Warren Christopher's rumored desire to retire from the Clinton cabinet. Christopher announced that he was leaving the cabinet shortly after Clinton's 1996 reelection.

The presidential role of chief of state surely has the least relevance for party leadership. In symbolizing the nation undivided, the president ostensibly puts partisanship aside. The problem here is that presidential roles cannot simply be discarded like hats. The basic contradiction between these two roles produces tension for the president and confusion throughout the political system.

President Nixon's attempts to deal with allegations concerning his involvement in the Watergate scandal while pursuing his ongoing presidential responsibilities illustrate this situation. In his January 1974 State of the Union address, Nixon bemoaned that "One year of Watergate is enough," and he asserted that in responding to congressional demands, he would never do "anything that weakens the office of the president of the United States or impairs the ability of the presidents of the future to make the great decisions that are so essential to this nation and to the world."[66]

A few weeks later, during a March 19 question-and-answer session before the National Association of Broadcasters, the president urged the House Judiciary Committee considering the issue of presidential impeachment to resolve the question quickly, asserting that "dragging out Watergate drags down America."[67]

The paradoxes of the president's role as party chief will remain unresolved. The president of all the people is the champion of a specific part of the electorate and the antagonist of another. Yet, in acknowledging the divisiveness inherent in presidential party leadership, Americans also must credit it with providing the means for presidential leadership in other roles. Without embodying specific powers, party leadership nevertheless typically enhances the president's power position in the political order. Contemporary trends that undermine presidential party leadership and widen the separation between president and party could diminish both the presidency and the party system.

NOTES

1. Woodrow Wilson, *Constitutional Government in the United States* (New York: Columbia University Press, 1980/1908), 67.

2. James MacGregor Burns, *Leadership* (New York: Harper and Row, 1978), 4.

3. Frank J. Sorauf, *Party Politics in America* (Boston: Little, Brown, 1968), 11–12.

4. This section draws on Harold F. Bass Jr., "Thomas Jefferson's Presidential Party Leadership" (Paper presented at the annual meeting of the American Political Science Association, Chicago, September 3–6, 1987). See also three works by Noble Cunningham Jr., *The Jeffersonian Republicans: The Formation of Party Organization, 1798–1801* (Chapel Hill: University of North Carolina Press, 1957); *The Jeffersonian Republicans in Power: Party Operations, 1801–1809* (Chapel Hill: University of North Carolina Press, 1963); and *The Process of Government under Jefferson* (Princeton, N.J.: Princeton University Press, 1978).

5. Robert V. Remini, "The Emergence of Political Parties and Their Effect on the Presidency," in *Power and the Presidency,* ed. Philip C. Dolce and George H. Skau (New York: Scribner's, 1976), 30–32.

6. This section draws on Harold F. Bass Jr., "The President and the National Party Organization," in *Presidents and Their Parties: Leadership or Neglect?,* ed. Robert Harmel (New York: Praeger, 1984), 59–89.

7. The traditional role and status of the national party convention is developed at length in Paul T. David, Ralph M. Goldman, and Richard C. Bain, *The Politics of National Party Conventions* (Washington, D.C.: Brookings, 1960).

8. See "Rule No. 31," *The Rules of the Republican Party* (Washington, D.C.: Republican National Committee, 1992), 15–16.

9. See Byron E. Shafer, *Bifurcated Politics: Evolution and Reform in the National Party Convention* (Cambridge, Mass.: Harvard University Press, 1988).

10. Three instructive studies of the national party committees are Hugh A. Bone, *Party Committees and National Politics* (Seattle: University of Washington Press, 1958); Cornelius P. Cotter and Bernard C. Hennessy, *Politics Without Power: The National Party Committees* (New York: Atherton, 1964); and Philip A. Klinkner, *The Losing Parties: Out-Party National Committees, 1956–1993* (New Haven, Conn.: Yale University Press, 1994).

11. Generally, see Cotter and Hennessy, *Politics Without Power,* chaps. 4–5, for a consideration of the traditional role and status of the national party chair.

12. See Bone, *Party Committees and National Politics,* chap. 2; Cotter and Hennessy, *Politics Without Power,* chaps. 6–9; and Cornelius P. Cotter and John F. Bibby, "Institutional Development of Parties and the Thesis of Party Decline," *Political Science Quarterly* 95 (spring 1980): 6–7.

13. Cotter and Bibby, "Institutional Development of Parties," 5.

14. *Charter and the Bylaws of the Democratic Party of the United States* (Washington, D.C.: Democratic National Committee, 1994), 3.

15. Paul Allen Beck and Frank J. Sorauf, *Party Politics in America,* 7th ed. (New York: HarperCollins, 1992), 104–105.

16. Cotter and Bibby, "Institutional Development of Parties," 6–7.

17. Cotter and Hennessy, *Politics Without Power,* 67–71, 78–80.

18. Theodore H. White, *The Making of the President 1972* (New York: Atheneum, 1973), 61.

19. Rowland Evans and Robert Novak, *Nixon in the White House: The Frustration of Power* (New York: New American Library, 1968) 71–74, 364.

20. Jeb S. Magruder, *An American Life: One Man's Road to Watergate* (New York: Atheneum, 1975), 178.

21. None of the nineteenth-century "accidental" presidents received a subsequent major party nomination. By contrast, all of their twentieth-century counterparts were nominated to succeed themselves as president.

22. Theodore H. White, *Breach of Faith: The Fall of Richard Nixon* (New York: Atheneum, 1975), 97.

23. Sources for this discussion include Malcolm E. Jewell and David Olson, *Political Parties and Elections in the American States,* 3d ed. (Belmont, Calif.: Wadsworth, 1988), chap. 3; Robert J. Huckshorn, *Party Leadership in the States* (Amherst: University of Massachusetts Press, 1976); and Cornelius P. Cotter et al., *Party Organizations in American Politics* (New York: Praeger, 1984).

24. Cotter et al., *Party Organizations in American Politics,* chap. 2.

25. Ibid., passim.

26. See E. E. Schattschneider, *Party Government* (New York: Rinehart, 1942), 129–133; Morton Grodzins, "American Political Parties and the American System," *Western Political Quarterly* (December 1960): 974–998.

27. Cotter and Bibby, "Institutional Development of Parties," 13–20; Charles Longley, "Party Reform and Party Nationalization: The Case of the Democrats," in *The Party Symbol: Readings on Political Parties,* ed. William Crotty (San Francisco: Freeman, 1980), 359–378; John F. Bibby, "Party Re-

newal in the National Republican Party," in *Party Renewal in America,* ed. Gerald Pomper (New York: Praeger, 1981), 102–115.

28. Harry S. Truman, "The President's News Conference of October 31, 1945," *Public Papers of the Presidents of the United States, Harry S. Truman, 1945* (Washington, D.C.: Government Printing Office, 1953), 456.

29. Dorothy G. Fowler, *The Cabinet Politician: The Postmaster General, 1829–1909* (New York: Columbia University Press, 1943), 302.

30. Hoover Commission, *Report on Organization of the Executive Branch of Government* (New York: McGraw-Hill, 1949), 224–225.

31. Richard Fenno, *The President's Cabinet: An Analysis in the Period from Wilson to Eisenhower* (Cambridge, Mass.: Harvard University Press, 1959), 70.

32. President's Committee on Administrative Management, *Administrative Management of the Government of the United States* (Washington, D.C.: Government Printing Office, 1937), 5.

33. See Thomas J. Weko, *The Politicizing Presidency: The White House Personnel Office, 1948-1994* (Lawrence: University Press of Kansas, 1995).

34. Herbert Kaufman, "The Growth of the Federal Personnel System," in *The Federal Government Service,* 2d ed., ed. Wallace S. Sayre (Englewood Cliffs, N.J.: Prentice-Hall, 1965), 40–53.

35. James A. Farley, *Behind the Ballot: The Personal History of a Politician* (New York: Harcourt, Brace, 1938), 223–238.

36. Kaufman, "Growth of the Federal Personnel System," 55.

37. James A. Farley, *Jim Farley's Story: The Roosevelt Years* (New York: Whittlesey House, 1948), 68.

38. Terry M. Moe, "The Politicized Presidency," in *The New Direction in American Politics,* ed. John E. Chubb and Paul E. Peterson (Washington, D.C.: Brookings, 1985), 260–261.

39. George C. Edwards III, *Presidential Influence in Congress* (San Francisco: Freeman, 1980), 125–188 passim. See also George C. Edwards III, *At the Margins: Presidential Leadership of Congress* (New Haven: Yale University Press, 1989).

40. Edwards, *Presidential Influence in Congress,* 129, citing Harry McPherson, *A Political Education* (Boston: Little, Brown, 1972), 197; and Russell D. Renka, "Legislative Leadership and Marginal Vote-Gaining Strategies in the Kennedy and Johnson Presidencies" (Paper delivered at the annual meeting of the Southwestern Political Science Association, Houston, Texas, April 1978, 26–27).

41. James Madison, "Federalist No. 51," in *The Federalist Papers,* Alexander Hamilton, James Madison, and John Jay (New York: Bantam, 1982), 262.

42. George C. Edwards III, *The Public Presidency: The Pursuit of Public Support* (New York: St. Martin's Press, 1983), 83–88.

43. Edwards, *Presidential Influence in Congress,* 77.

44. James W. Davis, *The President as Party Leader* (New York: Praeger, 1992).

45. "Million-Dollar Bill," *Time,* July 4, 1994, 31.

46. Roger G. Brown, "Presidents and Midterm Campaigners," in *Presidents and Their Parties,* 127.

47. Stephen E. Ambrose, *Eisenhower,* vol. 2, *The President* (New York: Simon & Shuster, 1984), 218–219.

48. There have been exceptions, notably in Franklin Roosevelt's first midterm election (1934) when the Democrats gained nine seats in the House and ten in the Senate. In 1902 the GOP under Theodore Roosevelt gained seats but lost ground to the Democrats because the House expanded in size. In 1838 the Democrats slightly improved their position when both parties added seats. In 1830 the Democrats gained two seats.

49. Sidney M. Milkis, "Presidents and Party Purges: With Special Emphasis on the Lessons of 1938," in *Presidents and Their Parties,* 167.

50. Henry J. Abraham, *The Judicial Process: An Introductory Analysis of the Courts of the United States, England, and France,* 6th ed. (New York: Oxford University Press, 1993), 66.

51. Walter F. Murphy and C. Herman Pritchett, *Courts, Judges, and Politics: An Introduction to the Judicial Process,* 4th ed. (New York: Random House, 1986), 150; citing Henry Cabot Lodge, *Selections from the Correspondence of Theodore Roosevelt and Henry Cabot Lodge, 1894–1918* (New York: Scribner's, 1925), vol. 1, 517–519.

52. Abraham, *The Judicial Process,* 71; citing *New York Times,* May 17, 1969, 1.

53. Ibid., 74; citing Lodge, *Correspondence of Theodore Roosevelt and Henry Cabot Lodge,* vol. 2, 228.

54. *The United States Government Manual, 1996/97* (Washington, D.C.: U.S. Government Printing Office, 1996), 68–73.

55. "Gallup Trend on Party Identification, 1937–1995," *Gallup Poll Monthly,* August 1995, 45.

56. See Fred I. Greenstein, *Children and Politics* (New Haven: Yale University Press, 1965); Robert D. Hess and Judith V. Torney, *The Development of Political Attitudes in Children* (Chicago: Aldine, 1967).

57. Edwards, *The Public Presidency,* 213.

58. The party-decline thesis finds expression in Walter Dean Burnham, *Critical Elections and the Mainsprings of American Politics* (New York: Norton, 1970); Gerald M. Pomper, "The Decline of the Party in American Elections," *Political Science Quarterly* 92 (spring 1977): 21–41; William J. Crotty and Gary C. Jacobson, *American Parties in Decline,* 2d ed. (New York: Harper and Row, 1987); and Martin P. Wattenberg, *The Decline of American Political Parties, 1952–1992* (Cambridge, Mass.: Harvard University Press, 1994).

59. Nelson W. Polsby, "Presidential Cabinet Making: Lessons for the Political System," *Political Science Quarterly* 93 (spring 1978): 19.

60. James David Barber, *The Presidential Character: Predicting Performance in the White House,* 4th ed. (New York: Prentice-Hall, 1992).

61. Fred I. Greenstein, *The Hidden Hand Presidency: Eisenhower as Leader* (New York: Basic Books, 1982).

62. Dwight D. Eisenhower, "The President's Press Conference of October 11, 1956," *Public Papers of the Presidents, Dwight D. Eisenhower, 1956* (Washington, D.C.: Government Printing Office, 1956), 891.

63. Ibid., 1957, "The President's News Conference of June 5, 1957," 435.

64. *New York Times,* January 15, 1960, 14.

65. See Warren Weaver Jr., "National Committee Scolds Carter for Bypassing State Party Chiefs," *New York Times,* April 2, 1977, 12.

66. Quoted in Congressional Quarterly, *Watergate: Chronology of a Crisis,* vol. 2 (Washington, D.C.: Congressional Quarterly, 1974), 228.

67. Ibid., 286.

SELECTED BIBLIOGRAPHY

Bone, Hugh A. *Party Committees and National Politics.* Seattle: University of Washington Press, 1958.

Brown, Roger G. "Party and Bureaucracy: From Kennedy to Reagan," *Political Science Quarterly* 97 (summer 1982): 279–294.

———. "The Presidency and the Political Parties." In *The Presidency and the Political System,* ed. Michael Nelson. Washington, D.C.: CQ Press, 1985.

———, and David M. Welborn. "Presidents and Their Parties: Performance and Prospects." *Presidential Studies Quarterly* 12 (summer 1982): 302–316.

Cotter, Cornelius P. "Eisenhower as Party Leader." *Political Science Quarterly* 98 (summer 1983): 255–284.

———, and John F. Bibby. "Institutional Development of Parties and the Thesis of Party Decline." *Political Science Quarterly* 95 (spring 1980): 1–27.

———, James L. Gibson, John F. Bibby, and Robert J. Huckshorn. *Party Organizations in American Politics.* New York: Praeger, 1984.

———, and Bernard D. Hennessy. *Politics Without Power: The National Party Committees.* New York: Atherton, 1964.

Cronin, Thomas E. "The Presidency and the Parties." In *Party Renewal in America,* ed. Gerald M. Pomper. New York: Praeger, 1980.

Davis, James W. *The President as Party Leader.* New York: Praeger, 1992.

Goldman, Ralph M. "Titular Leadership of Presidential Parties." In *The Presidency,* ed. Aaron Wildavsky. Boston: Little, Brown, 1969.

Harmel, Robert, ed. *Presidents and Their Parties: Leadership or Neglect?* New York: Praeger, 1984.

Kessel, John H. *Presidential Parties.* Homewood, Ill.: Dorsey, 1984.

Ketcham, Ralph. *Presidents above Party: The First American Presidency, 1789–1829.* Chapel Hill: University of North Carolina Press, 1984.

Milkis, Sidney M. "The Presidency and the Political Parties." In *The Presidency and the Political System,* ed. Michael Nelson. 4th ed. Washington, D.C.: CQ Press, 1994.

——. *The President and the Parties: The Transformation of the American Party System Since the New Deal.* New York: Oxford University Press, 1993.

Odegard, Peter H. "Presidential Leadership and Party Responsibility." *Annals of the American Academy of Political and Social Science* 307 (September 1956): 66–81.

Seligman, Lester. "The Presidential Office and the President as Party Leader (with a Postscript on the Kennedy-Nixon Era)." In *Parties and Elections in an Antiparty Age,* ed. Jeff Fishel. Bloomington: Indiana University Press, 1978.

CHAPTER 3

The President and the News Media

BY MARTHA JOYNT KUMAR

THE NEWS MEDIA are a president's lifeline to the citizenry. Television and radio networks, wire services, newspapers, and periodicals disseminate presidential statements, chronicle administration actions, and analyze administration programs and progress. They also serve as vehicles for opposing views. Although the mix among statements, facts, analysis, and opinion has varied through the years, the president's need for the news media has remained unchanged.

Since the earliest days of the young nation, presidents and their surrogates have sought out opportunities to publicize themselves and their administrations. For the early presidents, newspapers were the vehicle of choice to establish contact with the voting public, but today's technology has created a broader range of choices for conveying information, and presidents and their staffs have made quick use of them. At the same time, news organizations have moved from a time in the early days when they had to beg for entry into the halls of government for their representatives to a time when they expect government officials to be regularly accessible for on-the-record interviews and to provide reporters with a daily stream of statements for public consumption.

A conspicuous feature of the modern-day relationship between the White House and news organizations is the layer of hostility at its surface. "I have long since given up the thought that I could disabuse some of you of turning any substantive decision into anything but a political process," retorted President Bill Clinton in 1993 to a question directed to him by Brit Hume, the White House correspondent for ABC News.[1] The president was seething with frustration over what he considered to be frivolous and inaccurate coverage of him and his administration. But his comments were typical of remarks delivered at some point by almost every one of his predecessors. For their part, reporters have grievances against just about every president they encounter. When reporters believe the White House is withholding information, complaints abound. The resulting tension between the two sides receives great play in the pages of newspapers and on television news programs.

The harsh veneer that overlays the relationship between the president and news organizations belies the continuing working relationship existing below its surface. Two fundamental features characterize this enduring relationship: the mutual benefit of the president–news media association and the cooperation that suffuses the dealings of the White House and news organizations. Without these features, the relationship would not have

the importance it currently holds for each partner. Presidents need news organizations to reach their constituents, and reporters depend on the president for their copy. The president is central to the concept of news that is shared by a news organization's viewers and readers: people want to hear what the president is doing, thinking, and planning.

All presidents have valued the press. They have not necessarily liked the people who report or who publish or air the news, but they have understood that the media are an important vehicle for reaching the public. When the first president, George Washington (1789–1797), needed to explain his rationale for leaving his presidency to the public, he did so through the press. His farewell address was not spoken directly to Congress nor was it even presented as a speech. Instead, at President Washington's request it was printed as a communication to the people in the Pennsylvania's *Daily American Advertiser* on September 19, 1796. Philadelphia was the nation's capital at that time, so Washington chose a local newspaper as his venue. His choice of a newspaper for such an important statement confirmed his high regard for the press as a presidential resource.

Washington's successors also have recognized the value of news organizations. When President Ronald Reagan addressed the American public at the end of his eight years in office, he delivered a televised farewell speech from the Oval Office. He too chose the media as the vehicle to deliver his message to the people collectively.

Through the decades, new forms of media have changed the ways in which people receive information. Beginning in the late seventeenth century, newspapers played an active part in the political debate that surrounded the founding of the United States. The first colonial newspaper, *Publick Occurrences Both Forreign and Domestick,* was published in Boston on September 25, 1690, and its first issue happened to be its last. The *Boston News-Letter,* which followed in 1704, was the first continually published newspaper in colonial America.

While the Constitution was being drafted in the late eighteenth century, the citizens of major cities were able to read in more than one newspaper timely, solid political discussions of the emerging document. In New York, for example, newspapers were available four days a week,[2] and political information, either by subscription or through quick perusal in taverns or coffee houses, was plentiful. Indeed, essays by Alexander Hamilton, John Jay, and James Madison in support of the Constitution initially appeared as letters published in New York's *Independent*

Journal; they then were reprinted in newspapers around the country.

Unfortunately, once the Constitution was adopted, what had become a partisan and often vituperative press frequently failed to raise and seriously discuss important political questions in anything but the most partisan manner. Presidents and the members of their administrations spoke through newspapers designated as the vehicles for their official statements and viewpoints. The opposition regularly used the partisan press to launch attacks against specific presidents and their administrations.

In 1800, as Washington began to function as the nation's capital, the establishment of a newspaper, the *National Intelligencer,* marked the city's development. Similarly, as communities around the young nation matured, newspapers became an important aspect of their civic lives. By the turn of the century, 202 newspapers were being published nationwide.[3]

From 1861 to 1900, a second period emerged as the press changed its focus from serving presidential interests to getting a story quickly and attracting the largest number of readers possible. During these years, the White House began to take shape as an institution as the staff assumed new responsibilities, including daily dealings with reporters.

A third period, 1901–1932, covering the administration of Theodore Roosevelt through that of Herbert Hoover, saw the White House become a distinct beat for the press. Presidents began to hold regular meetings with reporters to receive their questions, and the position of presidential press secretary was established and the operating procedures of the office were developed. When Franklin Roosevelt became president, the modern period in president-press relations began.

Origins of Press Coverage:
1789–1860

In 1789, the federal government's first year, press access to the government was extremely limited. Earlier, neither the press nor the public had been admitted to the Constitutional Convention. After American independence, state legislatures generally were not open to the public nor was the Continental Congress. Moreover, no one in the government or in the press thought it their duty to provide a literal transcript of either debate or the statements of elected officials. Verbatim reports of congressional debates were not available until the *Congressional Globe* provided them for both houses beginning in 1851.[4] The *Congressional Record* became the publisher of debate in 1873. Both publications, however, made generous allowance for transcript "corrections" by the members.

At least four significant patterns established during this period continue to define relations between the president and the news media today. First, it was clearly recognized that the press—newspapers in those days—was a valuable resource for a governing president. Second, the reciprocity or mutual benefit

In 1754 Benjamin Franklin drew what is considered the first American editorial cartoon. In his *Pennsylvania Gazette,* Franklin published the drawing of a reptile divided into separate parts, each representing one of the colonial states.

that underlies the present-day relationship between the president and the news media was established. Third, presidential opponents came to see the news media as a major venue. Partisans acquired a means to oppose the president and his programs. Congress was their stage, but their line to the public was through the media. And, fourth, few rules governed political reporting as it developed in Washington. "Reporters" during this time included editors operating as journalists, letter writers who sent polemic messages back home, government employees who wrote newspaper copy on the side, and journalists who also lobbied for legislation. Some reporters were viewed as outsiders in the political system; others were among those consulted by the president. Some newsmen, such as early and midnineteenth-century newspaper publishers Joseph Gales, William Seaton, Francis Blair, and Amos Kendall, were among the glitterati of their time, socially and professionally recognized.

THE PRESS AS AN
EXECUTIVE RESOURCE

When George Washington took office, there were no national political parties. Nevertheless, a newspaper associated with the incoming president and his governing principles began to take shape just as the new president was to take the oath of office. The *Gazette of the United States* published its first issue in New York on April 15, 1789, fifteen days before Washington's inauguration. It moved to Philadelphia the next year when the government seat was relocated to that city.

Political parties grew out of the political programs that government leaders endorsed and sought to enact, and officials found such political organizations useful for articulating their ideas and broadening their coalitions of support. According to political scientist Richard Rubin, "newspapers formed around leadership blocs . . . linking political leaders to their mass constituencies."[5] Alexander Hamilton, a political figure with a very specific agenda, saw to the creation of the *Gazette of the United States;* John Fenno served as its editor. Hamilton, Vice President John Adams, and other Federalists contributed editorially and financially to the paper, which rapidly became the voice of the developing Federalist Party.[6] In fact, when Vice President Adams wrote a series of articles on American political history, he published them in the *Gazette* in 1790 and 1791. Later, as president, Adams (1797–1801) took no active role in establishing a newspaper as an organ for the government.

WASHINGTON NEWSPAPERS AND THE PATRONAGE FACTOR

Washington newspapers got their start with assistance from Thomas Jefferson who foresaw the need for an outlet to carry his voice beyond Washington. When the capital moved to the new federal town on the banks of the Potomac, Jefferson recommended to Samuel Harrison Smith, the owner of the Philadelphia newspaper the *Independent Gazetteer,* that he move to Washington and establish a newspaper there that would become the new administration's official voice. He did so, and on October 31, 1800, he published the first issue of the *National Intelligencer,* which began as a four-page paper appearing three times a week.

Once Thomas Jefferson became president (1801–1809), the fledgling newspaper became the official channel for information coming from the executive branch of government. "Over a faithful and comprehensive detail of facts will preside a spirit of investigation, a desire to enlighten, not only by fact, but by reason," editor Smith stated in the *National Intelligencer*'s second issue November 3, 1800. "The tendency of public measures, and the conduct of public men, will be examined with candour and truth."[7] While generally a source of anti-Federalist and later Whig views, the paper was never seen as partisan in the way many party organs were in the decades that followed.

The imprimatur of the new administration guaranteed the *Intelligencer*'s success. With no rivals in the new town, the *Intelligencer* could establish its roots and dominate an industry that would inevitably grow. James Madison (1809–1817) continued the governmental role of the *Intelligencer* as did James Monroe (1817–1825) and John Quincy Adams (1825–1829). Thus the *Intelligencer* served as the president's agent until President Andrew Jackson (1829–1837) moved first to the *United States Telegraph* and then in 1830 to the *Washington Globe.*[8] President Martin Van Buren (1837–1841) continued the presidential association with the *Globe.* The *Intelligencer* came back into favor with William Henry Harrison (1841), John Tyler (1841–1845), although not for all of his term, and Millard Fillmore (1850–1853). The Washington *Union,* a new paper, was favored by President James K. Polk (1845–1849), Franklin Pierce (1853–1857), and James Buchanan (1857–1861). Yet another paper, the Washington *Republic,* was created when President Zachary Taylor (1849–1850) took office. Other papers, then, sprouted up in Washington during the terms of the thirteen presidents from 1801 to 1860, but none

lived so long or was so closely associated with the institutions of government as the *Intelligencer,* which firmly established its reputation as the most reliable reporter of congressional debates.

Although both the administration and the nascent newspapers benefited from the popular press's role as a voice of the administration, the newspapers received another reward for their endeavor—patronage. According to historian William Ames, the federal government paid the newspapers to print proclamations, advertisements for bids, and other notices, as well as official documents such as treaties. Some of the documents were copied by other papers, thereby enhancing the *Intelligencer*'s importance as a news source.[9] Local and state newspapers regularly used information from the *Intelligencer* in their pages. At its high point, approximately six hundred papers were reprinting information gleaned from its pages.[10] Along with official administration pronouncements, speeches in both houses of Congress were reported, as well as news reports from the federal city.

In time the paper paid more attention to Congress than to the administration through whose efforts it had been established. Interestingly, the patronage potential at the congressional level was about equal to that at the executive branch level. Congressional patronage took the form of offers to the newspapers to publish debates, and the executive branch was profitable through the publication of newly enacted laws.

In 1829, when Andrew Jackson became president, reciprocity between the president and the press took a new form. Long comfortable with journalists, the new president surrounded himself with several ad hoc advisers (known as his kitchen cabinet), who included three journalists: Francis Blair, Amos Kendall, and Duff Green. Jackson also appointed his supporters to government positions, and, in a change from the way governmental positions had been filled previously, his appointees included journalists as well as party functionaries. Ben Perley Poore, a journalist in Washington in its early days, observed that the editors who supported President Jackson "claimed their rewards." But what they sought was different from the rewards given earlier to newspaper editors supporting a president. "They were not to be appeased by sops of Government advertising, or by the appointment of publisher of the laws of the United States in the respective States, but they demanded some of the most lucrative offices as their share of the spoils," Poore said.[11] In 1832 the *National Intelligencer* published the names of fifty-seven journalists who received appointments to positions in the federal government during Jackson's first term.[12]

NEWSPAPERS AS VENUES FOR PRESIDENTIAL OPPONENTS

As Alexander Hamilton pressed for government policies based on a broad reading of the Constitution, his opponents were quick to match his *Gazette of the United States* with a news outlet of their own. James Madison and Thomas Jefferson encouraged Philip Freneau to publish a newspaper in Philadelphia, which was at that time America's capital. The *National Gazette* was established October 31, 1791.

Then as now, no political figure was immune from the attack of newspapers. On the day he left office, George Washington found himself characterized most unfavorably in the *Aurora*, rival newspaper to Washington's *Gazette of the United States*. Editor Benny Bache described Washington as a "man who is the source of all the misfortunes of our country . . . no longer possessed of power to multiply evils upon the United States."[13] This was not the first stinging criticism of President Washington by the *Aurora* or other critics. Editor Bache, the grandson of Benjamin Franklin, was the most vitriolic of the critics of the Federalists. The severest attacks began with the discussion of the Jay Treaty between the United States and Great Britain, the first sharply partisan issue of the young nation.

At the end of his administration, President John Adams also had to contend with the attacks leveled at him by the Republican-slanted *National Intelligencer*. On its very first front page, an anonymous writer—"A Republican"—queried the legality of President Adams's actions as an executive. The Framers of the Constitution "understood that he should exercise *no participation in making the laws,* further than that of assenting to, or rejecting them, when submitted to him, after their formation."[14]

The Federalists responded to the vilification directed their way by enacting laws to stop the attacks on them. In 1798 Congress passed the Alien and Sedition Acts making it a crime to write or to publish "any false, scandalous and malicious" criticism of the federal government. The effect was to slow down, if not silence, the opposition. In total, twenty-five people were arrested and twelve trials were held, with eleven people convicted, including editors of newspapers as well as members of Congress. When Jefferson became president, he pardoned all convicted under the act.[15]

At this time, neither the stalwarts of the president nor the opposition newspapers believed it their duty to present both sides of a national political issue. Newspapers supporting a president did so wholeheartedly. Among papers, however, there was a difference in the vehemence of support. The *Intelligencer* was perhaps the most objective of the lot.

BIRTH OF THE WASHINGTON PRESS CORPS

With a twofold increase in national population between 1790 and 1820 and a burgeoning electorate (property ownership as a prerequisite for voting was abandoned), newspapers found themselves catering to an expanding audience. Concurrently, the Republican coalition began to break apart, and regional differences and splits over trade and tariffs began to surface. The result was that editors outside Washington were no longer willing to rely solely on the *Intelligencer* for news and views of the national government; only the *Intelligencer*'s debate summaries remained acceptable. By the 1820s correspondents from around the country were being sent to report on the government—the first Washington correspondents had arrived.

The nature of these reporters' work bore little semblance to the activities of the modern professional press corps. The beat then included purchasing news and, sometimes, even running for office. The job did not require focusing on a particular institution or territory; in fact, until the Civil War reporters roamed all around Washington placing little emphasis on any special agency or activity. Actually, Congress, not the president, was the dominant source of national government news. It was not until the late nineteenth century that the White House had news people assigned to it permanently. The White House itself lacked the staff to exploit the publicity opportunities available to it.

Congressional press galleries came into being in the 1840s. James Gordon Bennett, publisher of the *New York Herald*, sought congressional floor space for his stenographers and was granted a number of desks in what was called a "Reporters' Gallery." Created in July 1841, the gallery was located above the vice president's chair in the Senate. Here began the formal press's coverage of governmental institutions in Washington.

The first Washington correspondents were letter writers who sent back their impressions of the government at work. Beginning with the opening of the second session of the Seventeenth Congress in December 1822, Nathaniel Carter wrote articles for the *Albany Statesman and Evening Advertiser* under the title "Washington Correspondence." By 1827 the group of out-of-town staffers included Samuel Knapp, who wrote for the *Boston Gazette, Charleston Courier,* and *New York Advertiser*; Joseph Buckingham, who reported for the *Boston Gazette*; and James Gordon Bennett, who began his long career with a stint as the correspondent for the *New York Enquirer*. F. B. Marbut, in his *News from the Capital: The Story of Washington Reporting,* marked the year 1827 as the founding of the Washington press corps as a permanent institution. But there still were no organization and no rules to govern behavior.[16]

By their nature, the letter writers were able to engender stronger feelings in their work than the feelings aroused by the fairly bland summaries of debates and pamphlets typical of the *Intelligencer*. "Miserable slanderers—hirelings, hanging on to the skirts of literature, earning a miserable subsistence from their vile and dirty misrepresentations of the proceedings here, and many of them writing for both sides," complained Sen. John M. Niles of Connecticut, who felt the sting of their attacks.[17]

Without rules, there were no restrictions to participation in the press corps. Thus women, who were admitted to the House of Representatives in 1827 as floor observers, were able to work alongside their male colleagues so long as they reported to a newspaper.[18] Originally sent to Washington in 1850 to write a column for Horace Greeley's *New York Tribune*, Jane Swisshelm was the first woman gallery reporter and the first woman political correspondent. She recorded a session from the Senate press gallery on April 17, 1850, "greatly to the surprise of the Senators, the reporters, and others on the floor and in the galleries."[19] Other women failed to occupy the gallery as she had anticipated. While never a large group in the nineteenth century, women eventually made up 12 percent of the 167 correspondents accred-

Horace Greeley used his newspaper for crusades and causes. His *New York Tribune* was the first major paper to endorse the abolition of slavery and the first to introduce a separate editorial page.

ited to the press galleries of the two houses of Congress until their temporary disappearance from the scene in 1880.[20]

From the beginning, women's interests tended to differ from those of their male colleagues. In addition to reporting on Washington social activities, they were especially interested in the issues surrounding slavery. In 1831 Anne Royall, the woman whom journalism historian Frank Luther Mott has identified as writing the "forerunner of the modern Washington gossip column," published a weekly paper that focused on gossip and religion.[21] But she, like her successor Jane Swisshelm, was regarded as an outsider with little influence on those who governed.

Diversity also created differences in influence. Some news people were widely accepted in the halls of government and had close connections with those in power. President Andrew Jackson and *Globe* editor Amos Kendall had such a relationship, reports journalism historian Thomas C. Leonard. "The president himself called in Amos Kendall when he wished to make an address. This experienced newspaper editor took down what Jackson said and usually recast it before reading it back. Only after a lengthy exchange did Jackson know what he wished to say."[22]

EMERGING INDEPENDENCE OF THE PRESS

From 1789 to 1860, the media played a unique role in linking together national political institutions and the electorate and in enhancing the evolving two-party system. As Rubin observed,

Unlike the situation of present-day politics, both of the chief instruments of mass mobilization and communications, the party and the press, served to increase partisan organizational activity and reinforce lines of electoral cleavage. More effectively than substantive issues alone, the extensiveness of the press's political coverage, the penetrating partisanship of its new journalistic style, and the press's tight organizational links to the parties, all helped make possible a new and tumultuous era of American politics—the politics of mass mobilization in a firmly entrenched two-party system.[23]

Throughout the seventy years, the press, while becoming increasingly independent, remained an important presidential resource as each president's party sought to build a stable group of supporters with whom it could communicate. Also during this time, the number of newspapers grew in enormous increments, from approximately two hundred at the beginning of the nineteenth century to twelve hundred by the middle of Andrew Jackson's presidency. Newspapers had doubled again by 1860, but the vast growth came primarily through the proliferation of rural weeklies that accompanied the western expansion taking place during the first half of the nineteenth century.[24] At the same time, in the cities inexpensive dailies proliferated. The affordable price of these dailies earned them the name "penny press." Their sensational style of coverage was aimed at a wide popular audience. The papers did not espouse or depend on party principles or political subsidies. Financially independent through mass circulation and high advertising revenues, they proved harder for politicians to control.[25]

Technology also played an important part in the emerging independence of the press. Publishing costs plummeted with advances in printing and the use of advertising. The telegraph allowed news organizations to gather information more quickly but at a greater cost. In 1844 Samuel F. B. Morse tested his experimental telegraph cable, which ran from the Capitol to the Democratic convention assembled in Baltimore. The exchange between the two political centers demonstrated the validity of the telegraph and "demolished forever the Washington papers' monopoly on Washington reporting," noted Donald Ritchie, an authority on nineteenth-century reporting from Washington.[26]

The outbreak of the Mexican War in 1846 put news organizations on notice that the news must be provided as quickly as possible. Distance proved to be an obstacle to timely reporting. According to historian Frank Luther Mott, most news about the event took from two to four weeks to reach print.[27] Some newspapers, however, were willing to spend large sums of money to scoop the competition. In New Orleans, which was serving as a source of military supplies and thus a national combat center, there was great competition for news of the war. With nine newspapers jockeying for the latest information, the tab ran high. According to one account, "The *Picayune* sometimes sent fast boats equipped with composing rooms out to sea to meet the slower steamers from Vera Cruz; and by the time the boat had returned to harbor the type for the latest story was set and ready to be rushed to the *Picayune* presses."[28]

Papers in the East incurred even greater expenses because of gaps in the railroad system, requiring fill-in horseback transmittal to get information out of the South. Not until Richmond, Virginia, the southern-most point of the telegraph, could the news be put on the wire. The cost was so high that several news organizations joined forces to share both the news and the expenses incurred in gathering it. In May 1848 six papers assembled at the offices of the *New York Sun* to form an informal association to share foreign news. In 1856 a more formal association with the same membership became incorporated; it was known as the New York Associated Press.

The establishment of the Government Printing Office in 1860 contributed to the growing independence of the press from parties. With its creation, the newspapers lost their patronage plum. Coincidentally, Joseph Gales, senior editor of the *Intelligencer*, died in 1860, bringing to an end an era and the influence of a paper that at one time had so dominated the newspaper industry in Washington.

Establishment of Routines:
1861–1900

Between 1861 and 1900, several key developments transformed the news business and its relations with the White House. First, technological improvements allowed the diffusion of more news to a greater number of people throughout a larger geographical area. The telegraph, distribution of the news through wire services, and the invention of the linotype machine in 1886 made it possible to quickly mass produce and circulate papers featuring the latest information. Second, the rising professionalism of reporters added a new dimension to relations between the press and government institutions. For the first time, journalists established rules governing eligibility of persons to cover Congress. The aim was to limit access to congressional institutions to those who worked for valid news-gathering organizations. Third, in this period, too, the importance of the president as a center of news became clear and the White House itself became a distinct news beat. And, fourth, the increased attention to the White House led to the establishment of White House routines for the distribution of news. As the White House staff grew during the latter part of the nineteenth century, the distribution of information to journalists was among its important functions. And, increasingly, the president dealt directly with reporters but not on a routine basis. Not until shortly after the turn of the century could reporters expect to see and to question the president regularly.

TECHNOLOGY AND CONSOLIDATION

In this significant period, newspapers began to worry about the costs of news gathering—especially about how to transmit information quickly and at a lower cost. Efficiency in gathering news took precedence over a newspaper's relationship with the president; getting a story as soon as possible and making it dramatic was of primary importance. But with the country expanding, speed and accuracy were becoming more difficult. The

---

PUBLISHERS AND POLITICS

In the late nineteenth century, elected officials found publishers like Horace Greeley a force to be reckoned with. In 1872 Greeley ran for president on the Democratic ticket, receiving 44 percent of the vote. Other influential publishers of the time included Charles Dana of the *New York Sun*, James Gordon Bennett of the *New York Herald*, Henry J. Raymond of the *New York Times*, Joseph Pulitzer of the *New York World*, and William Randolph Hearst of the *New York Journal*.

None was chary about speaking on the issues of the day or about telling the president what course he should follow. They guided the growth of their newspapers, expressed their opinions in print and in person, and believed in the correctness of their high level of activity in the political world. Even policy positions were within their ken. In the spring of 1869, for example, Charles Dana of the *New York Sun* served as temporary chair of a public meeting in behalf of Cuban independence from Spain; the mayor of New York was the permanent chair.[1]

When Oscar King Davis, the *New York Times* Washington correspondent during Theodore Roosevelt's last years in office, spoke with the president about taking a position as a newspaper editor after leaving the White House, they discussed the influence of Charles Dana. According to Davis, Dana was a great editor because of his "keen and constant interest in everything that was going on all around the world and his determination to have something about it to print in the 'Sun.'"[2] The group proposing the position to Roosevelt wanted him for his "inspiration" since "that is what makes a great newspaper."[3]

And that is what Dana and the other publishers provided for their newspapers. They employed people to gather, edit, and write news, but the notion of what constituted news came from the direction of the publishers.

1. James Pollard, *The Presidents and the Press* (New York: Macmillan, 1947), 444.
2. Oscar King Davis, *Released for Publication* (New York: Houghton Mifflin, 1925), 138.
3. Ibid.

---

creation in 1856 of the New York Associated Press led to the rapid distribution of news through press associations. By 1914 participation in the New York Associated Press had risen from the original six newspapers to one hundred newspapers.[29]

Newspaper advances and consolidation made ties to political parties even less important. News became market-driven. The invention of the linotype machine allowed newspapers to run pictures and advertisements with graphics, making papers livelier. This development translated into more revenue to cover the burgeoning costs of printing the news. The telephone sped news to the home office. As rag replaced wood pulp, paper costs fell dramatically. Presidential scholar Elmer E. Cornwell Jr. found that the entire financial structure of journalism changed as the price of newsprint dropped from about 12 cents a pound in 1872 to 3 cents a pound in 1892.[30] Lower costs meant increased circulation so that between 1870 and 1890 daily circulation went up

222 percent with only a 63 percent increase in population. Cornwell suggested that increased literacy and the wider availability of cheap newspapers in attractive formats accounted for the rise.[31]

ADOPTION OF RULES AND STANDARDS

With so many of the Civil War battlefields located near the nation's capital, the new correspondents coming into Washington more than doubled the size of the press corps. By the end of the war, there were forty-nine correspondents listed in the congressional galleries.[32]

Out of the reporting of the war came demands from news organizations for objective news reports. "The heads of the Associated Press were troubled by the warped opinions and twisted reports in news columns, which had helped stir sectional antipathies before the war," noted Douglass Cater, a chronicler of the Washington press corps.[33] As the Associated Press developed, it required objectivity from its correspondents so that they would be able to appeal equally to all of its member newspapers.

In another development, reporters developed name recognition in a way they had not previously. The War Department, which designed and enforced censorship regulations, ruled that stories detailing the actions of war had to carry the name of the correspondent writing it. That began the practice of bylines for reporters, a custom retained after the war.

Despite all these rules, only after the Civil War were standards and rules for congressional coverage formalized. News organizations, in particular, wanted to make sure that journalists with congressional privileges were actually working for news organizations devoted to objective coverage of the government. There was no room in the press galleries for agents of persons or organizations seeking governmental actions in their behalf.

The line between lobbying and journalism became particularly murky during the years of industrial expansion. When the Crédit Mobilier scandal arose in the 1870s, the investigations disclosed that Washington correspondents were lobbying for the passage of specific bills. In 1875 the House decided to expel all journalists who had acted in behalf of legislation.[34]

The resulting questions that arose about the objectivity of the congressional community of correspondents led to the adoption of rules governing admittance to the press galleries and the use of its facilities. In 1879 a set of rules was adopted specifying who could serve as an accredited congressional correspondent. "These rules defined an accreditable correspondent as one whose primary salary came from sending telegraphic dispatches to daily newspapers. The rules also barred lobbying by any member of the press gallery; and prohibited all clerks from executive agencies (although not from congressional committees)," reported Donald Ritchie.[35]

As benign as the gallery rules sounded, their effect was to exclude women from representation because they either worked for weeklies or mailed in their columns on Washington society news to their newspapers.[36] Generally, editors did not believe women to be as astute as men or their pieces to be worth the transmittal costs. Women, however, continued to report from Washington because social reporting was such a central element of both Washington and the White House. Emily Briggs of the *Philadelphia Press* was an exception to the gallery rule as she became one of the first women correspondents to use the telegraph for "spot news" (important late-breaking information). Her dispatches contained "detailed accounts of the people and events she observed from the reporters' galleries or at an evening's social gathering."[37]

THE PRESIDENT AS A NEWS STORY

Down the road from the Capitol, the press was beginning to take an increased interest in the president. On the eve of the Civil War, the Associated Press assigned a correspondent, Henry Villard, to shadow the newly elected Abraham Lincoln (1861–1865) from December until he left Springfield, Illinois, for Washington in early February. Villard was to supply the Associated Press with regular dispatches about events in Springfield, which "was to become for a time the center of political gravitation."[38] The correspondent sat in on Lincoln's morning meetings with political visitors and was privy to all matters under review, including cabinet appointments. Villard went on to become an exceptionally inventive war correspondent who provided firsthand reports of important battles. His dispatches were closely followed by government officials, including the president. Villard was summoned by Lincoln to relate his account of the battle of Fredericksburg and to discuss with the president his assessments of the war.[39]

The first reporter ever assigned to cover a president-elect full time, Henry Villard followed Abraham Lincoln in 1860–1861, thus becoming a forerunner of the modern White House correspondent.

A White House press corps eventually evolved from the reporters who came to the White House for specific purposes. In the case of President Andrew Johnson (1865–1869), many reporters talked with him before his impeachment trial. Both the president and the press recognized the benefits their relationship could have: the president could explain his beliefs about the errors of the impeachment proceedings, and members of the press could report the results of the individual interviews each had had with the president.

In the years after Andrew Johnson left office, the presidency faced considerable congressional opposition. Presidents thus were forced to turn to the public for support of legislation favored by the White House. Interviews and presidential "swings around the circle" were particularly useful tools for eliciting public support. In fact, between 1860 and 1901, the availability of information about the president changed from being episodic to routine. And once individual presidential interviews and the distribution of information about the president were in place, reporters did not want to give up the regular presidential and staff contact.

With the cutting of political ties between newspaper editors and presidents, press relationships had become inherently less cozy. Gone were the days when a president could expect the counsel of an editor on the release of information. Instead, there was an emphasis on recording presidential statements and views. The interview replaced the edited speech. This innovation became a distinctive characteristic of American reporting built, in most respects, on the earlier tradition of printing the statements, debates, and speeches of elected officials. Now, however, reporters also were recording the intentions and desires of officials, including the president.[40]

The modern presidential interview has its roots in Andrew Johnson's presidency. In October 1865 Col. A. K. McClure of the *Franklin Repository* of Chambersburg, Pennsylvania, interviewed President Johnson.[41] McClure, in fact, simply asked the president about his policy intentions and published the president's answers in his newspaper. Over the next two and a half years, President Johnson, as noted earlier, held a dozen more interviews with reporters, seven of them in the year of his 1868 impeachment proceedings. Finally, his lawyers put an end to the sessions.

President Johnson's interviews were complemented by his tours through cities in the Midwest, including Chicago and St. Louis. On such tours, known as "swings around the circle," the president took his message to people outside of Washington. Although his appearances were heavily covered by the local media, in Johnson's case the local newspaper coverage worked to his detriment because his speeches led to the desertion of many of his supporters. As journalism historian Mark Wahlgren Summers described it:

When the president used an address to accuse members of Congress of plotting his assassination or to brand two of the most prominent Republicans on Capitol Hill traitors, when he compared himself to Christ or, in the presence of disabled veterans, posed the rhetorical question

of who had suffered for the Union more than himself, he did himself more damage than the most hostile editorial that radical partisans could have penned.[42]

Although Johnson's successor, Ulysses S. Grant (1869–1877), regularly gave interviews when he was in the field as a general, he gave few as president. Rutherford B. Hayes (1877–1881) also had few formal meetings or interviews with the press. President James A. Garfield (1881) had friends among the media, including Whitelaw Reid, the editor and publisher of the *New York Tribune,* but he gave only one interview, appearing April 24, 1881, just days before his assassination.[43] Chester A. Arthur (1881–1885) who followed him, kept his distance from the press. "From the standpoint of publicity," historian James Pollard noted, "he was perhaps less conspicuous than he had been . . . as customs collector."[44] By the time of Grover Cleveland's administration (1885–1889; 1893–1897) the press had expectations about what information the White House would provide journalists. Overcoming his natural antipathy for the press, Cleveland realized he needed to respond to press inquiries and issue statements through the newspapers when necessary, but he rarely confided in the press or had direct contacts.[45]

Like other presidents, Grover Cleveland received press attention as he traveled. Local reporters chronicled his every move as he took a "swing around the circle" through the western and southern United States. To the South, he brought a message of healing: "There is . . . fairness enough abroad in the land to insure a proper and substantial recognition of the good faith which you have exhibited. . . . [T]he educational advantages and the care which may be accorded to every class of your citizens have a relation to the general character of the entire country."[46]

DEVELOPMENT OF WHITE HOUSE PRESS OPERATIONS

The president's staff was quite minimal during the late nineteenth century. In 1871 President Grant was allowed only a private secretary, stenographer, a few executive clerks, a steward, and a messenger. They were paid out of a total payroll of $13,800, according to Leonard D. White, who has chronicled the development of administrations.[47]

Unfortunately, White House staff positions, including the position of private secretary, held little allure for would-be appointees. Yet President Garfield was wise enough to know that "the man who holds that place can do very much to make or mar the success of an administration" and "ought to be held in higher estimation than Secretary of State."[48] Candidates for the position shared neither his enthusiasm nor his confidence.

Dan Lamont, Grover Cleveland's secretary, counted among his responsibilities that of dispensing routine scheduling and other discretionary information to the press. David Barry, a Washington correspondent during those days, described Cleveland's press habits:

When he had something to communicate to the public he wrote it out and gave it to his private secretary to hand to representatives of the press associations. Mr. Cleveland early developed a fondness for making announcements in this formal way and it is a fact perhaps worth noting that he invariably selected Sunday evening for having his messages promulgated, evidently believing that on Monday morning the newspapers had ample space to devote to his utterances.[49]

President Cleveland released information primarily through a press syndicate headed by George F. Parker, one of the few newsmen Cleveland counted among his friends. This daily contact with the president allowed Parker to make specific recommendations to Cleveland such as suggesting that he provide advance texts of speeches to both friendly and oppositional news organizations. Cleveland's eagerness to reach the public overcame his reticence, and he saw that competent staff people provided reporters with solid presidential information. A Washington correspondent of that time, commenting on Lamont's importance to both reporters and to the president, observed that Lamont "had tact, judgment, knew what to say and how to say it, and what to do and how to do it. He let the 'boys' do most of the talking and guessing, but never allowed them to leave the White House with a wrong impression, or without thinking that they had got about all there was in the story."[50] For the first time, the White House staff was at the heart of the news operation.

Meanwhile, the interest in presidential activities was building. In 1896 William W. Price of the *Washington Evening Star* became the first correspondent to be based at the White House, and he brought to his beat a different approach than those of his predecessors. Price found that his old *modus operandi* from his days with a weekly newspaper in South Carolina—his main assignment had been to interview people leaving the trains as they arrived in town each day[51]—also was suited to the White House in 1896. According to historian George Juergens:

The idea of rounding up news simply by standing outside the White House and interviewing visitors as they arrived and departed was at once obvious and inspired. Price immediately struck a rich lode. It may be that the people he accosted opened up to him because of the sheer surprise at being asked questions under such circumstances. Within a few hours he had accumulated enough material to scrawl hurriedly a story that appeared in the *Star* that evening under the headline "AT THE WHITE HOUSE," the first installment of what would be a regular Price feature in the paper for the next two decades.[52]

The importance of news organizations to William McKinley's administration was presaged in his 1896 campaign. President McKinley (1897–1901) used the press to carry his advertisements and to report on his prepared speeches, which carefully enunciated his campaign themes. In addition, McKinley was the first presidential candidate to be filmed.[53]

Also during the McKinley administration, Congress appropriated the funds for a "secretary and two assistant secretaries, two executive clerks and four clerks, two of whom were telegraphers, as well as numerous doorkeepers and messengers," raising the total White House staff to approximately thirty.[54] Only this additional staff assistance made it possible to provide for the daily needs of the press.

CREATION OF A WHITE HOUSE PRESS FACILITY

By 1898, one year into the administration of William McKinley, White House routines for dealing with the press were in place, White House facilities were being made available on a regular basis for the exclusive use of reporters, and unwritten conventions were being observed by reporters in their dealings with the president. During the Spanish-American War noted journalist Ida Mae Tarbell described the White House press arrangements:

The President, as a matter of fact, has the newspaper man always with him. He is as much a part of the White House personnel as . . . the big police inspector at the door. Accommodations are furnished him there, and his privileges are well-defined and generally recognized. Thus in the outer reception-room of the business part of the White House, a corner containing a well furnished table and plenty of chairs is set aside for reporters. Here representatives of half a dozen or more papers are always to be found, and during Cabinet meetings and at moments of grave importance the number increases many fold. Here they write, note the visitors who are admitted to the President, catch the secretaries as they come and go, and here every evening about ten o'clock they gather around Secretary [John Addison] Porter for a kind of family talk, he discussing with them whatever the events of the day he thinks it wise to discuss.

It is in "Newspaper Row," as the east side of the great north portico is called, that the White House press correspondents flourish most vigorously. Here they gather by the score on exciting days, and, in the shadow of the great white pillars, watch for opportunities to waylay important officials as they come and go. Nobody can get in or out of the Executive Mansion without their seeing him, and it is here that most of the interviews, particularly with the cabinet officers, are held. Close to "Newspaper Row" is a long line of wheels belonging to messengers and telegraph boys, alert, swift little chaps, a half dozen of whom are always in waiting at the foot of the big columns, discussing the war, or on warm days catching the forty winks of sleep they are always sadly in need of.

It is part of the unwritten law of the White House that the newspaper men shall never approach the President as he passes to and fro near their alcove or crosses the portico to his carriage, unless he himself stops and talks to them. This he occasionally does, for he knows all of the reporters by name and treats them with uniform kindness. If a man disappears, Mr. McKinley is sure to inquire soon what has become of him, and if one falls ill, he asks regularly after him.[55]

Thus under McKinley, for the first time a place was set aside in the White House for the exclusive use of reporters and the staff assigned to deal with reporters on a regular basis. According to historian Lewis L. Gould, the "president's secretary, John Addison Porter, circulated constantly, and at noon and 4:00 p.m. he spoke formally with the newsmen."[56] By the end of the McKinley administration, the staff was clipping information and editorial opinion from newspapers for the president's daily perusal. Moreover, the release of major presidential messages and speeches had been coordinated so that all newspapers and press services would receive equal treatment.[57] By the time of McKinley's assassination in 1901, the following procedures were in place: presidential speeches and texts were distributed regularly to news organizations on an equal basis; permanent space was available for reporters in the White House; senior staff were responsible for the president's press relations; the White House was involved in making arrangements for the press traveling with the president; a press briefing was held daily; a rudimentary news summary was prepared for the president to read; and a press corps was assigned to cover the White House. These procedures remain at the heart of the arrangements provided today for those covering the president.

The present contours of the relationship between the president and the press were in place as well. Presidential statements and speeches were made available to reporters, and the president's staff answered questions about his actions and the nuances of policy. The White House had begun its routines of providing the reporters with information in forms they could best use, with an adequate amount of lead time to prepare their stories, and in a permanent place set aside for their use. Reporters, for their part, had established the White House as a beat. In addition, they had settled on the ways in which they gathered information and the importance of the interview to their concept of a story. Those interviews could be with staff members, departmental secretaries, or members of Congress. Their most important interview was the presidential one, but those interviews were not a hallmark of this period. That would come in the next stages.

The President Meets the Press:
1901–1932

Many of the formal structures and tacit understandings that underlie today's relationship between the president and the news media were shaped significantly in the period from 1901 to 1932. Four important developments marked this period.

First, the president became a central actor in a federal government expanding its scope of activity. At the turn of the century, and under the aegis of Theodore Roosevelt, the United States had become a world power and its president a world leader. On the domestic front, the president's policy agenda included railroad regulation, passage of a Pure Food and Drug Act, and initiation of government-sponsored conservation activities, including a conservation corps. The increase in activity generated a commensurate increase in public attention to the chief executive's activities.

A second development of this period was the establishment of the presidential press conference as an instrument through which the president could inform and respond to the Washington press corps. From a rather informal exchange in Theodore Roosevelt's administration, it assumed a more formal, public, and egalitarian form in the Wilson administration and continuing into those of Harding, Coolidge, and Hoover. Since its inception in March 1913, the press conference has proved enduring as a central meeting place for presidents and those who cover them and their administrations. In a related development, rules were established to govern both small private and large public

meetings between the president and reporters. Many of these rules remain the basis of today's interactions between the president and the press. Their mutual dependency evolved naturally as reporters struggled to define the nature of their relationship with the president in the larger context of news gathering. Over the course of this struggle, several prominent correspondents became confidants and advisers to presidents. This aspect of the relationship waned, however, in later periods as procedures established at the beginning of the century gradually shifted toward a more egalitarian model.

Third, in this era the White House press staff, headed by a presidential press secretary, became fully responsible for handling the president's daily relations with news organizations and for servicing the news needs of a White House press corps.

And, fourth, the presidency became an important institution for prominent news organizations to cover regularly.

THE PRESIDENT ON CENTER STAGE

When President Theodore Roosevelt (1901–1909) came into office, he was an important official but hardly a national news center; Congress, and particularly the Senate, held center stage. But all that soon changed. Washington correspondent Louis Ludlow described how:

It would not be stating the whole truth to say that [Roosevelt] made news. He was news. His very personality reflected news. He exuded news at every pore. Even the way in which he said and did things made news.

The ordinary person's conventional "I'm pleased to meet you" suggests nothing to write about, but when President Roosevelt exclaimed, "Dee-lighted!" and showed two glistening rows of ivories, he made copy for the press.[58]

Earlier presidents had chosen to distance themselves from reporters. Roosevelt preferred instead to capitalize on a personal relationship with the correspondents. He sought their friendship and encouraged their reporting. A magnetic force resulted, which drew correspondents to the White House when he was there and around the country when he was on the road on one of his many swings around the circle.

President Roosevelt turned to reporters to publicize himself and his policies. For him, the correspondents—not the publishers or editors—were important. Leo Rosten, chronicler of the creation of the Washington press corps, noted that Roosevelt, in what was fairly typical of his publicity style, called in about fifty correspondents to announce the creation of the First Conservation Congress.[59] Roosevelt "knew the value and potent influence of a news paragraph written as he wanted it written and disseminated through the proper influential channels better than any man who ever occupied the White House, before him, or since," assessed David Barry, a journalist who covered his administration. He also knew that "editorial articles do not mold public opinion" and that "editors are nowadays more apt to follow public opinion than to lead it."[60]

For Theodore Roosevelt, caring about news articles meant getting involved in their direction and preparation. He did not

Photographers covering the White House pose on the South Lawn in 1918.

hesitate to suggest possible news articles and news paragraphs to reporters, and once he even drafted himself what he wanted sent over the wires. When a bill to control railroad rates was being considered by the Senate, an attorney working for the Standard Oil Company sent a letter to selected senators suggesting how they should vote on individual elements of the bill. According to Barry, "The newspaper account of that incident created a world-wide sensation, and blocked the attempt of those who sought to amend the bill in behalf of certain interests, and the man who gave the story to the newspapers and who wrote the preliminary news item that was sent to the afternoon papers was the President of the United States himself."[61] When an issue was important to the president, he put his redoubtable energy into the publicity element in its passage.

In the spring of 1905, when congressional action on railroad rate regulation was stymied, President Roosevelt launched a publicity campaign that took him through the Southwest and the Midwest. He continued in October with a trip to the South. "Invoking the name of his mother as a native of Georgia, and of his two uncles as Confederate veterans, he made such legislation almost a matter of sectional loyalty. It was as if he 'himself fired the last two shots for the *Alabama* instead of his uncles.'"[62] Back at the White House, Roosevelt kept up his campaign for railroad regulation by providing reporters with information on malfeasance by the railroad companies. His multipronged publicity attack featured local as well as national reporters and news writers from both magazines and newspapers.

President William Howard Taft (1909–1913), in contrast, paid little attention to publicity preparations, including major speeches such as one on the Payne-Aldrich Bill, which he lauded as the "best tariff bill the Republican party ever passed."[63] The bill was in fact extremely unpopular, particularly in the congressional district of James A. Tawney of Minnesota whom Taft was

trying to aid with a campaign appearance. Later, Taft confessed that he had not prepared the speech until he was on the train to Winona.[64] Moreover, he had not sought information about the nature of the district and the issues alive in it. Unfortunately for Taft, Tawney went down to a resounding defeat.

President Woodrow Wilson (1913–1921), who shared with Roosevelt a sense for the importance of a public address, revived the custom of delivering his State of the Union address in person, a practice moribund since Jefferson's presidency. The more he had a hand in public addresses or in press conferences, he believed, the more likely that his words would be recorded faithfully and prominently displayed. His was a public presidency, and his choices of forums continually reinforced that theme. Wilson also used personal addresses before joint sessions of Congress to concentrate public attention on particular issues. Political scientist Elmer Cornwell calculated that in his first term Wilson made twelve appearances before the Congress, in addition to his State of the Union addresses.[65]

If vehicles other than newspapers had then existed, Wilson would have had an even larger choice of strategies for getting to the public. One of Wilson's few close associates in the press, Ray Stannard Baker, suggested that "the radio, if it had been in use at that time, might have proved a godsend to Wilson: for he would have been able to secure direct contact with his public, broadening his influence as the fragmentary reporting of his addresses could not do."[66]

America's entry into World War I stimulated President Wilson to establish a special vehicle to coordinate publicity information. The Committee on Public Information became the first sustained effort to coordinate White House information with that from the executive branch departments and agencies. George Creel, a Wilson appointee heading the group, carefully constructed an image of the president as chief executive and commander in chief. According to Cornwell, the Creel Committee saw the war in Wilsonian terms. "Mobilization, diplomacy, and peacemaking" were all orchestrated to "impress on the public a heightened sense of the importance of the presidency" and Wilson.[67] Among the publicity strategies devised by Creel was the *Official Bulletin,* which was distributed to post offices throughout the country as well as to military installations.

Succeeding presidents Harding, Coolidge, and Hoover relied primarily on press conferences to communicate their messages to the public but added professional speechwriters and use of the radio to the presidential communications arsenal. President Warren Harding (1921–1923) hired speechwriter Judson Welliver, who proved so successful that President Calvin Coolidge kept him on. Coolidge (1923–1929) was the first president to give his State of the Union message not only in person but also on radio. Recognizing that the new medium allowed him to speak directly with the citizens of the country and communicate both his persona and his brand of leadership, Coolidge began to broadcast a monthly radio program in 1924. President Herbert Hoover (1929–1933), too, used radio but preferred it only for traditional occasions such as the State of the Union address. "Radio as a presidential tool would not and could not come into its own until it was realized that only speeches prepared exclusively with an unseen radio audience in mind would make possible full exploitation of the medium," Cornwell suggested.[68] Presidential radio would have to wait for Franklin Roosevelt to shape fully its contours into a powerful force to promote programs and policy.

PRESIDENTIAL PRESS CONFERENCE

Theodore Roosevelt was the first president to make himself regularly available to reporters. He met with them at all hours of the day, individually and in groups, while he was at his desk, over a meal, and at unusual locations. Often his group meetings meant receiving a half dozen reporters while he was being shaved. Oscar King Davis, a correspondent for the *New York Times,* described the scene as he met the president at shaving time:

Every day, at one o'clock, Delaney, a colored messenger employed at the Treasury Department, came over to the White House and shaved the President. There was, of course, no regular barber's chair, but Delaney did the best he could with a big armchair. The shaving hour was always a good one to see the President, for it gave the interviewer a better chance to say what he wanted to say in full, as the President, with his face covered with lather and Delaney's razor sweeping over it, was rather at a disadvantage as to talking.[69]

Unlike his predecessors, Theodore Roosevelt was no stranger to regular give and take with reporters. As governor of New York, he had held daily press meetings and recognized the value of direct dealings with reporters and the efficient use of staff. Both this practice and his skillful staff followed him into the White House after William McKinley's assassination in 1901. William Loeb, his assistant from Albany, who had both an ability to deal with reporters and a knowledge of news gathering,

was able to enhance the likelihood of good play in what reporters produced.

Taft had a very different view of press relations. On the day of his inauguration, reporters received their "first, emphatic demonstration that it was not only a new President in the White House, but, in fact, a new man, and not at all the pleasant, genial, helpful, good-natured man we had known as Secretary of War."[70] Taft was no longer as cooperative with reporters as when he was a cabinet officer. The president's secretary, Fred Carpenter, informed reporters that when the president wanted to see the newsmen, he would send for them. Wednesdays were a possibility, but such meetings were totally at his direction. Reporters, then, had to resort to other means of acquiring presidential information—ones less favorable to the president. "Correspondents took advantage of the four mornings a week from 10:30 a.m. to noon that Taft set aside to see senators and representatives," historian George Juergens recounted. "They would feed questions to the president through their congressional contacts, on the understanding that nothing would be said about who was actually doing the asking."[71] Leaks also proved to be a fruitful source of information on the executive branch.

Woodrow Wilson, too, was most comfortable dealing with reporters at arm's length. But Wilson did bring reporters together as a group, which was the first step in the evolution of the formal modern press conference. These regularly scheduled gatherings were open to all reporters on an equal basis; members of the press chose the questions; and the president chose how and when to answer. The first formal press conference was held March 15, 1913, at 12:45 on a Saturday afternoon, eleven days after Wilson's inauguration. "Although no transcript exists of the dialogue in the Oval Office between the president and approximately 125 reporters, it is clear the session went badly," wrote Juergens.[72] A week later, the second conference attracted almost two hundred reporters, who this time headed for the East Room, the only White House room large enough to handle a group of that size. Clearly, then, the press conference was a successful idea even if Wilson did not enjoy the meetings.

Like Roosevelt, Wilson felt the press conference was a valuable publicity tool and one particularly suited to current issues; these gatherings led to positive articles on the front pages of major newspapers. In June 1913, for example, the president called on Congress to create a Federal Reserve system, and the next day the *New York Times* featured the story, commenting that "in the course of the day the President made a splendid defense of the currency bill." Generally, the *Times,* Cornwell found, gave great play to a presidential initiative, including a page-one story on the message and the press conference text.[73] In another conference, the president became his own assertive publicist when he suggested, "'There is one question, which, if I am properly informed, I would ask me, if I were you.'" He then emphasized that he had no intention of compromising on a wool provision in tariff legislation: "When you get a chance, just say that I am not the kind that considers compromises when I once take my position. Just note that down, so that there will be nothing more of the sort transmitted in the press."[74]

Reporters, having grown used to individual meetings with presidents, did not like Wilson's group sessions. The president reverted to his schoolmaster role toward undergraduates, noted Barry. "The newspaper men would, when they screwed up courage enough to do so, ask questions bearing upon various phases of the news of the day, and the president would answer or sidestep them as he chose, sometimes elucidating the subject with a little inside information but as a rule not throwing any new light on the subject."[75]

The reporters sensed the president disliked those meetings and always looked forward to their conclusion. In the early days of his term, conferences were held regularly on Mondays and Thursdays, but they dwindled early in 1915 to each Tuesday before being abandoned altogether. The sinking of the ocean liner *Lusitania* in May 1915 seemed to provide the excuse Wilson needed to cut back. His annoyance was directed generally at what he considered the time wasted in preparation and the poor quality of the questions posed to him.

Other presidents used press conferences to attract attention to matters of particular interest. Warren Harding structured his conferences to stimulate the exchange between the president and correspondents and thoroughly enjoyed the encounters. As former publisher of an Ohio newspaper, the Marion *Star*, Harding was used to the news-gathering business. He discussed cabinet meetings and problems in the conduct of his office at twice-weekly sessions. Not reluctant to talk, Harding spoke on a background basis (words can be used without attributing them to the president), but he often went "off the record" (neither the words nor their source may be cited). *(See "Classifications of White House Information," p. 126.)* Reporters were expected to keep these off-the-record discussions private, but there was inevitable seepage into the public domain. Harding's concern with this eventuality stemmed more from possible inadvertent errors than unwanted publicity. Ground rules, therefore, were initiated to require reporters to submit in writing the questions to be put to the president. The rules were relaxed during the course of Harding's term, but they did not prevent a presidential gaffe when Harding responded to a written question about the provisions in the Four Power Treaty being negotiated by the Conference for the Limitation of Armaments related to the protection of the Japanese islands.[76] While those negotiating the treaty intended such protection, the president responded that the treaty itself did not. Secretary of State Charles Evans Hughes intervened, and that evening the White House issued a statement correcting the president's misstatement.

Calvin Coolidge continued to require that questions be submitted in advance when he succeeded Harding, and, like Harding, Coolidge spoke with reporters from his office in the West Wing of the White House. But without the bond of a shared profession, he lacked ease in dealing with the press. "As the reporters, between fifty and one hundred in number, stood silent-

ly in the executive office taking notes, the president leafed through the pile of written queries and answered those which he wished to answer, ignoring the others," described F. B. Marbut.[77] Another Washington correspondent, J. Fred Essary, who covered the administration, told of reporters collectively responding to this habit by all writing the same question. Leafing through the pile, Coolidge picked out the final one in the stack. "I have here a question about the condition of the children in Porto Rico," said Coolidge to the group of newsmen, none of whom had asked that question.[78] Neither the reporters nor the president divulged the true content of the question they had actually submitted.

What frustrated reporters most was the paucity of material for their stories. "What he says is mostly noncommittal, neutral, evasive," complained Frank Kent of the *Baltimore Sun*. "To many questions he replies that he has no exact information on the subject but expects to have it shortly, or that he is informed some department has the matter in hand and is handling it in a satisfactory manner. Even when his replies are definite, which is rare, they are flat and meatless."[79] Other Coolidge practices rankled reporters as well. For example, they chafed under the new rule that the president could not be quoted either directly or indirectly. Thus in order to use information, reporters created a contrivance: the White House spokesman.[80]

President Hoover also required presubmitted questions, but he tightened the time frame to twenty-four hours in advance and, like Coolidge, made his own choice of responses. By now reporters were restive, and they regarded Hoover as a roadblock to the release of information. As the economy worsened in 1931, so did Hoover's press relations. From the beginning of June until the end of November 1932, Hoover held only eight press conferences.[81] By the end of the administration, not many reporters attended the few conferences that were held.

NEW RULES GOVERNING THE RELATIONSHIP

As open as President Theodore Roosevelt was to certain reporters, he had a set of rules—and punishments—governing his relationships with correspondents and news organizations. Roosevelt's rules were not negotiated, they were announced. On his first day in office he invited David Barry and three colleagues to the White House to discuss their relationship. His confidence in them would be demonstrated by keeping them apprised, he declared, but "if any of the reporters should at any time violate a confidence or publish news that the President thought ought not to be published, he should be punished by having legitimate news withheld from him."[82] During his years as governor, such a punishment had been leveled against a reporter in Albany, Roosevelt told them, and that man still would not be privy to any White House news.[83] Members of the press corps consigned to the Roosevelt-invented Ananais Club faced a news blackout.

President Taft, like Roosevelt, set the rules. Taft kept personal contacts with reporters at a minimum, allowing press relations to be handled through his staff and only occasionally meeting with individual correspondents, such as Oscar King Davis. He selected the publications he would favor with a response, usually those with which he had had a long-standing acquaintance or friendship. President Wilson's rules, in contrast, focused on group settings and equal presidential access. Press conference information was "just between us" when the president said so. Otherwise, material could be used without attribution to the president himself.

Herbert Hoover established a formal set of rules to govern the terms of the release of information provided in press conferences. His rules included three tiers of information. First, information on the record could be quoted directly as the president's words. For the second tier, material could be used but without the president's name. At the third tier was information given on a confidential basis with the understanding that it would not be used in any way. The device of the "White House spokesman" was put to rest in the Hoover years,[84] but these three distinctions continue to form the basis of White House information policies. (See "Classifications of White House Information," p. 126.)

President Hoover had trouble with reporters—not over the rules but over the manner in which he sought to apply them. The Hoover White House sought to prevent the distribution of official information, something it could not accomplish. At a press conference on October 6, 1931, Hoover tried to prevent the publication of reports that a conference on the depression and unemployment would be held at the White House. "He said there would be no announcement, not even a statement of the persons attending or of the general program discussed," wrote Leo Rosten. "He told the newspapermen not to 'waylay' participants as they left the conference." But waylay them they did. Richard Oulahan of the *New York Times* and Hay Hayden of the *Detroit News* warned "the President that it would be out of the question to expect the newspapermen not to supply the public with information about one of the most important events of the year."[85] Rebellion was reporters' only recourse. Armed with a petition of more than one hundred signatories, they appealed to the Board of Governors of the National Press Club to create a committee to consider the problem of the administration's refusal to provide information on government activities.[86]

PRESS CORPS CONFIDANTS AND ADVISERS

As the twentieth century began, there was a well-laid history of journalistic advice to presidents. During Andrew Jackson's administration, Amos Kendall had helped the president to craft speeches. Journalist George F. Parker had advised President Cleveland on the release of information to the press, and, to facilitate the process, Parker had formed a press syndicate to handle the distribution of White House information. By his own account, Parker met frequently with the president, and in Cleveland's second term the two discussed cabinet selections. Cleveland had not yet decided on any appointees, Parker said. "At this

interview, I had occasion to bring forward and to discuss the names of five men fitted to become Mr. Cleveland's advisers," Parker related. "Of these, two declined appointment, and the remainder were sworn into his Cabinet after his second inauguration."[87] The definition of *conflict of interest* was fuzzy in those days. There was no widely held understanding among reporters that newspaper work precluded participation in White House decision making.

In the administration of Theodore Roosevelt, as reporters eagerly sought a close relationship, he, in turn, gave credence to their opinions and, most especially, to their knowledge. Correspondents often served as his foils and advisers as illustrated by the role they played in preparing presidential speeches. His preparation for a major address on transportation suggested the routine he often employed. "The President had laboriously prepared his great speech on the transportation problem . . . and Secretary [William] Loeb called in the correspondents in order that the President might 'try it on the dog' before he went out to Indianapolis to deliver it," observed journalist Louis Ludlow. When the president read his speech, "warm words of approbation came from different correspondents." Only one correspondent remained silent, Judson Welliver, who only recently had come to Washington from Iowa. When Roosevelt asked Welliver what he thought, the correspondent responded that he did not "think much of it." After prodding by the president, Welliver continued: "I have studied this subject a long time and I tell you that you are going about this business in the wrong way." Welliver's fellow correspondents were astonished. "No other correspondent had ever dared to start a rough house with the impetuous President. But Roosevelt craved fuller information. He pressed Welliver for his detailed views," recounted Ludlow. At a second encounter the next evening, President Roosevelt and Welliver redrafted the Indianapolis speech and the president "from that night became a staunch advocate of the railroad valuation plan," wrote Ludlow. Welliver emerged as a valuable informal aide. He remained at the White House for several administrations and, among other things, handled press relations and speech writing for President Harding. In the Roosevelt administration, however, he was there as a journalist, yet that did not preclude his involvement in White House decisions and actions.[88]

As much as William Howard Taft disdained reporters' advice, there were times when he paid attention. During the 1908 election campaign, Oscar Davis was concerned that Taft had not defined a theme in his speeches. Davis and fellow Washington correspondent Dick Lindsay, representing the *Kansas City Star and Times,* urged Taft to become more involved in developing speeches with specific themes. "So Lindsay and I kept at Mr. Taft to prepare some speeches," Davis said. "We pointed out several issues that he might well discuss, and he replied that he had handled them all in his speech of acceptance." That night, Davis and Lindsay spent hours tearing apart the nomination acceptance speech. The next day they gave Taft a series of speeches dealing with discrete topics. Ultimately he did not give them, but, significantly, the correspondents had felt free to make their suggestions.[89]

OFFICE OF PRESS SECRETARY

The foundation for the office of press secretary was laid in the late nineteenth-century administrations of Cleveland and McKinley with the work of staff members Dan Lamont, George Cortelyou, and John Addison Porter. They stood in for the reluctant presidents and for the first time provided official White House information and guidance in behalf of the chief executives they served. (Earlier, the presidential private secretary, the equivalent of the contemporary chief of staff, had served as the president's surrogate, preparing information and providing news-gathering arrangements.) George Cortelyou, secretary to McKinley, handled all press relations as well as the president's congressional contacts. This required him to organize whatever information the president might need and also preside over the White House staff. Employed by three presidents, Cortelyou saw his work for Theodore Roosevelt bring him particular attention, in part because as a master publicist the president added luster to his secretaries' reputations. Both Cortelyou and William Loeb had more press exposure than their predecessors precisely because Roosevelt was so publicity-prone.

Notable also before the formal creation in 1930 of the press secretary's position were Joseph Tumulty (Wilson), who shaped and broadened the task of presidential press relations still further, and secretaries Charles Norton (Taft), Judson Welliver (Harding), and George B. Christian (Harding), who maintained the traditions set by their predecessors, paving the way for many of the practices in use today. They provided the speech texts reporters needed, arranged press conferences, held daily briefings, answered questions, and sought to represent the interests of reporters to press-shy presidents.

William Loeb's familiarity with press routines and with Roosevelt's penchant for publicity went back to his service during Roosevelt's New York governorship. This relationship was of inestimable value to both the president and the press, according to Henry L. Stoddard, a Washington correspondent at the time:

No one ever knew every thought, purpose and mood of a President as Loeb knew Roosevelt's. He was in truth the President's other self;—he was the one man who could act for Roosevelt in full confidence that he was doing as the President would have him to do. There is not much in the Roosevelt Administration that does not, in some way, bear the impress of Loeb's judgment.[90]

Loeb also knew the rules reporters lived by, and he worked on stories with individual reporters.

The styles of those handling presidential press relations usually reflected the interests of their presidents. A press-shy president, William Howard Taft first chose Fred Carpenter, a man with curiously little interest in either directing press inquiries to the president or pleading the cases of journalists. After Carpenter was succeeded by Charles Norton, relations with reporters

took an upswing. As described by Oscar Davis, "We began to get back into something of our old status with Mr. Taft, and it was no longer such a rare thing to get an appointment with him, even on very short notice."[91]

Joseph Tumulty, secretary to President Wilson, struggled to pick up the slack when Wilson's news conferences ceased in 1915. Tumulty became the intermediary between "these two entities whose contacts otherwise remained at best formal and reserved."[92] In addition, Tumulty was able to interpret successfully President Wilson's thoughts and actions. David Lawrence, who served as a Washington correspondent during that period, reported that "time and again, Secretary Tumulty revealed the President's views and articulated the administration viewpoint with more skill than the President showed in his conferences with the newspapermen."[93] He put the best face on the president's actions and made a good case with his boss for release of information to reporters. Tumulty also was familiar with reporters' routines and convinced the president that advance preparation of speeches encouraged wide public circulation. Press associations required a full week to distribute speeches to member papers. Once World War I had begun and President Wilson's clearinghouse for the release of all government information, the Committee on Public Information, was established, Tumulty discontinued his daily briefings and his publicity work.

In the Coolidge White House, for the first time, the responsibility for arrangements for the press traveling with the president was added to other staff duties. In the Hoover administration the first presidential press secretary, George Akerson, was appointed. With Congress providing funding for three secretarial positions instead of the traditional one, the president was able to have one senior aide devote his full attention to press matters. Akerson instituted twice-daily briefings and also provided space for photographers in the renovated White House West Wing. But he was not regarded as an especially able staff person and his successor, Theodore G. Joslin, was held in even lower esteem.[94] It remained for Stephen T. Early to shape the position during his years as the press secretary to President Franklin Roosevelt.

ORGANIZATION OF THE PRESS CORPS

After the congressional Standing Committee on the Press Galleries was formed, needs beyond the creation of rules of appropriate professional conduct for the press emerged. In 1908 news organizations banded together to form the National Press Club. Located in a building across from the Treasury Department, the Press Club provided a place where Washington institutions could quickly distribute press releases to a large number of news organizations. "The news from the Government departments and various publicity agencies are delivered at the club every day and are spread out on a long table. Every member of the club is at liberty to help himself to this literary free lunch," Louis Ludlow reported.[95] The National Press Club, however, did not coordinate or distribute the news. With many bureaus for out-of-town newspapers located in the building, the assembled journalists fell into a social as well as professional camaraderie.

Common interests brought together another group. On February 25, 1914, the White House Correspondents Association was established. Its first task was to address the difficulty of getting reporters to accept certain tacit understandings that arose from presidential press conferences. On July 17, 1913, when Woodrow Wilson went off the record, several reporters violated the unspoken agreement that governed the reporting of such remarks. Before this incident, the president had indicated when something was off the record and reporters had respected his wish. "The violation threatened for a time to end the conferences altogether," reported George Juergens. Instead, reporters allowed Joseph Tumulty, the president's secretary, to decide who would be allowed to attend conferences. "When eleven charter members came together several months later to found an organization through which reporters would handle the responsibility themselves, the press demonstrated a new level of professionalism," noted Juergens.[96] The organization was most important for legitimating the notion that there was an amorphous group that could be characterized as the White House press corps. (In reality, the organization has not served as much more than a social one, organizing an annual dinner attended by the president and those who cover the White House.)

The Modern White House Publicity Apparatus

When Franklin Roosevelt (1933–1945) assumed the office of president, approximately thirty-five people were on the White House payroll.[97] By 1995 that figure had increased to 430—four hundred full-time employees plus thirty detailees from government agencies.[98] The enormous increase in staff during the years has related directly to the development of the presidency and the White House as the policy center of the American political system. Throughout most of the twentieth century, the public and the various elites in and around government have come to expect the president to initiate policy action. With this responsibility has come the need to communicate an administration's programs to the president's many constituencies.

PUBLICIZING ADMINISTRATION POLICY

The turbulent times of the early 1930s saw the president become the dominant force in the American political system. Congress depended on the chief executive to introduce legislation to serve as its agenda, its members waited on the president's budget before formulating its appropriations and revenue measures, and the people depended on the president to give notice of the condition of the nation. When Franklin Roosevelt took office in 1933, financial disaster was looming. The public prayed for the president to find a way to create a stable economy and to communicate a sense of hope for the future to each citizen.

Those in government also expected two things from the president: action and communication. They wanted something

done to restore the nation and expected the president to communicate with them about his plans. Roosevelt delivered on both points. In his administration, executive action and communication reached new levels. Indeed, the high level of public expectation of a president's policy performance that crystallized in the Roosevelt years served as a base on which to build for those who followed him. Through his policy initiatives and his explanations of his actions, President Roosevelt established the standards by which his successors would be judged.

On March 5, 1933, the nation tuned into Franklin Roosevelt's inauguration speech to hear him articulate the path to stability. His specific solutions were laid out in only the most general of terms, but here was leadership. "In declaring there was nothing to fear but fear, Roosevelt had minted no new platitude; Hoover had said the same thing repeatedly for three years," wrote historian William E. Leuchtenburg. "Yet Roosevelt had nonetheless made his greatest single contribution to the politics of the 1930's: the instillation of hope and courage in the people."[99] Later that day, Roosevelt ordered a national bank holiday and called for Congress to come into session March 9. The strong inaugural speech, together with the promise to pay attention to the instability of the banks, lent confidence to a shaken populace. The president's banking message was read to Congress on March 9, and the accompanying bill was considered and passed by both houses within six and a half hours. It was signed by the chief executive an hour later. One week after his inauguration, the president reported to the nation through radio. In what became the first of twenty-seven "fireside chats," the president called on the public to return their money to the banks. What followed, then, was not the drain on the banks that many observers had expected. Instead, people heeded the president's request and deposited funds in the reopened banks. In seven days, noted Leuchtenburg, Roosevelt was able to "make an impression which Hoover had never been able to create—of a man who knew how to lead and had faith in the future."[100]

Roosevelt reached for a new medium to go directly to the public: radio. The president had a voice that could and did soothe a nation, and he appreciated the lack of distortion radio could provide. "Radio for the first time put the president and his public in face-to-face contact," observed Elmer Cornwell in *Presidential Leadership of Public Opinion.* "Cutting, paraphrasing, quoting out of context, adverse editorial comment, and other alleged newspaper practices which annoyed Chief Executives were ruled out."[101]

"Fireside chats" built support for the president and his programs, and only occasionally for his legislative initiatives (in only four out of the twenty-seven chats did the president very clearly discuss legislation under consideration).[102] The first half dozen chats, wrote Cornwell, "found the President carefully reviewing . . . the steps that the New Deal had taken to deal with the depression, the new legislation that had been passed, and the programs that had been set up."[103] Later presidents adopted his strategy of using the latest electronic technology to make direct contact with the people.

The forceful FDR transformed presidential press relations. He held 998 Oval Office news conferences during his twelve years in office.

From 1933 to 1968, Washington took on even greater importance in addressing domestic problems. By the end of the period, there were government programs for consumer protection, medical care for the poor and elderly, rent subsidies for the poor, housing, food stamps, automobile safety, airport and hospital construction, environmental protection, aid to higher education, and equal employment. The initiative for most of these pieces of legislation came from the president, and only under his aegis was the legislation passed.

The nature of the times also led to a concentration of presidential power. Crisis was the prevailing condition. Sometimes, as for the depression, it was an economic crisis; at other times a war gripped the nation. World War II, the Korean War, and the Vietnam War all took place during this thirty-five year period. The cold war that existed between the United States and the Soviet Union precipitated the undercurrents that ran through most foreign and defense policies. Crises involve a president as few other situations do. It was only natural that the president became the focal point of the nation and that the news media became his path to its citizens. Both presidents and news organizations are elevated in crisis situations.

The demands for new policies were matched by expectations that the president would effectively communicate his actions to his various publics. This required the existence of a communications operation that would provide in a timely way both the documents and the people to elaborate on their importance. To meet these expectations, presidents and their staffs created a publicity operation that could respond to the increased communications demands on the president. Thus from 1933 to 1968,

the duties of the presidential press secretary were further defined and developed and a Press Office was created to handle the distribution of information. Today, the White House press corps has come to rely on the press secretary's daily briefing and on the regular distribution of information through Press Office officials to reporters as they put together their stories on presidential activities.

GROWING PRESIDENTIAL VULNERABILITY

Beginning in 1968 the presidency developed a vulnerability it did not have earlier. The president and his staff were required to perform as the public expected in an environment of declining political resources. With the decentralization of Congress in the 1970s, which placed great authority with subcommittee chairs, presidential policy action became a much more difficult process because so many more people had the power to shape legislation. Political parties began to have less meaning to the average voter than in Roosevelt's time, making it is more difficult for presidents to appeal successfully for public support. Presidents themselves were another source of vulnerability. In 1974 Richard Nixon became the first president to resign his office; he was threatened with impeachment because of the illegal activities undertaken by those who worked in his name and because of evidence that he had obstructed justice in his attempts to thwart a federal investigation. When Nixon entered office, he replaced a president, Lyndon Johnson, who had lost public support through a discredited Vietnam policy.

In the years 1933–1968, the president represented the public

The *Washington Post*'s Bob Woodward, left, and Carl Bernstein, right, broke many of the Watergate stories that led to President Nixon's eventual resignation.

trust. When a problem surfaced in the society, it was directed his way for solution. Since 1969, however, some presidents and many White House staff members have been charged—in print, on the air, and in the halls of Congress—with misusing that trust. Presidents or their staffs have been accused of, among other things, violating the law, using the office for private gain, having financial irregularities in previous business transactions and political campaigns, promoting failed policies, and being "out of touch" with public sentiment and need. Perhaps reflecting this trend, which has run through the past thirty years, no president except for Ronald Reagan has served two full terms.

In the face of an increasingly restless and skeptical press, the White House has sought new avenues of publicity and additional communications structures to direct the selling of the president and the president's program. President Nixon overhauled the White House communications structure to take account of the new vulnerability. He created additional structures and redesigned the traditional ones. Because the Press Office operation was focused only on one segment of the nation's press—the Washington press corps—the Nixon administration, concluding correctly that there were other press elements on which to draw—created the Office of Communications as a complement to the existing Press Office. The Office of Communications handled three aspects of presidential publicity: the out-of-town press (newspapers with regional and local focus, not national papers such as the *New York Times, Washington Post,* and *Wall Street Journal*) and the specialty press (newspapers and magazines that target a specific audience, such as Hispanic readers), long-range planning, and coordination of executive branch public information officers. The parallel staff organizations of daily operations and future planning continue to define the White House communications operations nearly thirty years later.

Today, one of the central activities of the White House staff is publicizing the president and the president's program. The approximately one hundred staff members (out of the four hundred full-time White House employees)[104] of the frontline publicity units—including the Press Office and the Office of Communications—answer the questions of reporters, make arrangements for their travel, and prepare documents, such as transcripts of the press secretary's daily briefing. The Press Office also ensures that reporters are able to see and question the president regularly. In recent years, the Office of Communications has expanded the White House press functions to include the preparation of materials for the out-of-town and specialty press. In addition, its functions include managing the television appearances of administration spokespersons, coordinating administration information, and supplying speeches for the president.

Others in the White House who are concerned with the communications element of the president's program and publicity matters are the chief of staff, who manages the president's time and the information going into the Oval Office; the people who schedule the president's appointments and make advance preparations for presidential appearances; and those responsible for managing the president's relations with the Congress, interest groups, and political constituencies. Thus almost all of the White House senior staff are concerned with presidential publicity.

A brief survey of the president's top staff indicates the importance of publicity to their work. In 1996 sixteen White House staff members were at the top salary level of $125,000; the chief of staff earned $133,600. Of those sixteen people, three (the press secretary, the communications coordinator, and the speech writing and research assistant) had jobs directly related to communications. Of the remaining thirteen, almost all had a significant communications element in their work. The national security adviser and the director of the National Economic Council briefed the press at times of important administration initiatives and crises, and they regularly answered the queries of reporters. Others, such as those who handled legislative relations, public liaison, and political affairs, used publicity as a major strategy in building support for the president's program. The first lady's chief of staff also considered publicity matters. The only two people in the top salary range who did not have a direct communications component to their work were the deputy counsel and the cabinet secretary. They could have elected to answer reporters' questions, however. These figures suggest that presidential publicity is important in the operations of practically every warren within the White House. After all, the decisions that rise to the presidential level are those that cannot be solved elsewhere. Once a presidential judgment is made, acceptance most often has to be sold to the reluctant.

THE PRESIDENTIAL PRESS SECRETARY

In the years from Franklin Roosevelt's administration through that of Lyndon Johnson, the White House press operation consisted of the press secretary and the Press Office. In the Nixon administration, however, the press operation was bifurcated. As noted, a long-range planning operation, the Office of Communications, was created to emphasize coordination among White House and departmental units. The Press Office continued to handle the daily publicity routines under the guidance of the press secretary. *(See Table 3-1.)*

Standard-Setters: Stephen T. Early and James C. Hagerty

"Steve and I thought that it would be best that straight news for use from this office should always be without direct quotations," declared Franklin Roosevelt at his first presidential press conference. "In other words, I do not want to be directly quoted, unless direct quotations are given out by Steve in writing."[105] With these words, Roosevelt defined an important role for his press secretary. Steve Early listened to the president, who relied on him to serve daily as his spokesperson throughout his administration. He would provide a presidential or administration viewpoint with skillful accuracy.

Early had known the future president since 1913 when the young Roosevelt came to Washington as assistant secretary of the navy. Early was then a reporter for the Associated Press covering the military beat. The two kept in touch over the next twenty years and earned each other's trust. Roosevelt viewed Early as a person who knew his craft. Thus Roosevelt had faith in Early's recommendation to establish a different press relationship outside of the prevailing rules. "This new deal in press relations was largely the handiwork of Roosevelt's hard-driving, hot-tempered press secretary, Steve Early," wrote Patrick Anderson in *The President's Men*.[106] "Before accepting the job, Early demanded Roosevelt's assurance that he would cooperate in a liberalized press policy." Mutual trust and respect served both men well.

President Eisenhower had similar confidence in his press secretary, James C. Hagerty. At a crucial juncture in his presidency, Eisenhower confirmed this stance. While on vacation in Denver in September 1955, President Eisenhower suffered a heart attack. Afterward, Eisenhower reportedly told his doctor: "Tell Jim to take over." Once Hagerty arrived in Denver, he did in fact take over. "Jim represented the sole link between the presidential sick room and the anxious public," noted Cornwell. "As such he held the center of news interest to the unheard of extent of having *his* press conferences reproduced verbatim in the *New York Times*."[107] Because President Eisenhower had three illnesses—the heart attack, ileitis (1956), and a minor stroke (1957)—Hagerty was the president's only link with the public for several months at a time. Eisenhower did not have a press conference for five months after his heart attack and two months after his ileitis operation. "In a sense, then," observed Cornwell, "the mythical 'White House spokesman' of the Coolidge era had at last been clothed with flesh and respectability."[108] Even in good health, Eisenhower kept his press secretary well informed. According to Hagerty, "For eight years I knew everything he did,

TABLE 3-1 Presidential Press Secretaries, 1929–1997

Press secretary	President	Years	Background[a]
George Akerson	Hoover	1929–1931	Reporter
Theodore G. Joslin	Hoover	1931–1933	AP reporter
Stephen T. Early	Roosevelt	1933–1945	AP, UPI reporter
Charles Ross	Truman	1945–1950	Reporter
Joseph H. Short	Truman	1950–1952	Reporter
Roger Tubby	Truman	1952–1953	Journalist
James C. Hagerty	Eisenhower	1953–1961	Reporter
Pierre E. Salinger	Kennedy	1961–1963	Investigative writer
	Johnson	1963–1964	
George Reedy	Johnson	1964–1965	UPI reporter
Bill Moyers	Johnson	1965–1967	Associate director, Peace Corps
George Christian	Johnson	1967–1969	Reporter
Ronald L. Ziegler	Nixon	1969–1974	Advertising
Jerald F. terHorst	Ford	1974	Bureau chief, newspaper
Ron H. Nessen	Ford	1974–1977	Journalist
Jody L. Powell	Carter	1977–1981	Advertising
James Brady[b]	Reagan	1981–1989	Congressional press aide
Larry Speakes	Reagan	1981–1987	Reporter
Marlin Fitzwater	Reagan	1987–1989	Government information aide
	Bush	1989–1993	
Dee Dee Myers	Clinton	1993–1994	Campaign aide
Michael McCurry	Clinton	1995–	Congressional press aide

NOTE: a. Early training. b. Although Brady was severely wounded in the 1981 assassination attempt, his title remained press secretary until 1989. Speakes's title was assistant to the president and principal deputy press secretary; Fitzwater's title was assistant to the president for press relations. Fitzwater's title became White House press secretary in the Bush administration.

and if I wasn't in his office when he made a decision, even including the secretary of state, he'd tell John Foster Dulles, 'stop in at Jim's office as you go out and tell him what we decided.'"[109] Eisenhower depended on the press secretary in a way that the presidents before and after him have not.

Previous contact with the press appears to be a significant determinant of presidential inclinations. "[Theodore] Roosevelt, Truman, Kennedy, and Johnson had all dealt with the press for decades before entering the White House," Patrick Anderson wrote, and

all rightly felt that they could more skillfully persuade, inform, or deceive the press, as the case demanded, than their Press Secretaries. Eisenhower was different. He disliked the cajolery, the deception, the self-promotion of press relations, and he was happy to delegate it all to Hagerty, as he delegated political affairs to [Chief of Staff Sherman] Adams.[110]

Thus the president's inclinations have served as a particularly important element in the nature of the duties of the press secretary. In the case of Pierre Salinger (1961–1963, John Kennedy; 1963–1964, Lyndon Johnson), the inclinations of his presidents were to conduct their own dealings with reporters and not report contacts to Salinger.

Early and Hagerty were model press secretaries because each

was able to serve his president's interests effectively. Yet each could at the same time convey to the reporters that they too were being taken care of and that the press secretary was their best source of information. One White House reporter who worked under both men compared the strengths of each:

Early could give you a long think-piece on the Administration's attitude toward the gold standard. Hagerty knows just what makes a good still picture, the exact amount of lighting needed for television, and exactly when to break up a press conference in order to make deadlines for home editions on the East Coast.[111]

What these two men had in common was their leaders' confidence and an ability to deal effectively with news organizations. They had different ways of carrying out their duties, but each excelled. Early is remembered for the quality of information he provided and Hagerty for the way in which he serviced the news and technological needs of those who covered the White House.

Relationship with Press Corps

At least part of the success enjoyed by Steve Early and James Hagerty stemmed from the willingness of the press corps and the press secretary to cooperate with each other to a degree that is no longer found. An unusual, although not unique, example of cooperation between presidential candidate Dwight Eisenhower and the photographers covering him illustrates the sense of comity existing during those years. For much of the 1952 electoral campaign, Eisenhower traveled around the country by train. On one trip, an enterprising photographer observed that the Eisenhowers had the habit of rising early and going to the back of their train car where local townspeople often assembled to greet them. Very early on one such morning a photographer was waiting for the Eisenhowers when they made their five-thirty appearance. He took photos and sent them to his home office. Soon his colleagues received demands from their parent offices asking for comparable pictures. The photographers appealed to Press Secretary Hagerty to intervene. Undaunted, Hagerty persuaded the Eisenhowers to don bathrobes later that day and to replicate the scene at the end of the train so the other photographers would have their own pictures for their home offices. The Eisenhowers were agreeable, and the photographers were thankful both to the Eisenhowers and to Hagerty.[112] Such a scene could not be repeated today.

Press Secretary Marlin Fitzwater described a different relationship with the White House press corps during his ten years on the job in the Reagan and Bush White Houses. "The White House press corps gathers every morning like a pride of lions. It snarls and growls, sleeps and creeps, and occasionally loves, but it is always hungry," Fitzwater observed.[113] The relationship between the White House and the press plays itself out in the daily briefing. In that spotlight,

each reporter has a hold on you, an invisible string tied to your belt buckle that pulls and tugs with each question, as if you were tied to the ground near anthills, and they torture you with repetitive questions. When they see that your mouth is dry, and you have squandered every ounce of knowledge, and you have probably made at least one embar-

Marlin Fitzwater from 1987 to 1992 worked as press secretary for Presidents Ronald Reagan and George Bush.

rassing slip that will elicit ridicule from White House colleagues and a frown from the president, then Helen [Thomas] twists until she can see over her shoulder, and decides if the lions have any fight left.[114]

The senior White House correspondent (a position United Press International reporter Helen Thomas held in the 1980s and 1990s) calls an end to the briefing, not the press secretary. The tenor of the briefing provides an indicator of the mutual mistrust evident in public White House settings.

The atmosphere of acrimony is fueled by the formal setting that now dominates the dissemination of official White House information. When Hagerty was Eisenhower's press secretary, reporters were stationed right across the hall from his room on the first floor of the West Wing. Checking in with the press secretary was quite easy given the short distance between their quarters. Douglass Cater described the scene:

A special room has been aside for the press, its typewriters, its telephones, its poker table. There are twenty to thirty White House 'regulars'—reporters whose sole assignment is to cover this tiny beat. . . . Just across the entrance hall, the Press Secretary has offices, connected by private corridor to the President's own office. He is the hourly spokesman of the President, the constant stand-in for the public image of the Presidency. Two and three times daily he meets with the regulars and any other reporters who may wander in.[115]

Today the informality is gone; the poker table an artifact. The press secretary steps behind a podium in the briefing room at an announced time—a time not always observed—to respond to the queries of those who are seated in the forty-eight assigned chairs. A formal setting, it emphasizes the differences between those on either side of the dais. In these sessions, routine information coexists with hotter requests for a response to a president's policy critics. If a secretary is weak in providing information, the secretary's influence both inside and outside the White House is strongly reduced.

Functions of the Press Secretary

From administration to administration, there is continuity in the tasks performed by the press secretary. No matter who is serving in the post, the demands made by the president, the White House staff, and the press corps all call for the individual to serve as an accurate and sensitive conduit of information, to bring together and then organize a press staff, to advise the president on communications policy and then be responsible for its implementation, and, finally, to serve as an agent responsible for meeting the interests of the press corps, the White House staff, and the president.[116] From a staff point of view, the press secretary manages Press Office personnel and whatever units are subsumed in this domain. The secretary also is responsible for implementing and disseminating communications policy for the administration. As agent, the press secretary must carefully interweave representation of the interests of the president, the press, and the White House staff. Although the secretary is chosen by and is solely responsible to the president, the appointee must be able to articulate skillfully the interests of all three and help each to understand the others' points of view.

Conduit of Presidential Information. The conduit function includes the transmittal of information from the White House to the president's various publics. In this, the daily briefing is key. At the daily briefing reporters can expect to uncover a president's thinking on specific issues of interest to them. Often an hour or longer when there is a hot issue, briefings are held once a day and cover a broad range of topics. Good press secretaries must be able to field questions on diverse topics because the fast-moving queries cover a broad spectrum of concerns. Often the secretary must deal with an issue for which there are no instructions or guidelines. In fact, the value of a press secretary to an administration lies in his or her ability "to go before reporters and articulate the administration's position without being instructed on what to say, as well as . . . to provide the right emphasis on information the White House wishes reporters to present to their audiences."[117]

In something of a juggling act, a press secretary must be articulate in accurately representing the president's positions and at the same time provide informed answers to correspondents' queries. Without this dual skill, the secretary's influence will be minimal and reporters will look elsewhere for answers. Such was the case with the Clinton administration's first press secretary, *Dee Dee Myers.* Never in the information loop, Myers was not even given the office occupied by her predecessors. Reporters liked her but saw her as amiable rather than well in-

Jimmy Carter's press secretary, Jody Powell, left, was highly regarded by the press for his ability to speak for the president. A fellow Georgian, Powell had been a confidant, aide, and adviser to Carter for about ten years before his White House appointment.

formed. "She is often left out of what is going on," said one reporter. "She came out and said she didn't know anything about a staff shakeup and five minutes later the President in the Oval Office said they had been discussing it for five weeks."[118] Myers was not the first press secretary to be perceived as uninformed. Others who acknowledged they felt left out of the information loop or about whom reporters expressed lack of confidence were Ronald L. Ziegler (1969–1974, Richard Nixon), Jerald F. ter-Horst (1974, Gerald Ford), Ron H. Nessen (1974–1976, Ford), and Larry Speakes (1981–1987, Ronald Reagan).

At the end of 1994 Myers left the Clinton administration and was replaced by Michael McCurry, who moved to the White House from his perch behind the podium at the State Department. Trained through answering tough questions but in a less-charged atmosphere, McCurry's transition to the White House podium was smooth and effective. Because many reporters already were well acquainted with McCurry from his years as a press secretary on Capitol Hill, he came to the White House with the benefit of recognition and respect. And in a symbolic victory, he was given the press secretary's office, a trophy denied to Myers.

In the post–Early and Hagerty period, Jimmy Carter's press secretary Jody Powell was the closest to Early and Hagerty in terms of his ability to speak for his president. "There was only one source [of information] when Carter was here," said Sam Donaldson, who served as the ABC White House correspondent in those years. "As long as you talked with Jody, you knew you weren't going to get beaten and if he didn't know, he would find out."[119] Powell had worked and traveled with Carter not only during his gubernatorial years but also through the long presidential campaign. He knew the president well and had honed the ability to speak for him even on individual issues they had not discussed. In relating the importance of Powell's access to Carter, Larry Speakes, principal deputy press secretary to Ronald Reagan, indicated that he was hurt by Reagan's reluctance to keep him fully informed. "In fairness to [Reagan], ninety percent of the politicians deal with press secretaries in the same fashion," Speakes related. "Two exceptions were Jimmy Carter, who gave extraordinary access to Jody Powell, and Dwight Eisenhower, who did the same with Jim Hagerty. It's no accident that Hagerty and Powell were two of the best press secretaries of all time."[120] Solid information, given in a timely manner, glosses over many imperfections. In Powell's case, that meant overlooking the administrative clutter that resulted from the press secretary's penchant for trying to control too many organizational units in the White House. Although no press secretaries in the post-Hagerty period have been able to speak for their presidents as effectively as Powell, two press secretaries whom reporters found valuable for the reliability of their information and their understanding of what reporters needed were George Christian (1967–1969, Lyndon Johnson) and Marlin Fitzwater (1987–1989, Ronald Reagan; 1989–1993, George Bush).

The conduit role also includes informal contacts with correspondents and news organizations. The press secretary must steer individual reporters toward an accurate story or away from an incorrect one. A press secretary who is wrong suffers publicly for it. Larry Speakes had such an experience as the principal spokesperson for President Reagan. In late October 1983, Bill Plante, CBS White House correspondent, went to Speakes for verification of a story. Plante said that he had information that the United States was amassing forces for an invasion of the island nation of Grenada. Speakes went to Adm. John Poindexter, deputy director of the National Security Council, to check out Plante's story and was told in no uncertain terms that there was nothing to the allegation. Speakes repeated Poindexter's words and deflected what would have been a scoop for Plante.[121] In the process, Speakes raised serious questions about his capacity to speak knowledgeably about White House activities.

Authenticity of information is sacrosanct. Use of one's own thoughts or words instead of those of the president brings an unhappy ending for any press secretary. Speakes also was the perpetrator of such a practice. In his book *Speaking Out: The Reagan Presidency from Inside the White House*, Speakes confessed to manufacturing presidential quotations:

I polished the quotes and told the press that while the two leaders stood together . . . the President said to [Soviet leader Mikhail] Gorbachev, "There is much that divides us, but I believe the world breathes easier because we are talking here together." CBS had me on the news Wednesday evening . . . and Chris Wallace said, "The talks were frank. The President's best statement came off-camera, aides quoting him as saying, 'The world breathes easier because we are talking together.'"[122]

Speakes was not the only one to venture into such muddy waters. Among correspondents, Bill Moyers had a similar reputation: "I never fully trusted Bill Moyers; he was interested in promoting himself and his programs. He ingratiated himself with the press corps. He was serving two masters and I distrust anyone who tries that," said one doubter.[123] Moyers appreciated policy and enjoyed talking about the merits of particular courses of action. Press secretaries, however, are judged according to their fidelity in representing the president, not their own abilities to explain the value of alternative courses of action.

As a conduit, a press secretary also must reverse the flow and make sure that press reports reach the president and the president's staff. Transcripts of the briefings are an extremely valuable source of press intelligence. Richard M. Cheney, chief of staff in the Ford administration, regularly read the transcripts to get "a feel for what is on the minds of the press."[124] The repetition of a question in one briefing can serve as an alert to staff members that the matter merits attention.

Secretary as Staff Chief. When Steve Early was press secretary, his staff consisted of one assistant, William Hassett, and secretarial help. James Hagerty's office operation was not much larger. He had two aides, Murray Snyder and Anne Wheaton, and secretarial help. The White House staff then was small by today's standards. In both cases, the secretary could talk regularly in an informal way with the president and with other staff members, eliminating the need for elaborate coordination mechanisms. In fact, both men, but especially Early, also often dealt with cabinet officers and members of Congress. Early's diary noted: "Throughout the day was kept busy on the telephones, as I am the only secretary here to talk with governors, Senators, and Cabinet officers, etc."[125] Hagerty had a more difficult time keeping up with the larger White House staff. He also was very particular that both White House staff and reporters coordinate any statements through him so that one clear voice would emerge. Moreover, the juggling act included bringing together the departmental information officers and keeping in touch with both White House staff members and even cabinet officers. *Time* noted the effectiveness of Hagerty's efforts to keep "the news systems of all the departments of Federal Government under his sure thumb." He met regularly with the press officers for the departments, scanned departmental news bulletins before they were released, and advised cabinet members who may have gotten themselves out on a limb and needed help.[126]

Other press secretaries have tried to maintain such control but failed. The daily routines exact too many demands to manage effectively departmental press officers who are bent on avoiding any curbs. Since the Nixon administration, the responsibility for coordinating public information officers has shifted to the purview of the communications adviser. In the Carter administration, Jody Powell tried to establish control, but both he and his deputy, Walter Wurfel, were snowed under just trying to attend to the daily routines.

To manage the Press Office staff today, a press secretary must hold several meetings a day, unlike the single gathering Early enjoyed. At these meetings, information received from both reporters and officials is exchanged and assignments are divided up. In the morning staffers go over issues raised in the day's newspapers and television and radio programs, which are the first clues to questions likely to come up at reporters' briefings. At the senior staff meeting later in the morning, the press secretary looks for guidance on the issues that have emerged and are presented to the assembled group. The deputies will have spent the morning checking with the public information officers in the departments, particularly State and Defense, and, when relevant, domestic departments and agencies will be asked to comment on pertinent material arising at the senior staff meeting. When not in meetings, the press secretary and deputy secretaries search for more signals in talks with reporters who visit their offices or who are cruising the press room. Clinton press secretary Michael McCurry got early warning of press corps interests at the nine-fifteen morning meeting with reporters in his office. Referred to as the "gaggle," reporters asked questions arising from overnight stories and reviewed information on the day's schedule.

The Press Office has jurisdiction over the White House photographers and the staffers who manage the advance operation, news summary, and radio operation. *(See box, One Picture Is Worth a . . . , below.)* Begun in the Nixon administration, the

---

ONE PICTURE IS WORTH A . . .

The White House Photo Office is entrusted with the mission of making a historical record of the presidency. And it is no small task. In *The Ring of Power: The White House Staff and Its Expanding Role in Government*, Bradley Patterson recounted the enormity of the photo enterprise: "Every year, the photographer and his five assistants put 7,000 rolls of film into their cameras; some 150,000 frames are snapped, 70 percent of them producing pictures of archival quality."[1] During the Reagan years, six photographers worked in the White House photo shop, aided by four assistants; the technical processing staff of military personnel numbered forty.

Recording a president's time in office involves photographs of many types of occasions, official and personal. "Personal meetings, classified meetings, just personal things that happen," observed Bush photographer David Valdez about the subjects of his photographs, which included the president's grandchildren and dogs.[2] All presidential occasions—official and personal—are appropriate subjects for official photographs. The presence of the president is what makes a scene worth recording.

Presidential photographs are distributed to news organizations and also displayed on White House walls and in the homes of the president's supporters around the country. At the end of the Reagan administration, Reaganites queued up from the Roosevelt Room to the far corners of the White House lobby to have their pictures taken with the president who appointed them. And at the annual White House reception for correspondents, journalists and their spouses lined up to have their pictures taken with the president they covered. To their satisfaction, within days they received from the White House the photographs of them signed by the president.

The photographs distributed to news organizations usually are ones that will complement a theme the White House is then emphasizing in presidential speeches and appearances, in the press secretary's briefing, in the public remarks of senior White House staff members appearing on television news programs, and in officially released White House statements. In late 1995, for example, President Bill Clinton was spending much of his time debating the shape of the federal budget with Republican congressional leaders. In one such session, the president, harking back to his days as a professor at the University of Arkansas Law School, stood pointer in hand next to a board brought into the Oval Office to allow the president to lecture his "students"—Senate majority leader Robert J. Dole, Speaker of the House Newt Gingrich, and House majority leader Dick Armey, among others—who were seated comfortably around him.[3] When the picture later appeared in *Time,* the three congressional leaders objected to being used as presidential props.

What the Clinton communications team was trying to do in this instance differed little from the practices of most earlier administrations, which used presidential photographs to advance the personal and policy interests of the president. With the capacity to determine what pictures should be released and when, the White House can use its photographs to create positive impressions of the president.

Beginning with the administration of Franklin Roosevelt, the job of recording the president's activities was assigned to photographers employed by the National Park Service. The appointment of an official presidential photographer began with the administration of Lyndon B. Johnson, who appointed Yoichi Okamoto to the position. Although Okamoto was assigned to the Press Office, his salary was paid by the Defense Department and his film was processed by the White House Communications Agency, a division of the Army Signal Corps. Once Okamoto came onto the White House staff and the Photo Office was finally formed, the unit was maintained in succeeding administrations even though some, such as the Carter administration, did not designate an official photographer.

Some official presidential photographers have had a high profile, such as David Hume Kennerly, the Pulitzer Prize-winning photographer from *Time* who held that post in the Ford administration. Michael Evans in the first Reagan term also was well known.

Photographers are allowed into the Oval Office only when the president and the president's staff decree. In most administrations, the monopoly on presidential meetings and family pictures is sacrosanct. David Valdez, however, experienced different practices in the Reagan and Bush photo shops. "Under the Reagan administration," Valdez explained, "the White House Photo Office did two and three photo releases a day." The Bush White House, however, preferred to accommodate photographers from news organizations and let them record their own pictures of White House events rather than having the Photo Office control the pictures.

1. Bradley Patterson, *The Ring of Power: The White House Staff and Its Expanding Role in Government* (New York: Basic Books, 1988).

2. David Valdez, interview by Martha Joynt Kumar, Washington, D.C., January 12, 1993.

3. Nancy Gibbs, "The Inner Game," *Time,* January 15, 1996, 12–14.

news summary operation brings together in one place articles from regional and local papers. President Nixon analyzed the summary to provide an agenda for media action, and, according to Nixon aide John Ehrlichman, Nixon's marginal notes contained the responses he wanted his staff to make to news items found in the document. Other administrations have used summaries to emphasize coverage of the administration at state and local levels. As a similar resource, the Carter administration added a "radio actuality" line to its database, and it, too, has been maintained by successors. Audio clips of presidential speeches and statements are available daily for taping by local radio stations.

Communications Planning. Before the creation of the Office of Communications, the press secretary held primary responsibility for planning the administration's media strategies and communications policies. During the latter part of the Eisenhower administration, a particularly well-crafted and executed communications effort was devised by James Hagerty, who wanted Eisenhower's eight years to end on a high note with an image of the president as a world leader seeking peace. He recommended to Eisenhower that he focus on traveling worldwide during his last two years in office. The theme, "A Man of Peace," was suggested in a memorandum to the president, who accepted Hagerty's recommendations. During his December 1959 world tour, Eisenhower traveled 22,000 miles, visiting eleven countries in Asia and Europe.[127]

The press secretary's policy participation is almost always restricted to communications rather than substantive policy. For example, rarely would a president call on his press secretary to advise him on the wisdom or shape of a welfare policy. There is simply not enough time to get deeply involved. James Connor, secretary of the cabinet under President Ford, elucidated: "Ron Nessen's workload means that he can't be involved early on in the process. . . . Anyone . . . who comes late . . . is at a remarkable disadvantage. They don't know the state of play and by the time they have learned it, the decision has been made."[128] This in no way undermines the importance of the press secretary's work. Communications policy is paramount to articulate presidential positions and to persuade others to join forces. "In the contemporary White House, where almost every activity has a public relations impact, it means that the press secretary has to be the best-informed person there," observed political scientists Michael B. Grossman and Martha J. Kumar. "He needs to know what is going on, where it is taking place, and how it will affect the President's efforts to communicate with the media."[129]

Agent. James Hagerty, who understood the needs of the press as well as the presidential requirements for publicity, set the standard as agent. His predecessors in the Truman administration had only mixed success in servicing the press.

From the routine releases and general travel arrangements of earlier years, Hagerty stepped up the level of services given White House correspondents. When Eisenhower took his world tour, for example, Hagerty did the advance work for the trip and was able to provide reporters with a detailed itinerary that re-

counted hour by hour where the contingent would be. A thirty-seven-page document included everything Hagerty thought might be of interest to reporters as they prepared for the extended journey. "He would not only investigate such obvious matters as the availability of telephones and hotel accommodations, he would also find out where reporters could get their laundry done and whether the local voltage would power their electric razors."[130] Reporters were very grateful.

Once established, the high level of service continued. "Life as a peripatetic White House correspondent has its rewards. Aides make your hotel reservations and worry about your luggage, a pressroom with phones and fax machines awaits you at every stop; staffers hand out transcripts of the president's remarks a half hour after he has spoken," related Howard Kurtz, the media critic for the *Washington Post.* "On trips abroad, reporters are whisked past customs. Local regimes shower them with goodies. When the Turkish government provided a cruise and lavish dinner for Bush, it also rolled out a second boat with identical food for the press."[131]

THE OFFICE OF COMMUNICATIONS

The Office of Communications was created shortly after President Nixon took office in 1969 primarily to handle relations with the out-of-town and specialty press. The office serves multiple functions, which vary from administration to administration. As a White House organization, its parts are more distinct than the whole. Each administration determines its own publicity functions, and many place them differently on organizational charts. During the Carter administration, for example, there was a distinct Office of Communications for only one year. More specifically, Carter press secretary Jody Powell kept speech writing under his wing for most of the administration, while in the Ford, Reagan, and Clinton administrations it was largely located in the Office of Communications.

Such administrative flexibility does not seem to affect continuity. Although each unit appears in many different locations on the organizational chart, physically the units continue to occupy the same offices as their predecessors. The news summary staff, for example, remains housed in a warren on the top floor of the Old Executive Office Building. Speechwriters are well established on the first floor across from the media affairs people.

Although the Office of Communications has been controlled by the press secretary at times, the communications adviser, a senior-level official, is usually in charge. *(See Table 3-2, p. 111.)*

Media Affairs Unit

The media affairs unit lies at the heart of the Office of Communications. It maintains a television studio in the Old Executive Office Building and arranges radio and television interviews with administration figures—both on and off the premises. Most especially, the office deals with the news organizations that exist outside of Washington and have no local bureau—a group that includes television stations and the print press at the regional and local levels, as well as newspapers that target identi-

TABLE 3–2 Directors of the White House Office of Communications, 1969–1997

President	Director	Term
Richard Nixon	Herbert G. Klein	January 1969–June 1973
	Ken W. Clawson	January 1974–August 1974
Gerald R. Ford	Paul Miltich and James Holland[a]	August 1974–November 1974
	Gerald L. Warren[a]	November 1974–June 1975
	Margita White[a]	June 1975–June 1976
	David R. Gergen	July 1976–January 1977
Jimmy Carter	None[b]	January 1977–June 1978
	Gerald Rafshoon	July 1978–August 1979
	None[b]	September 1979–January 1981
Ronald Reagan	Frank A. Ursomarso	February 1981–June 1981
	David R. Gergen	June 1981–January 1984
	Michael A. McManus Jr. (acting director)	January 1984–January 1985
	Patrick Buchanan	February 1985–February 1987
	John O. Koehler	February 1987–March 1987
	Thomas C. Griscom	April 1987–June 1988
	Mari Maseng	July 1988–January 1989
George Bush	David F. Demarest Jr.	January 1989–August 1992
	Margaret Tutwiler	August 1992–January 1993
Bill Clinton	George R. Stephanopoulos	January 1993–May 1993
	Mark D. Gearan	May 1993–August 1995
	Donald Baer	August 1995–

SOURCE: John Anthony Maltese, *Spin Control* (Chapel Hill: University of North Carolina Press, 1994), 243.

NOTES: a. Communications Office under the jurisdiction of the Press Office. b. The functions of the Office of Communications performed by the deputy press secretaries and the Office of Media Liaison.

fied ethnic, racial, or gender groups. When there is a presidential statement or appearance of interest to a specific group, the White House sends information to the relevant news organizations. In addition, the office deals with a satellite technology base of organizations. Conus Communications, for example, is a satellite cooperative that provides news spots to independent television stations around the country. If a station asks for an interview with a home state official who is visiting the president that day, the White House correspondent for Conus provides the footage. To set up such an event, the correspondent would have to go through the designated television specialist in the media affairs office.

Recent presidents have been particularly receptive to appearances on radio and television news programs and talk shows. In his first year, President Clinton had interviews with 161 correspondents from local television stations. Media affairs arranged these sessions because most occurred while the president was visiting the cities where the stations were located. Although the staff had visions of regularly connecting the president with local television anchors around the country, the budget for such ac-

tivities proved meager. "The technique is an inefficient way of communicating because there are six hundred TV stations in the country, and the White House has no budget for satellite work and has to beg and borrow the money from various contingency funds or from federal agencies," explained Tom Rosenstiel, media critic for the *Los Angeles Times*.[132]

While satellites have proven to be outside of budget range, computers have connected the White House to interested individuals and to news organizations. For the White House, contacting the local media once meant sending statements and speeches by surface mail. Today, this is done by electronic mail via the Internet. Anyone with a computer and a modem can get into the White House list server and download the press secretary's briefing, selected presidential speeches, and interviews.

Public Affairs Unit

Under several recent administrations, the public affairs office coordinated administration spokespersons, including department publicity officers and administration officials appearing in behalf of the president and his programs. It also assembled information for administration spokespersons making public appearances, particularly the latest facts and figures proving administration successes. In the Reagan administration, it was a significant support unit, which included among its functions arranging television appearances. Although this office was closed during the Clinton administration, it could resurface in succeeding administrations.

Advance Unit

Assigned the task of making arrangements for press traveling with the president on trips outside of Washington, the advance unit arranges hotels and locations where reporters can write and file their stories, and facilitates communications links. This unit works closely with scheduling operations, which makes travel arrangements for the president and the White House staff, since the plans of both the press and the White House must be coordinated.

How the president is covered is a major concern in setting up the locations and choosing the times for presidential appearances. Michael Deaver, Reagan's trusted aide who designed and scripted the president's first-term appearances, was especially good at matching location and message. "The trip of the Demilitarized Zone on the border between North and South Korea was a symbolic high point of the Reagan years," said Deaver. "Standing there, staring across that buffer zone, drawing the contrast between freedom and oppression, this was what Ronald Reagan did best."[133]

Speech Writing Unit

Since the Reagan administration, speech writing usually has been housed in the Office of Communications. The staff is responsible for preparing the president's major addresses as well as routine remarks, such as those delivered in brief Rose Garden ceremonies. Message coordination is critical. An administration needs a strong presidential message to focus the attention of its personnel on one subject or issue.

Communications directors especially concerned with message—David R. Gergen (Ford, Reagan); Gerald Rafshoon (Carter); and Patrick Buchanan, Thomas C. Griscom, Mari Maseng (Reagan), among others—have kept speech writing within their organizational base. Interestingly, four communications directors—Gergen, Buchanan, Maseng, and Clinton director Donald Baer—had served earlier as presidential speechwriters. This exposure provided a sense of the importance of speech writing within the communications framework.

Relationship with Press Secretaries

Since the creation of the Office of Communications in the Nixon administration, Jody Powell has been the only press secretary with the extraordinary responsibility of stage managing long-range planning, speech writing, photographers, the news summary, radio actuality, and the out-of-town and specialty press operations. In the Ford, Reagan, Bush, and Clinton administrations, communications advisers were responsible individually for such functions as planning, speech writing, and the out-of-town and specialty press, but not for the daily operation as well.

The Office of Communications was subjected to exceptional scrutiny after the Watergate scandal of the Nixon administration. It was recognized that

at times, the office stepped over the line that separates legitimate appeals for public support from illegitimate tactics to induce or fabricate that support through the use of administration-sponsored letters and telegrams, the creation of supposedly independent citizens' committees to praise administration policy, and even threat of Internal Revenue Service investigations and antitrust suits against media organizations that painted the White House in an unfavorable light.[134]

In recent years, instead of controlling the office the press secretary has had to fight for independence from the office. In the Reagan years, communications advisers Tom Griscom and David Gergen had the Press Office within their domain. In the Clinton administration, the Press Office again was placed under the direction of the communications adviser until Michael McCurry joined as the press secretary.

THE COMMUNICATIONS ADVISER

The Office of Communications is headed by a senior-level official, whose duties are primarily administrative but also include participation in communications strategies. With a staff who ranges between fifty and one hundred people, the adviser spends a significant amount of time keeping management running smoothly. The "adviser" aspect of the role refers to developing and coordinating the president's public messages. Depending on the individual strengths of the office's occupants, the adviser also helps to build political support for the president and the administration's program.

An effective communications adviser provides news organizations with a convincing interpretation of presidential actions and policies and also designs strategies to coordinate and integrate administration ideas. Equally important are the creation of a presidential message and the coalescence of administration support around it.

The communications adviser also provides reporters with information on a background basis. In some administrations, for example, the communications adviser has regularly conducted a weekly briefing for the news magazines and another for the networks. The communications adviser sometimes has a public role as well. During the Clinton's first term, two communications advisers appeared frequently on television to provide a presidential version of events. Clinton advisers George R. Stephanopoulos and Mark D. Gearan were seen regularly on the weekday and Sunday morning television news show circuit.

The right surrogate needs to speak for the president in the right place at the right time. Communications advisers are responsible for finding that right person and coordinating the statements provided by public information officers from the departments with messages coming from the White House. Personnel from all sections of an administration must speak with one voice if they are to consolidate the sources of presidential support. During the Reagan administration, Friday or Saturday meetings were regularly devoted to long-range planning for coordinating legislative and communications strategy.[135] Without these meetings, the effective establishment of a presidential message relevant to the progress of the administration's legislative program would have been difficult if not impossible.

But communications advisers have not served without controversy in the White House. During the twenty-six years that the Office of Communications has existed, there have been twenty presidential communications advisers, ten press secretaries, and six presidents. Only five communications advisers have served two years or more: Herbert G. Klein (1969–1973, Nixon), David Gergen (1976, Ford; 1981–1984, Reagan), Patrick Buchanan (1985–1987, Reagan), David F. Demarest Jr. (1989–1992, Bush), and Mark Gearan (1993–1995, Clinton). The relatively high turnover of advisers points up the difficult nature of their tasks and the complexity of relationships. The adviser is charged with the smooth operation of the various units contained within the Office of Communications, yet the adviser's status derives from the ability to create and execute a successful presidential communications plan. The adviser's success depends on the president's success. If things go sour for the president, the communications adviser is often the first casualty.

Three general models have to date characterized the communications adviser: staff director, campaign adviser, and coalitions coordinator.

The staff chief type of director concentrates on administrative tasks. During his four and a half years in office, Klein, the longest-serving communications adviser, set up the operation and established the routines for disseminating information to the out-of-town press. He also focused on taking Nixon's message to groups of news organizations, such as the American Society of Newspaper Editors. In the Bush administration, David

Demarest directed his attention to the administrative aspects of the job rather than to developing a tightly coordinated message to sell to news organizations. With three and a half years of service, he stayed at his post almost as long as Klein. As a model, the communications adviser as an administrator seems to offend few.

In the campaign model, the director has the added responsibility of coordinating the president's reelection communications efforts. Gergen assumed the adviser role during Gerald Ford's presidential campaign and was followed by Gerald Rafshoon (1978–1979) who arrived to prepare for President Carter's reelection effort. Gergen and Rafshoon had the added burden of having to create a general strategy and set the tone for a presidential campaign in addition to the staff coordination required. Something had to give, and their strategies were devised to enhance the president's political strengths rather than the day-to-day unit operations.

Gergen remained until the end of the Ford administration, but Rafshoon left his desk after a year to run Carter's reelection campaign. Because Ford lost the election, the strength of Gergen's early success in the Ford administration was little noticed beyond Washington. During his tenure, however, Ford's support climbed dramatically. Part of the credit belonged to the controlled publicity operation that featured President Ford amid the trappings of the office as he carried out his duties.

During Ronald Reagan's reelection campaign, senior adviser Michael Deaver was able to closely control the communications operation by having his deputy, Michael A. McManus Jr., serve as its acting director during 1984. Reagan's last communications adviser, Mari Maseng, directed a campaign of another sort at the end of his second term. Focused on the notion of the legacy of the Reagan years, the campaign was designed to establish a strong finish for a president who was under fire in his last years in office.

During George Bush's reelection campaign, the communications adviser was Margaret Tutwiler, longtime assistant to James A. Baker III, who was responsible for directing the campaign. The resources of the office were used to emphasize the general communications assets of the president.

An example from the Reagan administration illustrates the third model, coalitions coordinator. In his second tour of duty as communications adviser, David Gergen directed his energies toward shaping political coalitions for governing. During the first three years of the Reagan administration, under Gergen's guidance, the office held 150 briefings for media and elite groups from outside Washington.[136] These meetings were specifically geared toward generating political support for the president's program. Along with senior advisers Michael Deaver, who understood the communications strengths of Ronald Reagan as well as the dynamics of television, and James Baker, who was familiar with the workings of power in Washington, Gergen developed clear messages together with strong communications plans to implement them. He also maintained a tightly controlled "line-of-the-day" operation throughout the administration. "Not only was the line spread to the departments through morning conference calls, but it was also accessible throughout the executive branch by computer," political scientist John Maltese reported.[137] When the reelection effort got under way, the system was broadened to include campaign officials.

At the beginning of Reagan's second term, Patrick Buchanan introduced a different agenda than that from Gergen's. Buchanan spent less time with reporters and gave more time to a conservative agenda. Instead of speaking on background to reporters about the president's program, he expressed his policy preferences publicly. For example, he wrote an article published in the *Washington Post* calling for congressional support of the Nicaraguan rebels. In participating in the upcoming vote, Buchanan wrote, "the Democratic Party will reveal whether it stands with Ronald Reagan and the resistance—or Daniel Ortega and the communists."[138] When the details of the Iran-contra affair became public, the White House sought a less combative communications director and one centered on the restoration of the presidential image. Thomas C. Griscom accompanied Sen. Howard Baker to the White House when the latter became chief of staff. Having served as press secretary to Baker when he was majority leader, Griscom had the knowledge and skills to work smoothly with the representatives of news organizations. He was followed as communications director by Mari Maseng, who took over to conduct "the legacy" campaign.

In 1993 the broad scope and the burdensome nature of the communications adviser's duties came under closer scrutiny when George Stephanopoulos left the position after four months. He had tried to develop overall communications planning while at the same time splitting the briefing duties with Press Secretary Dee Dee Myers. "As chief White House spokesman he was giving daily press briefings and returning some 150 telephone calls a day," revealed Maltese. "As a policy advisor, he met regularly with [Chief of Staff] McLarty and the president to discuss substantive issues."[139] But as Jody Powell had discovered, involvement in daily operations leaves no time to handle long-range planning. Thus Stephanopoulos gave up the communications and the briefing roles and took instead a less-visible senior position. The communications post then was taken by Mark D. Gearan, who held it for two years before leaving the White House to head the Peace Corps. Although Gearan made many public appearances to explain the president's positions and actions, others, including Stephanopoulos, also helped to create the administration's messages.

The Modern Presidential News Conference

The most important of the direct exchanges of information between the president and the press is the presidential news (or press) conference. *(See "Presidential Press Conference," p. 98.)* Although each side has groused about the conduct and performance of the other in these exchanges, the news conference has proved to be a durable institution. Every president since

Woodrow Wilson convened the first news conference on March 15, 1913, has held conferences designed around a question-and-answer format. Reporters have asked the questions and presidents have responded. The exchange itself has evolved from a "just between us" basis in the Wilson administration to the public nature of today's conference, and the evolution from an off-the-record session to an official event has brought with it a variation in the way presidents have used press conferences.

Many presidents have not been enthusiastic about the use of press conferences and have tried to use them to suit their own purposes. Presidents from Harry Truman through Lyndon Johnson held approximately two press conferences a month. Since President Johnson, there has been little stability either in the numbers or in the location of press conferences; the only presidents to hold at least two conferences a month have been George Bush and Bill Clinton. In the administrations of Richard Nixon and Ronald Reagan, news conferences were reduced to the lowest numbers the presidents and their staffs could manage. (See Table 3-3.)

Presidential press conferences have endured because both presidents and reporters have found them to be useful. For the president, the primary distinction of the press conference is its usefulness in advancing policy and electoral goals; it is an opportunity to explain policies and seek support for them. Moreover, conferences can be timed to coincide with legislative initiatives or foreign policy events.

The press conference is the closest the president gets to having a conversation with the nation. In response to a reporter's question at one of the gatherings, President Eisenhower spoke of the importance of the press conference as a communication device:

The presidency is not merely an institution. In the minds of the American public, the President is also a personality. They are interested in his thinking. . . . At the same time, they believe the President, who is the one official with the Vice President that is elected by the whole country, should be able to speak to the whole country in some way. . . . I believe [what] they want to see is the President, probably, capable of going through the whole range of subjects that can be fired at him and giving to the average citizen some concept of what he is thinking about the whole works. . . . [T]he press conference is a very fine latter-day American institution.[140]

Other than the press conference, there is no established forum where a president regularly submits to questions. Advisers and cabinet officers cannot be expected to engage in the rigorous questioning of the president that reporters favor in press conferences. The president is, however, in a vulnerable position when appearing before correspondents. Reporters and the public may find this an attractive feature of the press conference, but it represents an element of concern for the president and the White House staff. For that reason, as the event has become increasingly public, presidents and their staffs have had to invest a considerable amount of time in preparations for the conference. The presidential briefing books that appeared in the Truman administration have been maintained ever since. Staff members

TABLE 3–3 Presidential News Conferences, 1933–1995

President (term)	Number of conferences	Months in office	Average
Franklin D. Roosevelt (March 4, 1933– April 12, 1945)	998	145	6.9 per month 82.6 per year
Harry S. Truman (April 12, 1945– Jan. 20, 1953)	324	94	3.4 per month 41.4 per year
Dwight D. Eisenhower (Jan. 20, 1953– Jan. 20, 1961)	193	96	2.0 per month 24.1 per year
John F. Kennedy (Jan. 20, 1961– Nov. 22, 1963)	64	34	1.9 per month 22.6 per year
Lyndon B. Johnson (Nov. 22, 1963– Jan. 20, 1969)	135	62	2.2 per month 26.1 per year
Richard Nixon (Jan. 20, 1969– Aug. 9, 1974)	37	66	0.6 per month 6.7 per year
Gerald R. Ford (Aug. 9, 1974– Jan. 20, 1977)	39	30	1.3 per month 15.6 per year
Jimmy Carter (Jan. 20, 1977– Jan. 20, 1981)	59	48	1.2 per month 14.7 per year
Ronald Reagan (Jan. 20, 1981– Jan. 20, 1989)	44	96	0.5 per month 5.5 per year
George Bush (Jan. 20, 1989– Jan. 20, 1993)	142	48	3.0 per month 35.5 per year
Bill Clinton (Jan. 20, 1993– Jan. 20, 1996)[a]	113	36	3.1 per month 37.7 per year

SOURCES: All figures except those for Roosevelt were compiled by the author from *Public Papers of the President* (Washington, D.C.: Government Printing Office). The figures for Roosevelt were taken from Harold W. Stanley and Richard G. Niemi, *Vital Statistics on American Politics,* 5th ed. (Washington, D.C.: CQ Press, 1995), 53.

NOTES: Press conference totals include only those conferences that were numbered at the time as part of the series of press conferences for each president. Not included are events that later were labeled press conferences but were not given a number. Each month in office is counted only once. When two presidents served within one month, the month is allotted to the president who served the majority of days in the month.   a. First three years of term.

also pose questions to the president in preparatory rounds. Both of these practices reduce the risks the president faces when appearing before reporters. It is fairly easy to predict almost all the questions that will be raised.

Besides presenting the president with an opportunity to communicate with the public, the conference has the added advantage of ensuring that the president is brought up to speed on existing problems and what is going on in the bureaucracy on particular policies. The *Washington Post* reporter David S. Broder has explained the importance of a press conference to a president: "The reporters' questions often short-circuit the offi-

President George Bush preferred casual press conferences, such as this one at his vacation home in Kennebunkport, Maine, in September 1989.

cial channels, layers of bureaucracy, and tiers of staff advisers that insulate a President from the real world."[141] In this way, President Nixon found out about problems in the Veterans Administration through a question posed by Sarah McClendon, owner of a news service providing Washington political information to small newspapers and radio stations.

Presidents who do not invest attention and time in preparation for press conferences put themselves at some risk. Because President Reagan, for example, did not like to prepare for press conferences, his staff sometimes had to correct his statements after he made them. *Washington Post* media critic Howard Kurtz explained the dramatic appeal of Reagan's press conferences: "The old actor was John Wayne, swaggering into the saloon to do battle with the villains of the press corps. Would he say something outrageous? Would he mangle the facts and force the White House to put out a correction?"[142] Even when Reagan made mistakes, the public did not seem to mind. But the president did, and he preferred to make speeches when he had a message to deliver. The Oval Office, joint sessions of Congress, and settings around the country and abroad with dramatic backdrops were the venues he preferred for delivering messages. He wanted a script to follow and a stage where he could deliver his lines.

Until the Bush administration, a president could reasonably expect his press conferences to be televised, but conferences held in the early afternoon attracted much smaller audiences than those held in the evening. Neither Bush nor Clinton favored the evening East Room event, preferring less formal settings. Bush held only two conferences at eight o'clock in the evening, and the second one was not televised by the regular networks because it was too close to the election and network executives believed that "equal time" questions could be raised. With cable television in so many homes today, the networks are no longer willing to commit evening time to a presidential press confer-

ence. If people want to watch a press conference, the networks contend, they can tune in CNN or C-SPAN (Cable Satellite Public Affairs Television).

Reporters also find press conferences useful. The gatherings give them an opportunity to take the president's measure; they think they learn a great deal about a president as a person through occasions in which the president must respond publicly to their questions. No other regular forum guarantees that the president will be called to respond to questions posed by people outside the administration. The absence of other forums increases the significance of the presidential news conference. In addition, reporters become part of a presidential event in a news conference. In televised conferences, their colleagues in the press corps, back at the office, and at corporate headquarters can watch them at work.

FRANKLIN ROOSEVELT AND THE PRESS CONFERENCE

President Franklin Roosevelt converted the presidential press conference "from the comatose institution he inherited from Herbert Hoover to a distinctly American device for informing the nation of what the President is contemplating and the President of what the nation is thinking."[143] He set a standard that, for frequency (an average of 6.9 conferences a month and 82.6 a year) has yet to be repeated.[144] At his twice-weekly Oval Office meetings, reporters no longer had to submit written questions, which allowed better access to the facts. Information could be attributed to the president, but direct quotations still were not used, except when Steve Early wrote out the quotations cleared for publication. Confident in his relationship with the press, Roosevelt was generous in sharing with reporters information that he would classify as "background" or "off the record." In more than half of his first 250 news conferences, the president raised the issues.[145] In the others, he left it to reporters to choose the questions and direct the flow of conversation. A true master of the press conference, Roosevelt had no imitators. For frequency, consistency, and close control, he was unmatched and a tough act to follow.

TRUMAN AND THE PRESS: FORMALIZING THE RELATIONSHIP

President Harry Truman, true to his nature, sought a more formal relationship with reporters. He cut back the number of conferences to once a week, for an average of 3.4 a month (41.4 a year) and a total of 324. Truman also moved the meeting place from the Oval Office to the Indian Treaty Room in the Executive Office Building. Here "the whole tone was shifted in the direction of a rather stiff interpellation, far removed from 'family' gatherings, as F.D.R. liked to call them."[146] Reporters now had seats instead of standing in haphazard fashion around the president's desk. When correspondents asked a question, they had to identify themselves and their publication. The formal setting robbed the conference of the spontaneity that had characterized sessions in the Roosevelt years. Transcripts were taken and audio recordings were made. Snippets of both were released under the president's name and with his voice. For the first time, electronic media competed for attention alongside the pencil press.

As the relationship between the president and the press became more formal during the Truman years, so did the preparation for the press conferences. And as the conferences became more public, measures had to be introduced to reduce the risks inherent in open, public exchanges. Opening presidential statements at the conference provided such a buffer because they gave the president an opportunity to state his positions on issues of his choosing, as did the process of briefing the president before the conference. Elmer Cornwell found that President Truman began with formal statements in 63 percent of the con-

ferences held his first two years in office and 52 percent of the conferences held the last two years as president.[147] Not only did this practice reduce the inherent risks of openness by directing attention to the issues of the president's choosing, but, as with Roosevelt's issue statements, the president could selectively respond to the news media when the attention was focused on him.

Presidential preparations for the press conferences were the responsibility of Truman's press secretary and consisted mainly of preparing the president to answer questions the secretary anticipated would be asked. Staff members joined the press secretary for collective sessions to brief the president. By the end of the administration, the briefing book—introduced by Roger Tubby, who became acting press secretary after the death of Joseph H. Short—was being used. It included about forty possible questions for the president's perusal the night before the conference.[148] The staff might then go over the material with the president one last time before the conference began.

EISENHOWER AND KENNEDY: TELEVISED CONFERENCES

By the time Dwight Eisenhower was elected, the serendipitous encounter between president and press of Theodore Roosevelt's day had metamorphosed to the scripted event of the Truman administration. President Eisenhower proceeded to build on the formal and public nature of the press conference, with reporters kept even further at arm's length. Radio had allowed Truman extra space; Eisenhower used television in the same way. Although the technology for transmission was still cumbersome, James Hagerty, Eisenhower's press secretary, capitalized on this direct link to the public and encouraged the improvement of lighting.

Hagerty's real innovation was to provide full television cov-

Eisenhower was the first president to hold a televised news conference. But before the film was released to the public, it was edited by his press secretary, James Hagerty.

erage of news conferences, beginning in 1955. The films of conferences were released to news organizations later in the day the conferences occurred. The Eisenhower press conference tape was subject to editing as television stations individually kept only what each considered to be the most newsworthy portions; newspaper reporters treated presidential statements in a similar fashion. President Kennedy was the first president to have his press conferences broadcast live.

Hagerty's interest lay in having the public serve as the main audience rather than reporters who might be critical. After one conference Hagerty wrote in his diary: "[President Eisenhower] upset at press reaction. . . . I'm glad we released the tape of the statement to radio, TV, and newsreels . . . .[W]e'll go directly to the people."[149] He also noted in his diary that reporters would drop by and tell him what questions they were going to ask. "[Chalmers] Roberts of the *Washington Post* told me that he was going to ask the President the same question he had asked Churchill. Namely, what are the possibilities for peaceful co-existence between Soviet Russia and Communist China on the one hand and non-communist nations on the other?"[150] The spontaneous appearances of press conferences, then, were not always real. Prepared statements also were used by Eisenhower but not nearly as frequently as some of his predecessors. Retreating even further from President Roosevelt's twice-weekly and Truman's once-a-week conferences, President Eisenhower held press conferences only once every two weeks, or an average of 2.0 a month (24.1 a year) for a total of 193 during his administration.

By President Kennedy's election, new electronic equipment offered new opportunities for presidential publicity. The president's news conferences could be televised live without concern about lighting difficulties. By then, almost half the households in the United States had television sets. President Kennedy, long comfortable with the print and electronic media, had no hesitation about live conferences and held them with a frequency similar to that of Eisenhower. His total conferences numbered sixty-four, or an average of 1.9 per month (22.6 per year). As the press conference became a higher-profile event, preparations became more extensive. Briefing books, practice sessions, and increasing amounts of staff time were devoted to conferences. The conferences, broadcast live throughout the country, were held in the afternoons in the State Department auditorium, which could accommodate a large press contingent.

JOHNSON, NIXON, AND REAGAN: AVOIDING THE TRADITIONAL CONFERENCE

Beginning with President Johnson, the notion of what constituted a press conference changed. Instead of counting as press conferences only those meetings held in a set forum, such as the Indian Treaty Room or the State Department auditorium, and announced in advance, Johnson often included impromptu sessions where few questions were asked. He might appear in the press room at five o'clock or take a walk around the residence and have reporters ask him questions while he moved at a fair speed. Of the forty-one press conferences he held in 1966, for example, twenty were impromptu sessions and most did not have television coverage. His average was 2.2 a month (26.1 per year), for a total of 135.

President Nixon did not like the formal setting either, but he saw no need to include other types of sessions with reporters. Instead, he avoided them altogether. His average was 0.6 a month (6.7 a year), with a total of thirty-seven held. And when they were held, they were extremely contentious events.

Ronald Reagan also avoided press conferences. Somewhat like Nixon, he averaged 0.5 a month (5.5 a year), for a total of forty-four. His conferences were not contentious in the same way that Nixon's were, but in some, such as the ones he held to answer questions on the Iran-contra affair, he came off poorly. Because Reagan was able to present himself and his policies in so many other venues, he avoided press conferences. When he did have them, he used the East Room as a venue. In addition, Reagan held them at night in order to minimize the impact of the analysis of news organizations. If the sessions were held in the afternoon before the evening news programs, the networks assessed his performances and pointed out where his answers were weak. Evening conferences avoided those assessments. Because President Reagan was so successful communicating his message from a set stage, he could afford to opt for few press conferences.

FORD, CARTER, AND BUSH: REGULAR CONFERENCES

President Ford sought to ameliorate the bitterness that pervaded the relationship between the president and the press after Watergate. He was open with reporters, offering to hold press conferences and to schedule interviews regularly. He held thirty-nine conferences, with an average of 1.3 a month (15.6 a year) during his time in office. He also conducted interviews with televisions anchors, such as Walter Cronkite, Tom Brokaw, and Barbara Walters, and with leading columnists and journalists. In addition to holding comparatively regular conferences, Ford met with local correspondents when he traveled around the country. Meetings with the press were an aspect of restoring trust in the presidency.

Jimmy Carter had no liking for the White House press corps. To expand his contacts with the press, he scheduled meetings with out-of-town editors. Carter generally met with the White House press corps every two weeks and with the out-of-town press on alternate weeks. Thus he had far more press appearances than his predecessors. But counting only his regular press conferences with the White House press corps, he held an average of 1.2 a month (14.7 a year). These fifty-nine press conferences were almost evenly matched by the number of question-and-answer sessions he held with the out-of-town press held in the Cabinet Room. His conferences fell off during his last two years, however, with only six held in his last year and twelve the year before.

President Gerald R. Ford holds an impromptu press conference in the Oval Office in another attempt to restore openness to the presidency after the closed administration and secrets of the Richard Nixon.

Almost all of Carter's press conferences were held in Room 450 of the Old Executive Office Building, an auditorium lacking the trappings of office. Five of his last seven conferences, however, were held in the opulent setting of the East Room with four of those held at nine o'clock in the evening when the viewing audience would be the greatest. In preparing for his reelection campaign, Carter found the formal White House setting an appropriate one to dramatize his incumbency. The evening sessions allowed him to get access to a larger viewing audience than the afternoon sessions. However, Carter reduced the number of conferences in his final year as he felt the coverage he received did not justify the work that went into preparing for them.

Although Reagan dealt with reporters chiefly through the intermediary of the White House staff, Bush preferred to deal directly with reporters. Where Reagan had few press conferences, Bush followed earlier precedents by bringing back the press conference as a tool for communicating regularly with the public, although he did not hold the high-profile evening events favored by President Reagan. President Bush made frequent use of the conference during his first three years in office. His total of 142 averaged out to 3.0 a month (35.5 a year). His conferences almost always were held in the Press Office briefing room, and he added something new to the press conference with his fairly regular practice of holding joint sessions with heads of state (35.2 percent of his press conferences were joint sessions). In his final year, particularly once he began his reelection campaign, he no longer held conferences with the same regularity. Like his predecessors, he found them less useful than he first imagined them to be. And he found other ways to deal with news organizations.

CLINTON: JOINT PRESS CONFERENCES

President Clinton followed the practice first established by President Bush of holding joint press conferences with visiting foreign leaders—63.7 percent of the 113 conferences held during Clinton's first three years in office fell into this category. In 1993 he held thirty-eight conferences, and in twenty-five (65.8 percent) of those he was accompanied by a world leader. In 1994 the numbers were similar; he held forty-five conferences of which 28 (62.2 percent) were joint sessions. In 1995 President Clinton held twenty-seven conferences, nineteen (70.4 percent) of which were held with leaders of other countries. An average of 3.1 conferences a month (37.7 a year) were held over the three years.

Reporters usually find the joint conferences restrictive as the expectation is that reporters' questions will revolve around the work the two leaders accomplished in their meetings. Having so many other opportunities to see and hear President Clinton, however, reporters did not seem particularly restive with the press conference arrangements. Clinton was often available for questions from the pool reporters at photo opportunities. In addition, he spoke in Washington, at the White House and around the country on a regular basis. He also was available for a large number of radio and television interviews with hosts from stations around the country, and he appeared on the CNN's *Larry King Live* and MTV, venues that had proven so successful for him during his first presidential campaign.

The Modern White House Press Corps

"The White House is the gilded cage of American journalism," declared media critic Howard Kurtz.[151] It is an assignment that fills the new recruit with anticipation of journalistic bravura. After all, few people can say that they spend their days in the West Wing of the White House less than fifty feet from where the president is meeting with officials, digesting information and preparing to take actions, and making decisions. But correspondents soon realize that the only information accessible is that scrupulously selected, either officially or unofficially, for dissemination. A White House press pass provides merely the privilege to wait—wait for a briefing; wait to see the president; wait until a press conference is called; wait to see the press secretary; wait to see senior officials; wait to have phone calls returned. There may be propinquity to power, but there is little control over when and how the news is gathered.

WHO COVERS THE WHITE HOUSE

A White House press pass is issued to relatively few correspondents—currently they number 1,700, almost unchanged from the Reagan years.[152] The first step toward qualification is accreditation to the congressional press galleries. Accredited correspondents in the four congressional press galleries fall into the following categories: newspapers, 2,000; periodicals, 1,835; radio and television, 2,527; and photographers, 354.[153] To qualify for a pass for any of the congressional press galleries, a person must work for an independent news organization with a Washington bureau and live in or around Washington. The second step toward qualification for the White House press corps is a formal request to the White House from the bureau chief of the correspondent's news organization seeking clearance for the correspondent to represent the bureau at the White House on a regular basis. A Secret Service review follows. For a valid reason, the Secret Service can deny entrance to a correspondent, but a negative decision can be appealed through the court system.

Beyond those with press credentials, others can apply for a day's admittance to the White House. If, for example, several out-of-town reporters wish to attend a presidential press conference, they can apply through their news organizations' Washington bureaus. Accordingly, an almost limitless number can come in for specified reasons on a short-term basis. Nevertheless, rarely are all forty-eight seats in the briefing room filled.

Exceptions occur when it is believed the president will come in to personally name an appointee to a major administration post, or is ready to present legislation to Capitol Hill, or when the scent of trouble prevails. Then the seats fill up and people stand along the walls.

The White House is among the prestige beats in Washington. Some, like correspondent Stewart Alsop in 1968, found it to be the assignment with the greatest status. But in his 1981 study of the Washington press corps, Stephen Hess found that the White House beat had slipped in prestige—from first place to fifth.[154] Diplomacy, law, and politics are equally lustrous and are distinguished by the flexibility of the subjects the reporters might cover and of the approaches that reporters can take toward structuring their stories. The White House has less latitude.

Demographically, in 1981 the White House reporter was male (86.2 percent), white (89.7 percent), and thirty to thirty-nine years old (58.6 percent); over half of reporters (55.2 percent) had had some graduate school work.[155] Today, one clear difference is the growing number of women assigned to the White House beat and the importance of the copy they produce. Since the Hess study was completed, the *New York Times* and *Washington Post* have both regularly posted women to presidential coverage.

On a day-to-day basis it is the White House press corps to whom the president and the presidents's staff pitch their best stuff. Nevertheless, in the larger scheme of things, news outlet owners, columnists, and television anchors may receive special attention. Columnists may get special interviews with senior officials, and, on occasion, with the president. Television anchors also may get one-on-one time, and, occasionally, publishers are invited to dine with the president, especially when the poll numbers fall or successes seem in doubt. But it is the nature of the news itself that makes the regulars important. "A large part of the success of public affairs depends on the newspaper-

Generally, press secretaries and sometimes presidents make announcements to the White House press corps in the White House Press Room, which is about fifty feet from the Oval Office.

men—not so much the editorial writers, because we can live down what they say, as upon the news writers, because the news is the atmosphere of public affairs," Woodrow Wilson suggested in his first presidential press conference.[156] News is the context in which an administration operates. Maintaining some control over its content is essential to laying a foundation for policy initiatives and for the president's personal popularity. Time spent advancing either one is regarded as time efficiently spent.

THE OFFICIAL STORY

Through the Press Office, the press secretary, senior staff officials, and the president, the official story is available to all reporters who cover the White House. On a typical day, reporters may have access to written announcements, briefings, individual meetings with White House staffers, and presidential appearances from which they prepare their coverage. The official story is the basic story. For Carl Cannon, White House correspondent for the *Baltimore Sun*, President Clinton himself provided a good measure of what was needed for a story. "If you want to cover something, you have to listen to Clinton," Cannon said. "He will give you a road map of where he is going. You can write off of what he is saying and then call the Press Office and then call sources."[157] With Clinton, who talked to a large number of people, building a presidential story was not as difficult as it was in some earlier administrations.

In the morning as they enter the White House, correspondents go to the Press Room. (Occupying a low-level, one-story building that links the West Wing to the main White House, it was the site of Franklin Roosevelt's swimming pool. In 1969 President Nixon filled in the pool and had press facilities built on top.) A reporter's typical day is fairly routine. The first item of business in the morning is to check the bins on a wall near the entrance to the Press Room for printed announcements, statements, and schedules. These items provide early indications of the shape of the day's activities. At about a quarter past nine o'clock in the morning reporters begin to assemble outside the office of the press secretary. For approximately fifteen minutes, the secretary goes through the president's schedule for the day and answers questions for the perhaps twelve to twenty assembled reporters. In addition, the secretary provides a White House response to overnight developments. The correspondents gathered there heavily represent the wire services, radio, and television—that is, those who need a continual flow of news. They cannot wait until the one o'clock briefing to get information for their news audiences.

While press officers prepare for the noon briefing, reporters call in to their news organizations' Washington bureaus to set up their schedules. Then reporters might check around with people in the White House to see when or if there will be an opportunity to see the president. If the president is making an appearance, such as brief remarks in the Rose Garden to the Future Farmers of America, will there be an opportunity to ask questions? The Rose Garden is large enough to accommodate all reporters for presidential appearances. By contrast, only a few reporters are allowed in the Oval Office.

Each day press pools are established to allocate coverage when a presidential appearance takes place in a limited space such as the Oval Office or the Cabinet Room. The pool is composed of representatives of all of the television networks (including the independent ones), the wire services, and radio; photographers representing newspapers, magazines, and the wire services; technical people to operate the lights and the sound recording system; and a representative of the print press. The group is ushered into a presidential meeting and often is allowed, and sometimes even encouraged, to ask the president a question or two. It is the responsibility of the representative of the print press to write up a report for distribution to the entire White House press corps. The Press Office then distributes the official transcripts of the presidential question-and-answer sessions along with copies of the pool reports. In instances where official transcripts are made available, the pool reports focus almost exclusively on providing color. If, however, as happens on the road, the president speaks informally to people he meets publicly or exchanges remarks with citizens, the print pool reporter must use his or her old skills of reporting exchanges of words as well as describing the event itself.

All the facts must be included in the pool report to guarantee that those who were not present will have everything, not just a summary. The pool report for a typical White House ceremony provides an example. In May 1993 President Clinton met at the White House with a group of Cuban Americans to commemorate the ninety-first anniversary of Cuban independence. The group gathered under a tent on the South Lawn. "HRC [Hillary Rodham Clinton] wore a blue skirt, red blazer and a red, white, and blue star-spangled scarf. The President, with not a hair out of place, wore his customary ventless blue suit," the report stated. "He then launched into a defense of his budget plan and a plea for the group's help in getting it passed. Nothing particularly new here; he criticized the Boren plan as 'this so-called alternative proposal' and said, in effect, it would rob from the poor and give to the rich." The report ended with identifications of those on the dais.[158]

The press secretary's briefing is the central event in the daily distribution of official White House information. Whatever the president and the president's staff decide must be highlighted is presented in an opening statement. The press secretary then takes questions from the media. After the briefing, which may last from a half hour to an hour, depending on the day's issues, reporters call their home offices to discuss their stories. When the Press Office puts on a "lid," there is an interruption in distribution, and the media can feel free to go to lunch as no news will be distributed in their absence. If something big occurred, the Press Office staff would page reporters on their beepers and summon them back to the White House.

Other briefings also take place in a normal day. A senior official, such as the national security adviser, the head of the Office of Management and Budget, or the head of the Council of Economic Advisers, might give a briefing on a policy or action under discussion.

In the late afternoon when reporters have their stories together, some may want to check the accuracy of their information with the Press Office. The press secretary or staff members are available to check the validity of a story. Those from the "prestige press" (*New York Times, Washington Post,* and *Wall Street Journal*) and the networks are more likely to get first priority, but others also can rely on verification. Inaccurate stories, even in obscure publications, are a hazard as far as the Press Office is concerned because that information can leach into the prestige press.

THE UNOFFICIAL RECORD

Official presidential news is distributed to all correspondents at approximately the same time and in the same format, but not all presidential information is distributed in an official manner. Certain kinds of news are released on the basis of whom the reporter represents, the identity of the reporter, or the kind of information in which he or she specializes. Special consideration is generally given to television, prestige newspapers, news magazines, and the wire services. In some cases, a particular reporter is sought out, and in others it is the news organization the person represents, such as the *New York Times, Washington Post, Newsweek, Time,* or one of the big three networks. Unequal distribution also occurs with the specific kinds of information to be released. Not all reporters are looking for the same thing; some specialize in particular stories and the bits and pieces of information that go into them.

Images for Television

Since the Eisenhower administration, most Press Offices have sent their best stuff television's way. Television offers the direct access to the public that the other news formats do not. Television coverage has increased immeasurably since Eisenhower's day. In 1994, 98 percent of the population had television sets and 62 percent had cable compared with 9 percent with televisions in 1950 and 87 percent in 1960.[159] Only negligible numbers of Americans had cable until 1980.

Larry Speakes, press secretary to Ronald Reagan—the president who made perhaps the most effective use of the medium, told how television was woven into strategies for presenting the administration's policies. "Underlying our whole theory of disseminating information in the White House was our knowledge that the American people get their news and form their judgments based largely on what they see on television," Speakes wrote. The Reagan White House, then, learned to think "like a television producer" in order to dramatize its story. The formula was

a minute and thirty seconds of pictures to tell the story, and a good solid soundbite with some news. So when Reagan was pushing education, the visual was of him sitting at a little desk and talking to a group

of students, or with the football team and some cheerleaders, or in a science lab. Then we would have an educators' forum where the President would make a newsworthy statement. We knew very quickly that the rule was no pictures, no television piece, no matter how important our news was.[160]

During the Reagan years, the White House staff expended a great deal of effort on designing communications strategies. This was especially true in Reagan's first term when news was thought of primarily in terms of television images. The senior staff members Michael Deaver, David Gergen, and James Baker were very good at picking ways to publicize a policy visually, highlight the picture with a good presidential speech, and tie it in with a policy under consideration on the Hill. If the president's schedule revealed that there was no event with particular appeal for television, they would tell the press there would be no coverage of the day. "There was no need to have cameras in there and reporters trying to ask questions that would embarrass the President unless we could get our story on T.V.," said Speakes. The White House chose which networks would receive information.

Throughout the Reagan years, we not only played to television, we based all of our television judgments strictly on audience size. If ABC's 'Good Morning, America' was the leading morning show, which it was during most of Reagan's term, they got our number-one person on a given subject, like George Shultz on foreign policy. On the evening shows, when Dan Rather was the leader, we'd put our number-one guy on there. We played entirely to the ratings, and made no bones about it.[161]

The administration guest lists for the Sunday television programs involved the same calculations: put the top official on ABC's *This Week*.

Although television was being used by the White House, its correspondents also profited. The public tuned in to watch the president when he spoke, whether it was from the Oval Office or the shores of Normandy. And they liked what they saw. Television reporters basked in the reflected glory of the president they covered. Sam Donaldson got his own evening television magazine program, which he shared with former Nixon White House Press Office aide Diane Sawyer. Lesley Stahl, the CBS White House correspondent, was selected to cohost the television news magazine program *60 Minutes*. Earlier, she had had the host position on *Face the Nation*. When she left to go to *60 Minutes*, *Face the Nation* was taken over by Bob Schieffer, another former CBS White House correspondent. Judy Woodruff, an NBC White House correspondent, moved on to a coanchor position on the Public Broadcasting Company's news program the *MacNeil-Lehrer News Hour*. From there she moved to the anchor slot on CNN's *Inside Politics*. Thus White House television correspondents during the Reagan years did very well. Reagan's good pictures included them.

In the years since Ronald Reagan, television, specifically the three networks, has not fared as well at the White House. George Bush avoided comparisons with the master performer by choosing other venues in which to release information. Having a decidedly less aggressive policy agenda, Bush did not need prime-time exposure to the public; a Washington hand of long standing, he was comfortable talking with reporters in less formal settings. While Reagan's venues included prime-time television appearances, which guaranteed maximum exposure, Bush chose non-peak hours for his press conferences—held in the Press Office briefing room—which ensured minimum attention. In the Clinton years, network correspondents found their air time shrinking once the Republicans took control of the House of Representatives and the Senate in the 1994 midterm elections. Political momentum moved to Capitol Hill as the 104th Congress took office. Later in 1995, however, the president was again at the top of the news even though he was often sharing top billing with the Republicans heading the House and the Senate.

Prestige Newspapers

All newspapers are not equal at the White House, nor anywhere else in Washington. The *Washington Post, Wall Street Journal, New York Times*, and, sometimes, *Los Angeles Times* are more likely to get the big stories and explanations of policy decisions and presidential actions than the regional papers because of their broad and deep reach into the Washington political community. "In dealing with the daily newspapers, [the Reagan administration's] starting point was always the *Washington Post*," explained Press Secretary Larry Speakes. "It had a slight edge in importance over *The New York Times*, simply because it hit the doorstep first, and all of Washington spun off the *Post*—including Congress, the Supreme Court, and everybody in the administration." [162]

The solid financial bases of both the *Post* and the *New York Times* and the keen interests their readers have in White House activities combine for strong institutional and personal coverage of the president and the president's staff. Each paper has two correspondents covering the White House, which allows a certain flexibility in coverage: only one person needs do the "body watch"—that is, close coverage of the president. That person picks up official announcements, hears the press secretary's pronouncements, and views the president. Being there when and if the unexpected or the unthinkable occurs is essential. The other correspondent is free to work the phones and seek information from the unofficial sources. *(See box, How a Reporter Gets the Story, right.)*

News Magazines

Each administration treats news magazines with care. *Time, Newsweek,* and *U.S. News and World Report* all receive special consideration from the White House, traditionally at the end of the week. These background briefings allow the White House to give them what they need for their weekend deadlines. During the first Reagan term, the White House paid obeisance to the three news magazines in a way Reagan's predecessors and successors have not. "Every news magazine would see every senior

---

HOW A REPORTER GETS THE STORY

How do reporters sniff out a good story? Ann Devroy of the *Washington Post,* known to be particularly enterprising in her White House coverage, wrote a sweeping series of articles in the early 1990s on the finances of Bush chief of staff John H. Sununu and his propensity to travel at the expense of others, including businesses and taxpayers.[1] A look at how the series was developed demonstrates the way a good story comes about.

The elements here were an enterprising reporter, a newspaper that supported the development of the story, and the willingness of people with collaborative information to come forward. According to *Washington Post* media critic Howard Kurtz, during the Bush administration Devroy noticed that Sununu was traveling most weekends, yet his financial standing did not suggest that his salary could support that level of travel. Devroy and Charles Babcock of the *Post* used the Freedom of Information Act to pry loose Sununu's travel records. The result was a string of stories on his misuse of privilege during his tenure as chief of staff. Sununu, however, refused to cooperate with reporters, or, for that matter, with staff members seeking information on his conduct. "I'm not going to give them a damn thing," Sununu told Press Secretary Marlin Fitzwater. "It's none of their business. Every trip I made was authorized on behalf of the president."[2]

Once he was wounded, the many people he had offended during his two years in office sensed his vulnerability. "Those who provide reporters with their daily scraps of information—congressmen, Cabinet aides, Republican activists, midlevel staffers—had also been trampled by Sununu, and were only too happy to use the press to even the score."[3] In the end the disgruntled staff and critics got what they wanted: the resignation of John Sununu from his post as chief of staff.

1. Howard Kurtz, *Media Circus: The Trouble with America's Newspapers* (New York: Times Books, 1993), 255–260.
2. Marlin Fitzwater, *Call the Briefing: Bush and Reagan, Sam and Helen: A Decade with Presidents and the Press* (New York: Times Books, 1995), 177.
3. Kurtz, *Media Circus,* 256.

---

official for thirty minutes every week," said Larry Speakes, who managed the policy. "No newspaper or network enjoyed that privilege. The senior staff liked the idea that they could remain totally anonymous, that they would never identify you." [163] In the Bush administration, the White House continued a policy of special attention. On Thursday afternoons, Press Secretary Marlin Fitzwater arranged special briefings attended only by the magazines.

Briefings for news magazines concentrate on atmospherics, as do the news magazines themselves. They are interested in describing for their readers what the Oval Office looks like and how the president interacts with others as he makes decisions that will or will not change the world. Although the White House may complain about the excessive interest in detail, the staff makes sure that correspondents have the information they need. The staff also is interested in servicing other, lesser-known magazines such as the *National Journal*. Its circulation is small, but the *National Journal* is popular within the Washington community. It favors articles on governmental issues and presumes a fairly sophisticated understanding of the political system on the part of its readers. When Richard Nixon was president, John Ehrlichman, the domestic policy chief, gave a weekly half-hour appointment to Dom Bonafede, the *National Journal*'s White House correspondent, because he viewed the *National Journal* as a "channel of communication to Congress and the bureaucracy."[164] President Carter was so taken with articles in the *National Journal* that he regularly added a copy to the more traditional news magazines he received.

Wire Services

The wire services (Associated Press, United Press International, and Reuters) continually transmit information to their member news outlets—such as newspapers, radio, television, and online services—so their correspondents must generate a steady flow of material. While newspapers, news magazines, and, to a lesser extent, television, are looking for the scoop, wire services exist on official information. They record what a president says and does. The statements, announcements, and briefings are their lifeblood as throughout the day information flows to news outlets all over the country and to many parts of the world. Their deadlines follow events as they make sure that radio stations and newspapers get information as quickly as it can be delivered. Radio, too, works off a steady flow, but its deadlines are less frequent with demand centered around hourly newscasts or insertions in scheduled programs.

Reporters with Niches

Some reporters covering the White House have carved out information niches, which may be particularly useful in describing the operations of the White House or the personality of a president. *New York Times* correspondent Maureen Dowd, for example, explained an important aspect of President Bush and his administration by focusing on the personalities and behavior of those in power. Because George Bush came into office without a long, articulated agenda, who he was became unusually important. "What I'm interested in is character and how character can be traced in terms of its effect on policy and people—what compromises they're willing to make, how they see women, how they see blacks because of their background," Dowd explained. Character was especially pertinent to an understanding of the Bush administration. "His whole attitude is, we know best. We are the elite ruling class. We've been bred to run the country," Dowd said.[165]

In an earlier time, John Osborne was known for the details he collected on the operation of the Nixon White House. His *New Republic* column, "The Nixon Watch," was later retitled "White House Watch" during the years he chronicled the Ford and Carter administrations. His column was particularly useful for those who were following palace intrigues and the elements of an administration's decision-making process. For those providing the information to Osborne, there was a reward. James Fallows, chief speechwriter for President Carter, noted that Osborne was "kind to his sources, which makes him worthwhile to talk to."[166] After all, the higher one is on the White House staff chain, the greater the need to bank credit with a news source. In the Reagan years, *Washington Post* White House correspondent Lou Cannon commandeered much of the same kind of information that Osborne had once featured; he collected and published "Reaganisms" of the week. Regular readers of his column looked forward to their publication and insiders no doubt knew that there was mileage in providing them.

Dynamics of the Current Relationship

The relationship between the White House and the press corps based there is shaped by the continuing need each has for the other. The White House, for its part, seeks to provide reporters with a continual flow of news. Reporters try to get from the press secretary and from others in the White House, including the president, answers to the questions they believe to be important. Along the way, skirmishes erupt. In part, the contention that exists between them flows from the mistrust that has in recent decades colored how each views the other.

A LEGACY OF MUTUAL MISTRUST

Perhaps nowhere is the veneer of hostility in the relationship between the White House and the press more apparent than in the public statements traded between the press corps and recent former press secretaries. Each believes itself victimized by the other. Reporters feel they are used by the White House. "You are a stenographer for functionaries determined to put their spin on events," observed Kurtz.[167] Press Secretary Larry Speakes saw his role as one of the few against the many. "For my six years as White House spokesman, it was Us Against Them," he wrote. "Us was a handful of relatively underpaid but dedicated public servants in the White House press office. Them was the entire White House press corps, dozens strong, many of them Rich and Famous and Powerful."[168] It was a no-win game. Each viewed the other as having the advantage, yet each needed the other's cooperation to do an effective job.

Watergate was the primary source of the mistrust that exists today between the two sides. The press has yet to recover from the stream of lies from the Press Office and from other White House locations, including President Nixon himself. But the mistrust also had earlier roots in the way in which reporters were misinformed by President Eisenhower and his administration during the U-2 affair in May 1960. An American intelligence plane had been shot down over the Soviet Union and its pilot captured. Believing that all evidence of the plane and pilot would disintegrate, the government first stated that the aircraft was a weather plane that had strayed slightly off course. When the Soviets produced the pilot and evidence that it was an intelligence plane, President Eisenhower admitted the truth and defended the need for such surveillance now and in the future.

Mistrust escalated on an almost daily basis during Lyndon Johnson's years as president. In the early days of the administration, the press found the president unwilling to answer questions about his relationship as Senate majority leader with his protégé Bobby Baker, who held the position of secretary of the Senate. Eventually, Baker pleaded guilty to corruption charges and went to jail. Johnson remained silent about their relationship. As the administration progressed, reporters deplored other silences. By far the greatest source of friction was over the lack of accurate information on the progress of the Vietnam War. The misinformation provided by President Johnson on the circumstances surrounding the attacks by the North Vietnamese on two U.S. destroyers, the *Maddox* and the *C. Turner Joy,* resulted in congressional passage in 1964 of the Tonkin Gulf resolution, which commended the president for his handling of the crisis. After the first reports of torpedo attacks were sent to the Pentagon, the task force commander on the *Maddox* sent a telegram asking for a complete evaluation of the incident. "Review of action makes many recorded contacts and torpedoes fired appear doubtful. Freak weather effects and overeager sonarman may have accounted for many reports. No actual sightings by *Maddox,*" the telegram read.[169] But President Johnson chose not to review the facts, and only much later did the telegram become public. When it did become public, along with other facts about the alleged attack on the destroyers, members of the press corps questioned the versions of events provided by the president and the White House staff. Other incidents during the Johnson years also raised the issue of the value of information coming from the White House.

This, then, was the legacy carried into the Nixon administration. By the time President Nixon resigned his office, mistrust had been a major element in the relationship between the president and the news media for a full fifteen years. And it has not disappeared in the years since. Reporters are quick to question a president's motives or to go with a story calling a president's action into question. The details can come later. President Clinton acknowledged the mistrust existing between himself and the press: "I think the most important thing is that we attempt, you and I, to create an atmosphere of trust and respect and that you at least know that I'm going to do my best to be honest with you and I think you're going to be honest with me."[170]

The Twenty-four-Hour News Day

In the past, the news cycle was built around information coming out of the morning public events, the daily briefing, and whatever afternoon activity there was. Television spots and newspaper stories came together in the late afternoon when all of the day's pieces were fitted together. Today, the dynamics of coverage are different because day and night the events that unfold around the world are featured on the television news programs. Questions asked at the press secretary's daily briefing are frequently drawn from stories developed during the day and reported on radio and television news programs, especially CNN. Thus press secretaries do not have the same control over the briefings they once had. At times, the pace of events is so fast that the briefing becomes less of a White House publicity resource than it traditionally was. "In 1980 the White House dealt with three networks who controlled 90 percent of the viewing audience. The news cycle ended at 6:30 with the network news broadcasts," said Tom Rosenstiel of *Newsweek.* "Today the news cycle never ends."[171] *(See box, How the Twenty-four-Hour News Day Works, p. 125.)*

With such a news cycle, stories are constantly developing in a way that makes it difficult for the White House to control. If staff members can get well ahead of events, they have a greater chance of shaping the stories produced. But such efforts are not likely to come from the podium in the briefing room. Instead, the press secretary is likely to choose a strategy of aiming information at the outlets with the greatest impact such as the *New York Times* and the *Washington Post.* When the White House was ready to announce U.S. recognition of Vietnam in 1995, information was provided to the newspapers to round out reporters' stories. Thus the stories contained detailed information on the efforts of the Vietnamese government to track down missing U.S. servicemen. Special background briefings are used in such circumstances to provide the detailed information that such stories require. The briefing is not useful as a setting to prepare for a major news event. And once the story breaks, the briefing is often after the fact.

A Question of Standards

The expansion and diversification of news brought about by developments such as cable television and satellite technology have had a profound effect on the news business. Today, newspapers work on the assumption that their readers already know about, through television, the major news developments occurring overnight. When officials in Washington go to their doorsteps in the morning, they are ahead of the newspaper lying there and that fact changes the aims of news organizations. More emphasis is now placed on explaining why something has happened than on describing the outlines of the actions. Even the networks have been affected by the rapid transmittal of information. David Gergen told of a conversation he had with veteran network executive Larry Grossman: "When Larry Grossman became president of NBC News he told me that his greatest challenge was figuring out how to make the news fresh when so many people had already seen the national and international news stories that the network provided to local stations."[172] When cable arose in the 1980s, it put increasing pressure on news organizations to come up with a new angle for their traditional morning and evening news programs and their Sunday morning interviews. In 1981, 25.2 percent of American households received cable programming while in 1994 the number had risen to 62.4 percent.[173]

The need to find an attractive way to package information has grown more critical with the demise of many newspapers.

HOW THE TWENTY-FOUR-HOUR NEWS DAY WORKS

During the early months of the Clinton administration, seven members of the White House Travel Office were fired. Press Secretary Dee Dee Myers stated in her briefing that the people were relieved of their jobs because of "serious mismanagement. We believe that all of the seven individuals were part of a poor management operation."[1] Questions were immediately directed her way calling for solid information backing up the charges. As the week wore on, supporting information was hard to find. While five of the seven were later rehired by the federal government, only one person, Billy Dale, the head of the office, was brought to trial on criminal charges. He later was found not guilty.[2]

The incident crested on a Friday when the Press Office altered its normal briefing routine. Myers canceled her usual briefing and Communications Adviser George Stephanopoulos continually put off his afternoon one. During the day the White House staff consistently remained behind events. Around noon, Wolf Blitzer, CNN's senior White House correspondent, filed a news story from the White House. At the same time, Stephanopoulos and his staff could be seen in his office clustered around the television set watching Blitzer's report. Blitzer gave details of a memo raising questions of whether the Travel Office malfeasance issue was first brought up by someone who earlier had proposed to take over the travel operation. The memo raised the issue of personal gain as an element in the firings of the Travel Office staff.

At approximately one-thirty in the afternoon, Robert J. Dole, minority leader of the Senate, rose to the floor demanding that the White House get out information on the mismanagement charges. His information came from a Reuters wire story based on Blitzer's CNN news spot. "There are media reports that now suggest the firings were planned as long as three months ago, as part of [a] political coup at the nonpartisan White House travel office," Dole stated. "It had never been done before," he added.[3] All these activities took place in less than two hours. By the time Stephanopoulos held his news briefing three hours later, he found himself having to respond to news reports and official statements that he had had no hand in shaping. The story clearly had washed over the White House with the staff exercising little control over it. That is what happens in a twenty-four-hour news cycle.

1. Press briefing by Dee Dee Myers, May 19, 1993, 5.
2. Toni Locy, "Fired Travel Office Director Acquitted of Embezzlement," *Washington Post*, November 17, 1995, A1.
3. U.S. Congress, Senate, *Congressional Record*, daily ed., 103d Cong., May 21, 1993, S6314.

In 1909 there were 2,600 daily newspapers. That number fell to 1,556 in 1994.[174] In the time between the administrations of Harry Truman and Bill Clinton, the percentage of the population receiving newspapers dropped from 37.0 percent to 22.6 percent.[175] Often a fresh angle on events takes the form of news analysis. "A lot of what we do is what I call souffle journalism," said John Broder, White House correspondent for the *Los Angeles Times*.[176] The mix of story-as-souffle includes "a recipe that calls for one part information mixed with two parts attitude and two parts conjecture. And after twenty-four hours or so, the analysis it contains has fallen flat." Each newspaper has to provide something different and that often can turn out to be the perspective of the reporter. For the *Los Angeles Times* that has meant allowing reporters more latitude in describing presidential initiatives. James Risen, economics correspondent for the paper, told Tom Rosenstiel that "we definitely are willing to write what we think about [the Clinton] budget in a way we were not, say, in the budget package of 1990."[177] Such latitude leads to statements predicting the road ahead. Rosenstiel cited one budget article written by Risen that began by saying: "A few simple statistics go a long way toward explaining why the [Clinton budget deficit plan] may not work, despite the best intentions of its authors." Predictions of doom precede a discussion of the facts of the plan itself.

The impact of news analysis is made more dramatic by the trend among news organizations toward cutting back the space they provide for a president's version of events. Thirty years ago, newspapers regularly provided the transcripts of news conferences. Today, press conference information is contained in news articles, not verbatim transcripts, and the same is true for speeches. Transcript space is provided only for the most important statements, addresses, and speeches.

With the expansion of cable television, the networks are less compelled to give the president prime time for a news conference. In fact, when President Clinton gave his first prime-time conference in June 1993, NBC was the only one of the three networks to carry it live, and it cut away after thirty minutes. The networks give presidents less attention than they once received, but cable television provides contemporaneous coverage of their actions. Major presidential addresses are regularly carried live on CNN. C-SPAN provides interviews with White House reporters and officials as well as full-length coverage of presidential speeches and the press secretary's daily briefing. Major news organizations continue to commit resources to important stories and reporters provide extensive coverage of presidential remarks on prominent issues. "The president ought to be allowed to say what he wants to say to the American people before it is dissected and taken apart," states *Washington Post* correspondent Ann Devroy.[178] "We probably write more presidential speech stories than anyone."

In the case of the recognition of the Vietnamese government, the *Washington Post* provided a transcript of perhaps 75 percent of the speech; a piece by Devroy focusing on President Clinton's speech, the ceremony, and those who opposed the action; a color piece featuring an area draft resister who now lives in Stockholm; and an article on the mixed emotions stirred by the presidential action. The Devroy piece reviewed the president's statement, quoted the detractors of the policy, including Senate Majority Leader Robert Dole, and provided a description of the scene in the White House East Room, including who was there supporting the presidential action. The *New York Times* provided the full text, a White House story, a news analysis, and four separate articles viewing the action from the perspectives of investors, families, those in Vietnam, and refugees in California. All in all, both publications provided the reader with what President Clinton had earlier asked reporters that he be granted: "The only thing I ever ask is, if I have a response and I have a side, let that get out, and we'll let this conflict unfold."[179]

Classifications of White House Information

A president can elect to speak in an official posture or to make unofficial statements. The standard distinctions presidents and their surrogates use to release information fall into three categories: on the record, on background, and off the record.

ON-THE-RECORD INFORMATION

"On the record" means that a government official is speaking for attribution. The statement is officially given and made publicly available. An example of an official statement was President Clinton's declaration of recognition of the government of Vietnam: "Saying the time was at hand to 'bind up our own wounds,' President Clinton today extended full diplomatic recognition to Vietnam."[180] Reporters can use official statements in whatever form they wish.

BACKGROUND INFORMATION

"On background" means that the information may be used but not attached to the name of the official who gave it, even if that official was the president. An example of information coming out of a background session appeared in a *Washington Post* article: "Clinton, sources said, also probably will recommend new efforts to prevent companies from benefiting from affirmative action if they are not really owned by minorities."[181] No name is attached to the information provided; instead, epithets such as "an administration official" or "sources" are used.

Background information has become the coin of the realm for members of the White House staff. The staff of 430 people represent many different voices, which often find their way into reporters' copy. Dissenting words frequently appear in the prestige newspapers and in the news magazines. And sometimes staff members intentionally provide reporters with a statement that is at cross-purposes with a presidential proposal. With photocopy and fax machines as plentiful as they are, reporters frequently receive memoranda that could embarrass the president and some staff members. During the Ford administration, memoranda appeared in print so persistently that Donald Rumsfeld, President Ford's chief of staff, warned White House staff members with one of his Rumsfeld's Rules: "Assume that most everything you say or do will be on the front page of the *Washington Post* the next morning. It may well be. For many reasons, including that, conduct yourself accordingly."[182] In the 1993 Travel Office case, Wolf Blitzer, CNN's senior White House correspondent, received a memo that caused substantial problems for the president and his publicity team. *(See box, How the Twenty-four-Hour News Day Works, p. 125.)*

Background briefings are used on a regular basis to prepare reporters for legislative and administrative initiatives, such as the budget; trips, particularly foreign travel; and important speeches, such as the State of the Union address. Background information also is used to set up a policy proposal so that when the president gives a speech, reporters understand what actually is being said. In addition, the buildup brings the president a stream of articles beforehand that actually set up the speech. Such articles most likely will appear in the *Washington Post,* especially if the speech is to be delivered locally. When President Clinton spoke at the National Archives on July 19, 1995, outlining his affirmative action proposals, advance publicity provided a prepared audience. During the week before the event, the *Post* published two articles by White House correspondent John Harris announcing the speech and detailing its elements. The first article appeared on July 12. The piece, "Clinton Reassures Black Caucus on Affirmative Action Policies," indicated that Clinton would present his conclusions on what affirmative action policies the government should adopt. Three days later, Harris's second article, "Clinton to Push Set-Aside Programs for Poor," this one on the front page, detailed the direction of the speech with some degree of specificity about "set-aside" programs and the president's intention to reaffirm "what the government is already doing." The article cited "administration officials" (five times), "sources" (once), and "senior officials" (once). The one official named in the body of the piece was Clinton's press secretary, Michael McCurry. From that one citation, one can extrapolate where, either directly or indirectly, much of the remaining information originated. News of the speech was later broadcast on television and radio and carried in other newspapers. Thus through careful use of background strategies, the White House was able to get a week's worth of page-one and -two publicity.

From time to time the background information on policy proposals is provided by the major administration figures who are knowledgeable about a policy or issue up for discussion. If it is a budget briefing, the director of the Office of Management and Budget may conduct the briefing for reporters. Any reporter covering the issue, not just White House correspondents, may attend these briefings. Typically, they are held in Room 450 of the Old Executive Office Building, which is a large enough setting to accommodate all the correspondents news organizations might like to send.

Another use of background information is to float "trial balloons." If a policy turns out to be unpopular, the president and the staff can back away without having made a solid commitment to it. Theodore Roosevelt regularly used "trial balloons." Succeeding administrations have found them an equally important device because of the flexibility they provide. For example, staff members in the Ford and Carter administrations mentioned the idea of placing heavy energy taxes on gasoline. But the administrations backed off when it was clear that strong coalitions, and perhaps insurmountable ones, would oppose the idea.

Prestige publications, in particular, benefit from being in the White House information loop. Knowing a few days or weeks ahead where the president is going to be or what the president is doing implies that the paper is all-knowing where the White House is concerned. When the *Washington Post* was able to scoop its competition with the news that President Bush was planning to lift the next day the economic sanctions that the U.S. government had imposed on goods from South Africa, the news of the impending action was put on the front page. President Bush's statement about the lifting of sanctions and related actions, when it finally appeared, was placed near the end of section A.[183] From a White House staff member's point of view, providing such information banks credits with a reporter.

OFF-THE-RECORD INFORMATION

Off-the-record information is supposed to stay under one's hat. The terms under which it is given call for the reporter not to use the material in any way. Through the twentieth century, as presidents have moved to center stage in the nation's political life, the terms under which they have distributed information have changed substantially. At the beginning of the 1900s, presidents spoke only on an off-the-record basis. Reporters understood that they were to keep the president's counsel when they spoke with Theodore Roosevelt while he was being shaved. They also understood the consequences of breaking the rule. At the end of the century, however, a president's statements are made for attribution with almost no off-the-record statements. Even a president's brief responses to a reporter's queries during daily activities—climbing into a helicopter, walking with a head of state, responding to a tourist's question while jogging—are recorded by television, radio, and reporters' tape recorders. All become public and officially uttered statements.

In social situations, however, where reporters or members of news organizations are present, a president's remarks are off the record. Recent presidents have occasionally hosted social events, especially dinners, designed to have reporters get to know them. Although presidents Eisenhower, Nixon, and Reagan did not hold such sessions, Presidents Kennedy, Johnson, Ford, Carter, and Bush, some occasionally and some regularly, met socially with representatives of news organizations. Presidents Kennedy, Johnson, and Bush met informally with reporters as social friends. President Kennedy often dined with reporters such as Stewart Alsop, Charles Bartlett, a columnist for the *Chattanooga Times,* Rowland Evans of the *Herald Tribune,* and Ben Bradlee, who at the time was with *Newsweek.* A longtime member of the Washington scene, President Johnson had friends among the press from his years in Congress. At the behest of his communications adviser Gerald Rafshoon, President Carter held a group of off-the-record dinners for members of news organizations, including publishers, network executives, anchors for television news programs, editors, and bureau chiefs. The idea was to let them meet the president in an informal setting since few in

Washington had a sense of who Carter was. He came to the White House with few friends in Washington, including from among the media. President Bush enjoyed reporters' company fishing, boating, playing horseshoes, golf, and tennis. All of the contacts that presidents have with news organization personnel are helpful in that each side gets to know the other. But that does not necessarily translate into positive copy. That depends on what the president does.

PROVIDING AND PLUGGING LEAKS

Although a very large portion of the information provided to reporters on a background basis from White House officials carries the imprimatur of the president and the president's senior staff, there are unauthorized disclosures as well. Those are the ones that make presidents angry; every president, in fact, gets upset about leaked information. Lyndon Johnson had a White House staff member, Marvin Watson, check the visitor logs to see which reporters staff members were talking to. He also directly asked staff members to tell him of their contacts with reporters. President Carter was upset by leaks and tried to find out their sources on a couple of occasions, including one occasion when there were only four people in the room. Often the information provided is given on background in an effort to distance oneself from it. The senior staff themselves sometimes leak information they want to see printed but not to be associated with. For example, Carter press secretary Jody Powell floated what proved to be a false rumor about Republican senator Charles Percy of Illinois, who was then a vocal opponent of Budget Director Bert Lance. Lance was, at the time, under fire in the Senate. Powell told reporters that Percy had used business aircraft and offices while serving in his capacity as a senator.[184] When the *Chicago Sun-Times* revealed that Powell was floating the story, he came in for heavy criticism.

President Reagan's chief of staff, James Baker, regularly provided reporters with background information, but some Reagan staff members, such as senior adviser Edwin Meese, regarded this practice as leaking. Another viewpoint was expressed by David Gergen, in whose direction White House eyes often turned when he was on the staff and the path of a leak was being traced. What Meese viewed as a leak, Gergen explained, was an instance in which "the goal was to talk it through, to give us a historical context and some background to *why* things were going the way they were and what the President was trying to accomplish."[185]

Despite the pervasive patterns of leaking in the Reagan years, President Bush made clear his antipathy toward leaks. Presidential speechwriter John Podhoretz described the policy:

He signaled the seriousness of his intent during the 1988 transition when he informed a longtime friend and aide that she would not be given a job in the administration because she had had unauthorized conversations with reporters. The example terrified White House staffers, and with the exception of the focused and controlled leaking campaigns against [unpopular chief of staffs] John Sununu and subsequently Sam Skinner, Bush mostly got his wish.[186]

One of the reasons for the low level of unauthorized disclosures was Sununu's interest in tracking leaks. "This was due in part to Ed Rogers, John Sununu's assistant, who was official Leak Inquisitor—if a staffer was told by his secretary that Ed Rogers was on the line, it would fill him with fear and trembling." But the person who cared most about leaks was Bush himself. When the *New York Times* obtained a cable sent by William Reilly, the EPA administrator, from the 1992 summit on the environment held in Rio de Janeiro, President Bush sought to find out who had given it to *Times* reporter Keith Schneider:

He ordered an investigation of all outgoing White House phone calls and selected his favorite suspect, David Mcintosh, a member of Dan Quayle's staff. On a Saturday morning from Camp David, the president called Quayle and began reading from the logs: At 4:09 Tuesday afternoon the staffer had called Keith Schneider's office, and he'd better have a damn good explanation.[187]

Like all presidents who chase leaks, Bush did not find conclusive results. But the search process let off some presidential steam.

Phases in the Relationship with the News Media

No matter who is president and who is reporting, the chief executive and news organizations need one another. When governing requires building support on an issue-by-issue basis to create coalitions, news organizations provide the strongest support-building link to an attentive public. For that reason and others, the president invests large personal and staff resources to ensure that certain media serve the administration's interests. Weekly radio addresses, occasional press conferences and speeches, and White House appearances are effective channels for conveying the president's words and image. Both for the president personally and for the White House staff, news organizations provide not only the hardware to connect technically with the citizenry but also the interpretive link to relay the significance and meaning of the president's words and actions.

The White House press and communications advisers choose settings where the images and words transmitted by the media showcase the president in the way they prefer. In response, the media transmit their judgments on the importance of what the president said and did not say. To news organizations, the president is a top story—the most important continuing subject in national politics. On a day-in and day-out basis, the president receives more air time and print space than any other individual in the national government.

With mutual need creating the context of the relationship between the president and the news media, continuities tend to define the relationship more clearly than differences. Indeed, the relation between the two institutions becomes one of oscillating rhythms as within the span of each administration patterns repeat themselves with predictable regularity. As described in *Portraying the President: The White House and the Media* by Grossman and Kumar, the phases of alliance, competition, and detachment appear sequentially in most administrations.[188] The

President Bill Clinton takes questions during a Rose Garden press conference.

number of months and years making up each phase will vary, but every incoming president can expect to experience similar cycles. In short, the president and the press contend with one another in different degrees of cooperation and contention but with enduring regularity.

ALLIANCE

At the outset of most administrations, the interests and needs of both partners are fairly similar—and, indeed, they soon converge. The central stories of this period tend to introduce the new president and the presidential team, as well as their goals. For their part, presidents generally promise an open administration. Richard Nixon, for example, declared that he and his aides would be "open to new ideas . . . open to the critics as well as those who support us."[189] Others made similar declarations, and, in fact, an open administration works well in the early months. For their part, reporters want to write the kinds of stories that will generate goodwill for the president. For that reason, most chief executives and their staff come into office with the intention of making information available to reporters. Only when reporters begin asking for information that White House staff members do not want to release does the information flow reduce to a trickle.

Almost every modern president has realized his advantage and acted on the early opportunities to use news organizations as they announce staff decisions and describe goals. President Bill Clinton, however, was an exception to this rule. He came into office believing erroneously that the news media would grant him a "honeymoon." But grace periods never have been a formal practice. Instead, it has been the merging of interests that has resulted in early favorable stories. Thus less than six months after coming into office, Clinton complained aloud that he had not been given the honeymoon he anticipated. From the start, then, a contentious relationship was established between the president and the press.

The Clinton administration got off to a bad start with the press by banning reporters from the upper Press Office, an area traditionally open to them. As a result, the stories about denied access sat side by side—and dominated—the routine stories on the new administration and its personnel. Even the traditional stories on new appointees did not work favorably for the Clinton team. Beginning with Zoë Baird, a corporate lawyer nominated to head the Justice Department, several high-profile nominees ran headfirst into a wall of negative publicity. The health care task force proceedings that were not released to the public suffered the same fate. Through diffidence or arrogance, then, the new administration created and shaped its own elective crises. To further exacerbate its problems, a group of critics presented themselves earlier than normal when a new president takes office. In most administrations, critics are reluctant to surface in the early postelection months. Instead, they prefer to show support for the new team and to become critics only when they sense some weakening in the coalition behind the new leader. But as early as election night, the Senate minority leader, Robert Dole, indicated that he would not provide the new president with any automatic support. Because he had received only 43 percent of the popular vote, Bill Clinton's critics gave him no allowances for mistakes.

The unusually early and negative stories about the Clinton team were a product of two factors: elective crises unwittingly fueled by the administration and the immediate surfacing of critics. Reporters sometimes will write negative postelection stories, but rarely to the extent that they were evident in the opening days of the Clinton administration.

COMPETITION

When negative stories begin, an administration must decide whether to tamper with the information flow. Generally, two types of information control are available to the new president: shutting off the information spigot altogether or generating more positive stories. Some presidents find that their staff members are leaking damaging information to the press about the administration and its programs. *(See "Providing and Plugging Leaks," p. 127.)* Lyndon Johnson monitored reporters' communications with senior assistants and tracked the journalists' copy to determine what presidential aides might have said. Some presidents may even manipulate the access enjoyed by reporters as they cover the White House.

To generate more positive coverage of the president, the president's press and communications aides must prepare presidential appearances with great care. The settings and frequency of public presentations are manipulated to emphasize the president's strong points. For Ronald Reagan, who sometimes performed poorly at press conferences, that meant holding down the number of press conferences in favor of Oval Office speeches; Jimmy Carter preferred the opposite mix. George Bush curried favor with reporters rather than deny them access or manipulate the settings of his presentations. Bill Clinton, who moved almost directly into the competition phase because of the prominent place taken by his critics, sought to establish an advantage in his relationship with the press by avoiding the White House press corps. He turned instead to less-established settings, such as radio call-in programs, CNN's *Larry King Live*, and MTV.

DETACHMENT

After expending a great deal of effort manipulating settings and people, presidents and their staffs ultimately realize that all the effort produced less than what they sought. As a result, the staff cuts back on its effort to shape the stories of reporters through direct presidential-press contact. Jimmy Carter drastically reduced the number of his press conferences in his final year and a half in office; he had twenty-two in his first year but only six in his last year. George Bush also held fewer press conferences in his last year—twenty-two compared with thirty-one his first year. Even Reagan, who held few press conferences, staged fewer his last year in the White House; he held twelve his first two years in office and seven in the final two. Detachment also means that the president spends little time entertaining the members of news organizations, until perhaps, as the clock winds down the president begins to think about a spot in the history books.

From administration to administration, alliance, competition, and detachment are predictable phases in the relationship between the president and the press. The phases begin and end depending on the kinds of activity the president undertakes at key junctures in the term. The president may be upset at the information appearing in news stories, but articles generally reflect real political problems. Perception of problems with the press is endemic to the office, but, in fact, reporters are not the president's problem; the problem lies with the critics who talk with reporters. Yet most presidents persist in seeing reporters as the problem.

NOTES

1. "The One-Question News Conference," *Washington Post*, June 15, 1993, A13.

2. Richard B. Morris, *The Forging of the Union, 1781–1789* (New York: Harper and Row, 1987), 23.

3. Frank Luther Mott, *American Journalism, A History: 1690–1960* (New York: Macmillan, 1962), 113 n. 1.

4. Donald A. Ritchie, *Press Gallery: Congress and the Washington Correspondents* (Cambridge, Mass.: Harvard University Press, 1991), 30.

5. Richard Rubin, *Press, Party, and Presidency* (New York: Norton, 1981), 10.

6. Ibid., 12.

7. *National Intelligencer and Washington Advertiser*, November 5, 1800.

8. Mott, *American Journalism*, 179.

9. William Ames, *A History of the National Intelligencer* (Chapel Hill: University of North Carolina, 1972), 114.

10. Ritchie, *Press Gallery*, 17.

11. Ben: Perley Poore, *Perley's Reminiscences of Sixty Years in the National Metropolis*, vol. 1 (Philadelphia: Hubbard Brothers, 1886), 96.

12. Mott, *American Journalism*, 180.

13. James Pollard, *The Presidents and the Press* (New York: Macmillan, 1947), 26.

14. *National Intelligencer and Washington Advertiser*, October 31, 1800, 1.

15. This discussion comes from James Morton Smith, "Alien and Sedition Acts," *Encyclopedia of the American Presidency*, vol. 1, ed. Leonard W. Levy and Louis Fisher (New York: Simon and Schuster, 1994), 47.

16. F. B. Marbut, *News from the Capital: The Story of Washington Reporting* (Carbondale: Southern Illinois University Press, 1971), 30–31.

17. See the discussion in Ritchie, *Press Gallery*, 22.

18. Poore, *Perley's Reminiscences*, 77–78.

19. As quoted in Marbut, *News from the Capital*, 96.

20. Poore, *Perley's Reminiscences*, 77–78.

21. Mott, *American Journalism*, 312.

22. Thomas C. Leonard, *The Power of the Press: The Birth of American Political Reporting* (New York: Oxford University Press, 1986), 78–79.

23. Rubin, *Press, Party, and Presidency*, 52.

24. Ritchie, *Press Gallery*, 23.

25. Ibid., 23.

26. Ibid., 30.

27. Mott, *American Journalism*, 250.

28. Ibid., 249.

29. By 1940 the AP had increased to fourteen hundred newspapers. From this success other wire services, including the United Press Association, which was established in 1907, came into being and expanded from approximately five hundred clients in 1914 to fourteen hundred clients in 1940. Ibid., 710.

30. Elmer E. Cornwell Jr., *Presidential Leadership of Public Opinion* (Bloomington: Indiana University Press, 1965), 11.

31. Ibid.

32. Douglass Cater, *The Fourth Branch of Government* (New York: Vintage, 1959), 85.

33. Ibid., 85–86.

34. Ritchie, *Press Gallery*, 108.

35. Ibid., 109.

36. Ibid., 145.

37. Ibid., 154.

38. Henry Villard, *Memoirs of Henry Villard: Journalist and Financier, 1835–1900*, vol. 1 (Boston: Houghton Mifflin, 1904), 140.

39. Pollard, *Presidents and the Press*, 351.

40. The first published discussion with a president came as a result of an interview that James Gordon Bennett conducted with Martin Van Buren. James Pollard, who chronicled the relationship of each president with the press, characterized the interview as more of a recitation of the publisher's impressions after talking with President Van Buren than an interview. It appeared on January 12, 1839, and "although it caused no sensation at the time," Pollard noted, "it set a precedent." Ibid., 189–190.

41. Ibid., 413. There is some dispute as to which was the first interview granted by President Johnson. Frank Luther Mott indicated that J. B. McCullagh of the St. Louis *Globe-Democrat* was the first to interview a president. See Mott, *American Journalism*, 370.

42. Mark Whalgren Summers, *The Press Gang: Newspapers and Politics 1865–1878* (Chapel Hill: University of North Carolina Press, 1994), 32.

43. Pollard, *Presidents and the Press*, 485.

44. Ibid., 491.

45. Ibid., 501.

46. W. U. Hensel, *Life and Public Services of Grover Cleveland* (Philadelphia: Hubbard Brothers, 1888), 233–234.

47. Leonard D. White, *The Republican Era: A Study in Administrative History 1869–1901* (New York: Free Press, 1965), 101.

48. Ibid., 103.

49. As quoted in Pollard, *Presidents and the Press*, 517.

50. O. O. Stealey *Twenty Years in the Press Gallery* (New York: Publishers Printing, 1906), 34.

51. George Juergens, *News from the White House: The Presidential-Press Relationship in the Progressive Era* (Chicago: University of Chicago Press, 1981), 14–15.

52. Ibid., 15.

53. Lewis L. Gould, *The Presidency of William McKinley* (Lawrence: Regents Press of Kansas, 1980), 3, 11–12.

54. Ibid., 241; White, *Republican Era*, 102.

55. Ida Mae Tarbell, "President McKinley in War Times," *McClure's Magazine*, May 1898–October 1898, 98, 214.

56. Gould, *Presidency of William McKinley*, 38.

57. Ibid., 241.

58. Louis Ludlow, *From Cornfield to Press Gallery* (Washington, D.C.: W. F. Roberts, 1924), 321.

59. Leo Rosten, *The Washington Correspondents* (New York: Harcourt, Brace, 1937), 22.

60. David Barry, *Forty Years in Washington* (Boston: Little, Brown, 1924), 270.

61. Ibid., 271.

62. A *Washington Star* correspondent, as quoted in Juergens, *News for the White House*, 55–56.

63. Ibid., 114.

64. Oscar King Davis, *Released for Publication* (New York: Houghton Mifflin, 1925), 176.

65. Cornwell, *Presidential Leadership of Public Opinion*, 46.

66. Ibid., 45

67. Ibid., 49.

68. Ibid., 113.

69. Davis, *Released for Publication*, 136.

70. Ibid., 157.

71. Juergens, *News from the White House*, 97.

72. Ibid., 140.

73. Cornwell, *Presidential Leadership of Public Opinion*, 39.

74. Ibid., 41.

75. Barry, *Forty Years in Washington*, 309.

76. Marbut, *News from the Capital*, 174.

77. Ibid., 175.

78. Pollard, *Presidents and the Press*, 717–718.

79. Ibid., 719.

80. Marbut, *News from the Capital*, 175.

81. Rosten, *The Washington Correspondents*, 46.

82. Barry, *Forty Years in Washington*, 268.

83. Ibid., 269.

84. Rosten, *The Washington Correspondents*, 40.

85. Ibid., 44.

86. Ibid., 46.

87. George F. Parker, *Recollections of Grover Cleveland* (New York: Century, 1909), 174–176.

88. Ludlow, *From Cornfield to Press Gallery*, 328–329.

89. Davis, *Released for Publication*, 102.

90. Henry L. Stoddard, *As I Knew Them: Presidents and Politics from Grant to Coolidge* (New York: Harper and Brothers, 1927), 299–300.

91. Davis, *Released for Publication*, 184.

92. Cornwell, *Presidential Leadership of Public Opinion,* 43.

93. As quoted in ibid., 44.

94. Ibid., 109.

95. Ludlow, *From Cornfield to Press Gallery,* 269.

96. Juergens, *News from the White House,* 151.

97. John Hart, "White House Staff," in Levy and Fisher *Encyclopedia of the American Presidency,* vol. 4, 1641.

98. Ann Devroy, "Keeping a Campaign Pledge to Rein in Costs," *Washington Post,* July 3, 1995, A21.

99. William E. Leuchtenburg, *Franklin D. Roosevelt and the New Deal, 1932–1940* (New York: Harper Torchbooks, 1963), 42.

100. Ibid.

101. Cornwell, *Presidential Leadership of Public Opinion,* 255.

102. Ibid., 263.

103. Ibid.

104. These numbers are derived from the White House section of *The Capital Source* (Washington, D.C.: National Journal, 1994), 8–11. The listing includes approximately two hundred people, without counting such offices as National Security Council, National Economic Council, National Drug Control Policy, Environmental Policy, Domestic Policy Council, and Administration. For current distinctions of what falls outside of the White House proper for staffing purposes, see Ann Devroy, "Keeping a Campaign Pledge to Rein in Costs," *Washington Post,* July 3, 1995, A21.

105. Marbut, *News from the Capital,* 178.

106. Patrick Anderson, *The President's Men* (Garden City, N.Y.: Doubleday, 1968), 59.

107. Cornwell, *Presidential Leadership of Public Opinion,* 218.

108. Ibid., 220.

109. Transcript, James Hagerty oral history interview, March 2, 1967, Columbia Oral History Project, 56, as quoted in Michael B. Grossman and Martha J. Kumar, *Portraying the President: The White House and the News Media* (Baltimore: Johns Hopkins University Press, 1981), 153.

110. Anderson, *The President's Men,* 193.

111. Ibid., 182.

112. Dwight Eisenhower, *Mandate for Change, 1953–1956* (Garden City, N.Y.: Doubleday, 1963), 117.

113. Marlin Fitzwater, *Call the Briefing: Bush and Reagan, Sam and Helen, A Decade with Presidents and the Press* (New York: Times Books, 1995), 3.

114. Ibid., 105–106.

115. Douglass Cater, *The Fourth Branch of Government* (New York: Vintage, 1959), 23.

116. See the discussion of roles performed by the Press Secretary in Grossman and Kumar, *Portraying the President,* 136–149.

117. Ibid., 137–138.

118. A reporter on background, as quoted in Martha Joynt Kumar, "Freelancers and Fogmeisters: Party Control and White House Communications Activities" (Paper presented at the annual meeting of the American Political Science Association, Washington, D.C., September 2–5, 1993), 37.

119. Ibid.

120. Larry Speakes with Robert Pack, *Speaking Out: The Reagan Presidency from Inside the White House* (New York: Charles Scribner's Sons, 1988), 155.

121. Ibid., chap. 10.

122. Ibid., 136.

123. As quoted in Grossman and Kumar, *Portraying the President,* 152.

124. Ibid., 58.

125. As quoted in ibid., 153.

126. From Cornwell, *Presidential Leadership of Public Opinion,* 228.

127. Anderson, *President's Men,* 191.

128. As quoted in Grossman and Kumar, *Portraying the President,* 145.

129. Ibid.

130. Anderson, *President's Men,* 182.

131. Howard Kurtz, *Media Circus: The Trouble with America's Newspapers* (New York: Times Books, 1993), 249.

132. Tom Rosenstiel, *The Beat Goes On: President Clinton's First Year with the Media* (New York: Twentieth Century Fund, 1994), 14.

133. Michael K. Deaver, with Micky Herskowitz, *Behind the Scenes* (New York: William Morrow, 1987), 175.

134. John Anthony Maltese, "White House Office of Communications," in *Encyclopedia of the American Presidency,* vol. 4, ed. Leonard W. Levy and Louis Fisher (New York: Simon and Schuster, 1994), 1633–1634.

135. John Anthony Maltese, *Spin Control: The White House Office of Communications and the Management of Presidential News* (Chapel Hill: University of North Carolina, 1994), 186–187.

136. Ibid., 194.

137. Ibid., 198.

138. Ibid., 208.

139. Ibid., 235.

140. As quoted in David S. Broder, *Behind the Front Page* (New York: Simon and Schuster, 1987), 198–199.

141. Ibid., 200.

142. Kurtz, *Media Circus,* 251.

143. As quoted in Pollard, *Presidents and the Press,* 781.

144. Harold W. Stanley and Richard G. Niemi, *Vital Statistics on American Politics,* 5th ed. (Washington, D.C.: CQ Press, 1995), 53. All figures come from this source except those for Reagan, Bush, and Clinton, which are taken from the totals given in *Public Papers of the President.* Thus all figures, where available, are taken from the *Public Papers of the President.*

145. Cornwell, *Presidential Leadership of Public Opinion,* 157.

146. Ibid., 173.

147. Ibid., 170.

148. Ibid., 172.

149. Grossman and Kumar, *Portraying the President,* 243.

150. Ibid., 140.

151. Kurtz, *Media Circus,* 238.

152. Speakes, *Speaking Out,* 258.

153. The figures, as of July 11, 1995, were provided by the four separate congressional galleries. They are subject to fluctuations within a year.

154. Stephen Hess, *The Washington Reporters* (Washington, D.C.: Brookings, 1981), 49.

155. Ibid., 156–157.

156. As quoted in Cater, *Fourth Branch of Government,* 32.

157. Carl Cannon, telephone interview by author, July 8, 1995.

158. Pool report #1, May 20, 1993.

159. Stanley and Niemi, *Vital Statistics in American Politics,* 47.

160. Speakes, *Speaking Out,* 220.

161. Ibid.

162. Ibid., 227.

163. Speakes, *Speaking Out,* 231.

164. As quoted in Grossman and Kumar, *Portraying the President,* 32.

165. Kurtz, *Media Circus,* 255.

166. As quoted in Grossman and Kumar, *Portraying the President,* 171.

167. Kurtz, *Media Circus,* 238.

168. Speakes, *Speaking Out,* 217.

169. David Wise, *The Politics of Lying: Government Deception, Secrecy, and Power* (New York: Vintage, 1973), 62–63. In this, one of the most complete accounts of the incidents, Wise calls the Tonkin Gulf incident "the most crucial and disgraceful episode in the modern history of government lying."

170. Gwen Ifill, "President, in Prime Time, Is Spurned by Two Networks," *New York Times,* June 18, 1993, A19.

171. Tom Rosenstiel, telephone interview, July 13, 1995.

172. David Gergen, "Commentary," in *The Future of News: Television, Newspapers, Wire Services, Newsmagazines,* ed. Philip S. Cook, Douglas Gomery, and Lawrence W. Lichty (Baltimore: Johns Hopkins University Press, 1992), 207.

173. Stanley and Niemi, *Vital Statistics on American Politics,* 47.

174. Ibid., 50, for the 1994 figure. For the 1909 figure, see "Ready Reckoner of Advertising Rates and Circulations," *Editor and Publisher Interna-

tional Yearbook (New York: Editor and Publisher, 1994), front matter (un-numbered).

175. Stanley and Niemi, *Vital Statistics on American Politics,* 50.

176. Rosenstiel, *The Beat Goes On,* 31.

177. Ibid.

178. Ann Devroy, telephone interview, July 5, 1995.

179. Ifill, "President, in Prime Time, Is Spurned by Two Networks."

180. Alison Mitchell, "U.S. Grants Full Ties to Hanoi; Time for Healing, Clinton Says," *New York Times,* July 12, 1995, A1.

181. John F. Harris, "Clinton to Push Set-Aside Programs for Poor," *Washington Post,* July 15, 1995, A5.

182. Donald Rumsfeld, "Rumsfeld's Rules," in *The Presidency in Transition,* vol. 6, ed. James P. Pfiffner and Gordon Hoxie (New York: Center for the Study of the Presidency, 1989), 40.

183. Kurtz, *Media Circus,* 242.

184. Grossman and Kumar, *Portraying the President,* 175.

185. Mark Hertsgaard, *On Bended Knee: The Press and the Reagan Presidency* (New York: Farrar, Straus, Giroux, 1988), 41.

186. John Podhoretz, *Hell of a Ride: Backstage at the White House Follies 1989–1993* (New York: Simon and Schuster, 1993), 56.

187. Ibid., 60.

188. Grossman and Kumar, *Portraying the President,* 273–298.

189. As quoted in Rowland Evans Jr. and Robert D. Novak, *Nixon in the White House* (New York: Random House, 1971), 33–34.

SELECTED BIBLIOGRAPHY

Broder, David S. *Behind the Front Page.* New York: Simon and Schuster, 1987.

Cater, Douglass. *The Fourth Branch of Government.* New York: Vintage, 1959.

Davis, Oscar King. *Released for Publication.* New York: Houghton Mifflin, 1925.

Fitzwater, Marlin. *Call the Briefing!: Bush and Reagan, Sam and Helen: A Decade with Presidents and the Press.* New York: Times Books, 1995.

Grossman, Michael B., and Martha J. Kumar. *Portraying the President: The White House and the News Media.* Baltimore: Johns Hopkins University Press, 1981.

Hertsgaard, Mark. *On Bended Knee: The Press and the Reagan Presidency.* New York: Farrar, Straus, Giroux, 1988.

Hess, Stephen. *The Washington Reporters.* Washington, D.C.: Brookings, 1981.

Juergens, George. *News from the White House: The Presidential-Press Relationship in the Progressive Era.* Chicago: University of Chicago Press, 1981.

Kurtz, Howard. *Media Circus: The Trouble with America's Newspapers.* New York: Times Books, 1993.

Leonard, Thomas C. *The Power of the Press: The Birth of American Political Reporting.* New York: Oxford University Press, 1986.

Ludlow, Louis. *From Cornfield to Press Gallery.* Washington, D.C.: W. F. Roberts, 1924.

Maltese, John Anthony. *Spin Control: The White House Office of Communications and the Management of Presidential News.* Chapel Hill: University of North Carolina Press, 1994.

Marbut, F. B. *News from the Capital: The Story of Washington Reporting.* Carbondale: Southern Illinois University Press, 1971.

Pollard, James. *The Presidents and the Press.* New York: Macmillan, 1947.

Poore, Ben Perley. *Perley's Reminiscences of Sixty Years in the National Metropolis.* Vol. I. Philadelphia: Hubbard Brothers, 1886.

Ritchie, Donald A. *Press Gallery: Congress and the Washington Correspondents.* Cambridge, Mass.: Harvard University Press, 1991.

Rosenstiel, Tom. *The Beat Goes On: President Clinton's First Year with the Media.* New York: Twentieth Century Fund, 1994.

Rosten, Leo. *The Washington Correspondents.* New York: Harcourt, Brace, 1937.

Rubin, Richard. *Press, Party, and Presidency.* New York: Norton, 1981.

Speakes, Larry, with Robert Pack. *Speaking Out: The Reagan Presidency from Inside the White House.* New York: Charles Scribner's Sons, 1988.

Summers, Mark Whalgren. *The Press Gang: Newspapers and Politics 1865–1878.* Chapel Hill: University of North Carolina Press, 1994.

CHAPTER 4

Public Support and Opinion

BY CHARLES C. EUCHNER

D EMOCRACY BEGINS with the consent of the governed. But unless citizens have the mechanisms they need to relay their desires and opinions to the government, the government cannot claim the support of the people. Without public support, which provides a guiding vision of the identity and interest of the community, the government can degenerate into raw power politics. The government can, in short, lose its legitimacy.

Elections are the most obvious way that people tell the government what they think and what they want. But elections are blunt instruments. They occur only periodically. The issues in campaigns change, and the positions of candidates and parties often are unclear. As for the electorate, it usually renders an inchoate verdict. Elections express tendencies, not certainties.

People communicate with the government in other ways as well. They call, write, fax, or send electronic mail and telegrams to elected officials. They march in Washington to show their intensity and numbers. They also express their views in letters to newspapers or calls to radio or television programs, which often are monitored by political actors. Finally, they work through interest groups and political parties to make their views known.

People in government—especially elected officials like the president—fret daily about how the public will react to new government policies and actions. When the public indicates a strong preference for a certain course of action, politicians pay heed. Public support also is a political resource. Presidents can bolster their bargaining positions with Congress, for example, by referring to their high approval ratings in public opinion surveys. Likewise, presidents can bolster institutional support for their policy initiatives by referring to public support for the initiatives.

Public opinion, however, is not everything. Democratic processes also involve bargaining among elite groups, negotiating with foreign countries, struggling over legal definitions, controlling public institutions such as schools and utilities, and managing major economic institutions.

But even if public support is just one element of politics, it is an important one. Political scientist E. E. Schattschneider has argued that politicians always have tried to bolster their positions by claiming support from ever-expanding segments of the population.[1] But after the nation's suffrage was expanded to almost all citizens, politicians had to turn to other ways of widening the "sphere" of politics. Public opinion polls offered one way to bolster claims of support. Demonstrations, letters, telegrams,

telephone calls, and feedback from key party leaders, elected officials, and interest groups also indicated support.

Understanding the role of public opinion in the presidency requires first understanding the fundamental levels and sources of support for the presidency as an office and then determining how specific presidents work with that support. All presidents enjoy a basic reserve of support because of the public's near reverence of the office. But individual presidents experience a complex, constantly changing level of support for their programs and styles of leadership.

The President's Relationship with the Public

The American public has deep psychological bonds with all of its presidents. Those bonds may be strained by specific events and the conflicting interests of the population, but they are a foundation for the president's oscillating relationship with the public.[2]

Most schools teach Americans to respect the presidency, even when they find fault with a specific president on important issues. The media, economic enterprises, voluntary associations, cultural events, and even some religious institutions also promote a general respect for the office. This fundamental support for the presidency creates a basic reserve of popular support that occupants of the Oval Office can use in developing backing for their specific programs and actions.

The presidency is revered largely because the chief executive is the most visible single figure in American life. All but a tiny segment of the population knows who the president is at a given moment. In comparison, a 1995 national survey found that only 48 percent of the population knew one of their two senators, 33 percent knew their House member, and 24 percent could name both of their senators. In fact, the U.S. president is well known throughout the world.[3]

As the only government officials who represent the entire population, the president and the vice president are unique in American politics. Other elected officials—members of Congress, governors, and local government officials—have parochial outlooks. The Supreme Court has a national constituency, but its members are appointed, and its role in American politics is obscure and usually limited to narrow legal argumentation. The president is the only person who can profess to speak for the "national interest" and the "general will" of the people. As com-

The single most visible figure in American life, the president is covered by the media as both a personality and government official.

political scientist Fred I. Greenstein, is evident in the different attitudes of adults to the office of the presidency and the specific president in office. Political actors use this generalized support for the office to generate specific support for the incumbent in times of scandal and during reelection campaigns. It is common for the president's backers in difficult times to ask for public support by referring to "the president" rather than the specific name of the president. Richard Nixon's 1972 campaign slogan was "Reelect the President" rather than "Reelect Richard Nixon."

The childhood lesson that the president is benign and patriotic comes to the surface any time the nation faces a crisis. A military attack such as that on Pearl Harbor, a technological challenge such as the *Sputnik* launch, or a nation's sorrow over such tragedies as the assassination of John F. Kennedy caused the public to offer the president unquestioned, almost paternal loyalty for at least a short period.

Because the average citizen knows little about politics, he or she tends to identify with the president's personality as a shortcut to dealing with the complexities of the government. If citizens can develop "trust" of the president's personality, they can feel safe leaving the complexities of governing to the chief executive. Because the president is covered in the media as a personality as well as a government official, citizens are able to develop a vicarious relationship with the president.

On this subject, Murray Edelman, a leading student of the political uses of symbols and language, has written:

Because it is apparently intolerable for men to admit the key role of accident, or ignorance, and of unplanned processes in their affairs, the leader serves a vital function by personifying or reifying the processes. As an individual, he can be blamed and given "responsibility" in a way that processes cannot. Incumbents of high public office therefore become objects of acclaim for the satisfied, scapegoats for the unsatisfied, and symbols of aspiration or of whatever is opposed.[5]

mander in chief, the president projects this appearance to the rest of the world.

The prestige of the presidency is enhanced by the president's role as head of state as well as the top government official. Other nations, such as Great Britain and Japan, give symbolic functions to a queen or emperor and leave the job of governing to someone else. But the president is the embodiment of the state in the United States. Much of the emotional attachment that Americans give to the nation as a whole, therefore, also is transferred to the president.

On a more basic level, the first political figure that children learn about is the president. Children perceive this figure to be a uniquely benevolent, intelligent, powerful, and even-handed person. Although people grow up to be more skeptical of specific presidents, they retain the early lesson that the presidency is a special, important, stabilizing office usually deserving of awe.[4] One of the first tests of presidential candidates is that of "looking presidential."

The "legacy of juvenile learning," to use the terminology of

The public has a tendency to "project" its desires on the president—in other words, to interpret the president's actions to fit with the way it would like the president to be. Psychologists speak of citizens reducing "cognitive dissonance," or avoiding unpleasant facts or interpretations that might undercut a preferred view of the world. The citizen's desire to believe in the strength and stability of the system causes this identification with the president. This process becomes evident when the president uses vague language to appeal to groups with different goals. Even when the president's actions produce clear winners and losers, both groups often interpret the actions in a way that makes the actions coincide with their own desires.

The public's emotional attachment to the president does not always work in the president's favor. Presidents who have complex or contradictory personas can confuse and even anger the public. According to scholar Garry Wills, President Bill Clinton's early drop in popularity stemmed from his frequent movement between the world of "dogpatch" Arkansas politics and culture and the sophisticated and calculating world of national politics.

"He was as much at home with his mother, the Elvis groupie, as he was with his wife, the legal scholar. Not bad training for a politician—or so one would think. But onlookers can be puzzled by the blur of transitions as he takes them through time warps from one world to the other."[6] A president needs a consistent persona to exploit the national psychological yearning for a strong father figure.

The public's psychological needs for strong leadership contribute to a steady base of presidential support. One study has confirmed the proposition "Persons having great needs for strong guidance, regimen, and a well-ordered society will probably score more highly on measures of general support for the president than individuals who do not have such needs."[7]

As for their overall views of government and politics, Americans tend to be less ideological and more pragmatic than citizens of other countries. Surveys show that most Americans place themselves in the "moderate," or middle, part of the political spectrum.[8] They share common fears about big government, suspicion of elites, support for basic political rights, and the desire to assert American interests in foreign policy surely but quickly. America's cultural consensus, however, has frayed in the past generation. Since the late 1960s, sociologist James Davison Hunter writes, Americans have been engaged in bitter "culture wars" over the very meaning of the ideas and symbols, such as family, once central to a common national ethos.[9] These tensions have made presidential leadership more difficult. Presidents dare not stray too far from the national symbols, yet the meanings of the symbols are being increasingly contested.

Forms of Public Expression

In the years before public opinion polling became a regular part of politics and government, the measures of public support were rough and sporadic. This unscientific measurement of public support fit the original desires of the Founders. The drafters of the Constitution had been wary of the pressures that public sentiments would have on the government's operation. The Constitution therefore contains limits to the influence of public opinion, such as indirect election of the president and Senate (before the Seventeenth Amendment), "checks and balances" among the branches of government, a divided legislature, an independent national judiciary appointed for life, and a federal system of national and state governments.

Institutions usually mediated public opinion in the nation's first century. As former corporate executive Chester Barnard has noted, to gauge public opinion nineteenth-century legislators "read the local newspapers, toured their districts, and talked with voters, received letters from the home state, and entertained delegations which claimed to speak for large and important blocks of voters."[10]

Polling dominates modern presidents' efforts to gauge public opinion, but the White House still pays attention to the more traditional means of assessing public opinion. These vehicles provide the much-needed "texture" for understanding the mood of the country that is not captured by polling data. Other vehicles for measuring opinion—such as computer networks—promise to gain importance in the future.[11]

PARTY AND OTHER ORGANIZATIONS

Until World War II, state and local party organizations provided the most regular and reliable information on political attitudes. Party leaders were in touch with voters about issues ranging from trade to internal improvements. Attitudes toward political matters were revealed by local party meetings, as well as by the outside efforts of reform organizations and petition drives. If an issue persisted, officials at higher levels often began to pay attention to it. Much of the reform impulse in national politics around the turn of the century came from the activities of parties and reform organizations in states and cities.

As states and localities passed reform legislation for the organization of city government and the regulation of business, national leaders began to shift their ways of doing business. Woodrow Wilson's legislative program was, for some, a response to the demands of reform organizations in the states. Franklin D. Roosevelt kept a regular watch on party organizations in cities such as New York, Chicago, Philadelphia, and Detroit.

Party organizations did not just offer a rough measurement of public opinion; parties also stabilized and developed the support of particular groups. Because party membership demanded some commitment, political figures could be more certain of their popular standing with active citizens. Polls, however, measure the opinions of *uncommitted* as well as committed citizens. As political scientist Theodore J. Lowi has written: "The moorings of the voters are now so loose that, regardless of any partisan consistency displayed in local elections (which is lessening too), their relationship to the presidency is highly personal."[12]

The rise of third parties in the prepolling years offered a dramatic demonstration of changes in public opinion. When the two major parties did not address developing political issues, new parties developed to give voice to those concerns. Public opinion found expression in third parties on issues such as slavery, agriculture policy, monetary policy, women's rights, and labor relations.

Interest groups and elected officials have long been vehicles for transmitting opinion information to the president. The Kennedy administration kept a finger on the pulse of the civil rights movement through contacts with leaders of the National Association for the Advancement of Colored People and other organizations. Presidents regularly visit economic leaders in groups such as the U.S. Chamber of Commerce and the Business Roundtable, as well as social groups and the organizations of causes such as environmentalism and women's rights.

PUBLIC DEMONSTRATIONS

Public events—demonstrations, parades, strikes, and riots—have provided the president and other government leaders with

Despite reliance on polls as the chief measure of public opinion, presidents also heed the dramatic expressions of public demonstrations. Here abortion rights supporters march in 1995 against violence at health clinics.

dramatic expressions of public opinion throughout U.S. history. Protests and demonstrations have taken on, among other issues, slavery, tariffs, women's rights, gay rights, ethnic and religious divisions, Prohibition, wars, abuses of monopolies, capital-labor disputes, agricultural problems, the death penalty, civil rights, welfare rights, school busing, abortion, education, and drug abuse. But with the development of more regular and "scientific" means of measuring public opinion, public events have declined in importance.

Demonstrations expressed public opinion most vividly during the 1880s and 1890s when farmers, workers, and owners of small businesses took to the streets to demand government regulation of corporations and basic protections and assistance programs. The protest movements of that period were instrumental in forming populist organizations and campaigns as well as in structuring the countermovements of the progressives and conservatives.[13]

Despite the dominance in recent years of polls as expressions of public opinion, citizens have used demonstrations since the 1960s to express their opinions on civil rights, abortion, gay and women's rights, and involvement in war. People who either do

not have the ballot or find the ballot to be an empty gesture tend to favor protest as a way of expressing their opinions. Political scientist Benjamin Ginsberg has found that nations with well-established voting procedures are not the scene of demonstrations when economic conditions change for the worse. But the citizens of nations with less reliable voting procedures, such as Latin American countries, must take to the streets to express their opinions.[14] These findings suggest that formal procedures for expressing opinion preclude the spontaneous development and expression of opinion.

Studies also show that lower-income people are more likely to take part in demonstrations than they are to vote. Underrepresented in voting booths and many surveys, these people go to the streets to express their opinions about a wide range of issues. This form of participation occurs especially during times of crisis, as Frances Fox Piven and Richard A. Cloward demonstrated in their analyses of civil rights, workers, tenant, and welfare rights movements.[15]

Demonstrations continue to offer a gauge of the sentiments of selected groups. In 1982 one million people gathered at New York City's Central Park to protest against President Ronald Reagan's nuclear arms buildup and refusal to rule out U.S. initiation of nuclear conflict with the Soviet Union. The administration publicly dismissed the demonstration, the largest in American history, but understood its intensity. Reagan's political strategists attempted to put Reagan in situations where he could assuage the fears of people concerned about the danger of nuclear war.[16] Opponents of the administration's policies in Central America also applied pressure in protests and demonstrations.

During the Bush and Clinton administrations, activists staged protests to express themselves on, among other things, abortion, the Persian Gulf War, and the admission of gays to the military. Although protests were once considered a tool of the left, the right also took to protests as a way of acquainting elected officials with its likes and dislikes. In October 1995, Nation of Islam leader Louis Farrakhan organized a "Million Man March" in Washington. African American men from all across the country came to the march and pledged to commit themselves to their families and their communities. As is the case for all demonstrations, part of the reason for the march was internal: to send a message to African American men about the importance of solidarity and responsibility. The march also demonstrated the numbers and intensity of middle-class African American men.

NEWSPAPERS, TELEVISION, AND RADIO

Until the Civil War, newspapers were partisan sheets designed not so much to deliver news as to persuade or agitate a fiercely partisan audience. The fortunes of a newspaper—especially the size of its circulation, advertising, and the reaction it received from elites and the general public—provided a rough barometer of the public mood. Newspapers also indicated party strength because they depended on the parties for advertising and readership, and party strength provided clues about the popularity of presidents.

Newspapers were as important in shaping public opinion as in measuring it. James Bryce, the noted British analyst of American politics, wrote of readers' acceptance of partisan newspaper versions of events: "They could not be at the trouble of sifting the evidence."[17]

With the newspaper boom of the late nineteenth century, newspapers dropped their blatant partisan ties. Readership of the New York *World,* the nation's first mass-circulation newspaper, rose from 15,000 to 1.5 million between 1883 and 1898.[18] Because newspapers were cheap and geared toward the general public, they reached every class of people. Many cities had a dozen or more newspapers with distinct readerships. The news pages, letter columns, and advertising space all gave indications about the tenor and trend of popular opinion. Today, with daily newspaper readership in decline, news and opinion columns have become less reliable indicators of the public mood. Other media provide vehicles for gauging elite and mass opinion.

Radio and television talk shows became major forces in the creation and expression of political opinions in the 1980s and 1990s. Programs featuring personalities such as Larry King, Rush Limbaugh, and Jerry Williams offered running commentary with call-ins from listeners across the country. Callers to such programs tend to express intense viewpoints on issues. The radio hosts, in particular, feed into public passions with their strong rhetoric and exhortations to flood offices in Washington with telephone calls and faxes. Even when the shows do not take calls from listeners, their ratings-conscious hosts are savvy pulse-takers of the popular mood.

The White House has attempted to tap into the passions of talk radio. President Clinton invited talk-show hosts to set up their broadcasting operations on the White House lawn during an early push for health care reform in 1994. White House operatives appear on some programs as guests. President Clinton himself appeared several times on the nationally syndicated *Imus in the Morning* radio program.

LETTER WRITING

One of the most common forms of public expression is letter writing to the president and other public officials.[19] In the nation's early years, letter writing was a practice used mostly by economic and educational elites. As the nation expanded its notion of democracy, and as the government extended its reach during times of crisis, the letter-writing population grew to include not only elites but the whole literate public. Then, with the growth of mass communications, the letter became a regular tool of instantaneous public opinion pressure. The first major letter-writing campaign persuaded George Washington to seek a second term as president in 1792.

Like other forms of political activity, letter-writing booms during periods of national crisis. During periods of "normalcy" before the New Deal, the number of letters written per 10,000 literate adults ranged from 4.7 in 1900 during William McKin-ley's administration to 11.8 during Herbert C. Hoover's administration before the 1929 economic crash. The letter-writing rate increased during the crises of the Civil War (44 letters per 10,000 literate adults) and World War I (47). A major—and permanent—change came with the presidency of Franklin Roosevelt. Roosevelt's mail rate reached 160 during the Great Depression and fell to 111 during the relative calm of the late 1930s.

Until recent years, most letters were the work of persons acting on their own initiative. According to one study, less than 10 percent of Franklin Roosevelt's third-term mail could be linked to interest groups: "Mail is very often a means through which unorganized and transitory interests make themselves heard."[20]

Headline events are most likely to spur letter writing. State of the Union addresses, presidential speeches on television, press conferences, congressional hearings, wars and other military events, major appointments, Supreme Court decisions, international summits or meetings, and political scandals spark mass letter writing. The top letter-writing events in recent years included the Vietnam War, the Watergate scandal, the energy crisis, the proposed nomination of Robert H. Bork to the Supreme Court, crisis events in the Middle East and in the cold war with the Soviet Union, and the Iran-contra affair.

Many letter-writing campaigns are instigated by prominent officials during controversial political events. Sen. Joseph R. McCarthy of Wisconsin, for example, initiated a deluge of letters to President Dwight D. Eisenhower urging that the United States cut ties with countries doing business with the People's Republic of China. Members of Congress who regularly correspond with voters urge constituents to write letters to the president on key issues.

The president, too, sometimes calls for letters to the White House and to Congress to indicate support for presidential policies. Full-time White House staffers read and keep track of letters the president receives to determine the general flow of opinion.

Interest groups have begun to play a more prominent role in spurring letter writing. National organizations and grassroots organizations often circulate postcards and letters on specific issues for supporters to sign and send to the White House and Congress. Interest groups also print advertisements in newspapers urging a barrage of letters to elected officials. Interest groups with vast memberships are capable of managing letter-writing blitzkriegs to the president, to members of Congress, and to state officials. But those letters often rate only cursory consideration because the recipients can see that they are not spontaneous. They do, however, reinforce the sense of vulnerability of some elected officials.

Even though polls have replaced letters as the regular means for assessing public opinion, letters can provide clues about concerns that are submerged in the restricted format of surveys. In 1954, for example, the Democratic National Committee received a number of letters from people concerned about the effects of inflation on pensions. It was the first indication that inflation was a prime concern among the elderly. Letters thus can draw attention to issues that pollsters do not include in their surveys.

Besides giving the president a means of measuring public opinion, letter writing provides a way for the public to pressure other politicians in Washington. The power of letters was vividly underscored in the mid-1980s when both President Reagan and Democratic representative Daniel Rostenkowski of Illinois appealed to television audiences to write to them about tax reform issues. The president and congressional leaders both used letters to bolster their arguments during the tax reform procedures.

Letter writing, then, still influences both large- and small-scale policy initiatives, but, as might be expected, this once intimate form of communication has become part of the larger process of technologically sophisticated politics, driven by advances in computers and telecommunications technologies.

A new form of letters—messages sent electronically via computers (and popularly known as electronic mail or "e-mail")—provides modern presidents with public reaction to major policy initiatives. Most computer network services also provide forums for members to speak out on major issues.[21] The Clinton administration, which received unprecedented numbers of letters, telephone calls, and other communications during its first year in office, assigned a full-time staffer to gather and analyze the electronic mail messages to the president and vice president. Clinton also recruited volunteers from the Washington area to process the thousands of letters received daily in the early months of his administration.

TELEPHONE CALLS AND TELEGRAMS

For immediate reactions to political events, telephone calls and telegrams have replaced letters and have augmented the increasing use of overnight polls.

Telegrams provide a tangible if biased indication of support. White House officials referred to the volume of positive telegrams they received to bolster their credibility during such crises as the Watergate scandal, the Vietnam War, the explosion of the space shuttle *Challenger,* and the congressional hearings over the Reagan administration's secret dealings in the Iran-contra affair.

Vice-presidential candidate Nixon survived a major crisis in 1952 when he appealed on television for telegrams expressing support for his continued candidacy. Nixon's "Checkers speech" produced, according to Nixon's own reckoning, between one million and two million telegrams and permitted him to stay on the Republican ticket despite the controversy over the propriety of a fund for his personal expenses.

During the Iran-contra investigation in 1987, White House officials and backers pointed to the thousands of telegrams sent to fired National Security Council aide Oliver North as a sign of public support. North brought bags of the telegrams to the congressional hearings, giving both himself and the White House a boost during the administration's greatest crisis.

Also during the Iran-contra affair, Reagan referred to the deluge of supportive telephone calls he had received. "After my speech, some 84 percent of those people who called in supported me," Reagan said. "It was the biggest outpouring of calls they've ever had. The letters coming in are in my favor."[22]

Formal Surveys and Polling

Presidents and other political figures have used surveys since the early nineteenth century, but only since the development of sophisticated systems of communications and analysis have surveys and polls become a major part of White House efforts to measure and shape public opinion.

Polling data are often sketchy and contradictory, but they at least reduce the uncertainty under which the president operates. As President Reagan's pollster, Richard Wirthlin, suggested, polling is "the science of ABC—almost being certain."[23]

EARLY POLLS

The first poll in the United States was a straw poll measuring support for presidential candidates John Quincy Adams and Andrew Jackson; it appeared in the *Harrisburg Pennsylvanian* in 1824. With the rise of mass-circulation newspapers in the 1880s, polls became regular features. Newspapers such as the *New York Herald Tribune, Los Angeles Times,* and *St. Louis Republic* all regularly published poll results. A 1936 survey of *Literary Digest* readers, which predicted that Alfred Landon would defeat Franklin Roosevelt for the presidency, both damaged polling's credibility and helped to pave the way for more sophisticated surveys. The *Digest*'s huge mistake—Roosevelt won by a landslide—was attributed to the built-in bias of the polling sample, which consisted of the magazine's predominantly Republican, well-to-do readers.

The founder of modern polling was George Gallup, whose surveys helped his mother-in-law to win election as secretary of state in Iowa in 1932. Gallup wrote a doctoral thesis on sampling techniques and in 1935, with Elmo Roper and Archibald Crossley, founded the independent Gallup poll, which was the leader in scientific polling for decades. Gallup was a key figure in giving polling its scientific credentials by using large, representative sample sizes and carefully worded questions.

Franklin Roosevelt was the first president to use polling data regularly to interpret the public's reactions to the political and policy actions of the administration. As U.S. involvement in World War II became more likely in the late 1930s, Roosevelt received advice from Gallup on how to frame his rhetoric on possible U.S. involvement. Around the same time, Princeton University professor Hadley Cantril conducted surveys to determine the supply and demand of housing and consumer goods as well as public attitudes about the war. Cantril later polled members of the military about their housing and supply conditions during the war.

New York lawyer and congressional candidate Jacob K. Javits

In the Fish Room (now called the Roosevelt Room) across from the Oval Office, President Lyndon Johnson set up charts displaying his private polls before the 1964 election.

is thought to have been the first candidate for a public office to commission a private political poll (1946).[24] Harry S. Truman in 1948 and Dwight D. Eisenhower in 1952 used polls to develop campaign appeals. With the availability of regular information about voter attitudes, elections and governing became more and more intertwined.

John F. Kennedy hired pollster Louis Harris two years before his successful 1960 presidential campaign to gauge support and develop strategy. After that, polls gradually developed into a daily part of government action and the flow of news and academic analysis. By 1962 virtually all gubernatorial candidates, two-thirds of all Senate candidates, and half the winning candidates for the House of Representatives were commissioning polls sometime during their campaigns.

Lyndon B. Johnson was the first president to hire a pollster for the White House staff, Hadley Cantril's son Albert. The administration also consulted pollster Oliver Quayle regularly. Throughout his term, Johnson kept a steady stream of polling data flowing into the White House from every state. Academics working at Johnson's presidential library in Austin, Texas, have found dozens of memorandums and poll results among Johnson's papers.

When faced with growing opposition to the Vietnam War, Johnson frequently referred to polls that suggested that a majority of Americans favored the administration's war policies. Johnson rejected arguments that most of the nation was uninformed and that those who were knowledgeable about the war opposed it. When polls showed a majority of Americans opposing the war effort, Johnson moved toward a decision against seeking a second full term in office.

Nixon's public relations campaigns were based on the idea of the "silent majority," which the president claimed backed his administration's policies on Vietnam, civil rights, crime, regulation, social programs and budget priorities, and the Watergate

affair. The lack of widespread opposition to his policies, Nixon argued, could be interpreted to be approval. Nixon's argument, in effect, gave as much weight to people with no strong feelings or knowledge as to those with well-informed, strong views.

Nixon regularly used polls to help formulate policy statements and to plan strategies for dealing with Congress and interest groups. When polls showed that he was personally popular with blue-collar workers, Nixon decided to ignore the opposition of labor union leadership on issues such as wage and price controls.

CURRENT PUBLIC OPINION EFFORTS

Polls became pervasive in U.S. politics in the 1970s. In 1972 no newspapers conducted their own polls; they relied on private polling organizations. But by the end of the decade, most major news organizations were conducting regular surveys, which became an important part of determining which stories were "news." Today, dozens of newspapers and magazines, television and radio stations, government agencies, business firms, universities, and private organizations commission surveys of political and social attitudes and habits. Surveys are so pervasive that pollsters now ask survey questions about polling itself.[25] Polling also has become a daily part of White House operations. This practice began with the presidency of Jimmy Carter.

Carter's Use of Polls

Jimmy Carter became president with no Washington experience and an uncertain ideology; he therefore did not have a strong sense of his role in the government. His campaign was successful partly because of the work of Patrick Caddell, a pollster who was one of the top architects of the campaign agenda. Once in the White House, Carter regularly sought advice from Caddell, and polling data assumed a prominent role in presidential decision making.[26] In fact, Carter often relied on polls to tell him what other presidents, such as Ronald Reagan, gleaned from their own internal ideological "compasses."

Perhaps the most significant moment of Carter's presidency was the nationally televised speech he delivered about the country's moral lassitude. During a gas shortage in the summer of 1979, Carter planned to deliver a speech to promote a variety of energy conservation and development initiatives. While working on the address, however, he decided that it would fail to move a public that already had heard four such presidential speeches. Caddell gave Carter polling data and a memorandum recommending a shift in emphasis. Carter's decision to act on the data was one of his presidency's fateful moments.

Caddell's data suggested that the public would react cynically to another call for energy conservation. The memorandum said that the public had become "completely inured" to warnings about the energy crisis and would not make sacrifices because of cynicism about both the government and the oil industry.[27] Caddell argued that the breakdown of faith in U.S. institutions could be overcome only with a dramatic call for common cause and sacrifice. Caddell had been making that argument to Carter at least since the 1976 campaign.[28]

Carter's speech—which analyzed a "crisis of confidence" in the American public—originally was well received. But a series of cabinet firings, which Carter acknowledged handling "very poorly," then created an atmosphere of crisis—not so much in the nation as in the administration.[29] The "malaise" speech, as it came to be known, became a source of ridicule rather than national unity.

Reagan's Use of Polls

Despite widespread criticism of Carter's reliance on polls, Reagan brought campaign pollster Richard Wirthlin with him to the White House in 1981. While consistently articulating the basic themes of small government and international power, Reagan developed his rhetoric and policy proposals based on data supplied by polls and focus groups. Annual funding from the Republican National Committee (RNC) of about $900,000 allowed Wirthlin's firm, Decision Making Information, to conduct the most extensive and expensive polls ever undertaken on behalf of a president.

Wirthlin's surveys and regular "tracking" polls—in which changes in a sample of opinion were followed daily—affected administration policy in several areas. Reagan's "honeymoon" poll results encouraged the president to seek dramatic tax and budget legislation in early 1981. Later data, as well as an outcry from legislative leaders and interest groups, persuaded Reagan to drop plans for wholesale changes in Social Security. Early in 1982, administration officials feared that the economic slump would lead to big midterm losses for congressional Republicans. Polling data showed widespread support for giving the administration's tax policies a chance, but they also revealed disturbing declines in support from blue-collar voters. When polls began to show a decline in the percentage of the public urging the ad-

ministration to "continue as is," Reagan agreed to budget and tax compromises with Congress.[30] Polling data also guided administration actions on the nomination of Sandra Day O'Connor to the Supreme Court, U.S. involvement in the Lebanese civil war, Reagan's visit to the Bitburg cemetery in West Germany, and tax reform.

Wirthlin's most extensive polling took place in early 1987, when the administration struggled to control the effects of disclosures that the White House had secretly sold arms to Iran in exchange for help in releasing American hostages in Lebanon and that profits from the sales went to help rebels fight the government of Nicaragua. During the first six or seven weeks of the year, Wirthlin conducted rounds of interviews with 25,000 people—more people than most pollsters interview in an entire year.[31]

The Reagan administration, attentive every day to poll results, orchestrated a number of dramatic events that provided surges of support. Foreign summits, Oval Office speeches, military attacks on Libya and Grenada, emotional public appearances after tragedies such as the truck bombing of the marine barracks in Lebanon and the space shuttle *Challenger* explosion, and strongly worded statements after terrorist attacks and the Soviet attack on the Korean Air Lines plane—all provided "rally points" for Reagan.

Wirthlin's polling measured not only public attitudes toward issues, but also the public's emotional response to the president and his program. Wirthlin asked voters about how they felt toward President Reagan and his political rivals. When voters expressed doubts about the president's empathy and stability in international affairs, Wirthlin scripted public events and television advertisements that depicted Reagan as a person concerned about ordinary people's lives. The spots helped to strengthen the public's trust and emotional attachment to Reagan.

Presidents typically do not use polls to determine major policy stances. But polls do give the president information about what issues to highlight and downplay. Polls might not determine presidential policy and strategy, but they help to guide it. In a period of tumult, such guidance can be critical.

Polling in the Bush Years

George Bush lacked Reagan's strong ideology, and he could not claim that his election was a mandate for particular policies. He therefore had to rely increasingly on survey data over the course of his term—he rarely used pollsters during his first year in office, however—to help him formulate his policy pronouncements and to demonstrate to Congress that these policies had public support. Because of his tenuous mandate, Bush needed concrete evidence of public support as an extra political resource. With high approval ratings, the president could tell Congress and other parts of the political establishment that "the people" supported White House initiatives.

After the Persian Gulf War, President Bush may have paid too much attention to the polls, which showed his public approval ratings hovering near 90 percent. Bush and his advisers concluded that the American public was solidly behind the president, when in fact the polls represented a temporary surge of support. Because the president is the symbol of the nation as a whole, Bush benefited from the inclination of Americans to "rally 'round the flag" in a national emergency. But soon the nation turned its attention to other concerns, such as a slack economic recovery and a crisis in the health care system.

Bush's inability to develop a coherent domestic policy agenda has been attributed to his overreliance on polls. Bush reacted to public opinion on such things as the budget deficit, economic recession, civil rights, and the Los Angeles riots of 1992. His overreaction to some opinion surveys prompted him to expend valuable time and resources advocating constitutional amendments mandating a balanced budget and banning flag burning as a form of protest. The president, however, did not have an overall policy framework. Thus the public viewed his disconnected initiatives skeptically. Bush's reliance on survey data in his unsuccessful reelection campaign of 1992 reveals one of the main pitfalls of polling. Surveys underscored the importance of shoring up the conservative movement within the Republican Party, and Bush attempted to do just that during the party convention and fall campaign. Yet in the process he alienated his broader pool of potential voters, many of whom eventually cast their ballots for Democrat Bill Clinton or independent H. Ross Perot.

Clinton and the Perils of Polls

Bill Clinton won the presidency in 1992 with only 43 percent of the popular vote. Sensitive to the need to attract a broader base, Clinton used polls to figure out how to appeal to the independents who had voted for Texas billionaire Perot. But Clinton's desire to appeal to the broad electorate undermined his focus and resulted in the image of a waffling politician.

All recent presidents have arranged for their national party organizations to pay for polling that assists the White House. Thus the Democratic National Committee paid pollster Stanley Greenberg $1,986,410 for polling in Clinton's first year in the White House. Greenberg conducted several polls and focus groups each week for Clinton.

To many critics, Clinton's use of polls was far too obvious. Frank Luntz, a pollster who tracked public opinion for the opposition Republican Party, remarked on the fit between Clinton's public rhetoric and survey data:

When I conduct focus groups, from Topeka to New York, I quite literally hear, word for word, the same things Bill Clinton is saying. I know it's not because people are copying Bill Clinton. It's what they think and feel. That's what's so critical about Clinton—he understands what people feel, not just what they think. He's a pollster's dream because he can internalize what Stan Greenberg tells him. Words from focus groups become Bill Clinton's words.[32]

Clinton's aides denied that the president used polling data to guide basic decisions, but they admitted that polling was used to

Two months before he was sworn in as president, President-elect Bill Clinton solicited opinions from residents and business owners of a Washington, D.C., neighborhood.

help package and sell the president's proposals. One adviser to the president said: "With Bill Clinton, you are working with someone who knows what he believes and wants to know better ways of describing those positions. We shouldn't change [policy positions], but we should help him communicate them. Stan does an excellent job testing and analyzing the different options for the messages."[33] Clinton used polling data to package the 1993 budget-deficit reduction proposal. Clinton described his plan as "5-3-1" at a press conference—$5 in budget cuts for every $3 in additional taxes on the wealthy and $1 in additional taxes on the middle class—after surveys showed the formulation resonated with voters.[34]

Reliance on polling data, however, can provide a false sense of support. When they first announced their intention to overhaul the nation's health care system in 1993, President Clinton and First Lady Hillary Rodham Clinton appeared to enjoy the broad support of the public. But support for reform was "soft." When the blueprint for reform was delayed for months, Republican opponents and interest groups mounted a long-term campaign to cast the plan as dangerous "social engineering." By the time congressional allies had scheduled a vote, public support had dropped precipitously.

Reliance on polls to help guide decision making creates other dilemmas. Attention to short-term fluctuations in the public mood can undermine a president's ability to develop stable policies over the long term. Presidents, who typically experience the same patterns of support, may find attempts to alter those patterns distracting. Such attempts also can produce cynicism among the public.

Factors in Presidential Popularity

Presidential popularity tends to decline throughout the four-year term in office, with short-term increases after important international events and at the beginning of a reelection campaign or at the end of the term. Since 1945, the Gallup poll has surveyed Americans about once a month to determine popular support for the president. The identical question—"Do you approve or disapprove of the way [the incumbent] is handling his job as president?"—has produced data that track presidents' relations with the public.

Presidents between 1953 and 1969 attracted the support of 75 percent of the public, with a standard deviation of 3.1 percentage points; the approval ratings of presidents serving between 1969 and 1984 was 59.7 percent, with a standard deviation of 8.6 percentage points. The overall mean was 62 percent in the early period and 48.1 percent in the later period.[35]

Every president enjoys a honeymoon period in which the nation gives the new chief executive broad, general support.[36] An administration's early days are considered the best time for a president to pass difficult legislation, such as Carter's energy program or Reagan's tax- and budget-cutting packages.

After his third month in office, Truman received a rating of 87 percent; for the same period Kennedy received a rating of 83 percent. Lyndon Johnson had a rating of 80 percent after his second month, and Gerald R. Ford and Carter had early 71 percent ratings.[37] Elected with just 43 percent of the vote in 1992, Clinton's ratings never reached higher than 59 percent in his first four years in office, and he had an approval rating of 38 percent by June of his first year.[38]

Political scientist Samuel Kernell has argued that a president's popularity throughout the four-year term is partly determined by the results of previous polls.[39] Poll results do not vary much from month to month—mostly because only a small segment of the population is likely to veer very far from its orientations, but also because of the public's inertia and use of previous polls to judge the president. Presidents therefore have a strong base of support at the beginning of their term. The key question for the president is how quickly the support will decline.

Since the beginning of the Gallup survey, public approval of the president has ranged from a low of 14 percent for Carter to a high of 89 percent for Bush.[40] The approval rating for Nixon during the final days of perhaps the greatest crisis of the modern presidency—the Watergate affair, which led to Nixon's resignation August 9, 1974—was 23 percent.

The oscillation of support within an administration was greatest during the Truman presidency. Truman's support varied by as much as 64 percentage points, from a low of 23 percent to a high of 87 percent. Eisenhower had the most consistent support. In his first term, approval scores were almost always between 60 and 80 percent, and in his second term the scores largely ranged between 50 and 70 percent.

Of recent presidents, George Bush experienced the greatest highs and lows in public opinion polls. Bush's popularity fell 57 points in Gallup surveys from a high of 89 percent, after the Persian Gulf War in March 1991, to a low of 32 percent in July 1992. Major events, such as the invasion of Panama and the Persian Gulf War, gave Bush increased support. Other developments, such as the stalemate with Congress over the federal budget and the controversy over White House chief of staff John Sununu, hurt the president.[41] Bush's historic approval ratings after the 1991 war in the Persian Gulf probably caused complacency in the White House. Advisers justified Bush's inattention to major domestic issues by pointing to his high poll ratings. When his ratings fell, Bush struggled to define his goals and achievements.

The average levels of support for presidents have varied widely. Kennedy received the highest average rate of support, 70 percent, during his shortened presidency. Other average levels of support were: Eisenhower, 65 percent; Johnson, 55 percent; Nixon, 52 percent; Ford, 47 percent; Carter, 46 percent; Reagan, 53 percent; Bush, 61 percent; and Clinton, 49 percent (1993–1994).[42]

Public orientations change between, as well as during, administrations. Political scientist Stephen Skowronek has argued that presidents live in "political time"—that is, they are forced to respond to the legacies and ideals of their most recent predecessors. To establish their own identities, presidents must distance themselves from their predecessors, but the process of distancing can itself place undue importance on the previous president's legacy. Presidents present themselves as "mirror images" of their predecessors. Reagan depicted himself as a decisive leader in contrast to Carter's image of vacillation. Bush offered the image of an engaged, energetic insider to contrast himself with the hands-off and forgetful Reagan. Clinton's enthusiasm for domestic policy provided a stark contrast with Bush's indifference to domestic affairs and fascination with world politics. In a time of constant change, Skowronek suggests, presidents can break free of their predecessors' legacies and set their own agendas. They can avoid having to fulfill the expectations set by the previous occupants of the Oval Office and instead develop their distinct approaches to the presidency.[43]

PATTERNS OF SUPPORT

Studies by political scientists John E. Mueller and James A. Stimson suggest that public support of the president follows regular patterns, no matter who is president and what policies the president pursues. Mueller argues that the president's popularity declines steadily, virtually in a straight line, after the first several months in office.[44] Stimson argues that popularity ratings follow the form of a parabola, a curve that slowly declines before flattening out and then rising slightly late in the term.[45] Stimson writes: "The president, in this theory, is largely a passive observer of his downsliding popularity."[46]

Both Mueller and Stimson agree that the trend is interrupted—but only temporarily—by "rally points" such as U.S. military involvement overseas, the release of favorable economic news, assassination attempts, and campaign activities. Such events can give a president a spurt of approval. But even if a president benefits from public attention to highly visible news, the basic trend of decline is immutable.[47] According to Mueller, after an average approval rating of 69 percent early in the term, the president's rating will fall about 6 percentage points each year. Because of a "coalition of minorities" effect—in which groups aggrieved by administration policies slowly but steadily build an antiadministration coalition—presidential popularity ratings steadily decline.

Stimson and Mueller disagree, however, about the dynamic aspects of public opinion. A president's popularity at a given point cannot be considered an isolated judgment of the president, Stimson argues. Instead, one month's approval rating feeds into and influences the next. Rather than simply reflecting the accumulation of grievances, as Mueller argues, the decline in popularity results from the public's changing psychological relationship with the president. Early in the term, the president benefits from a sense of excitement and promise. As the term progresses, the president not only disappoints different parts of the public, but also develops an overall persona that many people come to dislike. The popularity decline, in other words, is greater than the sum of the disappointments.

Although the public usually pays little attention to politics and does not know much about presidents, from the media excitement and soaring rhetoric accompanying a new administration, the public develops high expectations of the new president. The two factors—inattentiveness and high expectations—are a dangerous combination for presidents. As political scientist Thomas E. Cronin has observed,

The significance of the textbook presidency is that the whole is greater than the sum of the parts. It presents a cumulative presidential image, a legacy of past glories and impressive performances . . . which endows the White House with a singular mystique and almost magical qualities. According to this image . . . only men of the caliber of Lincoln, the Roosevelts, or Wilson can seize the chalice of opportunity, create the vision, and rally the American public around that vision.[48]

The public, in effect, wants the president to lead them to the promised land, but it does not appreciate the rockiness of the terrain.

The public's response, Stimson points out, is not just a steady decline of support but a deep disappointment, reflected in the fast decline of support. The decline then bottoms out and rises slightly at the end of the term, both because of the public's desire to correct its overreaction and because of the president's return to more simplistic rhetoric as the reelection campaign approaches. A study by political scientists Paul Brace and Barbara Hinckley found the same pattern of decline followed by resurgence.[49]

President Reagan's first-term surge in popularity was unusual. After first- and second-year approval ratings similar to Carter's and Nixon's, Reagan's support surged in his third and fourth years. A January 1983 poll put Reagan's popularity at 35 percent; by his second inauguration it was almost 62 percent. Scholars attributed the surge to favorable economic trends, such as lower inflation and interest rates, and to adept use of public events to rally the nation around the president's leadership. Another cause might have been the nation's desire for a leader in whom it could place faith. After the assassination of President Kennedy and the failed presidencies of Johnson, Nixon, Ford, and Carter, the public may have decided to believe in Reagan's leadership just to give the nation the stability it had lacked since the 1950s.

After one year in office, Clinton had a lower approval rating than most recent presidents: 54 percent in the Gallup poll. His rating was lower than those for Bush (80), Kennedy (78), Eisenhower (70), Johnson (69), and Nixon (63), but higher than those of Carter (52), Reagan (47), Ford (46), and Truman (43).[50] Clinton was hurt in his first year in office by an uncoordinated policy agenda, missteps on appointments, and indecision on major foreign policy issues. Yet Clinton scored important legislative victories on deficit-reduction legislation, a free trade treaty, and a variety of bills that had been vetoed by President Bush (such as a law mandating unpaid leaves of absence for workers to tend to family emergencies, as well as a law mandating the use of the automobile registration process for voter registration).

Brace and Hinckley contend that presidents tend to lose support in greater and greater increments through the first thirty months of their presidencies, at which point approval ratings begin to climb. Presidents and their supporters then take steps to boost popularity in anticipation of the reelection campaign. If a president is reelected, the inauguration period is marked by even greater popularity, but it diminishes quickly in the new term.[51]

According to Brace and Hinckley, four main types of events affect presidential popularity. *Positive acts* are events that a president can control and that produce gains in popularity, such as foreign policy initiatives and announcements of aid to groups and regions. *Hard choices* are events that the president can control but that can produce declines in popularity, such as budget cutbacks or controversial domestic policy initiatives. *Good luck* and *bad luck* refer to events beyond the president's control that produce positive and negative effects on public support, such as changes in the world economy. In recent history, nondiscretionary events—ones the president cannot control—have outnumbered discretionary events by a ratio of almost two to one. Negative events outnumber positive events.

Presidents often respond to "bad luck" events by taking actions on other issues where they can exert greater control. Reagan's reactions to negative events was a case study in using the office's control over some policies to neutralize the negative effects of others. Brace and Hinckley discovered that

Reagan showed a more reactive pattern [than Eisenhower and Nixon] in his second term. Action in the Persian Gulf occurred within the same month as the beginning of the Iran-Contra hearings in May 1987. In June, as the hearings on the scandal continued, the reflagging of Kuwaiti tankers began. In April 1988, as the Edwin Meese scandal led to an investigation of the Justice Department, the marines entered Panama. Reagan's polls fell somewhat during this period, but they remained remarkably stable given the barrage of negative events.[52]

Reagan hoped to maintain his popularity in his second term so that he could earn a place in history as a beloved leader and also help his vice president succeed him in office. Simply serving out two terms was an achievement of sorts in an age of divisive and cynical politics; the last president to serve two full terms was Dwight Eisenhower, from 1953 to 1961.

Second-term presidents are generally less popular than first-term presidents. Eisenhower, Johnson, Nixon, and Reagan all had lower support scores after their second inaugurations. Johnson and Nixon were driven from the White House at least partly by depressed opinion scores.[53] Reagan's second term was marred by the Iran-contra scandal, an uncertain domestic agenda, and splits within the ranks of the Republican Party. Many critics said Reagan assumed a greater mandate for his policy agenda than election results and polls indicated.[54]

The second-term decline has several explanations. First, the president is a "lame duck," without the prospect of a bold reelection campaign to inspire supporters. The public, Congress, and key bureaucrats expect to be involved in national politics after the president's departure, which makes the president's position on long-term issues less and less relevant. Second, problems are more difficult to explain away with reference to the mistakes of the previous president. Reagan constantly referred to the "mess" left him by Carter, but the public was less willing to blame Carter the longer Reagan was in office. Third, the best members of the administration often leave office soon after the president's re-election, creating the aura of a provisional and "second-string" team less deserving of respect. The president also loses top political operatives as they go to work for other politicians who will be involved in public life after the president leaves office. Finally, other politicians, who want to develop an independent base and perhaps succeed the president, try to develop their own political messages distinct from that of the president, reducing the reinforcement that the president's message receives.

Patterns of support also have their partisan aspects. Public approval seems to work differently for Republican and Democratic presidents. Because of their more diverse constituencies, and a lower level of loyalty from their own party followers, Democratic presidents suffer greater declines in popularity than do Republican presidents. The key groups in Democratic coalitions—nonwhites, Catholics, Jews, easterners, manual laborers, and union families—disagree with each other on major issues. The Republican coalitions—whites, Protestants, midwesterners,

westerners, and recently southerners—usually share basic values and so are less likely to be critical of their own presidents than the more diverse Democrats of their top officeholders. For example, Johnson lost 34 points in approval ratings among Democrats between June 1965 and August 1968, and Carter lost 38 points between March 1977 and April 1980. By contrast, Republicans Nixon and Reagan did not lose significant support within their own party until scandals developed in their second terms. Even then, Reagan rallied at the end of his term.[55] Starting with a lower base, Clinton fell 20 points between January and June of his first year in office. Clinton rallied at several points, but it was not until 1996 that his support had rebounded to stay above the 50 percent mark for a sustained period.

The exception to this general rule was Bush. Bush lost support among all segments of the population—Republicans, Democrats, and independents between the elections of 1988 and 1992, when his support among Republican voters fell from 91 to 73 percent; his share among Democrats fell from 17 to 10 percent, and his support from independents fell from 55 to 32 percent.[56] Independent Perot's visibility in the last year of Bush's presidency played a major part in the declines. Bush's own uncertain political agenda, especially after the Gulf War, also contributed. Still, Bush's Republican drop-off in support was smaller than the typical Democratic drop-off.

STEADINESS DURING THE CYCLES

Throughout the cycles of presidential approval, some groups within the public consistently support or oppose the president, while "swing" groups fluctuate greatly and cause the ups and downs of presidential approval. Segments of the population react to public events according to their education, income, gender, and political involvement.

The president usually can depend on support from "partisans," citizens who are members of the same party, and opposition from members of the opposing party. The groups expressing support for the Vietnam War switched with Republican Nixon's move into the White House and Johnson's move out—that is, Republicans generally opposed the war under Johnson but supported it under Nixon. Unless presidents deeply offend the basic tenets of party, they usually can count on party identifiers for support. Many of those people actually will be registered with the party, and others will just "lean" toward the party—and rely on the party for cues—on most issues.

Besides these "partisans," the president also must deal with a set of "believers," a small minority of the population with fully developed ideological stances on a wide range of economic, social, and political issues. Believers are committed to a cause, such as the security of Israel or free-market values. They also have "psychological predispositions" on issues ranging from military activity to community values. Presidents can count on consistent behavior by believers, just as they can count on consistent behavior by partisans. But the consistency depends on the issue rather than the party affiliation.

Another group—the "followers"—is willing to follow the president's lead on a wide range of issues, especially foreign affairs, simply because the president is the president. This group often associates its support for the president with patriotism—a "my president, right or wrong" attitude.[57]

The battle for public opinion, then, centers on the opinions of the less-aligned, more independent citizen. Among the best-educated and involved elements of the citizenry, those who identify with a party rely on partisan cues in assessing the president. Independents, in contrast, react to shifting news events without the anchoring effects of partisanship. If they know that a president is struggling with Congress, they may lower their opinions of that person because of the conflict. If they see the president take a strong stand on an issue, they may raise their opinions of the officeholder.[58] In addition, changes in presidential evaluations tend to occur most rapidly among the best-educated citizens and those who are most attentive to news events. Those with less education and involvement do not closely follow political news and so are less able to react to changing political fortunes.

WHY SUPPORT DECLINES

No matter which model best depicts the trends of approval, it is clear that presidential approval usually declines throughout a term of office. There are several explanations for the decline:

• Inevitable disappointment after high expectations. Presidential campaigns are exercises in popular education and excitement. As the nation prepares to select its next leader, the candidates attempt to depict the positive changes that would occur in their administrations as dramatically as possible.[59]

The public—usually inattentive to politics—gradually gets to know prospective presidents and develops personal attachments to the personalities of the leading contenders. As the media explore the candidates' personal backgrounds, voters get an intimate view of the persons who might lead the next government.

When the president takes office, the public has unrealistic expectations of what might be accomplished. Thus when people begin to see the president's weaknesses, they view the president less and less favorably. Even when the public supports the president's stances and policies on specific issues, it might be critical of the administration's inability to achieve all that was promised. And even when the president is able to deliver on a specific program, support among certain groups may decline because the program yields less impressive results than were expected.

• Accumulation of grievances. When taking the oath of office for the first time, the president has not yet damaged the material fortunes of any segment of society. Even the most skeptical observers—such as business leaders under a Democratic administration or labor leaders under a Republican administration—are willing to suspend judgment of the new president.

As the president submits federal budgets, adopts legislative programs, and uses the "bully pulpit" to promote various social causes, different groups develop specific grievances with the administration. Any public policy decision helps some groups at the expense of others. Even defense and economic policies—which, the president argues, benefit all members of society—have clear winners and losers. High levels of military spending helps out defense contractors and towns where bases are located but undermines other programs facing severe funding restrictions in the budget.

As the president builds a record, some groups develop into consistent winners and others into consistent losers. The greater the number of policy areas affected by White House involvement, the greater is the number of groups affected negatively by policy decisions. Even if a group receives some benefits as well as losses because of the administration's policies, the group's support for the president likely will decline because of unhappiness with the losses. The result of the accumulation of grievances—or the "coalition of minorities effect"—is that groups dissatisfied with government policy are more likely to organize than groups satisfied with the government.[60]

Political scientist Richard A. Brody has linked presidential popularity to the amount of "good" and "bad" news the public receives in the media. Brody's model posits that the public keeps a running score of the news about politics and the economy and rewards presidents who have presided over periods full of good news—regardless of their role in creating that news.[61]

• Manipulation of the political calendar for electoral advantage. When first taking office, the president has one overriding goal: to create the best possible circumstances for a reelection campaign four years later. Secondary goals include passage of important policies and improvement of the president's party strength in Congress and state governments.

These goals demand different kinds of presidential popularity at different points in the nation's electoral cycles. The president will try to time the administration's policies and pronouncements to produce the support necessary for the crucial electoral and policy-making decisions. Most presidents, for example, are willing to see their popularity decline after the first year in office. The first year is usually the best time for achieving budgetary and other legislative goals, which require high levels of popularity. After a couple years of lower levels of support—during which the White House might pursue policy goals through executive action and more modest or bipartisan legislative action—the president seeks to boost public support in time for the reelection campaign.

• Persisting problems. Major national problems—many of which, when first exposed publicly, give the president broad support—develop into liabilities for the president if they are not resolved quickly.

The Korean War, Vietnam War, Watergate scandal, Iran hostage crisis, fears about drug trafficking and abuse, and American involvement in the Lebanese civil war all gained the president broad public support when they first came to the public's attention. But after those problems remained unsolved for one or more years, the public became disenchanted and turned against the president.

President Carter's experience with Iran was a dramatic example. When Iranian students stormed the American embassy in Tehran and took fifty-two Americans hostage on November 4, 1979, Carter's popularity jumped dramatically. His approval rating, which was 14 percent on October 30, rose to 38 percent on November 13 and almost 58 percent the next January 22. But as the crisis dragged into the summer months, Carter's popularity ratings dipped into the low 30s.

• Evidence of a breach of faith. Because they feel they have a highly personal relationship with the president, Americans are more likely to lose confidence in the chief executive over a personal moral failing, such as lying, than over ineffective, dangerous, or even immoral policies.

President Nixon's slide in public opinion did not come with revelations that his administration had undertaken questionable activities, such as illegally bombing Cambodia during the Vietnam War, destabilizing the Marxist regime of Chilean leader Salvador Allende, and presiding over a number of unethical campaign practices. The slide came instead with revelations that he had consistently covered up such activities.

Controversial Reagan administration policies in Central America, the Middle East, Iran, and South Africa did not cause Reagan as much trouble as the public's concern that he may have lied about his activities. When former White House aide Oliver North acknowledged and even bragged about breaking the law (shredding government documents, lying to Congress, diverting government funds to Nicaraguan rebels), the White House experienced a loss of support.

George Bush's popularity during his last year in office was marred by a number of problems, such as the continued rule of Saddam Hussein in Iraq, civil war in Somalia and the old Yugoslavia, persisting bitterness with a Democratic Congress, stagnant trade talks with Japan, and an economic recession. Bush's experience in foreign affairs, a boon most of his presidency, came to be seen as a sign of indifference to domestic problems.

Bill Clinton battled the "character" question throughout the first four years of his presidency. Even though public opinion polls showed little interest in the specific controversies that dogged Clinton—such as the Whitewater investigation, allegations of sexual infidelity and harassment, and investigations of cabinet officials—the public consistently expressed doubts about Clinton's values.

ISSUES AFFECTING PRESIDENTIAL POPULARITY

The relative importance of foreign affairs and domestic politics to presidential popularity is difficult to determine. In foreign affairs, the public is quick to unite behind the president because the source of concern is external. Domestic policy, however, usually involves internal divisions, so public support is less monolithic.

Domestic Affairs

The condition of the national economy can help or hurt a president's level of popularity, but not always in simple ways. People who hold the government responsible for the economy's overall performance—and their own economic fortunes—are likely to judge the president according to data about inflation, unemployment, interest rates, and so on. But about half of the population—those with a philosophy of "economic individualism"—are likely to take responsibility for their own economic fortunes. Generally, the more a person follows media accounts of the economy, the more that person holds the president responsible for the state of the economy. Partisanship biases a person's assessment of the economy. People are more willing to excuse poor economic trends when a president of their party is occupying the White House.[62]

Referring to the election adage that people vote according to "pocketbook issues," some students of public opinion maintain that a president is only as popular as the economic conditions allow. During periods of high unemployment or high inflation, the president's popularity is bound to suffer. As the nation's most visible public figure, the president bears the brunt of voter anxiety about the economic health of the country. Likewise, presidents benefit when economic conditions are good.

The experience of twentieth-century presidents lends some support to the pocketbook interpretation of presidential popularity. The most dramatic example of a president suffering from poor economic conditions was Herbert Hoover, president when the Great Crash of October 1929 plunged the nation into its severest depression. The popularity of Hoover's successor, Franklin Roosevelt, appeared to decline at the end of his second term when the nation experienced another economic downturn. Historian David Green has argued that the failure of the New Deal to produce prosperity forced Roosevelt to shift political tactics by 1938. To distract the nation from the economic slump, Roosevelt launched public campaigns against "reactionaries" at home and fascists abroad.[63]

Eisenhower's popularity ratings—the steadiest ever recorded for a president—declined when the nation entered a deep recession in 1958. The first poll of the year gave Eisenhower a 60 percent approval rate; by the time of the midterm congressional elections, it was down to 52 percent. Eisenhower also had the highest disapproval scores of his two terms during 1958—as high as 36 percent. More important, Eisenhower's Republicans were thrashed in the congressional campaign, losing forty-seven House seats and fifteen Senate seats.

The 1970s were a particularly difficult time for the U.S. economy, with, at various times, double-digit inflation and unemployment rates, a trebling of energy prices, high interest rates, and unprecedented trade and budget deficits. The conditions led one president, Nixon, to make drastic changes in the U.S.

With high rates of unemployment and food lines like this across the nation, in 1932 Americans voted their "pocketbooks" and gave Franklin D. Roosevelt a landslide victory over the incumbent Herbert Hoover.

and world monetary systems and to impose wage and price controls for the first time in peacetime.

Presidents occupying the Oval Office during periods of economic stagnation have struggled to maintain a moderate level of popularity. Johnson, Nixon, Ford, Carter, and Reagan all suffered in the polls during perilous economic times. As political scientist Kristen R. Monroe has pointed out, economic factors such as unemployment and inflation may have both an immediate and a cumulative effect. The public has a "lagged response" to inflation—that is, one single monthly increase in inflation will have a political effect for as many as eleven months. Monroe has written: "The lagged impact suggests that the public has a long memory. The public is not easily distracted by sudden declines in inflation which directly precede an election."[64]

President Clinton presided over a strong economy in his first two years in office but gained comparatively weak approval ratings. Confusion over his legislative agenda, controversy over political appointments and his proposal to lift the ban on homosexuals serving in the military, and the Whitewater investigation hurt Clinton. Nevertheless, the president rallied after legislative passage of his budget bill and the North American Free Trade Agreement (NAFTA) in 1993 and speeches on economic and health care initiatives. By the summer of 1994 weak personal approval ratings again threatened Clinton's proposals for health care reform on Capitol Hill; Democratic leaders in Congress introduced their own bills and stressed that their plans were "not the Clinton plan."

The election of Republican majorities to both houses of Congress in November 1994 radically changed the focus on the debate. Instead of national health insurance, Republicans proposed eliminating the entitlement to Medicaid for poor Americans, cutting the growth of Medicare, and other reforms. Throughout 1995 and into 1996, Clinton battled with Republicans over these reforms and a budget deal that would balance the federal budget in seven years. As polls showed the public supporting the White House stance on budget priorities, Clinton was able to regain some control of the national agenda. This along with continued good economic news was enough to carry Clinton to victory in the 1996 presidential campaign.

Other pocketbook issues affecting presidential popularity include tax rates, the strength of social welfare programs, and perceptions of government efficiency. All these factors affect the public's sense of economic well-being and, perhaps, its view of the president's performance. In fact, studies show that economic problems are more likely to damage a president's popularity than economic well-being is likely to boost the president's standing.[65]

Domestic events outside the economic sphere affect presidential popularity as well. Domestic disturbances such as the urban riots of the 1960s, controversial issues such as abortion and gay and lesbian rights, presidential appointments, and domestic scandals all tend to damage the president's popularity.

The Foreign Policy Explanation

Because pocketbook and other domestic issues do not provide the popularity boosts that most presidents seek, they often turn instead to a series of foreign policy events to help them regain their popularity.[66] Most analysts attributed President Reagan's strong rebound from low poll ratings during his first term to improvements in the economy. According to one study, the rise in Reagan's approval rating from 35 percent to 61 percent "seems to have been caused almost entirely by changes in economic conditions in the country."[67] Theodore Lowi maintains, however, that the economic improvements took place too gradually and affected people too little to produce Reagan's dramatic turnaround.[68] (Indeed, Reagan's ratings on specific economic issues—such as inflation, budget deficits, and efforts to get the country out of the recession and to help groups in economic distress—were very negative.) According to Lowi, Reagan's approval rating improved significantly after *foreign policy events* with which he associated publicly, such as the bombing of the U.S. embassy in Lebanon, the Soviet attack on the Korean Air Lines plane, the redeployment of marines in Lebanon, changes of leadership in the Soviet Union, and the invasion of Grenada.

Thus as Lowi has suggested, foreign policy events of short duration help a president's public standing, even if the event itself is not considered a "success" for the president. Domestic politics has a less certain effect on ratings. Positive economic news is considered the most useful domestic event for a president, but many experts question how much it can help a president's overall standing. Other domestic events—such as the passage of major spending programs or regulatory policies—are more divisive since they almost always produce clear losers as well as winners.

The president's tendency to become more involved in foreign policy as the term progresses may be an indicator of the public's inclination to "rally 'round the flag." Other reasons for greater presidential involvement in foreign policy exist—such as the greater experience and expertise acquired by the administration over time—but the steady decline in approval ratings may give the president a reason to look to foreign affairs as a way of boosting, at least temporary, public support. For example, the March 1947 announcement of the Truman Doctrine increased President's Truman's public support by 12 percentage points (from 48 percent to 60 percent); the surge endured over nine months. Likewise, trips to Europe in 1970 and Russia in 1972 upped Nixon's popularity by 7 and 9 percentage points, respectively, but the surges in support were short-lived—only two months.

The public's willingness to back a president in times of international crisis is almost complete. Franklin Roosevelt, for example, saw his public support rise from 72 percent to 84 percent after Japan's bombing of Pearl Harbor in 1941. President Kennedy marveled at his public support after an event that he acknowledged to be a complete failure: the aborted invasion of Cuba and attempted overthrow of Fidel Castro at the Bay of Pigs. Kennedy's public approval rating jumped from 73 to 83 percent after the disaster, with only 5 percent of the public giving negative views. A Democratic fund-raiser in Chicago after the Bay of Pigs invasion produced an overwhelming show of support for Kennedy.

Kennedy and other presidents have experienced surges of support after other major foreign policy events, whether or not they were "successes." In addition to the Bay of Pigs invasion, Kennedy's foreign policy crises included the Cuban Missile Crisis, the construction of the Berlin Wall to separate the eastern and western parts of Berlin, and the assassination of South Vietnamese president Ngo Dinh Diem. Incidents producing gains in other presidents' approval ratings have included: the Gulf of Tonkin crisis (Johnson); the early bombing of North Vietnam and Cambodia (Nixon); the *Mayaguez* incident and the fall of Saigon (Ford); the taking of American hostages at the U.S. embassy in Iran and the Soviet invasion of Afghanistan (Carter); terrorist attacks in Europe, the attack on a Korean Air Lines plane that strayed into Soviet territory, the Grenada invasion, the U.S. bombing of Libya, and the U.S. response to crises in the Philippines and Haiti (Reagan); the invasion of Panama, events leading up to the Gulf War, and the period during and after the war (Bush); and the American bombing of Iraq in retaliation for an alleged assassination plot against President Bush (Clinton).[69]

The rally effect is counteracted, two political scientists argue, when major "opinion leaders" such as public figures and the mass media express doubts about the president's policy. When the opinion leaders are divided or opposed to a president's policy, the public decides whether to support the president based on its judgment of the policy's success or failure.[70] President Bush's ups and down in public approval during and after the Persian Gulf crisis reflect the shift from elite unanimity to ambivalence. Bush rallied the public when he spoke frequently and clearly on the subject, but his ratings fell when he let others define or obscure the issues.[71]

Without decisive responses, foreign policy crises can produce "slump points" as well. Clinton's foreign policy was dogged by doubts from opinion leaders, and the policy actions in Somalia and Bosnia tended to produce ambiguous results. Yet Clinton's success in other areas—assistance to Russia's reform government, engagement in the peace process in the Middle East and Northern Ireland, and negotiation of world trade treaties—did not produce significant jumps in public support. Because the foreign policy victories were not accompanied by dramatic and continual good news in the media, they were easily overshadowed by his troubles on other issues.

In the post–cold war era, a time of uncertainty about the American role in the world, foreign policy presented mixed opportunities for presidents. For example, some 74 percent of the public approved of President Clinton's 1994 deployment of the U.S. military to the Persian Gulf in response to Iraq's massing of troops along the Kuwaiti border. But while 84 percent said they would support military action if Iraq invaded Kuwait, only 30 percent said they would support U.S. intervention without direct Iraqi belligerence. That put Clinton in a position of talking loudly but only occasionally being permitted to use the "stick" of American power.[72]

Presidents often can use the political structure of their support and opposition to initiate major changes in policy. In this context, they count on their supporters to back them despite their new policy and on their opponents to back them because of it. President Nixon, for example, was able to establish a polit-

Presidents often visit American troops abroad to build public support back home for military operations. President George Bush spent Thanksgiving Day 1990 with U.S. troops stationed in the Persian Gulf region before the outbreak of the Gulf War.

ical relationship with the People's Republic of China because of his career as an anticommunist. Nixon's allies could not resist their own president. Reagan also used his record of anticommunism to justify a risky initiative with communists—in this case, ambitious arms-limitation negotiations with the Soviet Union. Journalist Sidney Blumenthal wrote: "A Democrat, or even a traditional Republican, who returned from a Geneva summit praising Mikhail Gorbachev for being 'sincere' would be assailed as a naive appeaser. . . . Yet Reagan is unscathed. . . . Though Reagan has said and done things that would be considered weak in a Democratic president, he is seen as strong."[73] Polls showed that Reagan's record as an anticommunist helped him to neutralize right-wing opposition to agreements with the Soviets. As political scientist Lee Sigelman noted, "Americans may well reconsider their opposition on those dramatic occasions when the president rises above his own deeply help principles."[74]

It might be incorrect to ascribe paramount importance to either domestic or foreign policy issues for presidential popularity; both policy areas can increase or decrease the president's range of options. But perhaps domestic concerns provide a more durable base of popularity. Foreign policy events, by contrast, provide a dramatic but fleeting opportunity for the president to build popularity.

Links Between Opinion and Public Debate

Especially since the dawn of the media age, presidential popularity has been an important tool for attaining public policy goals. Presidents use information about their levels of public support to persuade Congress to go along with their proposals for foreign and domestic policies.

Particularly on issues on which the public has not formed strong opinions, presidents can shape public opinion simply by speaking out. The public's deep-seated desire to support its president gives the president opportunities to bring people's thinking more in line with that of the administration. A number of surveys have determined that the public is more willing to support an initiative if it knows the president proposed or backed the measure. For example, one researcher, Corey Rosen, found different samples showing different levels of support for proposals when respondents were either told or not told that the president backed the proposals.[75] The identification of the proposal with the president served to "personify" the policy and therefore to increase public support.

An unpopular president may produce a "reverse Midas" effect, damaging potentially popular policies. President Clinton's low popularity during congressional debate over health care reform in 1994 might have undermined public support for a compromise on the measure. When the Republican Party took control of Congress in 1995 for the first time in forty years, Clinton lost his stature as the nation's leading agenda-setter. The new Speaker of the House, Newt Gingrich of Georgia, temporarily dominated headlines with his leadership of the Republican campaign platform dubbed the "Contract with America." By early 1996, however, the Republican Congress had squandered its initiative on trying to force through cuts in Medicaid and Medicare, and President Clinton had regained some of his political footing.

Political scientist Lee Sigelman used one sample to determine that public support for a policy rises when respondents are told of the president's position. But Sigelman found that the public is less willing to go along with the president's policies as the president's position becomes more "radical."[76] The latter finding suggests that the president's prestige depends to a great extent on a strong base of public respect for the president's office. That respect is one of the nation's fundamental values. As presidents move away from the nation's other fundamental values with "radical" proposals, they might lose the public's automatic support.

History offers additional evidence for the academic findings of Rosen and Sigelman. Public support for President Truman's proposed aid to Greece and Turkey—which was not a prominent issue at the time—rose dramatically after Truman's 1947 speech on the matter.[77] Support for bombing Hanoi and Haiphong increased from 50 to 80 percent after the bombing there began in 1966.[78] Before Lyndon Johnson announced a halt to the bombing of North Vietnam on March 31, 1968, only 40 percent of the public opposed bombing the enemy. In early April, polls showed that 64 percent approved the bombing halt.

INFLUENCING CAPITOL HILL

The link between presidential approval ratings and support on Capitol Hill for the White House is not clear. Political scientist Richard E. Neustadt has argued that high approval ratings and poll support for specific policies help the president to persuade Congress to support key policy proposals.[79] But the record of postwar presidents suggests that the link is indirect and that other factors enter into the calculations of Congress and other actors.

One reason Congress pays attention to presidential popularity is that many members of Congress have no other regular barometer of the public mood. The president is the dominant figure in national politics, and when the public reacts to administration stands, members of Congress gain a sense of public opinion. Another reason is that the public generally expects Congress to cooperate with the president.[80]

Kent Hance, a Democratic representative from Texas, explained his support for Republican President Reagan's tax and budget initiatives in 1981: "Reagan won 72 percent of the vote in my district and he's a lot more popular now than he was on Election Day. It's mighty tough to go against a popular president in a district like mine."[81] Speaker Thomas P. "Tip" O'Neill Jr. pleaded with conservative Democrats to oppose the president's plan, but he concluded that the marginal representatives "go along with the will of the people, and the will of the people is to go along with the president."[82] When in November Reagan's public approval fell below 50 percent—a drop of 19 points since May—the White House encountered difficulties pushing the rest of its program. Budget cuts never made it to the floor of either chamber.[83]

In his statistical analysis of congressional roll-call votes and presidential popularity polls, political scientist George C. Edwards III confirmed that constituents expect their representatives to cooperate with the president, and that members of Congress respond to the general desires of their major supporters back home. According to Edwards, the relationship between presidential public support and success on Capitol Hill is modest. As a rule of thumb, the president gains 1.5 percentage points in congressional support for every 10 percentage point increase in public approval.[84] An increase in presidential support of 10 percentage points among Democrats produces a 3 to 4 percent

increase in Democratic support in the House of Representatives.[85] These strong results do not hold for Democrats in the Senate and Republicans in both chambers.

Yet Edwards notes that measures of aggregate support for the president may not tell the whole story. More revealing, he says, is congressional attention to the constituents in the district or state who support members. Edwards writes:

Presidential approval is likely to have its greatest positive impact on Congress when members of the legislature sense that the public supports the chief executive for his positions on issues as well as his general leadership or other characteristics. The strongest negative influence is likely to occur when there is dramatic, rapid decline in the president's approval level, undermining other sources of support. Neither of these situations is typical.[86]

Jon R. Bond and Richard Fleisher find Edwards's correlations "spurious" because of his failure to account for the natural biases of congressional party members regardless of the president's popularity.[87] Oddly, the correlation between presidential popularity and the success of the White House program on Capitol Hill is weaker on votes on important issues, to which the public pays more attention.[88] The president's popularity produces a greater effect on foreign policy votes in the House and domestic issues in the Senate. Of the presidents serving since the 1950s, Johnson demonstrated the closest correlation between popularity and success in Congress.[89]

Among members of Congress from the party not occupying the Oval Office, the relationship between presidential popularity and congressional support is mixed. Members of the party's "base" tend to respond somewhat favorably to a popular president of the other party. But members of Congress of the same party who face "cross pressures" about the White House program actually oppose the president more when the president is popular. "Most members of Congress know that very few voters are likely to have information about their votes on specific roll calls or about their support for the president," Bond and Fleisher write. "Voters are, however, more likely to be aware of a representative's general voting patterns reflected by party and ideology. Incumbents seldom lose because they support a popular president too little or support an unpopular president too much; they are more likely to lose because they are too liberal or too conservative for their constituents."[90]

SHAPING PUBLIC OPINION

The regularity of polling on every conceivable issue gives the president and other political figures the opportunity to shape public opinion and react to it.

Pollsters gather information daily about the ways all kinds of citizens think on a variety of issues, including many hypothetical situations. Polling data include combinations of conditions to which the polling subject can respond. Thus the president can anticipate the way the population—and specific groups of the population—will react to large and small initiatives on any issue imaginable. By analyzing polling data, the president can know, for example, what the Jewish population thinks about the administration's policies in the Middle East and what it thinks about different approaches to the broad problems as well as the minor elements of the situation.

Faced with the inevitable decline in popularity, the president is inclined to take dramatic, public actions to improve poll ratings. Presidential leadership, then, "tilts" toward dramatic actions designed to bolster approval ratings rather than concerted efforts and cooperation with other government officials to deal with complex problems.

George Gallup relates the public's desire for strong leadership to the president's sometimes feverish activity to boost ratings:

I would say that any sharp drop in popularity is likely to come from the president's inaction in the face of an important crisis. Inaction hurts a president more than anything else. A president can take some action, even a wrong one, and not lose his popularity. . . . People tend to judge a man by his goals, what he's trying to do, and not necessarily by what he accomplishes or how well he succeeds. People used to tell us over and over again about all the things that Roosevelt did wrong and then they would say, "I'm all for him, though, because his heart is in the right place; he's trying."[91]

Recent events appear to support Gallup's statement. Nixon's trips to the Soviet Union in 1974 during the height of the Watergate controversy, Ford's military action against Cambodia after the attack on the *Mayaguez*, Carter's dramatic disavowal of his previous approach to the Soviet Union after its invasion of Afghanistan, Carter's high-profile response to the Iranian seizure of hostages, and Reagan's attacks on Grenada and Libya—all led to a boost in the president's ratings. President Clinton's eventual decision in 1995 to send troops to Bosnia was in this context preferable to his continued stance of noncommitment of U.S. forces.

The Judgment on Public Opinion Polling

Changes in the measurement of public opinion fundamentally altered the way groups press political demands and political leaders respond to those demands. Scholars have disagreed about whether a system with constant polling promotes or damages democracy.

Some argue that regular polling, more than infrequent elections, makes political leaders responsive to the wishes of the electorate. George Gallup, one of the pioneers of modern polling, has maintained that elected officials do a better job when they have "an accurate measure of the wishes, aspirations, and needs of different groups within the general public."[92] Behavior in office that is influenced by polls is a kind of rolling election campaign, with officials constantly on the lookout for ways to please and avoid displeasing the public.

Proponents of polling also stress the "scientific" nature of findings and the increasingly sophisticated views of the political landscape that well-done polls offer. If conducted comprehensively, proponents say, polls can offer a more complete picture of the political landscape than any other single tool.

The reliability of public opinion surveys varies widely. Polls with carefully worded questions and random samples of at least a thousand respondents are considered the most reliable. Polls with smaller sample sizes can be useful if designed well and analyzed rigorously. In recent years, fascination with public opinion has prompted many media outlets to conduct unscientific polls. Readers and viewers are invited to convey their opinion by calling a telephone number. Some polls use "900" numbers, which cost the caller about $1 to $2 a minute. These polls tend to reflect the opinions of the most opinionated people; their value lies mostly in entertainment.

Even large opinion samples can misjudge the mood of the population because they gauge the intensity of public preferences only roughly. "Focus groups"—small groups of selected voters, gathered for intensive interviews with professional surveyors—help to tap the more visceral feelings of key segments of the public. Early in his administration, President Clinton decided to postpone his promise for a middle-class tax cut after focus groups revealed that Clinton and Perot voters would not blame him for breaking the pledge.[93]

Surveys also can be misleading because of the way the data are presented. In 1976 reporters seeking to understand Carter's appeal speculated that Carter's religiosity tapped a wellspring of conservatism in the electorate. But when polls showed that Carter was as popular among nonreligious as religious people, reporters dropped the idea. One polling expert, however, took the analysis a step further by examining young voters. "Sure enough, those young, non-churchgoing Carter fans were masking the religion effect. When age was held constant, religion effect appeared. Revealing it took nothing more complicated than a three-way table."[94] A look at a single factor, then, can obscure the complex truths hidden in polling data.

Reliance on polling data in making policy and strategic decisions can be risky; especially on volatile issues, survey results can be erratic and inaccurate. Differences in the wording of survey questions—as well as different arrangements of the questions—can produce dramatically different responses. Dramatic events also can produce reactions that do not last long. For example, American public opinion in the months before the Persian Gulf War of 1991 was extremely unsteady. In some polls, the public appeared to favor the use of military force; in others, the public appeared reluctant. On the surface, public opinion seemed to change dramatically. But, according to Mueller, "the most remarkable aspect of public opinion on such matters was that it changed very little." Events such as failed peace talks increased the public's hawkishness, but such hawkishness "was essentially ephemeral."[95] Presidents, then, who do not carefully interpret polling data can find themselves embarking on policies that have only fleeting support.

Some students of American politics take the critique of polling a step further, arguing that polls can be a tool of manipulation. Political scientist Benjamin Ginsberg argues that polls have the effect of stifling public expression rather than measuring it in a neutral manner for voter-conscious political leaders.

According to Ginsberg, a regular assessment of a wide variety of public attitudes, in which a diverse range of issues is assessed according to the many demographic characteristics of survey respondents, enables the government to "manage" demands rather than deal with the complex problems that produce political demands. By determining which groups in society would object to certain governmental actions, the government is able to adapt its policies and presentation of those policies to avoid conflict. Many issues, then, never receive the full public discussion that they might receive if the public pulse were not so regularly tested.

To illustrate his argument, Ginsberg cites a federal conservation program that, according to surveys, had aroused opposition in southern communities. Rather than canceling the program or negotiating with citizens, administrators used polling data to pinpoint the public's most nagging concerns and used propaganda to dispel those concerns.

Opinion surveys provided officials with more or less reliable information about current popular sentiment, offered a guide to the character of the public relations efforts that might usefully be made, and served as means of measuring the effect of "information programs" on a target population. In essence, polling allowed officials a better opportunity to anticipate, regulate, and manipulate popular attitudes.[96]

Presidents Carter and Reagan employed full-time White House pollsters who monitored the vagaries of public opinion among all imaginable demographic groups. Today, other parts of the federal government—from executive departments and agencies to Congress—also use polls regularly to monitor and shape public opinion. To the extent that such polling allows public officials to head off a full discussion of major issues, critics argue, democracy is thwarted.

Also concerned about the way polling shapes the expression of public opinion, Ginsberg has pointed out that polling data channel political expression into formulations provided by the pollster that discourage group political action. Besides allowing government officials to manage public opinion, polls have four possible negative effects on democratic expression.

First, polling eliminates the cost of expressing an opinion, which reduces the influence of the people most concerned and knowledgeable about various issues. Polls tally the preferences of cross sections of the population, which include people who do not know or care about issues. The respondent's knowledge and the issue's salience are usually ignored. "Polls, in effect, submerge individuals with strongly held views in a more apathetic mass public."[97]

Second, polls shift the concern of public debate from behavior to attitudes. The demonstrations that once informed elites of mass opinion required people to engage directly in politics. Simply responding to survey questions, in contrast, requires just a few moments of time of a small sample of the public. Polls give the government the opportunity to shape opinion before it can enjoy full debate, thereby reducing public engagement.

Third, polls shift politics from the group to the individual. Before polls, citizens needed to band together to express their

desires and demands. Such a requirement served to build political institutions such as parties, unions, neighborhood groups, and farmer cooperatives. Active involvement in many such groups—especially parties and unions—has declined as public officials have turned to polls for information about public opinion.

Fourth, polls shift political expression from assertions to responses. Survey subjects can react only to the agenda of the pollster; they rarely make an independent assertion. The subjects that respondents—and therefore, the public—can discuss is thereby limited to the interests of pollsters.

Daniel Yankelovich, a leading analyst of public opinion, has called for the simplicity of opinion polls to be replaced by a more complex process of "public judgment." Most polls ask questions that people do not know much about, so their answers are shaky at best. For example, 63 percent of respondents in one poll said they favored a constitutional amendment to balance the federal budget. But when respondents were told that such a measure might require higher taxes, only 39 percent said they favored the amendment.[98]

Political scientist Philip E. Converse puts the proper use of polls and surveys into perspective:

Acquiring relevant public opinion data is not unlike the riverboat captain buying the latest mapping of sandbar configurations before embarking on a voyage. Few politicians consult poll data to find out what they should be thinking on the issues, or to carry out errands. But they have very little interest in flouting the will of their constituency in any tendentious, head-on way. Such data give them a sense of what postures to emphasize and avoid.[99]

NOTES

1. E. E. Schattschneider, *The Semisovereign People* (New York: Holt, Rinehart, and Winston, 1960).

2. This discussion relies mostly on the following studies by Fred I. Greenstein: "Popular Images of the President," *American Journal of Psychiatry* 122, no. 5 (November 1965): 523–529; "The Benevolent Leader: Children's Images of Presidential Authority," *American Political Science Review* 54 (December 1960): 934–943; "College Student Reactions to the Assassination of President Kennedy," in *Communication in Crisis,* ed. B. Greenberg and E. Parker (Stanford, Calif.: Stanford University Press, 1965); and "What the President Means to Americans," in *Choosing the President,* ed. James David Barber (Englewood Cliffs, N.J.: Prentice-Hall, 1974), 121–147. Also see Roberta S. Sigel, "Image of the American Presidency, Part II of An Exploration into Popular Views of Presidential Power," *Midwest Journal of Political Science* 10 (February 1966): 123–137.

3. Greenstein, "What the President Means to Americans," 125, 128–129; percentage figures are from *The Washington Post,* January 29, 1996, 6.

4. The respect for the presidency is not uniformly strong. Groups that are left out of the mainstream of economic and political life, such as African Americans and Appalachian whites, respond less favorably to mention of the presidency and specific presidents.

5. Murray Edelman, *The Symbolic Uses of Politics* (Urbana: University of Illinois Press, 1985), 78.

6. Garry Wills, "Clinton's Troubles," *The New York Review of Books,* September 22, 1994, 6.

7. Samuel Kernell, Peter W. Sperlich, and Aaron Wildavsky, "Public Support for Presidents," in *Perspectives on the Presidency,* ed. Aaron Wildavsky (Boston: Little, Brown, 1975), 150, 158–164.

8. For examinations of consensus in U.S. politics, see Louis Hartz, *The*

Liberal Tradition in America (New York: Harcourt, Brace, Jovanovich, 1955); Daniel Boorstin, *The Genius of American Democracy* (Chicago: University of Chicago Press, 1958); Daniel Bell, *The End of Ideology* (Glencoe, Ill.: Free Press, 1960); and Samuel H. Beer, "In Search of a New Political Philosophy," in *The New American Political System*, ed. Anthony King (Washington, D.C.: American Enterprise Institute, 1978), 5–44.

9. James Davison Hunter, *Culture Wars: The Struggle to Define America* (New York: Basic Books, 1991).

10. Quoted in Benjamin Ginsberg, *The Captive Public* (New York: Basic Books, 1986), 61.

11. For a suggestive survey of new opinion media, see William G. Mayer, "The Rise of the New Media," *Public Opinion Quarterly* 58 (spring 1994): 124–146.

12. Theodore J. Lowi, *The End of Liberalism* (New York: Norton, 1979), 91.

13. Richard A. Cloward and Frances Fox Piven, "Toward a Class-Based Realignment of American Politics: A Movement Strategy," *Social Policy* (winter 1983): 8.

14. Ginsberg, *Captive Public*, 56–57.

15. See Frances Fox Piven and Richard A. Cloward, *Regulating the Poor* (New York: Random House, 1972), and *Poor People's Movements* (New York: Random House, 1979).

16. See Pam Solo, *From Protest to Policy: Beyond the Freeze to Common Security* (Cambridge, Mass.: Ballinger, 1988).

17. Quoted in Michael E. McGerr, *The Decline of Popular Politics* (New York: Oxford University Press, 1986), 22.

18. Daniel Boorstin, *The Americans: The Democratic Experience* (New York: Random House, 1973), 403.

19. Leila Sussman, "Dear Mr. President," in *Readings in American Public Opinion*, ed. Edward E. Walker et al. (New York: American Book, 1968).

20. Barry Sussman, *What Americans Really Think* (New York: Pantheon Books, 1988), 336.

21. Graeme Browning, "Hot-Wiring Washington," *National Journal*, June 26, 1993, 1624–1629.

22. Sussman, *What Americans Really Think*, 226.

23. Quoted in James R. Beniger and Robert J. Guiffra Jr., "Public Opinion Polling: Command and Control in Presidential Campaigns," in *Presidential Selection*, ed. Alexander Heard and Michael Nelson (Durham, N.C.: Duke University Press, 1987), 189.

24. Larry J. Sabato, *The Rise of Political Consultants* (New York: Basic Books, 1981), 105.

25. Herbert Asher, *Polling and the Public*, 3d ed. (Washington, D.C.: CQ Press, 1995), 15.

26. For a critique of Caddell's conception of politics and polling, see Sidney Blumenthal, "Mr. Smith Goes to Washington," *New Republic*, February 6, 1984, 17–20.

27. Jimmy Carter, *Keeping Faith* (New York: Bantam Books, 1982), 114.

28. Sabato, *Rise of Political Consultants*, 74–75.

29. Carter, *Keeping Faith*, 123.

30. Laurence I. Barrett, *Gambling with History* (New York: Doubleday, 1983), 351–352.

31. Sussman, *What Americans Really Think*, 35–36.

32. Quoted in David Shribman, "Leadership by the Numbers," *Boston Globe*, May 29, 1994, 67.

33. Quoted in James A. Barnes, "Polls Apart," *National Journal*, July 7, 1993, 1751.

34. Ibid., 1753.

35. Jon R. Bond and Richard Fleisher, *The President in the Legislative Arena* (Chicago: University of Chicago Press, 1990), 179.

36. Some scholars argue that the honeymoon is no longer something a new president can rely on. See Karen S. Johnson, "The Honeymoon Period: Fact or Fiction," *Journalism Quarterly* 62 (winter 1985): 869–876. Theodore J. Lowi has argued that the honeymoon period offers the president's only real opportunity to achieve major policy initiatives—and that that period is getting shorter and shorter. See Lowi, *The Personal President:*

Power Invested, Promise Unfulfilled (Ithaca, N.Y.: Cornell University Press, 1985), 7–11.

37. Lyn Ragsdale, *Vital Statistics on the Presidency: Washington to Clinton* (Washington, D.C.: Congressional Quarterly, 1996), 194–209.

38. "Clinton Job Performance," *Gallup Poll Monthly*, June 1994.

39. Samuel Kernell, "Explaining Presidential Popularity," *American Political Science Review* 72 (1978): 506–522.

40. John Mueller, "The Polls—A Review: American Public Opinion and the Gulf War," *Public Opinion Quarterly*, 57 (1993): 84, 85; Gary King and Lyn Ragsdale, *The Elusive Executive: Discovering Statistical Patterns in the Presidency* (Washington, D.C.: Congressional Quarterly, 1988), 292–293.

41. "Bush Job Performance—Trend," *Gallup Poll Monthly*, November 1992, 24–27.

42. Ragsdale, *Vital Statistics on the Presidency*, 189.

43. Stephen Skowronek, *The Politics that Presidents Make: Leadership from John Adams to George Bush* (Cambridge, Mass.: Belknap Press, 1993).

44. See John E. Mueller, *War, Presidents, and Public Opinion* (Lanham, Md.: University Press of America, 1985). Mueller's shorter works include "Presidential Popularity from Truman to Johnson," *American Political Science Review* 64 (March 1970): 18–34; and "Trends in Popular Support for the Wars in Korea and Vietnam," *American Political Science Review* 65 (June 1971): 358–375.

45. James A. Stimson, "Public Support for American Presidents: A Cyclical Model," *Public Opinion Quarterly* 40 (spring 1976): 1–21.

46. Ibid., 10.

47. See the work by Mueller and Jong R. Lee, "Rallying Around the Flag: Foreign-Policy Events and Presidential Popularity," *Presidential Studies Quarterly* 7 (fall 1977): 252–256.

48. Thomas E. Cronin, *The State of the Presidency* (Boston: Little, Brown, 1980), 84.

49. Paul Brace and Barbara Hinckley, "The Structure of Presidential Approval: Constraints within and across Presidencies," *Journal of Politics* 53 (November 1991): 1003, 1012.

50. Janet Hook, "Clinton Sets Get-Tough Agenda, Hard Line on Social Reforms," *Congressional Quarterly Weekly Report*, January 29, 1994, 156.

51. Paul Brace and Barbara Hinckley, *Follow the Leader: Opinion Polls and the Modern Presidents* (New York: Basic Books, 1992), 101.

52. Ibid.

53. King and Ragsdale, *The Elusive Executive*, 296–307.

54. Jane Mayer and Doyle McManus, *Landslide: The Unmaking of the President, 1984–1986* (Boston: Houghton Mifflin, 1988).

55. David J. Lanoue, "The 'Teflon Factor': Ronald Reagan and Comparative Presidential Popularity," *Polity* 21 (spring 1989): 291.

56. Paul J. Quirk, "The Election," in *The Elections of 1988*, ed. Michael Nelson (Washington, D.C.: CQ Press, 1989), 82; Paul J. Quirk and Jon K. Dalager, "The Election: A 'New Democrat' and a New Kind of Presidential Campaign," in *The Elections of 1992*, ed. Michael Nelson (Washington, D.C.: CQ Press, 1993), 78.

57. This discussion relies on John E. Mueller, "Public Opinion and the President," in *The Presidency Reappraised*, ed. Rexford G. Tugwell and Thomas E. Cronin (New York: Praeger, 1974), 133–147. It should be emphasized that the categories overlap; for example, a citizen can have elements of both the partisan and the follower.

58. See ibid. and Richard A. Brody and Benjamin I. Page, "The Impact of Events on Presidential Popularity: The Johnson and Nixon Administrations," in Wildavsky, *Perspectives on the Presidency*, especially p. 145: "Foreign events reach people through news reports, [while] some domestic events, like real personal income, may be perceived without mediation."

59. Eric B. Herzik and Mary L. Dodson have suggested that the "climate of expectations" has more to do with the president's personal appeal than with programmatic plans ("The President and Public Expectations: A Research Note," *Presidential Studies Quarterly* 12 [spring 1982]: 168–173).

60. Mueller, "Presidential Popularity," 20–21.

61. Richard A. Brody, "Public Evaluations and Expectations and the Future of the Presidency," in *Problems and Prospects of Presidential Leadership*

in the 1980's, ed. James Sterling Young (New York: University Press of America, 1982), 45–49. Also see Stanley Kelley, *Interpreting Elections* (Princeton, N.J.: Princeton University Press, 1983), for a similar view of how voters make judgments.

62. Alan I. Abramowitz, David J. Lanoue, and Subha Ramesh, "Economic Conditions, Causal Attributions, and Political Evaluations in the 1984 Presidential Election," *Journal of Politics* 50 (November 1988): 848–863.

63. David Green, *Shaping Political Consciousness* (New York: Oxford University Press, 1988), 126–134.

64. Kristen R. Monroe, "Inflation and Presidential Popularity," *Presidential Studies Quarterly* 9 (summer 1979): 339. Also see Kristen R. Monroe, "Economic Influences on Presidential Popularity," *Public Opinion Quarterly* (1978): 360–370. Kim Ezra Sheinbaum and Ervin Sheinbaum ("Public Perceptions of Presidential Economic Performance: From Johnson to Carter," *Presidential Studies Quarterly* 12 [summer 1982]: 421–427) find a strong link between prosperity and popularity. Henry C. Kenski, in "The Impact of Economic Conditions on Presidential Popularity," *Journal of Politics* 39 (1977): 764–773, argues that high unemployment and inflation rates affect Republican and Democratic presidents differently.

65. Henry C. Kenski, "The Impact of Unemployment on Presidential Popularity from Eisenhower to Nixon," *Presidential Studies Quarterly* 7 (spring–summer 1977): 114–126.

66. Lowi's analysis of the spurts in presidential popularity is part of his overall critique of the public presidency. See Lowi, *Personal President.*

67. Thomas Ferguson and Joel Rogers, *Right Turn* (New York: Hill and Wang, 1986), 26.

68. Lowi points to other evidence against the pocketbook explanation for presidential popularity. Economic conditions improved in both 1968 and 1976 but did not help Presidents Johnson and Ford, whose high negative ratings and intense public opposition prevented one from campaigning for, and the other from winning, reelection.

69. For an analysis of this phenomenon, see Mueller, *War, Presidents, and Public Opinion.*

70. Richard A. Brody and Catherine R. Shapiro, "A Reconsideration of the Rally Phenomenon in Public Opinion," in *Political Behavior Annual,* ed. Samuel Long (Boulder, Colo.: Westview, 1989), 77–102.

71. Brugitte Lebens Nacos, "Presidential Leadership during the Persian Gulf Conflict," *Presidential Studies Quarterly,* 24 (summer 1994): 543–561.

72. David W. Moore and Lydia Saad, "Public Supports Actions against Iraq," *Gallup Poll Monthly,* October 1994, 14.

73. Quoted in Lee Sigelman, "Disarming the Opposition: The President, the Public, and the I.N.F. Treaty," *Public Opinion Quarterly* 54 (1990): 38.

74. Ibid., 46.

75. Corey Rosen, "A Test of Presidential Leadership of Public Opinion: The Split Ballot Technique," *Polity* 6 (1972): 282–290.

76. Lee Sigelman, "Gauging the Public Response to Presidential Leadership," *Presidential Studies Quarterly* 10 (summer 1980): 427–433.

77. Samuel Kernell, "The Truman Doctrine Speech: A Case Study of the Dynamics of Presidential Opinion Leadership," *Social Science History* 1 (fall 1976): 20–45.

78. See Mueller, *War, Presidents, and Public Opinion.*

79. Richard E. Neustadt, *Presidential Power* (New York: Wiley, 1980), 64–73.

80. See George C. Edwards III, "Presidential Influence in the House: Presidential Prestige as a Source of Presidential Power," *American Political Science Review* 70 (March 1976): 101–113.

81. Quoted in George C. Edwards III, *At the Margins: Presidential Leadership of Congress* (New Haven: Yale University Press, 1989), 116.

82. Ibid., 116.

83. Ibid., 117.

84. Ibid., 118.

85. Ibid., 120.

86. Ibid., 124–125.

87. Jon R. Bond and Richard Fleisher, *The President in the Legislative Arena* (Chicago: University of Chicago Press, 1990), 187.

88. Ibid., 182.

89. Ibid., 182–183.

90. Ibid., 194.

91. Quoted in Edelman, *Symbolic Uses of Politics,* 78.

92. Quoted in Ginsberg, *Captive Public,* 237.

93. Bob Woodward, *The Agenda: Inside the Clinton White House* (New York: Simon and Schuster, 1993), 72, 97.

94. Philip Meyer, "Polling as Political Science and Polling as Journalism," *Public Opinion Quarterly* 54 (1990): 451.

95. Mueller, "The Polls," 84, 85.

96. Ginsberg, *Captive Public,* 85.

97. Ibid., 65.

98. Daniel Yankelovich, *Coming to Public Judgement: Making Democracy Work in a Complex World* (Syracuse: University of Syracuse Press, 1991), 25.

99. Philip E. Converse, "Changing Conceptions of Public Opinion in the Political Process," *Public Opinion Quarterly* 51 (1987): 22.

SELECTED BIBLIOGRAPHY

Asher, Herbert. *Polling and the Public.* 3d ed. Washington, D.C.: CQ Press, 1995.

Bond, Jon R., and Richard Fleisher. *The President in the Legislative Arena.* Chicago: University of Chicago Press, 1990.

Edelman, Murray. *The Symbolic Uses of Politics.* Urbana: University of Illinois Press, 1985.

Edwards, George C., III. *At the Margins: Presidential Leadership of Congress.* New Haven: Yale University Press, 1989.

——. *Presidential Approval: A Sourcebook.* Baltimore: Johns Hopkins University Press, 1990.

Ginsberg, Benjamin. *The Captive Public.* New York: Basic Books, 1986.

Greenberg, Stanley. *Middle Class Dreams.* New York: Times Books, 1995.

Kernell, Samuel. *Going Public: New Strategies of Presidential Leadership.* 2d ed. Washington, D.C.: Congressional Quarterly, 1992.

Langston, Thomas. *With Reverence and Contempt: How Americans Think About Their President.* Baltimore: Johns Hopkins University Press, 1995.

Lanoue, David J. *From Camelot to the Teflon Presidency.* New York: Greenwood Press, 1988.

Lowi, Theodore J. *The Personal President.* Ithaca, N.Y.: Cornell University Press, 1985.

Mueller, John E. *War, Presidents, and Public Opinion.* Lanham, Md.: University Press of America, 1985.

Ragsdale, Lyn. *Vital Statistics on the Presidency: Washington to Clinton.* Washington, D.C.: Congressional Quarterly, 1996.

CHAPTER 5

The President and Interest Groups

BY CHARLES C. EUCHNER

AMERICANS tend to form private associations to pursue their political ends. Balancing the demands of these organized interests has been a major—and difficult—part of the president's job, particularly since the days of the New Deal and World War II.

An interest group is a set of people who form an association to promote ideals or pursue material benefits. Groups may know what ends they want to pursue, but their goals and tactics evolve according to their relationship with other forces in society. Because interest groups usually are seeking the kind of assistance available only from the public, they often go to the government with their claims.[1]

Constitutional Debate about "Factions"

Debate over the U.S. Constitution framed the major issues of interest group politics that occupy students of U.S. government today. After completion of the Constitution in Philadelphia in 1787, Federalists and Anti-Federalists debated how best to achieve adequate "energy" in the federal government and the presidency without stifling free debate and competition among social groups—notions central to a democratic society. The debate's basic tension has persisted to the modern day.

James Madison presented what has come to be the main justification for interest group politics.[2] In *Federalist* No. 10, Madison argued that separate, competing interests were inevitable in a free society and that efforts to snuff out this competition would require the drastic step of curbing free thought and action. The goal of government should not be to ban interest groups, Madison asserted, but to control them by competition. In *Federalist* No. 10, Madison wrote:

As long as the reason of man continues fallible, and he is at liberty to exercise it, different opinions will be formed. . . . From the protection of different and unequal faculties of acquiring property, the possession of different degrees and kinds of property immediately results; and from the influence of these on the sentiments and views of the respective proprietors ensues a division of the society into different interests and parties.[3]

Alexis de Tocqueville, a nineteenth-century French aristocrat, argued in his classic study *Democracy in America* that the "equality of conditions" and the lack of a feudal tradition in the United States gave Americans the freedom to pursue their interests by using large and small associations. Tocqueville wrote:

Americans of all ages, all conditions, and all dispositions, constantly form associations. They have not only commercial and manufacturing companies, but associations of a thousand other kinds—religious, moral, serious, futile, general or restricted, enormous or diminutive. . . . Wherever, at the head of some new undertaking, you see the government in France, or a man of rank in England, in the United States you will be sure to find an association.[4]

This being said, Tocqueville pointed out that the American condition was a double-edged sword. He feared that the United States would develop into a "tyranny of the majority" because equality would undermine citizens' willingness to be tolerant of people who expressed unpopular ideas or had different characteristics. But, he observed, equality and freedom of expression also enabled a variety of institutions—newspapers, the legal profession, and interest groups—to brake the tendency of majorities to impose their wills on the entire population.

When Tocqueville published his work in 1835 and 1840, interest groups existed mainly at the local level. State and local governments had control over most matters of public life, including property laws, banking and commerce, morals, education, use of land and resources, and criminal procedures. The states and localities also played an important part in developing "internal improvements," such as roads, canals, railroads, schools, hospitals, and agricultural enterprises.[5]

John C. Calhoun, one of the South's great champions in the nineteenth century, developed another doctrine of interest groups that had a profound effect on U.S. history. Calhoun's theory of "concurrent majorities" asserted that the legitimacy of national government action depended on the acquiescence of the interests affected by the action. The distinct interests of the states, Calhoun said, deserved protection from the larger interests of the nation. Calhoun argued that a state could "nullify," or veto, federal actions that usurped state independence.

Calhoun's home state of South Carolina invoked the doctrine of nullification after enactment of a tariff bill in 1828 that state officials considered discriminatory against the South. President Andrew Jackson responded by sending warships to the harbor of Charleston, and the state legislature soon revoked the act of nullification.

Even though Jackson defeated the most extreme form of concurrent majorities, the theory remained a part of U.S. politics. The notion that states' rights had priority over the national interest helped to bring about the Civil War. After the war, the states' rights view held considerable sway in the national political debate. In the compromise over the 1876 presidential election, the national government ceded considerable autonomy

President Calvin Coolidge meets with members of the Sioux Indian Republican Club in March 1925.

to the states over the issues of basic civil rights and commerce.

The states' rights view crumbled as the national government gained strength in the twentieth century, but a doctrine similar in many ways to Calhoun's theory arose. Especially since the Great Society of the 1960s, a practice that might be called "representational democracy" has guided policy making in national politics. This practice encourages or requires the government to gain the consent of groups affected by legislation or regulations before it implements such policies.

Critics today charge that the American system too easily accommodates groups of all kinds. Whereas Madison counted on interest groups to guard jealously against rivals, in fact groups reinforce each others' actions. Jonathan Rauch writes in *Demosclerosis* that interest groups seek to avoid conflict that would threaten a stable working environment. According to Rauch:

So why don't all these lobbies cancel each other out? . . . Lobbies work hard to avoid head-on confrontations with other lobbies, for exactly the same reason that politicians work to avoid confrontations with lobbies: challenge someone's sinecure, and you get his fist in your face. If the farmers tell the government, "We want you to kill the ranchers' subsidy and give us the money," they can count on a bruising fight with the cattlemen's association. On the other hand, if they say, "The ranchers are getting land-use subsidies, so please raise our price supports," they avoid antagonizing any powerful group directly.[6]

This kind of accommodation among interest groups is likely to continue. Interest groups do not have incentives to give up benefits, and the federal government lacks the political support to develop comprehensive policies that are accepted across the nation.

The "Two Republics" of U.S. History

According to political scientist Theodore J. Lowi, the United States has seen two distinct styles of government which he calls the first and second "republics." In its early years, the national government was a "patronage state" (its first republic) based on the demands for internal improvements by governments and businesses at the state and local levels.[7] The national party system, with the president at its apex, played an important role in the process of internal development. But that process remained fundamentally parochial—congressional and party leaders from the states merely vied for a fair share of patronage—until Franklin D. Roosevelt's New Deal programs of the 1930s.

Beginning with the administrations of Theodore Roosevelt and Woodrow Wilson, and gaining full strength during Franklin Roosevelt's New Deal, the federal government expanded its reach over general regulation of the economy (the second republic). Rather than simply dole out resources to discrete states and constituencies, the government began to play an important role in almost all aspects of political and economic life.

In time, the federal government regulated the everyday activities of a wide range of enterprises, such as banking, labor relations, transportation systems, the media, mining and development of natural resources, manufacturing, product safety, farming, the environment, and civil rights. Thus rather than simply seeking direct material rewards from the government—and then using those rewards as they wished—a wide variety of enterprises saw even the most mundane business practices regulated by the government. The government continued to offer material rewards, such as subsidies to farmers, but they had strings attached. Enterprises, then, recognized the need to establish a permanent presence in Washington to influence the federal agencies and committees that controlled the strings. As the government's regulation of many aspects of economic and social life increased, interest groups sprung up to influence the way the government controlled their affairs.

Modern Interest Group Politics

Interest group politics boomed with the New Deal of Franklin Roosevelt, and today interest groups are one of the most important facets of national politics. Estimates of the number of interest groups are not entirely reliable, but they are suggestive. A 1929 study estimated that at the time five hundred interest groups were at work in Washington. Fewer than five thousand groups were listed in the *Encyclopedia of Associations* in 1956. That number doubled to about ten thousand by 1970—and that number doubled by 1990. Between 1979 and 1990, about ten new groups were formed every week on average.[8]

But these figures underestimate the amount of interest group activity because of the even more extensive activity of national organizations at the state and local levels. For example, the Chamber of Commerce and the American Federation of Labor-Congress of Industrial Organizations (AFL-CIO) each count as one interest group in the Washington surveys, but they have many subdivisions across the nation. In 1996 the chamber had more than 215,000 businesses and 3,000 individuals as members, along with 5,000 state and local chapters. The AFL-CIO included some 13 million dues-paying members in more than seventy-eight affiliates.[9]

Political action committees (PACs) boomed in the 1970s and 1980s after election finance laws were changed in 1974.[10] PACs are essentially checkbook organizations run by interest groups that depend on sophisticated direct-mail techniques to raise money for election campaigns, lobbying, and research. Indeed, PACs have become a major contributor to federal and statewide campaigns. PACs do not, however, have the active membership programs and tangible benefits other groups such as the AFL-CIO. Originally, PACs were mostly connected to labor groups, but in the last two decades, PACs have proliferated and expanded to a wide range of interest groups. In November 1975, just 722 PACs were in business; by 1995 there were nearly 4,000.[11]

Interest groups have increased their role in national politics partly because of the decline of political parties, the increased fragmentation of Congress, the rise of regulatory politics, the greater complexity of many government issues, and changes in the style of campaigning. Interest groups represent the politics of specialization, whereas the political style in the United States previously was majority rule.

MODERN THEORIES OF INTEREST GROUPS

Since the rise of the modern bureaucratic state, scholars have developed theories to justify or explain the place of interest groups in politics. One of the predominant theories of U.S. politics used a market model to justify the role of interest groups in policy making. Sociologist Arthur F. Bentley argued in 1908 that pursuit of the public interest was misguided; the sum total of government, he asserted, was the result of groups competing for position and favor. Interest groups had a "representative quality" that ensured a degree of democratic activity as groups competed for influence.[12]

Political scientist David Truman argued in 1951 that the result of interest group competition and bargaining was a consensus on the public interest.[13] Truman's model resembled the economic model of British economist Adam Smith, which held that an "invisible hand" guided self-interested competition among firms toward the public interest. According to Truman, the interaction of groups enabled a variety of viewpoints and material interests to get a public hearing. The result was a democratic contest over policy at all levels. Political scientist Robert A. Dahl reached similar conclusions in a 1961 study of community power.[14]

Later students of interest groups disputed the cheery views of such pluralists as Bentley, Truman, and Dahl. Political scientist E. E. Schattschneider and sociologists C. Wright Mills and Floyd Hunter argued that the interests of economically disadvantaged groups do not receive adequate representation simply because they do not have the resources to press their causes.[15] These scholars maintained that the makeup of the interest group "universe" had an elite bias.[16]

In perhaps the most influential work to question the assumption that citizens easily form groups to represent their interests, economist Mancur Olson pointed out that many groups with a definite stake in government actions have difficulty organizing because of limited resources and limited incentives for individuals to join the cause.[17] Group formation is most likely to occur when groups offer material incentives or even coerce prospective members. Labor unions, which automatically deduct dues from workers' paychecks, exercise a form of membership coercion. Because the less-advantaged groups in society have a smaller "surplus" to spend on political action, they lose out in the competition for influence over the government.

Another critique of interest group politics stresses the "overload" of modern bureaucratic politics. Sociologist Daniel Bell argues that economic conflicts have increasingly fallen to the federal government to resolve, needing entitlements to paper over fundamental contradictions between forces, such as the management–labor and business–environmentalist schisms. "One large question that the American system now confronts is whether it can find a way to resolve these conflicts. Lacking rules to mediate claims, the system will be under severe strains."[18]

A growing danger of the increased influence of interest groups is the erosion of government authority and legitimacy. Rather than integrating citizens into a process of mutual accommodation with a goal of the public interest, interest groups often isolate citizens from one another. The common purpose that is the hallmark of republican theory is lost to self-interested competition that does not recognize common social destiny.[19]

The autonomy given to many interest groups removes many policies from democratic deliberation and reduces the maneuvering room on issues that are on the public agenda. For example, the control given farmers over prices and land cultivation removes agriculture policy from the general debate about how society should allocate resources. And because they often are nonnegotiable, policies on agriculture, Social Security, Medicare, job training, and military spending reduce the options for the president and Congress on a wide variety of budget and social issues. In Theodore Lowi's view, by giving groups autonomy over parts of public policy, the public loses control over the wide range of interrelated issues. The system becomes inflexible; options for policy are closed.[20]

HOW INTEREST GROUPS VIEW THE WHITE HOUSE

Most students of U.S. national politics conclude that interest group activity is concentrated on the specific bureaucratic agencies and congressional committees that address the particular concerns of organized interests—not on the White House. For example, farmers deal with the Department of Agriculture and the congressional committees that allocate money to farm programs.

Interest groups do not concentrate on the White House for a number of reasons. First, the schedules of the president and top presidential aides are tight, so it is difficult even to get the president's time and attention. It is much easier to get the attention of a member of Congress or of a civil servant. One aide to President Lyndon B. Johnson explained: "There are 535 opportunities in Congress and only one in the White House. You get an hour to present your case before each representative, and only fifteen minutes once a year with the president. Where would you put your effort?"[21]

Second, the president's tenure in office is short compared to the terms of key bureaucrats and members of Congress. Postwar presidents have served an average of only five and a half years. Much of the president's time is spent learning the ropes or struggling with "lame duck" status.

Third, presidents usually devote their time to a few top priorities—and those priorities are shaped by previous alliances. Only occasionally can an interest group alter a president's set agenda.

Finally, the president is the nation's most public political figure, and interest groups usually operate best out of the glare of public attention where they can promote their interests through small legislative and regulatory means. Seeking a shift in import duties, for example, is a matter best addressed by Commerce Department bureaucrats, not by the president.

Even though interest groups favor the predictability of agencies and committees, many still maintain a relationship with the presidency. Since World War II, the White House has developed regular channels for interest groups to make and receive appeals. The size of the White House staff has increased greatly, with many officials assigned in some way to keeping track of interest groups. The most formal mechanism in the White House for dealing with interest groups is the Office of Public Liaison, created in the administrations of Richard Nixon and Gerald R. Ford.

Political scientist Robert H. Salisbury has noted that interest groups often "tend to gravitate toward the effective centers of power in a given political system." As the White House has become the initiator of the national political agenda, it has become the focus for at least some policy areas such as economic and security policy, and even smaller matters such as prayer in schools—even if the bulk of policies are better addressed in the bureaucracy and congressional committees. The White House may not be the focus of all interest group activity, but neither is it a place of last resort for groups.[22]

Interest groups do not become active only when a policy directly affects them. Effective lobbies make regular contact with political figures, often offering financial or logistical assistance and useful information even when no policy proposals are under discussion. Such assistance helps them to secure "access" when the issues in which they would like to have a say do arise. In 1993, for example, corporate interests—tobacco producers, automobile makers, airlines, breweries, electronics firms, and Japanese subsidiaries—provided $5 million in gifts and $7 million in unsecured loans to help finance the balls held to celebrate Bill Clinton's inauguration.[23] Such gifts could put subtle pressure on the White House to at least consider appeals of donors on controversial issues.

When the president attempts a major initiative—such as Ronald Reagan's tax- and budget-cutting initiatives of 1981 and his tax reform of 1986, or Clinton's deficit-reduction program of 1993 and health care legislation of 1994—interest groups respond in two ways. First, they recruit their members to contact congressional representatives. Second, they attempt to shape public opinion with advertising campaigns in the mass media. Both strategies effectively eliminated most of the important aspects of Clinton's health care reform plan.

Some authorities maintain that the president has an advantage in dealing with interest groups. For example, the White House "is less likely to be besieged at its most vulnerable points because lobbyists are less likely to know where those points are," observe political scientists Martha Joynt Kumar and Michael Baruch Grossman.[24] But the growth of the White House staff also has produced a separate arena in which interest groups can concentrate their appeals. White House officials who have served as unofficial spokespersons for interest groups include George Bush's first chief of staff, John H. Sununu (nuclear power interests), and Bill Clinton's first chief of staff, Thomas F. "Mack" McLarty (natural gas producers).

Although interest groups may have difficulty finding a point of entry into the White House, they do know their way around the executive bureaucracy. The White House must then struggle to exercise control over the huge and complex bureaucracy.

HOW THE WHITE HOUSE VIEWS AND DEALS WITH INTEREST GROUPS

Interest group politics have continued to grow and change with the inclusion of new groups in the political process. In the 1980s, a proliferation of groups on both the right and left presented a new challenge to leaders of both parties. Especially pronounced was the challenge from the right since its forces were better financed.

Former governors Jimmy Carter, Ronald Reagan, and Bill Clinton had no national political experience before becoming president and served at a time of party weakness. The fortunes of their legislative agendas turned in part on the bewildering interest group politics so widespread in the nation's capital. These presidents attempted to assemble viable coalitions on an issue-by-issue basis. But as they ventured into interest group politics, opposing groups allied to thwart their agendas—and party coalitions became even more vulnerable. Political scientist Joseph A. Pika has written, "In this way, presidents may have weakened political parties just at the time they were most needed as mechanisms to organize effective coalitions to pass legislative initiatives."[25]

An important part of Reagan's electoral strategy in 1980 was harnessing the so-called New Right, a wide range of groups that promoted an agenda that included tax cuts, reduced federal regulation, an end to legal abortions, a return to prayer in the schools, federal tax breaks for parochial schools, restricted gay rights, and a more rigid interpretation of civil rights. Reagan provided hortatory leadership, submitted legislation on some of these issues, and involved Christian organizations in drafting tuition tax credit legislation. But, overall, the New Right agenda was a low priority in Reagan's first term. Reagan held on to the groups' support, however, because they had nowhere else to go.

Presidents Carter and Reagan found themselves fighting large and small interest groups when their administrations tried to cut the federal budget. Social Security recipients, western water interests, military contractors, farmers, hospitals, and state and local governments all resisted the two administrations' budget axes. Carter expended great political capital early in his fights with western water interests, the nuclear power industry, oil companies, and many liberal groups that found his programs on welfare and health care stingy.

Reagan's budget-cutters were forced to look for relatively small savings—but were frustrated even there. The administration, for example, proposed that the Coast Guard charge commercial vessels and pleasure yachts for the $1 billion in services they receive at sea. The administration plan would have brought in $400 million. But the proposal was roundly criticized and, whittled down, produced only $8 million in new revenues. When Secretary of Education William J. Bennett proposed restrictions on college loans to prevent fraud, a wide range of university and student groups protested.[26]

President Bill Clinton's legislative successes—the 1993 tax and budget bill, passage of the North American Free Trade Agreement (NAFTA), anticrime legislation, and lobbying reforms—carried the visible imprint of interest group politics. Clinton's strategy involved attacking as well as negotiating with important interest groups. In his more successful efforts, Clinton assigned a staff member to assemble a workable coalition of interest groups that could be used to prod reluctant legislators. One such effort, the NAFTA campaign, was managed by Chicago political operative William Daley, the son and brother of two powerful Chicago mayors.

Calculating Interest Group Politics

The ongoing calculations of interest group politics at the White House take into account a number of factors. Perhaps the most important is which interests have supported the president's political campaigns and government initiatives. Just as when dealing with public opinion, the president must maintain the steady backing of a basic core of supporters and bring independents and opposition figures into alliances that will support different issues. For example, when campaigning for his tax-cutting initiative in 1981, President Reagan was able to count on the support of the large, organized business interests. To secure passage of the legislation, Reagan worked to bring other groups, such as labor unions and small businesses, into his alliance.

Interest group alliances shift from issue to issue. Most groups do not get involved in legislative or regulatory activity outside their direct interests; they only become active when they see a possible gain or threat in government initiatives. Large-scale policy making entails a wider array of competing groups than incremental policy making. As a result, presidents must consider the extent to which their initiatives will activate interest groups. Business and organized labor often switch sides depending on the issue. The two groups may work together on such issues as construction projects, banking regulation, and other legislation affecting economic "growth." But they will oppose each other on issues affecting the organization of the workplace, such as "common site" picketing (picketing of a workplace by workers not directly involved in the dispute), "right to work" rules (restrictions on union organizing), and workplace safety legislation.

Other factors in the calculations of shifting interest group politics are the salience of issues and the timing of events. As economist Anthony Downs has noted, issues are subject to a cycle of attention.[27] After a period of high publicity, most issues tend to fade from public consciousness. The president may try to focus attention on particular issues, but the public and interest groups will still react according to their own priorities at the time.

The president must respond to issues put on the public agenda by concerted interest group efforts. Likewise, the president must take into account—and influence, if possible—just how much attention the public is giving an issue and how groups are responding to that attention. In 1984 Reagan, long a critic of federal coercion of states, signed legislation to penalize states that did not increase the mandatory drinking age to twenty-one. This move followed a lengthy campaign by Mothers

During his presidency, Ronald Reagan frequently criticized federal coercion of states. In 1984, however, he signed legislation to penalize states that did not increase the mandatory drinking age to twenty-one after a lengthy campaign by Mothers Against Drunk Driving.

Against Drunk Driving (MADD) and other citizens' groups, which produced high public awareness of the problem. At a different time, Reagan may have resisted such legislation.

A final factor in the calculations is the relative strength of different interest groups. The membership, wealth, and status of advocacy organizations vary greatly. Most interest groups have just a few hundred members and budgets in the hundreds of thousands of dollars. Others, such as the American Association of Retired Persons (AARP), have multimillion dollar budgets, large memberships that can be deployed swiftly on various campaigns, and professional staffs and consultants to advise them. Many are connected with corporations that they can use for overhead expenses, expert advise, technology, and membership lists.

The White House examines the balance of power among interest groups on specific issues as it plans its strategy on how to deal with a particular issue. This is not to say that the president decides which side of the issue to take based on this balance of power, only whether to attempt to influence the issue and, if so, what tactics to use. For example, President Carter decided to withdraw the second Strategic Arms Limitation Talks (SALT) treaty from the Senate in 1980 after the Soviet Union's invasion of Afghanistan dramatically altered public opinion and the alignment of interest groups.[28] President Reagan decided to pursue "omnibus" budget reconciliation legislation in 1981 when a wide range of interest groups appeared ready to defeat the administration, issue by issue, in congressional committees. The package cut $130.6 billion from the federal budget over four years.[29]

The president's relationship with interest groups develops issue by issue. The president can rely on certain groups always to be supportive and others always to offer opposition; the president usually must seek the support of many fence-straddling groups. Groups traditionally aligning with Republican presidents include business, oil companies, conservative social and religious groups, and some farm groups. Traditional Democratic allies include many multinational firms, labor, environmental groups, feminists, and minorities.

Working behind the scenes, interest groups attempt to shape the details of major White House policy initiatives. Mark Bloomfield and Charles Walker developed the Bush administration's 1990 capital gains tax cut proposal. The proposal expanded the types of investments receiving tax preference from stocks and bonds to include other "passive" assets such as real estate and corporate structures. "Inclusion of timber and other assets," a confidential memorandum outlining the initiative advised, would bring the "timber industry, agricultural interests, heretofore reluctant small business organizations, and others into the private-sector capital-gains coalition." The memo also urged Bush to work more closely with the Capital Gains Coalition, a group of businesses actively lobbying on Capitol Hill.[30] Although the legislation did not pass, it helped to shape Bush's legislative relations.

Interest groups also pursue public strategies to promote their causes. As one example, interest groups have played an increasing role in the confirmation process for Supreme Court nominations. After bruising battles over Reagan's nomination of Robert H. Bork and Bush's nomination of Clarence Thomas, President Clinton was careful to select candidates with little in their records to spark controversy from interest groups. Thus it was only after lengthy searches that Clinton nominated Ruth Bader Ginsburg and Stephen G. Breyer to the high court. During the searches, Clinton floated many possibilities that were later withdrawn after objections from organized groups. Interior Secretary Bruce Babbitt was withdrawn from consideration in 1993 and 1994 after conservative groups complained about his liberal views and environmentalists expressed concern that they would lose their best advocate in the cabinet.

Cabinet positions also are subject to intense public lobbying. Recent casualties of interest group opposition include former Texas senator John G. Tower, President Bush's first nominee for secretary of defense. Morton Halperin, director of the Washington office of the American Civil Liberties Union (ACLU), saw his nomination for a high-level State Department position in the Clinton administration withdrawn after conservative groups complained about his past writings criticizing government policies on defense and intelligence gathering.

Using technologies that allow almost instant contact with organization members and key political figures, interest groups have undertaken a number of public campaigns in recent years to rouse the public on specific issues. Liberal organizations mobilized against the policies and nominees of the Reagan and Bush administrations. When Clinton won the presidency in 1992, conservatives mobilized. Floyd Brown, an independent political operative, sent a newsletter to 175,000 subscribers and regularly publicized charges against Clinton. Brown even sold an audiotape of Clinton talking with a woman who claimed to have had an affair with him. The Center for Security Policy, a conservative group that successfully opposed Clinton nominations, sent out triweekly "attack faxes" to one thousand public officials and opinion leaders.[31]

Sometimes the president is so concerned about the appearance of interest group activity that the White House will ask supporters to lobby discreetly or not at all. The Reagan administration kept a distance from Teamsters officials, for example, when they were under indictment for corruption in the mid-1980s. Also in the 1980s, responding to criticism that the Democrats were a party of special interests, Democratic leaders sought to create an image of independence from such supporters as African Americans and Hispanics, feminists, gays, and teachers. After the 1984 presidential campaign, Paul Kirk, chair of the Democratic National Committee, withdrew party recognition of seven party caucuses for specific groups.[32]

President Clinton in 1993 clashed bitterly with organized labor, a major Democratic constituency, over the North American Free Trade Agreement (NAFTA). Labor groups claimed that it would cost Americans jobs and damage the environment. The tensions over NAFTA lasted long after the successful, but very close, vote.

Inevitably, interest groups that support the president during election campaigns become disenchanted with the administration's performance. Organized labor, civil rights groups, mayors, social workers, and advocates of a national health system were disappointed with President Carter's policies—particularly after his budget and defense priorities shifted in a conservative direction during the second half of his term. This disappointment led many to urge Democratic senator Edward M. Kennedy of Massachusetts to challenge Carter for the 1980 nomination. The far right groups that supported Bush's candidacy in 1988 later were upset that Bush was not more vigorous in promoting their agenda, including prayer in the schools, tuition tax credits for private schools, and an antiabortion constitutional amendment.

Many in the right wing found a new voice in Patrick Buchanan, whose challenge of Bush in the 1992 primaries weakened the unity of the party.

The President's Staff and Interest Groups

Since the nation's earliest years, the president has assigned staff members to monitor important interest groups. Andrew Jackson's aides, for example, carefully gauged the activities and strength of bankers and businesses opposed to the Jackson administration (1829–1837). A little over a century later, Franklin D. Roosevelt's New Deal initiated governmental growth that gave hundreds of new groups reason to have a regular relationship with Washington politicians, including the president. Today, interest groups are so important to the presidency that the White House has an office—the Office of Public Liaison—devoted exclusively to monitoring and cajoling interest groups.

The president's relations with interest groups have not always been so direct as they are today. Before the expansion of the White House staff in the postwar era, the cabinet served as the main link between interest groups and the administration.[33] Cabinet officials tended to have strong ties to the groups whose affairs their departments oversaw, and over the years they developed an appreciation of the concerns of interest groups. Administrations also developed relations with interest groups through political parties and campaign organizations.

Many of the cabinet-level departments were designed to serve the interests of specific groups. The Departments of Agriculture, Commerce, and Labor were created after years of lobbying by farmers, business leaders, and unions. At first designed to be research centers, the departments later gave their clients influence over a wide range of programs. Other federal agencies created at the urging of interest groups include the Federal Reserve Board, Federal Trade Commission, and Environmental Protection Agency. Agencies even helped to create organizations for interest groups, as when the Department of Commerce helped to organize the U.S. Chamber of Commerce.

Departments develop strong ties to interest groups even if they were not created specifically to serve those groups. Political scientists have used images of "iron triangles" and "issue networks" to express the common outlooks and interests that develop among agencies and congressional committees and the groups they regulate.[34] Even some administration appointees develop protective views toward their agencies and the interest groups they work with.

To the extent that presidents need advice on issues, they rely on the information provided by the departments as well as the advice of a small staff in the White House and informal advisers. The interest-dominated departments are the incubators of presidential legislative initiatives. Bureaucrats interested in improving the status of their agencies develop programs that enlarge their involvement with interest groups.

Presidents frequently appoint interest group representatives to administration posts to gain their support. Less than 1 percent of the federal bureaucracy today is filled with presidential appointees, but strategic use of those posts can improve presidential relations with interest groups. The president appoints interest group representatives for a number of reasons: to gain insight into constituent groups or leverage in bargaining, to co-opt groups by giving them formal involvement in policy discussions, and simply to establish a common ground for dealing with those groups.

For some agencies, interest groups have almost absolute authority over presidential appointments. For example, the Justice Department must consider the likely ratings of judicial appointments by the American Bar Association. Appointments for the Federal Reserve Board, Treasury Department, Central Intelligence Agency (CIA), and Defense Department must meet the approval of their interest group establishments—bankers, businesses, academic experts, and defense contractors. President Carter dropped his nomination of Theodore C. Sorensen as CIA director after the intelligence community and conservative activists criticized it strongly.

Democratic presidents must get the blessings of African Americans, women's groups, environmental activists, consumer groups, real estate developers, multinationals, social workers, and organized labor for their major appointments because these groups are an important part of the Democratic coalition. Republican presidents must satisfy developers of natural resources, multinational and small business concerns, financial and insurance interests, conservative social groups, and defense contractors. President Carter withdrew his proposed nomination of John Dunlop for secretary of labor in 1976 because of opposition from African American and women's groups. Later, President Reagan consulted Moral Majority leader Jerry Falwell before appointing Sandra Day O'Connor to the Supreme Court because he was concerned that Falwell might oppose O'Connor over her vote as an Arizona state legislator for funding abortions.[35]

Who does not get an important cabinet position is often as revealing as who gets the post. Some Republican presidents have reached out to groups outside their coalition by appointing moderates to the Environmental Protection Agency and the Labor, Interior, and Energy Departments. Reagan, however, rebuffed those agencies' key clients by making appointments antagonistic to their concerns. Reagan's first secretary of interior, James G. Watt, had been a lawyer for a firm strongly opposed to restrictions on the development of natural resources. (Watt himself was associated with the Mountain States Legal Foundation, an interest group for developers and oil concerns.) Reagan's first energy chief, James B. Edwards, had no experience in the field and was told to do all he could to close down the department.

Tasks of the White House Staff

Kumar and Grossman have argued that the presidency's relationship with interest groups involves four basic roles, representing four distinct tasks for the administration. To enact its policies, the administration usually must deal with all four tasks at the same time. Assigned within the White House to carry out these tasks, the "marker" keeps track of the president's debts to particular groups and attempts to help those groups; the "communicant" gathers information about current interest group concerns; the "constructor" builds coalitions for specific policy initiatives; and the "broker" helps the administration and groups with different interests to negotiate their differences to give the president sufficiently broad backing for policy initiatives.[36]

The Reagan administration's action on its tax cuts in 1981 illustrates all four tasks. Partly to repay the business community for its support in the 1980 election, the administration proposed and shepherded through Congress legislation that would reduce the marginal tax rates on individuals by 30 percent over three years and would provide massive corporate tax relief. The original decision to push the legislation illustrates the "marker" task.

Before and after taking up the legislation, the White House acted as a communicant, sounding out diverse groups on tax and other issues. Staffers gathered information about which groups were likely to support and oppose the legislation and how strong and reliable they were.

White House constructors helped to build a coalition to back the legislation in Congress. A wide variety of groups joined the coalition, including the U.S. Chamber of Commerce, Business Roundtable, National Small Business Association, Moral Majority, and National Conservative Political Action Committee. Wayne Valis, a special assistant to the president, oversaw the coordination of interest group efforts.

Finally, the administration served as a broker to settle differences among the administration, congressional leaders, and interest groups. One result of the bargaining was a reduction of the tax cut from 30 to 25 percent and a delay of the legislation's implementation.

Interest group relations with the White House are most routine—and important—on budgetary matters. Interest groups develop relationships with bureaucrats in federal agencies throughout the year, and those agencies develop budget proposals in the last three months of the calendar year. The proposals work their way up the system to the cabinet secretaries and the president.

As it has grown in size, the White House staff has played a greater role in overseeing budget recommendations. The White House, often distrusting departmental recommendations, wants to create coherent domestic and foreign programs that often are impossible without top-down control. When departments and agencies do not agree on budget and program authorities, only the president and the White House staff can settle the differences.

In the Reagan administration, the Office of Management and Budget (OMB) played an important role not only in arbitrating budget claims but also in developing new federal regulations. Under a presidential order, OMB studied the impact of new regulations before they went into effect. White House and OMB purview over the budget and regulations meant a reduced role for interest groups. Before, public action on regulations extended simply to publication of the public's comments in the *Federal Register;* under Reagan, regulations came under the control of OMB. The close relationship that interest groups enjoyed with specific agencies was not enough for their wishes to prevail.

Critics of these developments focused on lack of expertise among the White House staff and OMB officials on the many complex matters under agency jurisdiction. The Reagan White House staff, as in previous administrations, was made up of political operatives, and OMB was staffed by political professionals and accountants—few of whom knew much if anything about the chemical issues involved in environmental regulations, for example, or the complex interrelationships between different components of tax and welfare policy.

Stung by criticism that his White House was not aggressively restricting the growth of regulations, President Bush created the Council on Competitiveness, chaired by Vice President Dan Quayle. The council, deliberating in strict secrecy, attempted to deal with contentious regulatory issues—issues dear to many special interests. Once again there was much criticism of this arrangement, which gave the impression of allowing private interests a chance at "backdoor rulemaking." One of the first executive orders President Clinton issued in 1993 disbanded the Council on Competitiveness and limited the role of OMB in reviewing new regulations. Clinton's executive order also required that OMB disclose all communications with federal agencies or outside parties during the course of its review.

A Greater White House Role

As the government extended its reach over more economic and social policy areas in the aftermath of World War II, conflicts developed between departments and agencies that re-

quired White House arbitration. The sheer size and the inertia of the bureaucracy created difficulties for presidents trying to exert "top-down" control. In response to the realization that the departments and interest groups could not be controlled without extra help, postwar presidents increased the size of the White House staff. Yet the staff often developed antagonistic relationships with the departments as it tried to formulate and implement programs consistent with the president's wishes. As a result, the president ceased to rely on the departments for key legislative proposals.

Although the White House was increasingly dominating the formation of legislative proposals and regulatory change, interest groups still had considerable reason to maintain regular contacts with federal departments. For the White House, contact with major interest groups became an important part of the president's strategy for mobilizing support on specific issues. First Lady Eleanor Roosevelt was one of Franklin Roosevelt's most important emissaries to some interest groups, such as African Americans and labor. Roosevelt also appointed White House aides James A. Farley, Harry Hopkins, Louis Howe, Adolph Berle, Raymond Moley, and Philleo Nash to stay in contact with interest groups as part of their jobs. But both Roosevelt and his successor, Harry S. Truman, expressed discomfort with assigning aides strictly to work with interest groups. Roosevelt informed his advisers that he did not want a formal White House apparatus because in theory it would attract people with vested interests.[37] Nevertheless, Roosevelt and Truman recognized the need to deal with interest groups. They wanted to work, however, through the Democratic National Committee since they considered interest groups to be part of the electoral coalition rather than a governing coalition.

Despite the lack of a large or formal White House apparatus

First Lady Eleanor Roosevelt was one of Franklin Roosevelt's most important emissaries to interest groups such as African Americans and labor. Here she speaks to members of the CIO, AFL, and unaffiliated unions in West Park, New York.

for dealing with interest groups, presidents always have constructed ad hoc coalitions of interest groups to pursue policies on specific issues. In fact, some of the great twentieth-century legislative campaigns resulted from presidential management of interest group lobbying. Notable examples include adoption of the constitutional amendment granting suffrage to women, the amendments for Prohibition and repeal of Prohibition, Franklin Roosevelt's attempt to gain control of the U.S. Supreme Court by increasing its size, the Truman administration's aid to Greece and Turkey and the subsequent Marshall Plan for postwar European economic recovery, civil rights legislation of the 1950s and 1960s, and Carter's energy package. To promote the Marshall Plan, the Truman administration formed a coalition of business, labor, religious, and charitable groups. Representatives of these interest groups met with administration officials to help develop the plan and sell it to Congress and the public.

Interest groups also are represented on a major scale on advisory committees, ad hoc groups formed to advise the president on specific policies. The New Deal expanded the use of ad hoc commissions; by 1939 eighty-two such committees advised the government. During World War II, some one thousand committees advised the Office of Price Administration alone. Three thousand committees were in operation in the late 1960s according to one survey.[38]

Recent presidential lobbying includes many examples of building coalitions of interest groups. In 1962 President Kennedy assembled a coalition of interest groups to promote the Trade Expansion Act. Nixon assigned aide Charles Colson to head a campaign to enlist interest group support for the 1969 antiballistic missile treaty with the Soviet Union. Nixon also put together coalitions for his "New Federalism" system of intergovernmental relations, for his economic programs, and for his two doomed Supreme Court nominations.

Nixon planned to create a White House office to oversee contacts with interest groups, but the Watergate scandal distracted him. Nixon's successor, Gerald R. Ford, created the Office of Public Liaison (OPL) in 1976. The new office supplemented the ad hoc efforts of the rest of the White House to stay in regular contact with key groups.

OPL has had an uneven history. The first full-time director was the Carter administration's Margaret "Midge" Costanza. Costanza made public her differences with the president as she courted "outsider" groups such as African Americans, women, and gays. Her most publicized differences with Carter concerned abortion: Carter opposed the use of federal funds for abortion, and Costanza openly favored federal support. Under Costanza, the office was oriented more toward advocacy than toward building coalitions for the president's policies.

After Carter replaced Costanza with Anne Wexler, the office became an effective instrument for White House lobbying. Costanza had complained that the office was strictly an outlet for meaningless public relations, but Wexler involved OPL in the policy formation and lobbying operations of the rest of the

White House. The office participated in the drafting of legislation from the beginning. One member of Carter's legislative liaison staff said of Wexler's OPL: "The public liaison folks have a pretty sophisticated operation for pinpointing potential interest group allies. When they pulled together a coalition, it could be pretty valuable on the Hill. I guess they had about 30,000 names and contacts on their computer for mobilization."[39]

Even with a sophisticated public liaison office, the president still usually entrusts the most important interest group assignments to specific staff members. Late in the Carter administration, even as OPL gained stature, the president called on Chief of Staff Hamilton Jordan to set up task forces to promote the administration's policies. Those task forces gradually won the administration praise from political professionals, but they came too late to promote much of Carter's agenda. The administration shifted its attention to the 1980 election just as it developed an effective way to build coalitions.

In addition to OPL and Jordan's task forces, the Carter administration relied on a number of interest group representatives on the White House staff and in agencies to reach out to interest groups. Carter appointed to his administration people affiliated with teachers' unions, Ralph Nader advocacy groups, and Jewish groups, as well as alternate energy developers, environmentalists, and social work veterans. Women's groups, African Americans, Hispanics, and labor leaders were consulted and given greater representation on courts and agencies.

Good interest group relations give the White House a public relations machine that reaches into every corner of the country. "The realtors can send out half a million Mailgrams within 24 hours," one observer noted. "If they have a hundred target congressmen, they can get out 100,000 Mailgrams targeted by district."[40] The Chamber of Commerce, Christian Coalition, AFL-CIO, American Federation of State, County, and Municipal Employees, National Education Association, and American Medical Association all can mobilize their many chapters and members within days. In many ways, the interest groups can be considered the new political machines of U.S. politics.

Carter both wooed and excoriated interest groups throughout his presidency, which created public confusion about his competence. For example, in 1979 Carter created a cabinet-level Department of Education to fulfill a promise to the National Education Association, the teachers' union that endorsed him in 1976 and 1980. Carter also made well-publicized efforts to promote groups such as evangelicals, organized labor, banks, some energy producers, and African Americans.

Most recent presidents have been accused of "pandering" to interest groups. But the presidency has found itself in an interest vortex that it cannot avoid. President Carter constantly expressed frustration with interest group politics. In his 1979 "crisis of confidence" speech and in his 1981 farewell address, Carter decried the effects of interest groups on national policy development. In his farewell address, he said:

We are increasingly drawn to single-issue groups and special-interest organizations to ensure that whatever else happens our own personal

President Ronald Reagan speaks to a gathering of the National Association of Evangelicals. Presidents frequently give speeches at the annual conventions of interest groups, especially to shore up presidential support.

views and our own personal interests are protected. This is a disturbing factor in American political life. It tends to distort our purposes. Because of the fragmented pressures of these special interests, it's very important that the office of the president be a strong one.[41]

Even when presidents are at odds with major interest groups, they must at least pay their respects to them, usually with appearances at annual conventions of the organizations. Occasional appearances and meetings are necessary expressions of good faith for the president who wishes to stand as a symbol for the whole nation.

The number of presidential appearances before groups has increased steadily in the postwar era. President Dwight D. Eisenhower attended meetings to deliver "minor" speeches an average of five times a year; President Johnson gave ten a year; President Reagan delivered twenty annually; President Clinton also gave about twenty.[42] Speeches to interest groups in Washington are far more numerous: Ford, Carter, and Reagan averaged about fifteen a month.[43]

The president often appears before interest groups to appeal for support on specific issues. Johnson appealed to leaders of civil rights organizations to keep the pressure on Congress for passage of the landmark Civil Rights Act of 1964. Reagan asked veterans' and Latin American groups to support the "contra" war against Nicaraguan government.

Presidential appearances before interest groups also can be pure symbolism—the head of state going before unfriendly groups to urge national unity. Nixon's speech before the AFL-CIO, Carter's speech before the Veterans of Foreign Wars, and Reagan's appearances before the National Association for the Advancement of Colored People (NAACP) are all examples.

The Interest Group Universe Today

Most of today's active interest groups are the offspring of past political and economic movements, and their survival and involvement in politics are one of the constraints on the activities of the president, the executive bureaucracy, and Congress. Yet the interest groups serve not just as constraints; they also offer politicians a means of mobilizing political activity.

Interest groups represent every conceivable group in the United States: big and small business, domestic and multinational manufacturers and services, banks and insurance companies, real estate developers, teachers, miners, lawyers, blue-collar workers, opponents of unions, the elderly, "peaceniks," military contractors, consumers, evangelicals, Jews, Arabs, Hispanics, gays, feminists, guardians of different notions of the "public interest," states and cities, government workers, secretaries, custodians, athletes, actors, environmentalists, developers of natural resources—and the list goes on and on. The interest group universe is so large that it contains innumerable internal contradictions. Within the set of interest groups concerned about military affairs, for example, there is often keen competition. Recent presidents sold weapons to influence the balance of power in the Middle East, provoking opposition from the nations or interests who felt put at a disadvantage.

To understand interest groups, it is important to understand their different goals and functions, resources, everyday activities, and long-term strategies.

GOALS AND FUNCTIONS

Interest groups form to promote a group's material interests in budget, tax, and regulatory proceedings in Washington; to express a group's ideology and desires; or to provide a group with a forum, services, and standards.

The U.S. Chamber of Commerce is an umbrella organization for more than 215,000 businesses and 3,000 individuals, 5,000 state and local chapters, and about 1,000 trade and professional associations. The chamber's annual $70 million budget allows extensive lobbying of both the federal and state governments. The chamber is dedicated to one overriding goal: improving the conditions for business expansion. Active in issues such as tax legislation, labor laws, and regulatory relief, the group has a definite ideology, but it is interested primarily in material concerns.

The chamber is the largest business organization in the United States. Other active business groups designed strictly to produce better conditions for economic activity include the Business Roundtable, oil lobbies, and the National Small Business Association.

The AFL-CIO also is designed to further the material benefits of its members. The organization has fourteen million dues-paying members in more than seventy-eight affiliates, including the Teamsters, the United Auto Workers, the United Mine Workers, and American Federation of Teachers. The AFL-CIO's job is simple: bargain for the best wages, benefits, and working conditions possible, and make the task of organizing workers as easy and efficient as possible.

The Chamber of Commerce and the AFL-CIO are interested mainly in material benefits for their members; other interest groups have more "expressive" agendas. Rather than simply seeking a share of federal largesse, they exist to promote their ideological or cultural values. Many of the evangelical and conservative groups that fall under the New Right umbrella were founded to promote values rather than material interests. Frustrated with what they perceive to be a decline in the moral values of the family, groups such as the Christian Coalition, National Right to Life Committee, and National Conservative Political Action Committee contribute generously to political campaigns and lobby hard in the White House and on Capitol Hill. They have promoted an antiabortion amendment to the Constitution, prayer in the schools, and tuition tax credits for private schools. They also have spoken out on foreign policy issues such as the war in Nicaragua and arms control. Other important ideologically oriented organizations include the Americans for Democratic Action, American Civil Liberties Union, Cato Institute, the Heritage Forum, and People for the American Way.

Professional organizations take on both material and expressive functions. The American Bar Association, American Medical Association (AMA), and American Association of State Colleges and Universities serve as protectors of professional standards and ideals, but they also want to defend the privileges of their members. The AMA, for example, is among the biggest contributors to political campaigns and actively defends the profession's material interests whenever Congress considers issues such as Medicare or hospital cost-containment legislation.

Since the 1970s there has been a boom in "public interest" lobbies. These groups do not promote the interests of any single sector but instead promote their nonpartisan vision of the general interest of all society. The members of these groups do not stand to receive special material benefits if their ideals are realized, but the policies they promote would help some groups at the expense of others. Prominent public interest groups include Common Cause, the League of Women Voters, the U.S. Public Interest Research Group and other organizations set up by consumer activist Ralph Nader, and the Consumer Federation of America.

RESOURCES AND EVERYDAY ACTIVITIES

The influence of interest groups differs according to their resources. Money, size of membership, technological sophistication (such as computer networks, direct-mail operations, fax machines, telephone banks, polling operations), expertise on issues, familiarity with the political process, political reputation and contacts, motivation, and leadership are the important factors defining an organization's strength.[44]

The everyday activities of most lobbies consist of unglamorous work such as monitoring legislation on Capitol Hill and regulatory action in agencies, researching issues, fund raising, surveying and responding to the concerns of membership, and staying in touch with congressional staff members.

Most interest groups have a legislative agenda that they would like to pursue, but they rarely have the opportunity to press specific proposals at the White House or on Capitol Hill. Usually they must form alliances with other groups on specific issues that the president, Congress, or federal departments are considering. An interest group's agenda, then, is pursued bit by bit rather than as a whole. This helps to explain why interest groups often become disenchanted with an administration that considers itself an ally: the interest group may consider its program to be the president's program, but presidents also must serve other, often conflicting groups and goals.

LONG-TERM STRATEGIES

Because of the slow pace of legislative action in Washington, lobbies must be content to pursue "incremental" change most of the time. But groups must do what they can to develop a wide range of large and small initiatives so they are able to act when opportunities for exerting influence arise.

Interest groups must decide whether they are going to use "insider" or "outsider" strategies to influence the president and the rest of the Washington establishment.[45] Insiders establish ties with a number of White House, agency, and congressional staffers and, depending on the administration, can play a role in writing legislation and regulations that affect their interests. Outsiders attempt to pressure the administration by putting the public spotlight on the issues they consider important.

Interest groups often move from outsider to insider roles with a change in administration. Many consumer protection and environmental protection groups moved from the outside to the inside with the election of Jimmy Carter in 1976. Carter appointed a number of "Naderites"—disciples of activist Ralph Nader—to top agency positions. Likewise, before Reagan was elected president, the Moral Majority and other conservative groups relied on public relations campaigns and insurgent candidates. After Reagan became president, however, the White House consulted these groups on many social initiatives. They actually helped to write tuition tax credit legislation.

Influencing the Balance of Power

Even if presidents are limited in their dealings with interest groups on particular issues, they influence the balance of power among competing interest groups. Presidential use of public opinion, budget priorities, and White House staff can enhance some groups and undercut others. In this way, the president can "set the table" for later political conflicts.

Political scientists Benjamin Ginsberg and Martin Shefter have identified three strategies that a president can use to shape the makeup of the interest group universe.[46] First, the president can try to transform the identities of established and nascent groups. Second, the president can "divide and conquer" existing alliances of groups and attempt to bring fragments of the old alliance under White House influence. Third, the president can attempt to bring estranged groups together on an issue in a movement where they find common interest.

Franklin Roosevelt provides a textbook example of presidential influence over interest group alignment. Roosevelt gave a number of groups—such as the elderly, African Americans, labor, and the "third of a nation" that was poor—a positive new identity that led to their involvement in Democratic politics. The New Deal offered a wide range of incentives to certain businesses to support the president, thereby chipping them away from a strong business alliance that had been hostile to previous liberal initiatives. Finally, by stressing the common desire for economic security, Roosevelt forged an alliance of ethnic groups in similarly vulnerable economic positions.[47]

Postwar presidencies steadily expanded the number of interest groups involved in national politics. The expansion of federal regulation of civil rights, workplace safety, consumer products, the environment, trade, energy production and prices, air travel, and home building continued through the Carter administration, regardless of the president's party. That regulatory expansion, added to the hundreds of federal programs and studies, increased the stake of interest groups in the federal government.

Lyndon B. Johnson's Great Society also led to the creation of many new interest groups. Domestic initiatives in housing, community development, job training, education, and health care included specific instructions to involve the communities and interests affected by the programs. The most famous example was the Economic Opportunity Act of 1964, which required some urban programs to be "developed, conducted, and administered with the maximum feasible participation of residents of the areas and members of the groups served." The "maximum feasible participation" provision was among the most controversial found in the 1960s programs. Proponents maintained that the provision allowed poor people to develop self-esteem and political skills so they could become self-sufficient members of society. Opponents argued that it simply gave antagonistic groups resources to undermine the government's efforts.[48]

A president's program does not need an explicit demand for participation to promote interest groups. In fact, such provisions have a minor effect compared to the way a president's budget priorities provide the resources and incentives for interest groups. Robert Reischauer, an official of the Urban League, has explained:

In each area of federal involvement a powerful network of interest groups developed. First there were the representatives of the recipient governments. These included not only interest groups representing governors, mayors, city managers, county executives, state legislators, and the like, but also recipient agency organizations such as chief state school officers, public welfare directors, and highway commissioners. All told, some seventy-two groups of this sort existed. A second element of the network consisted of the general providers of the services provided by the grants—organized teachers, builders of public housing, and so forth. The recipients of the services also formed an element in this network—ranging from welfare recipients to P.T.A. organizations to automobile clubs. Private-sector suppliers of the inputs needed to provide the services also joined the effort. These organizations might represent the producers of library shelves, manufacturers of school buses, book publishers, or asphalt suppliers. The academics and private-sector consulting firms that made a living evaluating existing programs and planning and designing new programs also formed an element in the support group for the grants strategy.[49]

The Reagan administration skillfully transformed the interest group balance of power.[50] First, the president gave greater visibility to many groups. Reagan attracted the support of southern white conservative groups by appealing not to past racial issues but to the moral concerns of their evangelical churches and organizations. The network of churches throughout the South served as a base for organizing on issues ranging from school prayer to nuclear arms policy. Reagan also helped to shift the focus of many blue-collar workers to patriotism and devotion to family issues such as opposition to abortion. The president appealed to middle-class voters not on the basis of federal programs—most of which they favored and he wanted to cut—but as overburdened taxpayers.

Reagan helped to ally groups long at odds. Protestants and Catholics came together with common concerns about abortion and other "moral" issues pertaining to personal values. Corporations and small domestic businesses—longtime antagonists on tariff, trade, and tax issues—united on environmental, consumer, and other regulatory concerns. Middle-class professionals, who often had sided with Democrats and liberals on social issues, were drawn to the Reagan camp with tax cuts.

Many groups and alliances split over Reagan initiatives—business and labor on issues of regulation, college-educated professionals over taxes, and beneficiaries of federal programs over tax and budget cuts. Business and labor, which previously had joined forces on many regulatory issues, for example, split in the late 1970s and early 1980s as deregulation led to the rise of nonunion firms that undersold unionized firms. Consumer groups also opposed former allies in business and labor.

Reagan managed as well to shift the focus of much interest group activity downward. His emphasis on nonfederal programs for addressing social problems increased the work of interest groups at the state level. The increased reliance on "public-private partnerships" and voluntarism limited the notion of public responsibility for social problems. Even though Reagan's tax policies reduced incentives for corporate giving, his celebration of voluntary action took some of the political pressure off the administration for its budget cuts.[51]

Finally, Reagan came to Washington determined to "defund" what he considered to be irresponsible liberal interest groups. Many groups, such as environmentalists and legal advocates, depended on the federal government for some support, but Reagan cut that support in 1981.

President Clinton entered office having an ambivalent approach toward interest groups. On the one hand, he considered himself a reformer sent to attack special-interest domination of the capital. On the other hand, he was a pragmatic politician eager to get along with powerful figures and enact a wide range of initiatives. "How can a new president turn his back on dozens of his advisers from inside the Beltway who make their living trading on influence and access?" asked Charles Lewis, president of the Center for Public Integrity. "He wants to be known as the candidate of change, but he's using all those old insider types because he wants to be effective."[52] The Washington establishment awaited Clinton's presidency nervously. The public policy magazine *National Journal* said the interest group "winners" from the change in administrations included the AIDS Action Council, American Gas Association, American Israel Public Affairs Committee, Association of Trial Lawyers of America, Progressive Policy Institute, and Cuban-American National Fund. Losers included the American Nuclear Energy Council, Association of Bank Holding Companies, Pharmaceutical Manufacturers Association, and Heritage Foundation.[53]

Interest groups with ties to the Democratic and liberal causes were uncertain whether to help Clinton or maintain their independence. Pamela Gilbert of Congress Watch said that liberal causes felt "emotionally odd" as Clinton took office. "We need a little group therapy, because we have these competing pressures on us," she said. "One is to work with a new Democratic administration and the other is to play our traditional outsider role, publicly criticizing what we don't like."[54] In the constantly shifting coalitions of modern American politics, most interest groups support the president on a case-by-case basis.

Congressional consideration of President Clinton's health care reform proposals in 1993 and 1994 dramatically displayed the modern role of interest groups. Groups representing business, labor, and the health care industry attacked Clinton's proposals one by one. The administration's options were limited from the beginning. Two solid Democratic allies—labor unions and senior citizens—opposed any changes in the tax status of worker health care benefits and reforms of Social Security and Medicare.

The most influential interests in the medical industry were the insurance companies and medical associations. Insurance companies like Aetna and Prudential supported the president's plan for "managed competition" because it put them at the center of delivery systems. Doctors' groups, led by the American Medical Association, resisted the president's plan for regulation of fees and the "alliances" that would oversee doctor-patient relationships. Smaller insurance companies, fearing that the giants would drive them out of business, opposed the Clinton plan. Pharmaceutical companies also criticized the plan because of the proposed regulation of drug prices. Teaching and research hospitals resisted the reform because of its emphasis on basic delivery and the fear that they would lose federal grants. Meanwhile, some citizens' groups attempted to steer policy making toward a more public plan such as that used in Canada. Citizens' groups in California succeeded in placing an initiative on the ballot that would mandate such a "single payer" plan in that state.

The decisive blow to comprehensive reform came from the National Federation of Independent Businesses (NFIB). The lobby of 600,000 owners of small businesses attacked the proposal for "employer mandates" to pay for health care. The NFIB claimed that Clinton's plan, which would have required businesses to pay up to 80 percent of health insurance costs, would eliminate as many as 1.5 million jobs. NFIB lobbyists wrote letters, attended rallies, and met personally with members of Congress and their staffers. NFIB members also appeared on television and other media outlets. The lobby focused its attention on undecided members of Congress from districts with high proportions of small businesses.

President Clinton and his wife, Hillary Rodham Clinton, the chief architect of the proposal, by turns took a hard line and a conciliatory line toward the interest groups. The first lady delivered blistering speeches against the pharmaceutical industry and doctors who benefited from the health care inflation of the 1980s. But she and the president also sought common ground with interest groups. When the usual politicking seemed to fail, the White House turned to parody, lampooning television commercials critical of the Clinton plan.

Any president's policies are bound to rouse interest groups that oppose the administration. Many groups develop or improve their organization in response to threats they perceive from the White House. President Nixon's grain export policies led to the creation of the American Agriculture Movement.[55] Independent oil companies organized on a large scale for the first time when President Carter pushed a windfall profits tax.[56] Labor, environmental, women's rights, Social Security, civil rights,

In May 1993 First Lady Hillary Rodham Clinton speaks to the union employees about health care reform. Facing fierce opposition from interest groups, the Clinton administration's efforts to overhaul the national health care system were unsuccessful by 1994.

and public interest groups improved their membership and fund-raising efforts in response to Reagan administration policies. Those groups used the negative images of administration officials such as Interior Secretary James G. Watt, Attorney General Edwin Meese III, and judge Robert Bork as part of their direct-mail fund-raising appeals and rallies. The Sierra Club's membership almost doubled from 180,000 to 300,000 during Watt's tenure at the Department of Interior.[57] A number of grassroots organizations developed sophisticated operations and national bases in their campaigns against Reagan's policies on Central America, nuclear arms, South Africa, and the environment. Some fifty thousand canvassers knocked on doors every night in the early 1980s with petitions and requests for donations for one cause or another.[58]

WHITE HOUSE EFFORTS TO ROUSE INTEREST GROUP SUPPORT

Presidents' interest group strategies fit somewhere between their attempts to control the huge bureaucracy and their efforts to appeal to the public at large. Interest groups have many of the open characteristics involved in public appeals, but groups also become intricately involved in the everyday machinery of the hundreds of agencies that develop and execute federal policy. Whatever the situation, the president needs interest group support for difficult policy battles. To gain support, the White House must mobilize both the public and the elites who are important players in the complex negotiations of congressional and bureaucratic politics.

Whether a president can persuade Congress to adopt the administration's policy proposals depends on how much pressure interest groups can bring to an issue. Interest groups offer the president a number of tools that can be used to prod Congress:

• Expertise and legitimacy. An organization that includes respected analysts of a political problem not only serves as a school for the president and the White House staff but also puts the reputations of the experts behind the White House.

• Membership and organization. Most interest groups do not have large, active memberships, but many have access to mailing lists and expertise in mobilizing the important participants in a political battle.

• Money for media campaigns. Even the most skeletal organizations often have financial resources for a media campaign. Recent battles over telecommunications and health care reform and passage of NAFTA have involved extensive broadcast and newspaper advertising to sway public opinion.

• A system of balancing political concerns. The participation of many interest groups in the policy-making process enables the president and members of Congress to engage in extensive bartering that goes far beyond the specific controversy. Votes for highly visible initiatives are won by promising members of Congress support on other, unrelated matters.

• Leadership. Interest groups include not only many nationally recognized names—such as John Sweeney of the AFL-CIO, Phyllis Schlafly of the Eagle Forum, Norman Lear of People for the American Way, and Ralph Reed of the Christian Coalition—but also sophisticated organizational operators. These groups can offer the kind of leadership that mobilizes whole segments of the population on issues important to the president.

Political battles occasionally develop into battles between two sets of interest groups and their White House and congressional allies. NAFTA-implementing legislation, passed under Clinton, and the 1981 budget cuts, enacted under Reagan, were two cases in which the battle lines between supporters and opponents were fairly clear, and uncommitted members of Congress were courted vigorously by both sides. Often, however, on a highly complex issue such as telecommunications reform, the lines are more fluid, and more negotiation occurs between interest groups and executive and legislative branch officials. In these cases, as legislation evolves, interest groups constantly reevaluate it, based on an assessment of how the legislation affects their core values and goals. Interest group activity determines the extent of the propaganda battle and the intricacy and duration of the maneuvering between the president and key members of Congress.

Telecommunications Overhaul: Freewheeling Negotiation

On February 8, 1996, President Clinton signed the long-awaited overhaul of the telecommunications industry into law. Appropriately for the measure that was designed to take American telecommunications into the twenty-first century, Clinton also logged onto the Internet and signed an electronic version of the bill in real time—the first president to do so. The passage of the Telecommunications Act of 1996 was a classic high-stakes contest among many affected interest groups. The outcome of the struggle was determined by bartering, public appeals, presidential leadership (much of it behind the scenes, in contrast to the highly public fight to round up votes for NAFTA), and the organizational strength of the various interest groups.

Billions of dollars were at stake when on November 22, 1993, bills were introduced in the House of Representatives to overhaul the U.S. telecommunications industry for the first time in sixty years. Technological innovations in data processing and communications had rendered existing legislation anachronistic. New digital technologies promised a convergence of telephone, television, and computer services, but existing legislation carefully separated and regulated the spheres in which local phone companies, long-distance phone companies, and cable television companies could operate. This regulation of the industry was stifling innovation. By unleashing full-blown competition in telecommunications, some argued, Congress would give companies more incentive to invest in these technologies and to realize more fully the potential of the "information superhighway."

Deregulation, however, would create winners and losers among many players. In order to gain support for passage of the legislation, Congress and the president would have to weigh the interests and organizational strength of the regional Bell companies, the cable industry, the long-distance phone companies, consumer advocates, supporters of service to rural (and therefore, high-cost) communities, family-values interest groups concerned with violence on television and pornography on the internet, First Amendment groups such as the ACLU, broadcast television interests and advertisers, equipment manufacturers, alarm-service providers, public television proponents and opponents, public utilities, electronic publishers, satellite companies, cellular phone service providers, and the members of Congress with ties to each of these players.

On a number of occasions between introduction of the legislation in November 1993 and enactment in February 1996 it appeared as though the whole effort would come to nothing. Every change, no matter how small, that was made to appease one interest group led other groups to reevaluate their support for the legislation.

In the end, no one was completely satisfied with the outcome. Bradley Stillman, telecommunications policy director of the Consumer Federation of America, for example, complained that the law deregulated cable TV rates without any assurance that a major competitor would come along.[59] Many Republican congressional leaders, including Dick Armey of Texas, objected that it did not deregulate the industry quickly enough or thoroughly enough.[60]

All players, including President Clinton, found something objectionable in the bill. But the final consensus was that any further tinkering would invite the whole, fragile house of cards to come crashing down.

Budget Cuts of 1981: Set Battle Lines

President Reagan's budget-cutting victory in the summer of 1981 was a classic contest between two sets of interest groups. Here, too, the outcome of the struggle was determined by bartering, public appeals, strong presidential leadership, and the organizational strength of interest groups.

The prospect of more than $160 billion in budget cuts over Reagan's first term in office activated a wide range of interest groups involved with domestic policy. The usual strategy of such groups was to work with the staff members of congressional committees and the federal agencies to restore proposed cuts, piece by piece, to the budget. This "micro" activity was to be supplemented by a publicity campaign that would show low public support for the budget cutting and put both the president and Congress on the defensive. The groups opposing the budget cut proposals included the AFL-CIO, NAACP, Urban League, U.S. Conference of Mayors, Children's Defense Fund, U.S. Public Interest Research Group, National Organization for Women, Operation PUSH, and American Association of Retired Persons.

President Reagan and his lieutenants thwarted the two-pronged interest group attack, however. First, the White House reduced the chances for "micro" response to the cuts by asking Republican Senate leaders to consider the cuts as a single budget package—that is, Congress would have one up-or-down vote on all the cuts. The all-or-nothing legislation reduced the possibilities for interest groups to appeal to friendly members of congressional committees. One observer noted: "Many hundreds of lobbying groups that had built strong relationships over the years with authorizing and appropriations committee members and aides have found themselves not so much without a sympathetic ear as without a way to leverage that sympathy to get more money."[61]

Second, by including in the package authorizing legislation as well as spending legislation—that is, legislation that allowed funding as well as legislation that actually funded the programs—Reagan forced Congress to deal with otherwise protected entitlement programs. If the authorization for a program were cut, it could not be funded later in that budget year.

And, third, the Reagan administration led supportive interest groups in its own public offensive in favor of the cuts. The groups Reagan brought into the administration's alliance included the Chamber of Commerce, National Association of Manufacturers, National Conservative Political Action Committee, Moral Majority, National Jaycees, National Federation of Independent Business, and American Medical Association. The

White House managed the interest groups' campaign. It selected key congressional districts where the administration might find support and instructed the interest groups to pressure House members from those districts. Lee Atwater, the president's assistant political director, explained:

The way we operate, within forty-eight hours any Congressman will know that he has had a major strike in his district. All of a sudden, Vice President Bush is in your district, Congressman Jack Kemp is in your district. Ten of your top contributors are calling you, the head of the local AMA, the head of the local realtors' group, local officials. Twenty letters come in. Within forty-eight hours, you're hit by paid media, free media, mail, phone, all asking you to support the president.[62]

The interest group politics of the budget cuts had an elaborate system of rewards and punishments. As Reagan sought congressional approval, he co-opted the United Auto Workers union by going along with import relief on Japanese automobiles. The president also punished two of his biggest Democratic foes, House Speaker Thomas P. "Tip" O'Neill Jr. and Sen. Edward Kennedy, by lifting duties on Taiwan and Korea—a move that hurt the shoe-making industry in their home state of Massachusetts.[63]

Under such a system of lobbying, the president depends on interest groups when bartering with reluctant budget-cutters in Congress. The cozy system of backroom bargaining between the White House staff and key congressional figures is not replaced, but it is supplemented by the mobilization of interest groups for the district pressure campaigns.

Reagan was not always so skillful in shaping interest group politics. During consideration of his tax-cut bill in 1981, Reagan watched as congressional leaders engaged interest groups in negotiations over tax benefits. David Stockman, Reagan's budget director, remembered: "Everyone was accusing everyone else of greed, and in same breath shouting *'What's in it for me?'*" If the budget no longer offered "ornaments" to offer constituents, the tax code did. The competition between White House and congressional versions of the tax bill gave interest groups the opportunity to expand their tax breaks. "Try as I have," Stockman mused, "it is virtually impossible to discern rationality in the behavior of any of the principal players."[64]

Interest group politics engages all modern presidents. President Carter won Senate approval of the Panama Canal treaties because of his ability to assemble a broad coalition of interest groups and his willingness to barter for the final crucial votes. Treaty opponents included Reagan, who had found the issue to be potent in the 1976 presidential campaign. Groups fighting the treaty included the American Conservative Union, Liberty Lobby, National States' Rights Party, and John Birch Society. Some fifteen hundred State Department officials led the fight for the treaty, backed by Common Cause, the National Education Association, AFL-CIO, National Jaycees, and business leaders. The interest groups were troops in a battle for public opinion to sway skeptical senators. At the beginning, only 8 percent of the public supported "giving up" the canal; by the time of the Senate vote, a majority favored the treaties. The emotional debate eventually worked to Carter's detriment, however. Leaders of the New Right later said the canal issue was the catalyst for their activism in the 1980 election campaign for Reagan and against Carter. The issue strengthened the memberships, treasuries, organization, and technological sophistication of groups within the New Right.

On issues affecting a wide number of groups, even presidents with less popular support can fashion a coalition strong enough to win on a particular vote. Clinton won approval of the 1993 budget and tax legislation and NAFTA by playing the "insider" game. On NAFTA, for example, Clinton used patronage agreements to gain the support of more than fifty members of the House of Representatives. Some of these deals provided special benefits for constituents—such as sugar growers, citrus farmers, and defense contractors—in the congressional districts of the representatives whose NAFTA votes Clinton obtained. Even if presidents do not enjoy a high personal standing with the public, they are able to use the executive branch's prodigious resources to pull together disparate groups.

THE USE OF THE "AD-HOCRACY"

When the White House faces a crisis or a seemingly intractable problem, the president often appoints representatives of interest groups to a commission to study the problem. Commissions have proved to be an effective way of using interest group representatives to overcome the difficulties of public wrangling by interest groups.

"Ad-hocracy," as the temporary commission has been called, offers several advantages to a president facing intransigent interest group politics.[65] First, the president can co-opt the interest groups by naming selected representatives to the panel. And even beyond that, the president can try to ensure favorable policy recommendations by "stacking" the panel. Second, the commission can stifle partisan debate by including members from both parties. Third, the commission can work in almost complete secrecy, thereby bypassing debilitating debate on each major issue that it faces. And, fourth, ad-hocracy can offer all-or-nothing proposals that preclude endless public bargaining after the report's release.

President Reagan, who enjoyed success with ad-hocracies, appointed special panels to address Social Security funding, the deployment strategy of the MX missile, the investigation of the Iran-contra affair, and the health crisis over acquired immune deficiency syndrome (AIDS). All of these issues proved too difficult for the normal public process of interest group bargaining—or at least the president thought he could defuse public controversy with a panel.

Social Security was in perilous financial shape, but efforts to trim benefits or raise taxes encountered well-orchestrated opposition campaigns. Democratic candidates campaigned emotionally and effectively against administration reform proposals in 1982. Reagan's 1983 commission helped to build support for more taxes.

The debate over the MX missile presented a different problem for the administration. Reagan was committed to the mobile missile program, but Republican supporters in the West were reluctant to see the missiles based in their home states. Commission recommendations skirted the most difficult turf issues.

President Bush used an ad-hocracy for an issue that was guaranteed to anger supporters of the military. With the end of the cold war, the demand for military bases declined dramatically. To remedy the situation, a bipartisan panel headed by former representative James A. Courter of New Jersey made recommendations for base closings. Democrats complained that the base closings were concentrated in Democratic districts, but the panel had the final authority to make specific decisions, knowing, however, that Congress could reject the committee's plan.

Soon after he became president, Bill Clinton appointed his wife, Hillary Rodham Clinton, to head a task force on health care reform. The Clintons hoped to avoid public wrangles over the controversial issue by operating in private. The five-hundred-member task force met in "cluster" groups to review and negotiate important details of the proposed reforms. Policy adviser Ira Magaziner managed the task force on a day-to-day basis.

But Clinton's attempt at ad-hocracy backfired. The group was so large that details about the plan leaked, providing opponents with an opportunity to attack the reform effort. The group also failed to produce their proposed reforms in time for legislative action within Clinton's first year. Outsiders complained about being excluded from deliberations. Some critics charged that the task force knew all along what policy approach it would propose—"managed competition"—and that it only pretended to consider other ideas carefully.

A commission can cause problems for the president if it recommends actions that antagonize the administration's supporters, but, generally, commissions are low-risk ventures. President Reagan was pleasantly surprised by the favorable publicity that his National Commission on Excellence in Education created. He initially had maintained that the commission was Education Secretary Terrel H. Bell's panel, not his. But when the report got rave reviews, Reagan adopted the commission and education issue as his own.

Reagan may have been the most successful president in his use of commissions, but he was not the first to try them. John Kennedy, a skeptic of bureaucratic routines, appointed a number of commissions to bypass the usual method of policy development by departments. The Kennedy efforts foundered, however, when the makeup of the commissions received criticism and possible proposals were leaked.

President Johnson used task forces to develop much of his Great Society domestic legislation. Johnson's panels were more secretive and tended to include more members of the affected groups than well-known intellectuals and experts. In addition, some task forces included a large number of officials from the White House and bureaucracy; others had strong interest group representation.

Task forces enabled Johnson and his special assistant, Joseph A. Califano, to maintain tight control of domestic policy. As an official in the U.S. Office of Education acknowledged, "Much policy development in education has moved from here to the White House."[66] Johnson's 1964 task forces were ad hoc efforts to develop a quick legislative package. In later years, the task forces were more entrenched. Fifty task forces worked on domestic programs in 1967. Most of the task forces recommended "incremental," or small-scale, adjustments to already existing policies and programs. But the task forces also proposed major initiatives.

PUBLIC EFFORTS BY INTEREST GROUPS

Textbooks of U.S. politics stress the "cozy," behind-the-scenes relationships between interest groups and government agencies and congressional committees. But many groups are not part of the secure federal establishment and must orchestrate large public demonstrations to influence the president and other parts of the government.

In recent years, protest has become a regular part of American politics. Protest traditionally has been a political strategy of groups excluded from mainstream of American life, such as minorities and poor people. But middle-class movements are increasingly resorting to protest and demonstrations to promote their interests.

A number of groups representing the "public interest" have arisen in recent years to pressure the president and Congress on a wide range of issues. United We Stand America, a rump group of 1992 independent presidential candidate H. Ross Perot, rallied followers and conducted door-to-door campaigns against the Clinton administration's trade, budget, health care, and Haiti initiatives. The Concord Coalition, founded in 1992 by former senators Warren B. Rudman, a New Hampshire Republican, and Paul Tsongas, a Massachusetts Democrat, lobbied for efforts to reduce the federal budget deficit and national debt.

Other outstanding examples of interest group efforts to influence the president and the rest of the government by "going public" include: the civil rights marches, starting in the 1950s; gay rights marches, beginning in the early 1970s; the protests against the Vietnam War and the movements for and against ratification of the Equal Rights Amendment in the 1970s; expressions of support and opposition to the Reagan administration's policies in Central America, particularly the activities of Lt. Col. Oliver North, in the late 1980s, as well as protests against Reagan's nuclear weapons policies; and the pro- and antiabortion movements of the 1980s and 1990s.

In the latter half of the twentieth century, the most sustained public protests in the United States have been those over the issues of civil rights and the Vietnam War. When African American organizations confronted the limits of the legal strategies of the NAACP and the state-by-state actions to protect rights, a series of protests helped to put the issue on the national agenda. Demonstrations and other "outsider" efforts by civil rights orga-

Frequently groups not part of the federal establishment organize large public demonstrations in an attempt to influence the government. In March 1963, from the steps of the Lincoln Memorial to the Washington Monument, thousands demonstrate for civil rights.

nizations forced Presidents Eisenhower, Kennedy, and Johnson to deal with the issue. The most dramatic demonstration was the 1963 march on Washington, capped by the Reverend Martin Luther King's "I Have a Dream" speech and a visit by civil rights leaders to the White House.

President Johnson first dismissed Vietnam War protests as unrepresentative of public opinion, but the protests succeeded in drawing attention to moral and tactical questions about the war in elite circles such as the media and universities. Extensive war coverage after protests helped to shift public opinion against the war and persuade Johnson to halt bombing in 1968.

Many protests fail to move the president, at least in any direct way. President Reagan stood by his nuclear arms policies—including the decision to base Pershing missiles in Europe—despite massive demonstrations in West Germany, Great Britain, and the United States. Reagan dismissed the protests, including a gathering of several hundred thousand people at New York's Central Park, and claimed that they were inspired and organized in part by Soviet agents. Reagan's aggressive moves toward arms control in his second term, however, suggest that the "peace" movement may have had an effect on him after all.

Sociologists Frances Fox Piven and Richard Cloward have argued that public protest and disruption historically have been necessary for poor people to obtain benefits from the federal government and the states. Protests develop when economic conditions decline, compelling the government to provide social welfare programs to serve as a "safety net." When the economy improves and public pressure declines, the government adopts restrictions on benefits.[67]

Public protest opens or narrows the space for political discussion and negotiation. On the one hand, demonstrations have brought new issues to the table of public debate—among them, civil rights, the Vietnam War, gay rights, military spending, abortion, and environmental protection. Debates about Social Security, however, have been restricted by the climate created by public lobbying against cuts in benefits. On the other hand, protest sometimes blunts the edge of a movement. Groups that mobilize followers for rallies may have difficulty translating their activism to sustained research and lobbying on Capitol Hill. Followers may mistake their expressions of opinion to be adequate political action.

CAMPAIGN PROMISES AND DEBTS

Despite the cynical view that candidates forget campaign promises as soon as they enter public office, studies have found that presidents at least attempt to honor most of their pledges. Presidents usually target those pledges to specific interest groups, so interest group influence on the White House can be understood to begin before a president even takes office.[68]

An analysis of Carter's 1976 campaign promises and later policies shows that he pursued the policies he promised in seven of ten policy areas. But because Carter's ambitious legislative agenda did not lead to success on many major issues, he often was under attack by interest groups even though he pursued many of his promises.

The areas in which Carter tried to honor pledges included: creation of a cabinet-level Department of Education (a promise to the National Education Association), creation of a consumer protection agency (Ralph Nader organizations), common-site picketing legislation (AFL-CIO), amnesty for Vietnam War draft dodgers (peace groups), deregulation of businesses such as the airline industry (business and labor groups), expansion of environmental regulations (the Wilderness Society and other environmental groups), and a new public works program (AFL-CIO and big-city mayors).

Other presidents have had similar records honoring campaign pledges. The Congress Kennedy faced was just as reluctant to enact his programs as the Congress faced years later by

Carter. Kennedy, however, tried to honor campaign promises and succeeded in a number of areas: the Peace Corps, minimum wage legislation, job training, trade expansion, regional development, arms control, the Alliance for Progress, and civil rights protections. Presidents Nixon and Reagan followed up on a number of campaign themes, such as a devolution of power to states and localities, a stronger U.S. military posture, free-trade policies, cuts in domestic programs, and reduced federal regulation of business and the environment. Nixon departed from his promises to some interest groups, however, by supporting improved relations with the Soviet Union and Communist China and strict regulation of the economy.

President Clinton was criticized by his party for abandoning campaign pledges. Early in his administration, Clinton postponed fulfillment of his pledge for a middle-class tax cut. Later, he had to compromise on issues such as homosexuals in the military and the treatment of Haitian refugees.

But Clinton risked his presidency to meet other campaign commitments. Clinton pushed anticrime legislation, health care reform, free trade treaties, and a package of tax increases and budget cuts to reduce the federal budget deficit. He also followed up on pledges to create a national service program for youths, make voter registration simpler, require employers to give leaves of absence to workers with family medical emergencies, and sign welfare reform legislation.

Despite their dedication to their candidate's campaign agenda, interest groups who see their candidate elected will later complain that the president should do better. White House officials will complain that interest groups do not understand the limits of political bargaining. One Carter official said of organized labor's impatience:

> The basic issue is not whether we support most of the things labor supports. We do! We had to make decisions about how much of our agenda could be dominated by labor-demanded bills in the first two years. Our decision to go with comprehensive welfare reform meant that health insurance had to wait. Not forever, but just intelligently delayed. . . . We're using a lot of credit in the Senate on the labor bill. But we get no thanks from [labor organizations].[69]

For the most part, interest groups do not feel that they can afford the luxury of gratitude to presidents. Lobbies develop long-term relationships with congressional committees and executive agencies. But because presidents serve for eight years at most, interest groups must act aggressively if they are to influence the White House.

Regulation of Lobbying

Lobbying is protected by First Amendment guarantees of the freedom of speech, but Congress has acted several times to monitor and regulate the kinds of contacts that interest groups can make with the president and Congress.

In the late 1970s, Congress, concerned about conflicts of interest in the White House and the bureaucracy, passed restrictions on the lobbying activities of former administration offi-

cials. Under the Ethics in Government Act of 1978, administration officials are not permitted to lobby for a year after they leave the government.

Two top Reagan advisers—Lyn Nofziger and Michael K. Deaver—were indicted for illegally contacting their former Reagan administration colleagues on behalf of clients after the two men had become lobbyists. Nofziger was convicted of illegal lobbying for a military contractor, and Deaver was convicted on three counts of perjury in connection with his lobbying work for the Canadian government.

The history of regulating lobbies has been spotty. Congress and the president have faced intense interest group resistance to any regulation of their activities. The legislation that has passed has been either so vaguely defined or restricted that lobbies' activities have been barely controlled.

The Revenue Act of 1934 denied tax-exempt status to groups that devoted a "substantial part" of their activities to influencing legislation. The provision enumerated vague definitions and no sanctions, and courts applied the law inconsistently. The Foreign Agents Registration Act of 1938 required representatives of foreign governments and organizations to register with the U.S. government. The act was the source of controversy when President Carter's brother, Billy, was hired by the Libyan government as a U.S. representative.

The Revenue Acts of 1938 and 1939 denied tax exemptions to corporations devoting a "substantial part" of their activities to propaganda and lobbying. The acts also stated that citizens' donations to such corporations were not tax deductible. The Federal Regulation of Lobbying Act of 1946, the most comprehensive legislation up to that time, required registration of anyone who was hired by someone else to lobby Congress. The act also required quarterly reports from registered lobbyists.

One of the issues Clinton campaigned on in 1992 was lobby reform. Three years later, in December 1995, Congress broke more than forty years of gridlock and passed legislation that required most lobbyists to disclose twice a year the issues that they lobbied on, the specific federal agencies or houses of Congress they contacted, and the amount of money spent on the effort.[70] *(See box, Lobbying Reform of 1995, p. 177.)*

When Clinton took office in 1993, he instituted new ethics standards for more than one thousand top appointees. Among other ethics guidelines, Clinton's executive order increased from one year to five years the period during which former executive branch officials are prohibited from lobbying their former agencies.

The regulation of interest groups is always several years behind the modern methods of lobbying. While former White House aides are forbidden from lobbying the executive branch, for example, they can still influence the political process directly as members of law firms or indirectly by giving advice to colleagues in lobbying firms. Activities of think tanks also are immune from the rules of lobbying.

At most, the government can create incentives that encourage or discourage the different kinds of petitioning of the gov-

LOBBYING REFORM OF 1995

A bill signed by President Bill Clinton in December 1995 was to give the public its most detailed look at the world of lobbying, which long operated behind closed doors. The bill stipulates that lobbyists who spend at least 20 percent of their time meeting with top executive branch officials, members of Congress, or their staff will have to disclose the names of their clients, the issues they are lobbying, and the amount of money they are spending. Lobbyists who are paid $5,000 or less, or organizations that use their own employees to lobby and spend $20,000 or less on those efforts, would not have to register.

The legislation closes loopholes in the 1946 Federal Regulation of Lobbying Act that allowed most lobbyists to avoid registering and required those who did to disclose only limited information about their activities. In July 1991 the General Accounting Office reported that almost 10,000 of the 13,500 individuals and organizations listed in the *Washington Representatives* directory were not registered as lobbyists.

In the Republican-dominated Congress, reluctant House Republican leaders were forced to bring the bill to the floor after proponents showed they had the votes either to attach the measure to another bill or to discharge the measure from committee. Veteran Republicans who had supported such a change for years, members of the feisty Republican class of 1994, and minority Democrats joined to force the bill to the floor. Once there, passage was all but assured since few lawmakers were willing to oppose the bill in an era of low public opinion of Congress.

SOURCE: Jonathan D. Salant, "Bill Would Open Windows on Lobbying Efforts," *Congressional Quarterly Weekly Report,* December 2, 1995, 3631–3633.

---

ernment undertaken by parties, interest groups, and the mass media. As the Framers of the Constitution recognized, attempts to stifle factions would endanger democracy. The government cannot eliminate the pressures of interest groups, but it can direct them in ways more conducive to deliberation and the public interest.

NOTES

1. For a comparative perspective on interest groups, see Frances Millard, *Pressure Politics in Industrial Societies* (London: Macmillan, 1986).

2. *Federalist* No. 10 was largely ignored by historians and theorists of American democracy until the early twentieth century. See David Rodgers, *Contested Truths* (New York: Basic Books, 1987), 185.

3. Clinton Rossiter, ed., *The Federalist Papers* (New York: New American Library, 1961), 78.

4. Alexis de Tocqueville, *Democracy in America* (New York: New American Library, 1956), 198.

5. Theodore J. Lowi, *The Personal President* (Ithaca, N.Y.: Cornell University Press, 1985), 22–41.

6. Jonathan Rauch, *Demosclerosis: The Silent Killer of American Government* (New York: Times Books, 1994), 135.

7. Theodore J. Lowi, *The End of Liberalism* (New York: Norton, 1979), 3–63.

8. Rauch, *Demosclerosis,* 39.

9. U.S. Chamber of Commerce; AFL-CIO.

10. The Federal Election Campaign Act amendments of 1974 limit donations to individual candidates to $1,000 and donations to groups to $5,000. This provision encourages donors to give to PACs rather than to candidates. *(See "The Campaign Finance System," p. 219, in Chapter 5.)*

11. Harold W. Stanley and Richard G. Niemi, *Vital Statistics on American Politics,* 5th ed. (Washington, D.C.: CQ Press, 1995), 161. Congressional PAC spending increased from $23 million in 1976 to $190 million in 1994. Also see Martha Joynt Kumar and Michael Baruch Grossman, "The President and Interest Groups," in *The Presidency and the Political System,* ed. Michael Nelson (Washington, D.C.: CQ Press, 1984), 288.

12. Arthur F. Bentley, *The Process of Government,* rev. ed. (San Antonio: Principia Press, 1949).

13. David Truman, *The Governmental Process* (New York: Knopf, 1951).

14. Robert A. Dahl, *Who Governs?* (New Haven, Conn.: Yale University Press, 1961).

15. E. E. Schattschneider, *The Semisovereign People* (New York: Holt, Rinehart, and Winston, 1960); C. Wright Mills, *The Power Elite* (New York: Oxford University Press, 1959); Floyd Hunter, *Community Power Structure* (Chapel Hill: University of North Carolina Press, 1953).

16. For a concise examination of the bias of interest group representation, see Kay Lehman Schlozman, "What Accent the Heavenly Chorus? Political Equality and the American Pressure System," *Journal of Politics* 46 (1984): 1006–1031.

17. Mancur Olson, *The Logic of Collective Action* (Cambridge, Mass.: Harvard University Press, 1965).

18. Daniel Bell, "The Revolution of Rising Entitlements," *Fortune,* April 1975, 99.

19. For a recent critique of the breakdown of a civic ethic because of individualist and interest group liberalism, see Benjamin Barber, *Strong Democracy* (Berkeley: University of California Press, 1984), especially pages 3–114. For a conservative statement of similar concerns, see Robert Nisbet, *The Twilight of Authority* (New York: Oxford University Press, 1975).

20. Lowi, *End of Liberalism,* 62.

21. Quoted in Paul Light, *The President's Agenda* (Baltimore: Johns Hopkins University Press, 1982), 94.

22. Joseph A. Pika, "Interest Groups and the Executive: Presidential Intervention," in *Interest Group Politics,* ed. Allen J. Cigler and Burdett A. Loomis (Washington, D.C.: CQ Press, 1983), 312.

23. Michael Kranish, "Corporate Cash Paves Way for Inaugural," *Boston Globe,* January 17, 1993.

24. Kumar and Grossman, "President and Interest Groups," 289.

25. Pika, "Interest Groups and the Executive," 301.

26. Alfred A. Malabre Jr., *Beyond Our Means* (New York: Vintage Books, 1987), 111–114.

27. Anthony Downs, "Up and Down with Ecology—The Issue Attention Cycle," *Public Interest* 28 (summer 1972): 38–50.

28. The Carter and Reagan administrations observed the terms of the arms treaty, but Carter decided that a public battle for ratification would be damaging politically. Carter, therefore, did not reap the usual public relations benefits of a major foreign policy event.

29. Reagan's budget-cutting strategy is discussed in Allen Schick, *Reconciliation and the Congressional Budget Process* (Washington, D.C.: American Enterprise Institute, 1981).

30. Jeffrey H. Birnbaum, *The Lobbyists: How Influence Peddlers Work Their Way in Washington* (New York: Times Books, 1993), 205–206.

31. Mary Curtius and John Aloysius Farrel, "Conservatives Hitting Hard at Clinton Policies," *Boston Globe,* March 21, 1994.

32. Larry J. Sabato, *The Party's Just Begun* (Glenview, Ill.: Scott Foresman, 1988).

33. The size of the White House staff increased from a few dozen under Franklin D. Roosevelt to 660 under Richard Nixon in 1971. After falling to 362 under President Reagan, the staff increased again under Bush and Clinton, to 400 by 1995. The Executive Office of the President was at its

largest—5,751—in 1974. See Lyn Ragsdale, *Vital Statistics on the Presidency* (Washington, D.C.: Congressional Quarterly, 1996), 258–260.

34. Thomas E. Cronin, *The State of the Presidency* (Boston: Little, Brown, 1980), 84.

35. Nelson W. Polsby, "Interest Groups and the Presidency: Trends in Political Intermediation in America," in *American Politics and Public Policy,* ed. Walter Dean Burnham and Martha Wagner Weinberg (Cambridge, Mass.: MIT Press, 1978), 46.

36. See Kumar and Grossman, "President and Interest Groups," 290–307.

37. Ibid., 284.

38. Pika, "Interest Groups and the Executive," 307–308.

39. Light, *President's Agenda,* 95.

40. Kumar and Grossman, "President and Interest Groups," 309.

41. "President Carter's Farewell Address," *Congressional Quarterly Weekly Report,* January 17, 1981, 156.

42. Ragsdale, *Vital Statistics on the Presidency,* 171–172.

43. Gary King and Lyn Ragsdale, *The Elusive Executive: Discovering Statistical Patterns in the Presidency* (Washington, D.C.: CQ Press, 1988), 254–259; Norman J. Ornstein and Shirley Elder, *Interest Groups, Lobbying, and Policymaking* (Washington, D.C.: CQ Press, 1978), 24, 37.

44. Ornstein and Elder, *Interest Groups, Lobbying, and Policymaking,* 69–79.

45. Ibid., 82–93.

46. The following discussion relies on Benjamin Ginsberg and Martin Shefter, "The Presidency and the Organization of Interests," in *The Presidency and the Political System,* ed. Michael Nelson (Washington, D.C.: CQ Press, 1988), 311–330.

47. Ibid., 311–333.

48. Maximum feasible participation never played as important a role as its promoters and detractors argued. Most organizations created by the provision eventually came under the control of local governments and other more conservative groups such as local businesses. But the principles behind the program—that interest groups can be created to promote policies and that interested parties should be consulted before policies affecting them are implemented—have remained part of American politics. Perhaps most important, the provision led to the development of a wide range of interest groups and trained a generation of government and interest group leaders. See Dennis R. Judd, *The Politics of American Cities: Power and Public Policy,* 2d ed. (Boston: Little, Brown, 1984), 311; and Daniel Patrick Moynihan, *Maximum Feasible Misunderstanding* (New York: Free Press, 1970).

49. Robert D. Reischauer, "Fiscal Federalism in the 1980's: Dismantling or Rationalizing the Great Society," in *The Great Society and Its Legacy,* ed. Marshall Kaplan and Peggy Cuciti (Durham, N.C.: Duke University Press, 1986), 187–188.

50. Ginsberg and Shefter, "Presidency and the Organization of Interests," 313–327.

51. Marc Bendick Jr. and Phyllis M. Levinson, "Private-Sector Initiatives or Public-Private Partnerships," in *The Reagan Presidency and the Governing of America,* ed. Lester M. Salamon and Michael S. Lund (Washington, D.C.: Urban Institute, 1984), 455–479.

52. Quoted in Peter H. Stone, "Lying in Wait," *National Journal,* November 21, 1992, 2661.

53. Ibid., 2656–2661.

54. Quoted in Kirk Victor, "Asleep at the Switch?" *National Journal,* January 16, 1993, 131.

55. Allan J. Cigler, "From Protest Group to Interest Group: The Making of American Agriculture Movement, Inc.," in *Interest Group Politics,* ed. Allan J. Cigler and Burdett A. Loomis (Washington, D.C.: CQ Press, 1988), 46–69.

56. Thomas Byrne Edsall, *The New Politics of Inequality* (New York: Norton, 1984), 99–103.

57. Jeff Fishel, *Presidents and Promises* (Washington, D.C.: CQ Press, 1985), 168.

58. John Herbers, "Grass-Roots Groups Go National," *New York Times Magazine,* September 4, 1983, 22–23, 42, 46, 48.

59. Dan Carney, *Congressional Quarterly Weekly Report,* February 3, 1996, 290.

60. Dan Carney, *Congressional Quarterly Weekly Report,* December 23, 1995, 3883.

61. Wolman and Teitelbaum, "Interest Groups and the Reagan Presidency," 308.

62. Quoted in Hedrick Smith, "The President as Coalition Builder: Reagan's First Year," in *Rethinking the Presidency,* ed. Thomas E. Cronin (Boston: Little, Brown, 1982), 280.

63. Ibid., 281.

64. David Stockman, *The Triumph of Politics: The Inside Story of the Reagan Revolution* (New York: Avon Books, 1987), 257.

65. Francis E. Rourke, *Bureaucracy, Politics, and Public Policy* (Boston: Little, Brown, 1984), 150.

66. Quoted in Norman C. Thomas and Harold L. Wolman, "Policy Formulation in the Institutionalized Presidency," in *The Presidential Advisory System,* ed. Thomas E. Cronin and Sanford D. Greenberg (New York: Harper and Row, 1969), 127. Also see Daniel Bell, "Government by Commission," in the same volume, 117–123.

67. Frances Fox Piven and Richard Cloward, *Regulating the Poor: The Functions of Public Relief* (New York: Random House, 1972).

68. See Fishel, *Presidents and Promises.*

69. Ibid., 93.

70. Jonathan D. Salant, "Bill Would Open Windows on Lobbying Efforts," *Congressional Quarterly Weekly Report,* December 2, 1995, 3631–3633.

SELECTED BIBLIOGRAPHY

Berry, Jeffrey. *The Interest Group Society.* Boston: Little, Brown, 1984.

Cigler, Allan J., and Burdett A. Loomis. *Interest Group Politics.* 4th ed. Washington, D.C.: CQ Press, 1994.

Heclo, Hugh. "Issue Networks and the Executive Establishment." In *The New American Political System,* ed. Anthony King. Washington, D.C.: American Enterprise Institute, 1978.

Lowi, Theodore J. *The End of Liberalism.* New York: Norton, 1979.

Ornstein, Norman J., and Shirley Elder. *Interest Groups, Lobbying, and Policymaking.* Washington, D.C.: CQ Press, 1978.

Schlozman, Kay Lehman. "What Accent the Heavenly Chorus: Political Equality and the American Pressure System." *Journal of Politics* 46 (1984): 1006–1031.

Index